Dr. David M. L...

As fantastic as *X-Files* episodes, but these things *really happened*:

- A part-time Christmas-tree salesman remote-viewed his way into the heart of a super-secret National Security Agency installation buried in the West Virginia mountains.

- The same psychic described previously unknown details of a high-tech Soviet military research facility—details that were later confirmed by spy satellite.

- A bizarre wave of paranormal visions haunted a group of scientists doing psychic research at Lawrence Livermore National Laboratory.

- A woman in Ohio psychically found the location of a crashed Soviet bomber in the jungles of Zaire, helping a CIA team to recover the wreckage before the Soviets got there—and earning praise from President Jimmy Carter.

- An Army remote viewer was the first in the U.S. intelligence community to describe the Soviets' new *Typhoon*-class submarine—while it was still indoors, under construction.

And those are just a few samples from this extraordinary story. . . .

QUANTITY SALES

Most Dell books are available at special quantity discounts when purchased in bulk by corporations, organizations, or groups. Special imprints, messages, and excerpts can be produced to meet your needs. For more information, write to: Dell Publishing, 1540 Broadway, New York, NY 10036. Attention: Special Markets.

INDIVIDUAL SALES

Are there any Dell books you want but cannot find in your local stores? If so, you can order them directly from us. You can get any Dell book currently in print. For a complete up-to-date listing of our books and information on how to order, write to: Dell Readers Service, Box DR, 1540 Broadway, New York, NY 10036.

REMOTE VIEWERS

The Secret History of America's Psychic Spies

JIM SCHNABEL

A Dell Book

Published by
Dell Publishing
a division of
Bantam Doubleday Dell Publishing Group, Inc.
1540 Broadway
New York, New York 10036

Grateful acknowledgment is made to Harcourt Brace & Company for permission to reprint an excerpt from "The Waste Land" in *Collected Poems 1909-1962* by T. S. Eliot, copyright 1936 by Harcourt Brace & Company, copyright © 1964, 1963 by T. S. Eliot, reprinted by permission of the publisher.

ISBN: 0-440-22306-7

Printed in the United States of America

Published simultaneously in Canada

February 1997

10 9 8 7 6 5 4 3 2 1

OPM

CONTENTS

BOOK THREE
A NEW AGE

A NOTE TO THE READER

THIS BOOK IS ABOUT THE PARANORMAL, A SUBJECT WHICH IN LATE-twentieth-century Western society is inseparable from controversy.

However, I hope the skeptical reader will bear in mind that this book was put together with the standard techniques of investigative journalism. I conducted numerous interviews with people who participated at all levels in the events I describe. I cross-checked stories among sources, and I gathered as much relevant documentary evidence as I could. In the back of the book I have noted the source(s) of each significant piece of information in the text. Were the subject of this book a different kind of classified government program—say, the effort to develop radar-evading Stealth aircraft—it would not be necessary to say any of this.

Because so many of the projects and operations discussed in these pages are still classified, some of my sources spoke to me on the condition that I identify them, as sources, in general terms only—e.g., "a former senior CIA official." This is the kind of practice commonly used, and often abused, in books about classified matters. However, most of the sources for this book spoke to me openly, "on the record." This is their story, not a dramatic invention of mine.

Jim Schnabel
August 1996

Marvellous as these methods of signalling may seem, there were medicine men who claimed that they could send their thoughts through the air and make things come to pass afar. Others could send their minds' eyes to distant places and discover what was happening. White explorers have written of these things, but to say just how it was done must remain for modern medicine men to tell us.

—Arthur C. Parker,
The Indian How Book,
1927

BOOK ONE

A CHEAP RADAR SYSTEM

[I]t seems to me that it would be a hell of a cheap radar system. And if the Russians have it and we don't, we are in serious trouble.

—Representative Charlie Rose (D-NC), House Select Committee on Intelligence, in a discussion about remote viewing, 1979

1
THE ZONE

THE DREAM FADED, AND MEL RILEY AWOKE. SIX O'CLOCK; THE SUN was not yet up. Brigitte, his wife, still lay asleep beside him. But the birds outside were awake and chattering, and they were Riley's usual alarm clock. He rose, showered, shaved, and dressed.

Riley was a morning person. He liked the dark calm of the predawn hours, the unsleeping stillness, half in this world, half in that. Downstairs in the kitchen he sat quietly, drinking coffee and smoking a cigarette, listening to his thoughts, watching through the window as the light changed on the trees and in the sky.

Riley was five feet eight, slim and fit, with wavy blond hair and an Irish, vaguely leprechaunish face. He had a tattoo on each arm—an eagle, a rabbit—and a large winged dragon across his chest. But it was Riley's eyes that people tended to notice. Sometimes with surprise, or merely concentration, they would open widely, intensely, as if Riley were about to hypnotize someone—or had already hypnotized himself and were staring inward at his own soul.

Thirty-three years old, Mel Riley was a staff sergeant in the U.S. Army. He and his wife and their two young daughters lived in a town house at Fort Meade, Maryland, about twenty-five miles northeast of Washington, D.C. "Meade," as its inhabitants abbreviated it, was the sprawling, townlike base for, among other things, the National Security Agency, the U.S. First Army, and a part of the Army's Intelligence and Security Command (INSCOM). Until recently, Riley had been a photo-interpreter at INSCOM, studying reconnaissance imagery from satellites and spy planes. But just now the Army was using him for something else.

Dressed in civilian clothes, which his new job required for security reasons, Riley drove the mile or so to work, past a golf course, parade grounds, a convenience store, and dozens of low buildings. Some of the buildings were brick, some were wood, some were named for dead generals, and some were simply numbered; many had obvious purposes, while others would always remain obscure. Riley's unit worked in two single-story wooden structures numbered 2560 and 2561. They were secluded beneath trees on a large open lot on the north side of Llewellyn Street, a quarter mile from Kimbrough Army Community Hospital. There beneath the trees, the buildings seemed strangely lonely and rural, almost forgotten. On the far end of 2560, the smaller building to the east, the land sloped down to an open field with a creek that ran south, under the road, into a park and a lake. To the north of the buildings was a field with sparse trees, photogenically bleak in winter. The two buildings were remnants of the great military construction boom of the Second World War, and had once housed a bakery school and mess hall. Here in September 1979, they looked like two cottages huddling together in the woods.

Riley parked in the driveway between the buildings. He walked up a set of wooden steps to a porchlike entrance near the right corner of 2561. He opened a heavy forest green metal door and went inside.

To a visitor, 2561 might have looked like a normal if somewhat makeshift military office. There was an entrance room, or foyer, with a secretary's desk, a refrigerator, a table with a coffeepot and mugs, and doors to two outer offices for the unit's commander and operations officer. Behind the secretary's desk, a narrow corridor led west, past half a dozen small cubicles with desks. The corridor terminated in a conference room.

There were still a few signs of the building's original function. Two large metal chimneys jutted from the roof of an old furnace room next to the entrance, and in the un-carpeted foyer the floor was covered with red heavy-duty tiles. Across the outer wall of the commander's office, next to the secretary's desk, lay a quarter-inch steel plate, a heat shield where a large oven had once stood. In the only hint of the current goings-on, someone had covered the plate with a painted mural, a dream of deep space: a supernova unfolding silently, in slow motion, across dark light-years.

The unit was known, formally, as "Special Action Branch," and was ostensibly attached to INSCOM head-quarters. But it took its orders from the Pentagon office of the Army's assistant chief of staff for intelligence, and its tasking requests originated from a variety of offices throughout the U.S. intelligence community: the Central Intelligence Agency, the Defense Intelligence Agency, even the President's National Security Council. The orders that came into the office, and the information that went out, were stamped not only with the standard Army intelligence SECRET, but with the Pentagon code word, GRILL FLAME. Only a few dozen officials in the intelligence community had been briefed on the existence of the Grill Flame project. "Access is limited," an Army memorandum of the time would note, "to those personnel approved on a 'by name' basis."

Riley was often the first to arrive at the unit in the morning; he would then go through the solitary routine of opening doors and safes, and making coffee. He had an office to himself in 2560, the operations building next door, but he would usually linger in 2561, where the rest of the unit had their offices. The nature of the unit's mission was such that he seldom had deskwork to do anyway.

On this morning, Riley had not been the first to arrive. Lieutenant Skip Atwater, the unit's operations officer, and Lieutenant Colonel Murray B. "Scotty" Watt, the unit's commander, were there waiting for him. Atwater was sandy-haired, droll and paunchy, a former enlisted man now in his late twenties. Watt was two decades older, a tall and husky man with a bulbous nose and a Boston accent. A new tasking had come in, they explained to Riley. It was a big one.

Riley walked over to the operations building. Atwater followed, carrying a large folder. After an entrance room—Riley's seldom-used office—there was a narrow hallway; the two men walked along it and into another small room. The room had a comfortable leather couch, with pillows and a blanket, and next to it a chair. The window had been bricked, plastered, and painted over.

Riley lay down on the couch. Atwater fastened a small microphone to his shirt, then turned off the light, and waited. This was Riley's cooling-off period, a time for him to settle his thoughts. The mental images he soon would seek—not just images but sounds, smells, tastes, textures, emotions, vestibular sensations—would be like faint, flickering signals from a faraway TV station, bent and bounced by the ionosphere, drowning in a storm of electronic noise. Now was the time to mute that noise.

Riley lay on his back in the dark. He felt his breathing slow, his heart rate drop. He imagined a large and empty suitcase lying open before him. In a heap, to one side of the suitcase, were all his anxieties and distractions. Riley began to place them into the suitcase, at first one by one and then by the armful. When they all had been put away, he closed the suitcase, locked it, and turned his back on it. For the next hour, he hoped, those distracting thoughts would stay locked inside that imaginary suitcase.

After the suitcase ritual came the diving ritual. Conjuring a new scene within his mind, Riley donned scuba gear and slipped from an evanescent boat into warm turquoise waters, fifty feet above a coral sand bottom. He drifted down, breathing slowly. He had a belt with small lead weights attached, and as he neared the bottom, he began to release the weights, slowing his descent. When he began to rise again, he released a trickle of air from his life vest. In this way he tried to stay motionless, in neutral buoyancy, ten feet above the bottom. The bottom was sleep. The mirrored, rippling surface far above him was full waking alertness. Each was an extreme to be avoided; Riley sought instead a narrow intermediate zone. He drifted up and down through it, now shedding weights, now shedding buoyant air, and each time he passed through this magical zone, he felt his mind connect to something, as if tuning in to that distant station.

Lieutenant Atwater meanwhile sat quietly, holding the folder. The outside of the folder was blank, except for a white label with a tasking reference number. Inside the folder was a piece of paper with a brief description of the target.

The target, sent in by Air Force intelligence, was a nuclear device that the Chinese had just developed and were evaluating at a remote facility in their western desert, near a dry lake known as Lop Nor. Foreign nuclear weapons programs were among the highest-priority targets for the U.S. intelligence community. The community evidently had word that the new device at Lop Nor existed, but it wanted to know much more: What was its design? Had it been tested? Air Force officials, anxious to supplement their more conventional intelligence efforts, had decided to task the men and women of Grill Flame.

"Are you ready, Mel?" asked Atwater.

"Uh-huh." Barely a murmur.

In a control room next door, Scotty Watt sat listening in with headphones. Atwater threw a switch near his chair, and inside the control room, a tape recorder began to roll.

"The target is an object," Atwater said to Riley. He neither opened the target folder nor gave Riley any further information. The folder itself, he knew, was only a prop, symbolizing that out there was a target, one that Riley should focus his mind on and should describe in as much detail as possible.

"Tell me what your impressions are," said Atwater.

Riley was floating in the turquoise waters, drifting down slowly, and now the signal grew and the static faded and there were glimpses and clipped sensations of metal and wires, electronics . . . a slender steel egg with a tritium yolk . . . And despite these dark impressions, with their aura of dread, Riley knew he was in the zone again, where he wanted to be, where he needed to be, and it was just about the best feeling in the world.

2

THE DREAM TEAM

I never liked to get into debates with the skeptics, because if you didn't believe that remote viewing was real, you hadn't done your homework.

We didn't know how to explain it, but we weren't so much interested in explaining it as in determining whether there was any practical use to it.

—Major General Edmund R. Thompson, Army Assistant Chief of Staff for Intelligence, 1977–81

MEL RILEY GREW UP IN THE CITY OF RACINE, WISCONSIN, JUST below Milwaukee on the western shore of Lake Michigan. He was the second of five children, three boys and two girls; his father was a machine repairman who worked for Borden, the dairy company, and his mother was a homemaker. Mel ran with the local pack of youngsters, but he also had a shy and solitary streak and a special love of the outdoors. As a teenager he would go out into the deep woods in late autumn, with a friend or two, camping out in the snow, hunting deer, and occasionally running into bears. In the summer there was canoeing and fishing. And sometimes even in downtown Racine, in a bar or a dance hall on a Saturday night, the spirit would move him and he would drive, alone or with his date, out to one of the cliffs on the east edge of town, staying up to watch the sun rise up over Lake Michigan.

The mind of any young person can be a jumble of altered states, but Mel at times seemed more altered than most. There was often about him a certain mild spaciness, a proneness to the zone. One summer day in preadolescence he was in an empty field near the lake, in a place where he was always finding arrowheads and other Native American artifacts. At some point a strange calm came upon him, and he smelled woodsmoke. He turned his head and saw an Indian village, with tepees, dogs, men and women, smoking meat, running children. Most of the village seemed oblivious of his presence, but some of the dogs barked, and one particularly tall and dignified Indian looked at him and seemed to wave. Then after a few more blinks of his eyes Riley's second sight grew dim, the warp in time was smoothed, and the village faded back into the field.

Riley was twenty-three years old, working in Racine as a machine repairman like his father, when he learned that he had been drafted by the Army. The date was July 7, 1969, two weeks before men would walk on the moon. Riley would later wonder if the journey he began that day had taken him farther.

At boot camp in Kentucky, there was a recruiter from Army intelligence, offering a special deal. If a draftee enlisted for three years instead of the usual two, he would be trained as a photo-interpreter. Riley signed up, and was sent to photo-interpreter school at Fort Holabird, in northern Maryland. From there he was sent to Germany, to the 7405th Operations Squadron, a special Army/Air Force unit at Rhein-Main Air Force Base in Wiesbaden. The unit's job was to fly covert reconnaissance missions through East Germany, zig-zagging along accepted air traffic corridors—usually between Wiesbaden and Berlin—in planes disguised as ordinary cargo planes. Looking down and sideways across miles of East German terrain, they would spy on armored divisions, airfields, radar sites, and whatever else they could reach with their special cameras and electronic-intercept gear.

Satellites would normally have been able to do the job more safely, but Eastern Europe was often blanketed by clouds, and in any case, Soviet bloc military officials generally knew when U.S. satellites were passing overhead. The aircraft Riley's unit flew could go in under the clouds, and weren't always recognizable as spy planes until they were practically on top of their targets—when doors would suddenly open all over the airframe, and camera lenses and radio and microwave antennas and infrared detector pods would start poking out. There was a panic button the crew could hit, in case an East German military jet decided to check them out, and then all the lenses and antennas and pods would pop back inside the airframe, like a turtle's limbs into its shell, and all the doors would close, and the plane would revert to its innocent, cargo-carrying state.

Riley's task, when he wasn't at his light-table in Wiesbaden scanning the photographic results of these missions, was to serve as an aerial observer on some of the missions themselves, peering out the aircraft window with binoculars and telling his colleagues where to aim their intelligence-gathering equipment.

Riley did well at this job, and earned a number of medals. He also developed a reputation as a fellow with a sixth sense. As an aerial observer, he seemed to have an unusually accurate intuition about where to head the plane or point the cameras. And as a photo analyst, he seemed able to see things in a reconnaissance image that no one else could see. One of his commendations came after he had analyzed a photo of an East German industrial area and found what seemed to be a new Soviet artillery piece, sitting on a flatcar in a rail yard. The artillery piece, which hadn't yet been seen in that particular area and was therefore significant to Army intelligence, was actually hidden by a canvas canopy. But Riley somehow had a feeling about what it was, and sketched it anyway. Satellite photographs later confirmed the sketch.

Riley was kept on in Wiesbaden for two three-year tours. Then, in 1976, he received word that he'd been ordered to a new posting, at Fort Meade, with something called the Operations Security Group. Operations security—"opsec" for short—simply meant the protection of sensitive operations from foreign espionage. Riley's new unit was a kind of Red-Team, its task being literally to spy on certain U.S. military facilities in an effort to find and correct security lapses. Riley's specific job was to analyze photographic intelligence on these installations—from satellites, aircraft, and even hand-held cameras at close range. One of his most memorable targets was the Army's experimental XM-1 tank (now the M-1), then undergoing gunnery trials at Aberdeen Proving Grounds, at the north end of Chesapeake Bay. Riley's team arranged to take into the Chesapeake near Aberdeen a U.S. Coast Guard boat outfitted with long-range cameras and other spy gear, to see if they could gather meaningful intelligence on the XM-1 trials. As they were sailing along, all systems go, a Russian freighter suddenly appeared and cruised past them in the shipping lanes, its own spy-cameras and antennas tactfully hidden.

Down the hall from Riley's office in building 4554 at Fort Meade was something called the Systems Exploitation Team, or "SET." It had been set up by the head of the Army Intelligence Agency, Brigadier General Edmund Thompson, and was meant to be a small, multidisciplinary group of creative, lateral thinkers, tackling the strangest and toughest military intelligence problems. They considered themselves an elite bunch.

One day, early in 1977, Riley was chatting with a friend at SET, a fellow sergeant named Bill Young. Riley noticed that Young had some unusual books on his shelf, books about "psi" phenomena such as extrasensory perception, psychokinesis, and out-of-body experiences. Young explained that the Soviets, and some of the Eastern European countries, were trying to use psi for military purposes—employing psychics, for example, to spy on intelligence targets in the United States. A Colonel Kowalski at SET was studying the situation, so far just informally. But who knew where it would lead? Maybe one day the United States would be employing its own psychic spies.

Riley's ears pricked up. Psychic spies? Would the Army ever undertake a project *that* bizarre? If it did, he certainly wanted to be involved.

Fresh from officer candidate training and espionage school at Fort Huachuca, Arizona, Skip Atwater arrived at Fort Meade in the summer of 1977. It was a time of great upheaval and acronymic confusion in the Army intelligence bureaucracy. The U.S. Army Intelligence Agency (USAINTA) was merging with the Army Security Agency (ASA) to form the all-in-one Intelligence and Security Command (INSCOM).* Atwater was assigned to one of the opsec teams, which now became part of SET, which in turn became SED—the Systems Exploitation *Detachment*—and was attached not to INSCOM but to the office of the assistant chief of staff for intelligence, the ACSI. The ACSI was now the former USAINTA commander, Edmund Thompson, who was now a major general.

By coincidence, Atwater ended up with the desk and the safe of SET's Colonel Kowalski, who had since moved

---

* ASA, responsible largely for foreign communications intercepts and Army communications security, had increasingly been treated as a kind of low-wage workforce by the National Security Agency. The NSA used ASA and other service personnel to help staff its hundreds of listening posts around the globe. The Army, by amalgamating ASA into INSCOM, was among other things trying to regain some control over its own people.

somewhere else. It was a nice coincidence, because Atwater, like Kowalski, had a strong interest in psi. Atwater spent hours going through the psi-related documents Kowalski had left behind.

Atwater—born Frederick Holmes Atwater, but nicknamed Skip—had grown up in Glendale, California, in a house on the edge of town with some land around it, plus dogs, cats, and even a goat and a donkey. His father was a dentist. His mother, a homemaker, had a strong belief in things paranormal and supernatural, and Atwater was similarly inclined. For a time in his teenage years, he seemed to be able to travel "out of body" almost at will, sometimes using his weird ability to float from his bed, through the walls of his house, across town, and into the bedroom of whatever high school girl he had chosen for that night (alas, like a ghost he could only gawk). Researchers might debate whether such experiences represented actual "astral travel," or ESP in the form of moving images, or merely vivid, fantasy-driven dreams, but to Atwater they were real enough.

Early in his military career, Atwater heard about Soviet and Eastern European psi research; he also heard rumors that the CIA had been responding with its own psi research, some of which had been wildly successful. For someone who had long been intrigued by the possibilities of the paranormal, it all sounded too good to be true. Mainstream scientists tended to reject psi research, calling it "pseudoscience," a morass of fraud and delusion. And yet the stories Atwater heard suggested that the U.S. and Soviet governments had simply decided to bypass mainstream science, embarking on nothing less than a paranormal arms race. And it was all a secret.

Atwater learned more after he arrived at Fort Meade. He learned that the CIA's psi research had been conducted since 1972, at Stanford Research Institute (SRI), a big scientific think-tank in Menlo Park, California. He learned that

SRI researchers, after experimenting with various psi phenomena, had decided to concentrate on clairvoyance—the psychic "seeing" of things otherwise hidden by obstacles or distance—for use in espionage. The SRI researchers, in rivalry with their Soviet counterparts, were attempting nothing less than the development of the perfect spies, human beings who, undetectably and at almost zero cost, could spy upon the most remote, sensitive, and heavily guarded locations. Throwing out the old labels for psychic phenomena, the SRI scientists were calling their clairvoyant techniques "remote viewing."*

At Fort Meade, Atwater began to argue that remote viewing represented a potential security threat, and should be studied in that light by the Army's opsec teams. He proposed to the head of SED, a Colonel Robert Keenan, that a small remote-viewing team be assembled. Its members, he suggested, could be screened for psychic abilities from the local population of Army intelligence personnel. Those selected for psychic duty wouldn't even have to leave their old units. They could come in to Fort Meade to do remote viewing a few hours a week, against targets chosen by the Opsec Group. They would be just another group of specialists working part-time for the opsec units, just like specialists in electronic intercepts and spy satellite photography. They would have a low profile and would cost the Army almost nothing. But they would enable the Army to determine how serious the Soviet remote-viewing threat might be. If it turned out that remote viewers didn't pose a serious threat to U.S. security, then so much the better.

Atwater's proposal went up the chain of command and was approved, remarkably, without any significant controversy. The proposal was eventually seen by the nominal overseer of SED, the Army's assistant chief of staff for intel-

* The early years of the SRI remote-viewing program are covered in Book Two.

ligence, Major General Thompson. Strange as it might have seemed, Thompson had considerable enthusiasm for the idea of psychic spying. He had been nurturing his own interest in psi, ever since reading Arthur Koestler's pro-paranormal book *The Roots of Coincidence* a few years earlier. Thompson also had heard about the remote-viewing work going on out at SRI, under the CIA's sponsorship. He liked the idea of getting the Army involved in remote viewing, but without having to rely too much on the CIA or SRI. He liked the idea of his own, secret unit of experimental psychic spies.

Atwater's project was initially given the code name Gondola Wish. As Atwater had suggested, it consumed minimal resources. Atwater was given a few thousand dollars in travel money, some cramped office space in building 4554 at Fort Meade—for which he had to scrounge carpets and furniture—and a commanding officer, Major Watt, whose volcanic temper was said to have left a cloud over his career. Some years before, while stationed in Panama, he had struck a fellow officer who had insulted his wife. Watt was never convicted of any offense, and in general he seemed an honorable and conscientious military officer, but since the incident, he felt, he hadn't been promoted as rapidly as he deserved. Atwater was told that Watt had been chosen for this assignment—obscure, and perhaps only temporary, but with the potential for enormous controversy—only because it was felt that he had so little to lose.*

Atwater's and Watt's first task was to select about a dozen potential psychics from the local population of Army intelligence personnel. To get an idea of the kind of person who would make a good remote viewer, the two officers visited SRI and talked to researchers there. The SRI researchers were somewhat evangelical on the subject of remote view-

* Watt later did receive a promotion to lieutenant colonel.

ing; they believed that remote-viewing ability was like musical ability: everyone had it to some degree. To find those who had the most ability, the SRI researchers said, the best thing to do was simply to test relatively large groups of people against remote-viewing targets, and see how well they did.

The problem was, Atwater and Watt didn't want it widely known that they were setting up a remote-viewing unit. They couldn't travel around giving military officers ESP tests. They needed a stealthier way of finding good psychics.

SRI researchers had already been wrestling with this problem for some time, running medical, neurological, and psychological profiles of their remote viewers, looking for attributes that stood out. So far, about all they had found was that artistic talent, visual-spatial intelligence, and creativity all tended to be associated with high remote-viewing scores. Also, SRI researchers believed that perceiving psi data with the mind's eye was like glimpsing a scene only briefly in real life. People who were good at describing and detailing such glimpses should, they reasoned, be good remote viewers.

But SRI researchers had to admit that even these attributes provided only a rough screening tool. As far as they were concerned, the best way to find good psychics, if one was limited to asking questions in interviews, was to ask the interviewees whether they had had any psychic experiences, or simply whether they believed in psi.

Back in Washington, Atwater and Watt quietly contacted INSCOM unit commanders at Fort Meade, and also at INSCOM's headquarters at Arlington Hall in northern Virginia, a military/civilian intelligence complex that had once been a private school for girls. The two officers asked the various INSCOM unit commanders to name people in their offices who fit the rough personality profile the SRI researchers had developed. Atwater and Watt also made the rounds of Army offices at the National Photographic Interpretation Center (NPIC) in southeast Washington, believing that photo-interpreters, with their visual skills, would probably make excellent candidates.

Generating a list of a few hundred candidates this way, Atwater and Watt then called the candidates in for personal interviews. The candidates were asked about their backgrounds, with particular emphasis on their paranormal beliefs and experiences. The candidates were told that it was just a general survey on psi that the INSCOM commander had ordered. But photo-interpreter Mel Riley, when he was called in, knew what the questions were really about. He had kept his ear to the ground, and realized he was being considered for Gondola Wish.

Following this first round of interviews, Atwater and Watt selected a few dozen of the most promising candidates, and then examined their personnel files. The two officers weren't just interested in raw psi potential. They realized they also needed to have men and women with competence and intelligence, and a willingness to learn new things. They didn't want an undisciplined group of crystal-ball gazers.

After going through the files, they cut the list of candidates down to about twenty, and called all of them in for a second interview. Mel Riley, who had made the cut again, was now told that the Army was thinking about setting up a special team, a team of people who would be trained as psychic spies for use in opsec missions. Was he interested in being on the team?

Riley didn't hesitate. He was definitely interested. It was about the sexiest military program he had ever heard of.

Not long afterwards, in early 1978, Riley was ordered to an eavesdropping-proof "secure room" across from Colonel Keenan's office in building 4554. When he arrived, he found himself with the other candidates—ten or eleven of them—plus Atwater and Watt, who gave a short briefing on the program and its reasons for being.

The unit was only experimental, warned Watt and Atwater; it might not survive long. The candidates assembled in the room would serve only part-time, perhaps a few hours per week, or as needed, and would officially remain attached to their old units. However, there was obviously an interest in the remote-viewing project at high levels. Perhaps if things went well, the project would expand, and Gondola Wish would usher in a new era in military espionage.

The group Atwater and Watt selected had, as expected, a heavy emphasis on photo-interpreters. Riley was one. Another was a tall, solid-looking former Navy petty officer named Hartleigh Trent. Now in his fifties, the graybeard of Gondola Wish (most of the others were in their late twenties or early thirties), Trent had been Riley's instructor for a course on overhead reconnaissance at Fort Holabird eight years before. He worked down at NPIC and also part-time for the opsec teams. Four other Army civilians in the group—Nancy Stern, Steve Hanson, Bud Duncan, and Steve Holloway*—were also photo-interpreters. Hanson was a devout Christian; when he started remote-viewing training, he would learn to "cool down" before a session by reading Bible verses.

There was a tall Army captain, Janice Rand, who worked in one of the INSCOM offices at Fort Meade. And there were several officers and civilians from the operations side of Army espionage. One was a counterintelligence specialist, Captain Ken Bell. Short, wiry, somewhat intense, he was into meditation. Another counterintelligence man was Fernand Gauvin, a dark-haired, handsome Rhode Islander, a civilian in his late forties. Gauvin had a long history of

---

* These are pseudonyms. See page 393 for a complete list of pseudonyms.

psychic experiences and transcendental yearnings, going back to his childhood. Somewhere in his teens he had belonged to a Catholic lay order, the Brothers of the Sacred Heart; he still went to mass regularly, but his faith now had a New Age tinge. He practiced yoga and meditation, experimented with altered states, and read books about spirit-mediums and auras. In 1975, he had had an unusual out-of-body-type experience, an encounter with some kind of benevolent, luminous, loving entity that had blown his mind. He still talked about it.

Gauvin and Bell worked down at Arlington Hall, home to some of the more James Bond-ish elements of the U.S. espionage community. Jackie Keith, another Arlington Hall civilian selected for Gondola Wish, worked in special ops, and always seemed to be involved in half a dozen cloak-and-dagger schemes, all going at once. Finally there was Joe McMoneagle, a bull-necked warrant officer; he was in charge of a group of technicians down at Arlington Hall, and had worked on special radio-intercept teams everywhere from the Bahamas to Cambodia and Vietnam.

For McMoneagle, Riley, and the others, it seemed fortunate that they were attached to Gondola Wish only part-time at first, because the project began with frustrating slowness, as if trying to avoid attention and controversy by doing as little as possible. There were no operations, only practice, and for a while there was not even practice.

The first remote-viewing session was undertaken by Mel Riley, lying on a couch in a makeshift remote-viewing room down the hall from the unit's small office in building 4554. Atwater sat by as his monitor. There was no control room, and Atwater merely held a portable cassette recorder to take down Riley's impressions. Scotty Watt, who himself was the target for the session, meanwhile walked over to a building a few hundred yards away, a guest house for visiting senior officers at Fort Meade.

The remote-viewing protocol in this case was one that

had been used for some of the experiments out at SRI, although it wasn't well-suited for use against actual intelligence targets. Researchers at SRI called it "outbound remote viewing," because an "outbound" experimenter (in this case, Watt) would go to a randomly selected site. The remote viewer would then try to describe the outbound experimenter's surroundings, by freehand sketching and by verbalizing the impressions that drifted into consciousness. Riley could try to go into a relatively deep, trancelike state, lying down on the couch in total darkness, murmuring his impressions and then waking up and sketching them afterwards. Or he could sit up on the couch during the session, with the room light dimly on, sketching his impressions as they came to him. Atwater encouraged experimentation. His guiding principle was pure Californian: *hey, whatever works for you.*

Riley sank down into what would become his preferred method, a mild eyes-closed trance in a darkened room, and described his impressions. He had glimpses of a manhole cover, a sidewalk, and a few other vaguely defined items. Afterwards he tried to sketch what he had seen. When Watt came back and took him to the target, Riley saw that he had identified some of its elements, but not very completely, and on the whole not very accurately. It wasn't an auspicious start.

Before any further practice sessions could be conducted, word came down from on high that remote viewing, somewhat belatedly, had been determined to be a form of "human use experimentation." The dark history of such experimentation in the military—in particular, the controversial studies of LSD and other potential "mind control" or "truth serum" drugs on servicemen in the 1950s and 1960s—meant that it now had to involve the informed consent of its participants, plus approval and oversight by the Army's human use review board. Riley and the others filled out sheafs of informed consent paperwork, while various medical officials were asked to sign off on the project. By the time the buck was passed all the way up to the Army's surgeon general, and a restart of the program was authorized, a few months had elapsed.

When the program resumed, the six most promising members of the team—Riley, Joe McMoneagle, Ken Bell, Fern Gauvin, Nancy Stern, and Hartleigh Trent—were selected to travel to SRI's campus in Menlo Park, California, to spend a couple of weeks as subjects in outbound remote-viewing experiments. They were told that they were going to SRI to learn the think tank's special remote-viewing methods. But in fact, Atwater and Watt primarily wanted SRI to evaluate the talents of the six, secretly naming the *three* who would be most useful as operational remote viewers. In the end, SRI sent the viewers back with the comment that all six seemed good enough to use in operations.

The others who had not gone to SRI would eventually fade from the remote-viewing scene. Some had problems with Gondola Wish anyway; it required them to turn up several hours per week, during normal work hours, but because of the project's secrecy they were generally not allowed to tell their ordinary bosses where they were really going. That was an impossible situation for some. Others had problems relaxing into the groove of remote viewing itself. Steve Hanson, in the throes of the zone, was apt to yank himself out of it with worries over whether he was doing it just right. *No, wait, that's not . . . Okay—No, wait . . .*

Mel Riley naturally was pleased that he had cleared this last hurdle, and as he began to spend an increasing amount of time at the remote-viewing unit, the quality of his experimental spying seemed to improve. One day he was asked to target Scotty Watt, and at the appointed time for the start of the session, he was in his zone, trying to tune in to Watt, wherever he was . . . Well, it was strange. Riley tasted chocolate. Just as if he were chewing a chocolate bar. He also saw, on the flickering screen of his mind, a glass jar filled with coins. Then he sensed a road, and a group of cars. Ten or fifteen minutes after the session was over, Watt walked into the office and drove Riley and Atwater out to where he had just been standing. It was a Volkswagen dealership, along a highway a few miles from Fort Meade. Riley couldn't figure out why he had tasted chocolate and had seen a jar of coins. Then Watt sheepishly admitted that he had arrived at the target a few minutes late; at the start of the session he had actually been at a 7-Eleven convenience store, where he had bought and eaten a chocolate bar. There on the counter next to the cash register had been one of those jars of coins for the March of Dimes.

It eventually occurred to some in the unit that training targets might be made a bit more interesting. Atwater, for example, had the idea of trying to win the Maryland lottery. He called for volunteers from among the remote viewers, and set up some informal "associative remote viewing" (ARV) experiments, in which objects were substituted for numbers as targets. For reasons that weren't entirely clear, numbers themselves were extremely difficult to remote-view directly. In ARV, a teddy bear might stand for 0, a baseball bat for 1, an orange for 2, and so on.

Atwater would assign these objects to numbers secretly. Then he would ask the viewers to enter trances and see into the future, describing the objects that he, Atwater, would present them with on the following day—those objects corresponding to the winning lottery numbers, which by then would have been published. If the RVers reported seeing rows of objects that Atwater had secretly chosen and that neatly translated into a lottery number, he would then place his bets accordingly. The idea was that the remote viewers were simply precognizing their own futures, instead of focusing on the lottery numbers themselves. Unfortunately, it never seemed to work.

Atwater also came up with a treasure-hunt scheme. Some nineteenth-century American adventurer had made a fortune out west, and then had taken it all back east, in the form of jewels and currency. According to the story, he had buried it all somewhere in Virginia, leaving in his writings cryptic clues to the treasure site. Riley and McMoneagle joined the chase and, with remote viewing, tried to narrow the search. Eventually they took a field trip to the general area where the treasure seemed to be, and looked around, driving along country roads and walking through pastures, waiting for a psychic jolt that would lead them in the right direction. They never found the treasure, though in one field, Riley and McMoneagle found an angry bull, and Riley still carries in his memory today the surreal image of McMoneagle—short, stout, not a sprinter—clearing a five-foot barb-wire fence while running uphill.

Major General Thompson, the Army's assistant chief of staff for intelligence, watched benignly over the unit during these first months, encouraged by its performance in practice sessions. And because those in Gondola Wish, and out at SRI, seemed to think that *anyone* could demonstrate some remote-viewing ability, the general eventually decided to give it a try himself.

Responding to the general's summons one day, Scotty Watt arrived with Mel Riley, by now regarded as a good monitor as well as a remote viewer. Riley sat down in Thompson's large Pentagon office, with the general and one of his staff officers, a Major Stone. Stone would be the outbound experimenter, the "beacon," while Thompson tried to remote-view him. Stone and Thompson agreed on a start time for the session, and then Stone left for the target; only he knew what it would be. At the appointed time, Thompson told his secretary to hold his calls. He prepared himself at his desk, with a small stack of blank white paper and a pen. Guided by Riley, he began to describe the images that came into his mind. He had a fleeting glimpse of a bulky, grand-looking building, and next to it a pool of water. He seemed to be looking down on it from a height. He guessed it was the Lincoln Memorial on the Mall near the Capitol; the memorial overlooks a shallow ornamental pool known as the Reflecting Pool.

A half hour or so later, Major Stone came back. It turned out that he had gone not to the Lincoln Memorial but to the Alexandria train station, several miles south of the Pentagon. It looked like a clear "miss," yet when Thompson visited the site, he saw only a few hundred yards away another bulky, grand-looking building, known as the Masonic Temple. It was much more prominent than the train station; in fact it dominated the western skyline of the old colonial section of Alexandria, and it also had a large pool of water close by its western side. Thompson decided he had actually zeroed in on the Temple—and had mistaken it for the Lincoln Memorial. A few weeks later, Thompson was flying out of Washington on official business, and as his plane lifted off from National Airport, heading south over the Potomac, he looked out the window and saw the old section of Alexandria laid out before him. Suddenly—*déjà vu*—it all fell into place. He decided that what he was seeing, from this unusually elevated angle, was merely a clearer version of what he had glimpsed during the remote-viewing session.

Gondola Wish had support not only from General Thompson but also, at least tacitly, from INSCOM commander William Rolya, Army Chief of Staff Edward C. "Shy" Meyer, and Secretary of the Army Clifford Alexander. Even so, the project's budgetary insignificance resulted in a number of practical annoyances for the remote viewers. Once in trance, for example, a remote viewer was apt to become highly sensitive to any sounds around him. Thus he needed a quiet room, preferably a very quiet room. But the small room set aside for remote viewing in 4554 was directly beneath a ladies' room. Riley and other remote viewers were constantly being flushed out of their zones by unwitting servicewomen on the floor above.

Worse, though, were the unexpected noises. One afternoon, Ken Bell was in the darkened viewing room, and Mel Riley was serving as his monitor. Bell liked to cool down by imagining a slowly spinning golden orb. All was quiet, and Bell was observing his orb, glowing and revolving, down in his zone, so deep, so quiet . . .

BOOOOM!

An earsplitting concussion shook the room; Bell was so shocked he seemed to levitate several feet off the couch before landing again and pulling his traumatized nervous system back together. It turned out that some general was retiring, and he was being saluted on the parade ground across the street with a battery of 155-millimeter howitzers.

Eventually, after persistent complaints about such incidents, the unit was moved to buildings 2560 and 2561 on Llewellyn Street, a half mile away. They weren't very attractive structures, and as it had been with the first suite of offices, much of the refurbishing had to be done by the remote viewers themselves. McMoneagle, something of an artist, put on the finishing touch by painting the deep-space mural on the old oven heat shield in 2561. But despite the makeshift, low-rent atmosphere of it all, the remote viewers quickly grew to like their new buildings; they were quiet, and there was much more space. There were three separate RV rooms in the "ops" building, 2560, plus a control room from which Scotty Watt, or visitors from tasking offices, could listen in and give instructions to the monitor as necessary.

Late in 1978, around the time of the move to the new buildings, Gondola Wish underwent a transformation, thanks to what a later Army memo would call "preliminary results and high level interest." The high-level interest came from General Thompson and others at the Pentagon and CIA, some of whom, for the last few years, had been sending intelligence taskings to the remote viewers out at SRI. These officials had heard about the Fort Meade remote viewers, and had decided that they wanted to be able to send taskings to them, too. The idea seemed to be that by consulting two independent sets of psychics, three thousand miles apart, they could compare what the two produced and get a better idea of how accurate the data were likely to be. In the long run, it was thought, the SRI group would focus on the scientific end of things, while the Fort Meade remote viewers would concentrate on operations.

Starting in late 1978, then, the Fort Meade unit began to move away from its originally envisioned function on the opsec teams. Although it would accept opsec-related targets, it would now be seen primarily as an offensive spying team, available for use by anyone in the intelligence community with the proper connections and clearances. To facilitate this role, General Thompson increased the unit's effective budget, and gave it three slots for full-time remote viewers: Mel Riley, Ken Bell, and Joe McMoneagle. The unit now became known as "Special Action Branch." Although it took its orders from General Thompson's office, it was essentially a psychic spying unit that was available to all approved customers in the intelligence community.

Marking this transition, the code name Gondola Wish disappeared. In its place came "Grill Flame," a Pentagon code name that referred to the overall remote-viewing program, encompassing both the Fort Meade unit and the work at SRI.

At its inception, Grill Flame was one of the most secret programs being run by the Pentagon. The secrecy was designed not just to protect the program from Soviet eyes, but—perhaps more important—to protect its supporters from the sheer mortification and embarrassment they would feel if the program were exposed. *Psychics in the Pentagon! The Army's crystal ball gazers!* Such a story would surely break one day. Almost every secret in Washington surfaced eventually. General Thompson and the others running Grill Flame simply hoped that that day would be a long time coming.

Many dozens of operational taskings later, in the late summer of 1979, Mel Riley remote-viewed the Chinese nuclear device at Lop Nor. On that first morning of the operation, he spent an hour on the remote-viewing couch, drifting in and out of the zone, describing to Skip Atwater what he saw and felt. Afterwards he sketched some impressions that had come to him. One stood out; it was a shape that looked like a basketball with two large funnels sticking out of opposite ends. A double-ended loudspeaker. An hourglass on its side. A bow tie. Riley didn't pretend to be a nuclear weapons engineer; he didn't know what it was.

After Riley had finished, it was Joe McMoneagle's turn, and he descended into his own quiet zone. McMoneagle's zone was so deep, he often began snoring during his cool-down period; when he reported back during the session, it was usually in sleepy, apneic murmurs, as if he were talking to someone in a dream. McMoneagle ended up drawing a detailed diagram of the device, including, at its center, the same hourglass-shaped object Riley had described. Ken Bell described the device too.

Atwater wrote a cover summary of the sessions and handed them over to the Air Force officials who had tasked the operation. They seemed to show great interest in the sketches of the hourglass-shaped device. "What is it?" Atwater wanted to know. "We can't tell you," replied one of the Air Force officials. "You don't have a CNWDI clearance."

CNWDI—"cinwiddie"—stood for Critical Nuclear

Weapons Design Information. The hourglass-shaped device, it turned out, was a design element the Chinese hadn't been thought capable of incorporating into their bombs.

Mel Riley and the other remote viewers were usually judged to have no "need to know" how well they had done, and consequently seldom did know. Only occasionally, they would be officially briefed, or Watt or Atwater would give them a pat on the back. If their target had been part of some major crisis, they might even get their feedback through the newspapers.

On this day, Riley knew at least that he couldn't be far off, for he was called back into the RV room in the afternoon, for another round. When he had drifted down to his zone, Atwater asked him to describe an "event" and gave him a set of geographical coordinates.

Riley now sensed a broad, bleak desert, and a series of wide concentric rings, miles in diameter, circling a central point marked by a tower or some other object. He sensed an airplane, a bomb being dropped, then . . . nothing. He wasn't sure what had happened. Later Joe McMoneagle took a turn. He described "a hell of an explosion," but sensed that the explosion had been a failure; it had not gone nuclear.

Riley would never know the full story behind that target, only that Atwater and Watt had seemed pleased afterward. But in fact, the remote-viewing operation had gone very well. The descriptions of the nuclear device, though hard to confirm, had elements that obviously made sense to U.S. weapons analysts, and at least suggested a starting point for analysis and further collection. The description of the failed test also made sense. The tasking had originated because U.S. intelligence had failed to detect a nuclear explosion at the Lop Nor test site on the day the test was expected. American spy satellites, U-2 reconnaissance planes rigged to gather airborne radioactive dust, and other collections systems all had come up empty. But the remote viewers' data had suggested a straightforward reason for the absence of a nuclear explosion: the bomb had exploded but had failed to go nuclear.

American officials eventually used other sources of intelligence to confirm what the remote viewers had detected. A plane carrying the new Chinese device had flown high over the testing site, ready to drop the bomb for an airburst over ground zero. For some reason, there had been one or more malfunctions. The bomb's parachute had failed to open, the bomb had burrowed into the ground, and the high-explosive detonators had fired improperly.* Though there had been a large, radioactively dirty blast, it had not been nuclear. The bomb had been a dud.

---

* The bomb was presumably thermonuclear, employing a conventional high-explosive blast to ignite a (plutonium or uranium) fission blast, in turn igniting a (deuterium-tritium) fusion reaction.

3
PSI-INT

You can't be involved in this for any length of time and not be convinced there's something here.

—former CIA official who tasked the Fort Meade unit

They seem like spectacular stories now. But back then they were an everyday thing, just what we did for a job.

—Skip Atwater

THE PENTAGON HAD A NEAT, COLD LIST OF ACRONYMS FOR ITS MAJOR forms of intelligence. HUMINT was traditional human intelligence, provided by foreign agents and their case officers; it was, so the joke went, the "second-oldest profession."

Then there was PHOTINT, photographic intelligence, which usually referred to satellite or spy-plane imagery, and was also sometimes called IMINT. The pictures U.S. intelligence could take from its spies in the skies included visible-light images, thermal infrared images, gamma-ray images, even wall- and ground-penetrating radar images.

SIGINT, signals intelligence, covered intercepts of virtually all electronic signals, while COMINT, communications intelligence, generally referred to signals from a telephone or a radio conversation. SIGINT/COMINT was rapidly becoming the most important intelligence-gathering technology. Led by the National Security Agency, whose staff was double that of the CIA, America's wiretappers, eavesdroppers, and code breakers gathered enormous quantities of sensitive data, including the most private and embarrassing moments in the lives of various foreign leaders. Trying to process it all was like drinking from a fire hose, and the NSA had to rely heavily on computers to automatically sift through intercepts for worthwhile material.

Finally, there was ELINT, electronic intelligence, a category whose boundaries often blurred with those of SIGINT, COMINT, and PHOTINT. Electronic intelligence usually referred to such things as the radar signatures of enemy air defense systems, and telemetry signals for missiles and satellites.

Together these four "conventional" INTs covered the world pretty well, and probably to a much more dramatic extent than the average citizen imagined. Even so, Atwater knew that intelligence consumers preferred not to rely on solitary sources of information. INTs were used together, to confirm and complement each other. One INT might only provide a tip in one direction, which could then be followed up by other INTs.

To the Grill Flame way of thinking, there was little reason not to consider PSI-INT too—psi-derived intelligence—as long as it provided accurate data from time to time. In straight espionage terms, there seemed little to lose, and much to gain. In the late 1970s, the traditional mainstay of spy work, the human intelligence that could penetrate to the heart of an enemy's capabilities and intentions, seemed to be on the wane. Following a number of scandals in the mid-1970s, including revelations of domestic spying, the CIA had come under unprecedented and often hostile scrutiny from Congress; thanks to that scrutiny, it was now increasingly reluctant to undertake sensitive HUMINT operations. Admiral Stansfield Turner, the

CIA's director during the Carter presidency, seemed to prefer arm's-length collection techniques, like satellite photography and communications intercepts. He was widely disliked at the Agency for having fired, abruptly in October 1977, two hundred case officers in CIA stations around the world. Given these cuts in America's HUMINT capability, and the new political context in which "clean" spying methods were favored, the concept of PSI-INT seemed ideal.

Riley and the other remote viewers had little access to the goings-on at higher levels; even so, they sensed that things were changing for the better, and their morale was rising. It seemed that they really were on the secret, cutting edge of something that would someday be very big—not just in military terms, but in the way human beings understood themselves and their universe. Riley and Atwater and the others would often broach these matters during quiet moments at the unit. They would talk about the history of psychic phenomena, and the possible explanations for it all, and where the pitfalls and limits might lie. Ken Bell, for example, believed that psi could never be used to make money; he had read too many stories about psychics who had become failures as soon as they tried to strike it rich. There was something about psi, he believed, that was intimately connected to human morality. Not everyone went along with Bell's theorem, but most agreed that modern science, with its denial of psi, was due for some profound changes.

In most outward respects, the unit looked like any other. Its members were concerned about promotions, and benefits, and military housing, and the eventual golden light of retirement with a pension. Even the office itself, except for McMoneagle's deep-space mural, seemed stereotypically ordinary, down to the little container of non-dairy-creamer powder next to the coffeepot, and the provocatively tight outfits worn by the typist, a young civilian named Jenny Davenport.

Still, the exotic beliefs the remote viewers held, and the fact that they were valued more for their innate abilities than for their education or military experience, fostered a more laid-back version of military culture, in which there was hardly ever any reference to rank. Sergeant Riley was just Mel. Lieutenant Atwater was "Skip," or "Fred." Remote viewers generally wore casual civilian clothes, and some didn't even wear shoes inside the office. The only discordant note was sounded by Major Watt, who hadn't chosen to be in the unit, wasn't particularly interested in the paranormal, and had an old-fashioned officer's brusqueness around enlisted personnel. He rubbed Riley the wrong way from the beginning.

Riley also found that the unit's laid-back, psi-oriented culture didn't always travel well, especially when it came to the home front. As career intelligence officers, dealing with classified information every day, Riley and the others had become used to keeping their work bottled up at the office. But some now found themselves unable even to tell their spouses in general terms what they did for the Army. It would have sounded too bizarre. *Honey, I lie on my back in a dark room, trying to use psychic powers to spy on people and places in foreign countries.* Better just to say that it was a new and interesting project, and highly classified. Parties and barbecues in which members of the unit mingled with their families were also problematic. When they occurred, the conversations tended to steer clear of the paranormal. Riley might talk about Wisconsin Indian tribes, or the beers of Germany; McMoneagle about camping, or Vietnam; Hartleigh Trent might talk about his cabin cruiser, and going fishing out on the Bay.

Trent, in fact, was one of the great characters in the unit, and Riley and McMoneagle became his close friends. He told a good story, but he never had to pull anyone's leg, for he'd had a long and interesting career. In his last years in the Navy he had helped to run a cold-weather survival school up in Maine, teaching Special Forces SEALs to build igloos in the snow and so forth. A restless tinkerer and inventor, Trent had built a large solar-powered hot-water heater at his house; it worked so well, one day when he showed it off to McMoneagle, that it started to melt some of its own copper pipes.

As near as Riley could tell, Trent had not told his wife about his part-time work as a military psychic. Trent apparently was also concerned about his mother, who was said to be religiously opposed to any dabbling in the paranormal. Riley could sympathize with his colleague. For a long time he wouldn't tell his own wife, Brigitte; all she knew was that he worked at a secret job somewhere, and didn't have to wear his uniform. In fact, since meeting her at the start of his Wiesbaden tour in 1970, Riley had told her very little of what he did for a living. Unsurprisingly, they had been drifting apart. Riley didn't know what the exact statistics were for marriages in which one partner worked in military intelligence, but he doubted that they were very hopeful.

Scotty Watt and Skip Atwater could work interchangeably if necessary, but they generally divided their responsibilities. Watt handled the bureaucratic end, and kept in touch with the network of Grill Flame customers. Atwater shaped incoming taskings into remote-viewing strategies, decided who would serve as monitor and viewer, and presented the final product. Along the way, he might deal with officials from other agencies, but usually only to make sure that the remote viewers were providing what was needed.

Ordinarily the first session for a remote viewer on a given target would be "blind"; in other words, the viewer would know only that there was a target—say, a "location," or an "event"—out there somewhere. Not only did this strange protocol work surprisingly well, but it was inherently self-correcting. If the target was, say, a tank factory in Minsk, and the viewer began to describe a South Pacific lagoon, his monitor would know that the viewer's psychic aim was wide of the mark. But if the viewer began to describe a large industrial facility with Russian-speaking workers, the monitor would be fairly certain that the remote viewer had begun to "access" the target—had tuned in—and might then allow him, before subsequent sessions, to have a look at some of the target material. Thus the monitor would be able to ask increasingly specific questions about the target. "Okay, Mel, you're on target so far. Here's a satellite photograph of the facility you've been describing. Now, you see that building right there? I want you to focus on that from now on. Tell me what's inside it."

Or the monitor might suggest a different approach to the target: "Mel, there is a man named Andrei Semyatin who works somewhere on the complex shown here in this photograph. Try to describe his surroundings at this moment." At times, thanks to the scarcity of personnel in the unit, Riley would come in early in the morning, would serve as the remote viewer in an initial session against a target, and then for the rest of the day (before he received feedback on his session) would serve as a monitor for other viewers on the same operation.

In the realm of scientific experiment, these wouldn't have been considered very rigorous protocols. To give the remote viewer any information about the target, while he was still attempting to remote-view it, would automatically cast doubt in a scientist's mind about the validity of the resulting data. And even if the remote viewer knew nothing about the target in advance, the monitor often knew, and could inadvertently coach the viewer toward the target through his questions and reactions. To do the process with proper scientific controls would mean keeping both the

RVer and the monitor blind to the target at all times during the operation.

But the thing was, when it came to operations, remote viewers didn't *have* to be very scientific. Scotty Watt would lose his temper more than once about what he saw as lax protocols and the need to avoid the appearance of cheating. Still, the clients weren't so much interested in the rigor of the process as they were in the accuracy and reliability— and above all, the usefulness—of the results. That left Atwater relatively free to try whatever worked best.

One of the things Atwater discovered, in the course of early experiments and operations, was that certain viewers had specific and often unique talents when it came to psychic perception. They were the kinds of talents one might imagine in comic book superheroes. Ken Bell, for example, had an extraordinary ability to "connect" with human targets, especially distressed or missing ones, determining such things as their concerns and intents, and whatever injuries they might have.

Mel Riley was valued for his artistic skill; Atwater knew that if Riley saw something in his mind's eye, he could render it on paper in sharp detail. Hartleigh Trent, for his part, was unusually good at taking directions at a target, in situations where other viewers might drift away in confusion. One time Atwater had Trent at a site in the Soviet Union. "I'm here, and there's a building over there," reported Trent. "What do you see to your right?" asked Atwater.

"I see a building, a metal building."

"Okay. What do you see to the left?"

"I see an open space, like a parking lot."

"And what do you see straight in front of you?"

Trent paused for a few seconds, getting his bearings, then said, "A transmission. I'm lying under a truck."

Joe McMoneagle was probably the best at picking up and sketching the details of technological targets. But he had far stranger talents, perhaps appropriately for a viewer whose zone was down on the very edge of dreams. In his hypnotic visions, the burly warrant officer seldom failed to see a green haze around any kind of radioactive or fissionable material. Whether it had something to do with the esoteric properties of matter and the universe, as McMoneagle himself believed, or whether it was that McMoneagle had simply read too many Superman cartoons as a kid (where deadly Kryptonite gave off the same greenish glow), the others thought it was a hell of a useful talent to have. McMoneagle sometimes also perceived radio frequency radiation—for example, from a broadcasting antenna—as a kind of orange flame.

Skeptics about psi often complained that if such a power really existed, its possessors would soon become so rich and influential that they would rule the world. But as Atwater and Riley and the others saw it, psi wasn't as powerful as all that. Like any other human faculty, it had a host of limitations. Numbers and letters—for example, a future lottery number or a name on a secret document—were nearly impossible to remote-view accurately. Researchers out at SRI believed this had something to do, unavoidably, with the way psi data were processed in the brain.

By contrast, visually dramatic targets whose locations were fixed and long established were usually the easiest to remote-view. The problem was, however, that in the intelligence world, these kinds of targets were also relatively easy to spy on by other, more conventional means—especially satellite imagery and communications intercepts. Even if it seemed that a remote viewer had penetrated a target more thoroughly than satellite systems and listening posts had, his data might be inherently difficult to verify. But RV data *had* to be verified somehow by other means, for it was of controversial value at the best of times; almost no one in the intelligence community would ever dare rely on it alone.

Despite this apparent quandary, the remote-viewing unit had regular customers, and kept busy most of the time. A surprising number of senior officials and analysts, scattered throughout the Pentagon and CIA bureaucracies, found it reassuring to have access to remote-viewing data, especially if it matched what they expected to find at a given site. There were cases when RV data on a site were actually used to guide subsequent penetrations of the site by other means. Riley, McMoneagle, and the others were asked by the CIA, Army special-ops teams, and even the Pentagon's Delta Force commando unit, to map the interiors of a number of foreign embassies and other sites around the world. The RV-derived maps were compared with what was already known about the buildings' interiors. In the cases where they seemed reasonably accurate, the maps were used to guide teams that then broke into the buildings to plant listening devices or to steal information, or to do whatever it was they were supposed to do.

Ironically, the taskings for which remote viewers could have been most useful were also the most difficult for them, and the most dreaded; they came to be known as "search problems," because the target was something, or someone, at an unknown location, and the task was to search for and find the location.

Under certain circumstances, search problems could be solved relatively quickly, for example if the search was focussed on a limited area. In one case in 1980, a target was brought in by one of the Grill Flame liaison officers from the National Security Agency. The NSA man brought a photograph of the outside of a U.S. consulate in the Mediterranean area. He explained that information seemed to be leaking out of the consulate to the Soviets. The NSA wanted to know how.

After an initial round of relatively "blind" remote-viewing sessions, followed by consultations with the NSA man, Atwater determined that Joe McMoneagle's information seemed most on target. He now showed McMoneagle the photo of the consulate and asked him to go inside. McMoneagle described and mapped out a particular area of the consulate; he said he saw a flamelike emanation, some kind of unusual electromagnetic signal, coming from a wall in a certain hallway, behind a water cooler. Atwater passed the session data to the NSA man, who nodded and said he wanted to know more; he wanted to know where the bug was sending its information.

So McMoneagle was sent back down into his zone, and Atwater asked him to scan the area around the consulate. The remote viewer soon found an apartment across the street that had its own unusual haze of electromagnetic emanations; it was the Soviet listening post, electronically tuning in to the radio signals from the bug in the consulate. But there was something else, McMoneagle said. Downstairs from the listening post, there was another apartment with strange emanations; there were Americans here.

The NSA man had to shake his head at that one. In the day or so since he had tasked the remote viewers, a special NSA investigation team at the consulate had discovered the Soviet listening post. It turned out the Soviets' receiving equipment was so badly designed that it inadvertently rebroadcast the signals it was pulling from the bug in the consulate. The Americans that McMoneagle detected in the lower apartment were the members of the NSA team, busy eavesdropping on the eavesdroppers.

It had been an impressive display of remote-viewing talent, but searches that were not so concentrated presented a much greater problem. Remote viewers often speculated about the reasons. Most seemed to believe that the longer a target had existed at a given site, the easier it was to remote-view. By contrast, the more a target moved around, the more it blurred on the screen of the RVer's perception.

And even when it seemed that the target itself—say, a missing person—could be perceived, remote viewers often found it impossible to describe the target's surroundings in enough detail to pinpoint the location. Sometimes McMoneagle or Bell would pick up words that seemed related to nearby towns or villages, but this tended to happen spontaneously and not always accurately. They were usually unable to move their perceptions around deliberately, to look at, say, the street signs at the nearest intersection. Even if they could, they probably wouldn't be able to read the signs.

When nothing else was working, the remote viewers might go over maps of the search area, moving their hands across it until some internal impulse told them they had hit the spot. Such "map-dowsing" techniques were never very reliable. But there were certainly some interesting search problems. One day in about 1979, a tasking that seemed particularly urgent came in. The target was an object that had been lost somewhere in the Mediterranean area; the remote viewers' job was to find it. As they began to run sessions, it became clear what the target was. McMoneagle sensed a green glow around it. The target was a nuclear weapon. The remote viewers' data suggested that it had accidentally dropped off a U.S. bomber's wing pod, into the sea near Spain, presumably during an official NATO exercise. Were the remote viewers right? They were never told.

In another case, around the same time, the unit was asked to predict the crash zone of Skylab, which had been decaying in its orbit and was expected to reenter Earth's atmosphere sometime in July 1979. At least half a dozen remote viewers attacked the problem. McMoneagle suggested that the big space station would impact in the South Pacific, somewhere around Australia and Indonesia. He was pretty close. A few weeks later, Skylab reentered over eastern Australia, blazed a trail westward in the sky across the big island, and rained hot metal debris on western Australia and the Indian Ocean.

One morning, around the time of the Skylab job, a tasking came in from the Pentagon via General Thompson's aide, Major Stone. Atwater was told simply that a Navy A-6 attack aircraft had been lost somewhere in the world. Could the Fort Meade remote viewers find it?

Ken Bell was sent against the target and was soon describing a wooded area, trees and bushes, and the charred remains of plane and crew. He felt that it was somewhere relatively close to where he was sitting at Fort Meade, certainly within a few hundred miles. He was unable to find the location on maps and had the impression that the wreckage was mostly obscured by terrain and foliage. But several times in the session, he found himself picking up the word "bald." He didn't know what it meant. Later, Atwater found out that the aircraft, whose terrain-following radar apparently had malfunctioned, had crashed into the side of a hill in the Blue Ridge Mountains of Virginia. The name of the hill was "Bald Knob."

Another search problem involved a U.S. helicopter that had gone down, for some reason, in a remote corner of Peru. A Pentagon satellite had picked up what seemed to be the copter's locator beacon, but the signal had died before anyone could triangulate in on it. On short notice, the RV unit at Fort Meade was asked to try to locate the downed craft. Atwater turned again to Ken Bell, who lay down on the leather couch in one of the RV rooms, and closed his eyes. The golden orb in his mind began to spin, and now Bell was high in the Andes, at the wreckage site. There was the pilot, and the copilot; he was with them— Suddenly, Bell was sobbing uncontrollably.

Atwater soon understood what was happening. Bell was tightly wound at the best of times, but now under trance conditions, with many of the normal inhibitory mechanisms of consciousness inoperative, he had become explosively sensitive to emotions evoked by the target. The helicopter's pilot and copilot were not only dead; they were broken and roasted. The horror of the scene had risen up and washed over him like a wave. It was too much; Atwater had to stop the session.

Other human targets were easier to deal with. One day a CIA official brought in a classic human-intelligence problem, one that case officers had to deal with all the time. The problem was this: The Agency had an agent on its payroll in a certain East European country. Like most important agents, he was subjected every year or so to a polygraph examination to check his truthfulness. His annual "poly" was coming up, but before that happened, the agent's case officer wanted to know what questions the Agency's polygrapher should ask. The target package, for Atwater, consisted simply of the case officer's name, and a date and time. The CIA official who had brought in the tasking wanted the remote viewers to spy on the case officer at that date and time, knowing that he would then be meeting with his agent. Setting it up this way, the Agency cleverly managed to target the agent without revealing that it had done so.

McMoneagle, given the target by Atwater, seemed to access it fairly quickly. He described two men meeting in a restaurant. He described a briefcase that one man—the agent—had with him. What's in the briefcase? Atwater asked McMoneagle. A lot of money, replied McMoneagle, who suggested that there were certain irregularities in the man's financial situation that the other man—the case officer—didn't know about. The session results were eventually cabled to the case officer overseas, and were also shown to the Agency's designated polygrapher. A week or so later, in a safe house or hotel room somewhere in Europe, the polygrapher met secretly with the agent for the examination. He began to grill him about possible financial irregu-larities. The agent denied everything. Then the polygrapher said, "What about all the money you had in that briefcase last week?" At this, the agent nearly fell out of his chair in astonishment. "How could you have known that?"

For the CIA and some other clients, it seemed, the more oblique forms of targeting were not just good for opera-tional security; they helped build confidence in what the remote viewers were saying. If the tasking didn't actually specify the information that was desired, but the remote viewers provided the information anyway, the client could be more sure they hadn't simply given him an educated guess.

One day in 1980, a CIA technical operations specialist named Norm Everheart brought a photograph to Fort Meade. The photograph depicted a foreign-looking man, somewhere in his mid-forties. He was the target.

Unknown to Atwater and the remote viewers, a similar photograph had landed on the desk of a government offi-cial somewhere in Scandinavia, a few weeks before, when the man in the photo had applied for a passport. He had appeared to be a local citizen. However, by a remarkable coincidence, a Western intelligence service had at the same time sent a warning to that same Scandinavian govern-ment, to the effect that the man was a KGB "illegal," a deep-cover officer who had assumed a foreign identity. The warning, with a photograph, had landed on the desk of the same official who had received the man's passport applica-tion.

The man was given a passport, and soon travelled to South Africa. But he did not travel alone; he was closely followed by a team of CIA and Scandinavian counterintel-ligence officers. The team notified South African counter-intelligence, pleading with them to leave the man alone while they tailed him to whatever his target happened to be. But the South Africans, perhaps worrying that some of their state secrets might be divulged this way, ignored the pleas and arrested the man within a day or so of his arrival. They put him under interrogation in a room somewhere in the coastal city of Cape Town.

The interrogation went nowhere. And although the group of Western counterintelligence officers were also given a chance to interrogate him, they too were unable to learn anything. Finally, a counterintelligence officer at CIA headquarters, a man named Jim Morris, came to Norm Everheart and sketched out the general facts of the case. Could the Grill Flame psychics lend a hand? There seemed to be nothing to lose.

Everheart was a rumpled-looking, mustachioed man in his forties who bore a resemblance to the early motion-picture actor Bert Lahr (think of the Lion character in *The Wizard of Oz*). A senior technical adviser to John McMahon, the CIA's deputy director for operations, Everheart had been asked by McMahon to serve as the chief coordinator for Grill Flame taskings from the CIA's Operations Directorate. Both Everheart and McMahon had been involved in psychic spying experiments since the early days of the CIA-sponsored work out at SRI. They had seen, and they had believed, and they were at least willing to give RV a try in operational situations.

Jim Morris, the counterintelligence man, told Everheart that he was primarily interested in answering one question about the KGB illegal. The man was assumed to be getting his instructions via shortwave radio, in some sort of code. The question was: how was the man decoding his messages?

Everheart brought the photograph of the KGB illegal over to Fort Meade one day, and gave it to Scotty Watt. Normally, Everheart couriered target packages over, and received the results back the same way, or sent the actual tasking officer himself out to Fort Meade. But ever since he had received his Grill Flame briefing from Scotty Watt in

1979, Watt had been encouraging him to come over to witness an operation for himself. This time, he did. Watt brought him over to the ops building, and ushered him into the control room. Inside the adjacent remote-viewing room, Skip Atwater was waiting while Ken Bell cooled down into a trance, watching his golden orb. As the session started, Norm Everheart listened in via headphones from the control room. He didn't know Bell's name—the identities of the viewers were the most classified aspect of the program—but what he heard astonished him.

Bell, down in his zone, began to describe a man sitting in an apartment on the second floor of a building, in some city bordered by an immense amount of water. The man was dressed oddly. His clothes weren't street clothes; they were more like pajamas. And they were gray. Like prison clothes, in fact.

The man was with two other people, dressed more normally. They didn't speak the languages he spoke. But he knew what they wanted from him—information—and he would never give it to them. He was adamant; it was as if he were having a conversation with himself, in his mind, about how sure he was that he would never give up his information.

At this point, Atwater quietly suggested that Bell "talk" to the KGB man, telepathically coaxing the information out of him. It was a strange technique, and perhaps only a metaphorical device that got remote viewers past psychological barriers within their own heads. But the remote viewers seemed to think that they *really were* "asking" their targets, and in any case, it had seemed to work for them on many occasions.

Bell tried; he telepathically asked the man what was happening. Why was he there? What did the other two men want from him? But it was no use. The KGB man was a rock; Bell's telepathic queries merely bounced off him. The session finally ended.

Norm Everheart was disappointed that the session hadn't produced more information. But he was enormously impressed with what he had heard. He knew few details of the case, but what the remote viewer had described had certainly sounded right. Everheart drove over to building 4554, to find a secure phone. He used it to call Jim Morris back at CIA headquarters, to tell him what the remote viewer had come up with. Morris confirmed it all: the upstairs room; the gray clothes; the two interrogators—everything.

Everheart now asked Morris if he could provide him with any personal details about the KGB man, or anything else that the remote viewer could focus on. Morris gave him the names—the actual Russian names—of the man's son and daughter.

Everheart thanked Morris, and drove back to building 2560. He had Watt schedule another remote-viewing session for the afternoon. After lunch, he came back to the ops building and put on the headphones again. Bell, down in his zone, was beginning to break through the KGB man's mental barriers. *Your son Sergei misses you,* he was whispering through the ether to the KGB man. *Your daughter Svetlana wonders when you'll be home.* And bit by bit, it seemed, information was coming back. Bell, from the depths of his zone, reported that the KGB man now had tears in his eyes. Bell was conducting one of the most bizarre interrogations—if it could be called that—in the history of intelligence work, and it seemed to be working. *Sergei wants me to take him skiing,* the KGB man seemed to muse sadly. *I promised him I would take him skiing.*

Yes, you promised, Bell responded. *You need to get home quickly to take him skiing.*

I need to get home. This was supposed to be my last tour anyway. I was about to retire, to go back to the USSR.

After a while of this, Bell decided that the man's mental barriers had been lowered enough, and he started to ask about more operational matters. In asking the KGB man about his possessions, he learned about a pocket calculator. Later, Mel Riley was run in a session against the same target, and also came up with a pocket calculator. Norm Everheart knew that pocket calculators, either unmodified or with special cryptographic chips, were commonly used by KGB illegals to code and decode messages.

Norm Everheart took the information back to CIA headquarters, and handed it over to Morris. In due course, Morris contacted the South African counterintelligence officials running the KGB man's interrogation. Asked about the calculator, they responded that they had found no such thing. Asked a second time, a few days later, they admitted that in fact one of their group had found a calculator among the KGB man's possessions, and had taken it home with him. No one ever confirmed whether the calculator had been used to decode messages, but Jim Morris and Norm Everheart were reasonably sure that it had. Thanks to the remote viewers, the case was closed.

The term "remote viewing" was, on the surface, a sanitized, high-tech synonym for the old term "clairvoyance." Clairvoyance, technically, was merely the ability to see things at a distance, in real time. In other words, it was a negation only of three-dimensional space. Yet Atwater, Riley, McMoneagle, and the others in the unit believed that remote viewers also could cross the fourth dimension—*time*.

They had no doubt, though, that time was the slipperiest dimension. Moving backward, into the past, was like travelling in a time machine with bugs in its software; you might not end up where you planned. In fact, there were many cases where remote viewers ended up in the past even when they had been sent to the present. More than once, Atwater had to tell Riley or McMoneagle or one of the others to ignore the interesting civilization they had alighted in, with its pyramids or human sacrifices or whatever, and move forward to, say, the terrorist training camp inhabiting that space in the present.

Moving beyond the present and into the future was a leap in the dark at the best of times. For some targets, it seemed to work with humdrum perfection, as if time, chance, and progress were only illusions conjured by Fate. For other targets, the future was opaque and confused, as if Fate were hopelessly unable to make up her mind.

One day, Skip Atwater was approached by a friend, Don Porter, who worked for INSCOM at Arlington Hall. Porter was about to travel to the Far East, to sit in on secret talks between military and civilian officials from North and South Korea. The talks were to be held in a certain farmhouse in the area of the demilitarized zone. Porter wanted Atwater's remote viewers to go to the farmhouse a week or so into the future when the conference should be under way. He wanted the viewers to get inside the heads of the North Korean delegates. What were their negotiating strategies? How far could they be pushed? Atwater, explaining that the future was a tricky business, agreed to give the task a try.

Remote viewers by now often served as monitors for operations, and this time Atwater appointed McMoneagle to that job. McMoneagle in turn ran Riley, Bell, and Trent against the target, asking them to describe the "event" he had in mind, at the coordinates of the farmhouse. Unfortunately, each remote viewer generated a different result, and none described a meeting, or even a farmhouse or the Korean countryside.

Atwater wasn't sure what to make of this, but McMoneagle had a theory. The apparent randomness of the responses, he suggested, was a sign that there was something wrong with the target. Perhaps the event at the given coordinates wasn't even going to occur. Perhaps there would be no meeting at all. Atwater went along with this suggestion, and relayed it to Porter. Not very impressed with what Atwater had to tell him, Porter took his scheduled flight to Korea anyway. A short time after he had arrived, he was told that the North Koreans, citing some excuse, had cancelled the meeting.

A similar operation unfolded in the early 1980s, when the CIA asked the remote-viewing unit to check out the new U.S. Embassy building in Moscow for possible Soviet bugs.

The new building was designed as a modern, comfortable replacement for the cramped and decaying structure that then housed the embassy staff. The catch was that the new building was only in the early stages of construction; the CIA wanted the remote viewers to look at the building *after* it had been finished, still a few years in the future.

The reason for the tasking was, for the CIA, painfully obvious. The new building was shaping up to be one of the worst security fiascoes in U.S. diplomatic history. Fearing that Russians would plant surveillance devices throughout the building during construction—especially the off-site construction of prefabricated components—CIA officials had argued loudly that only security-cleared U.S. firms and their employees should be allowed to take part in the construction. The Russians, for their part, had pounded the table and insisted that imported workers would not be allowed, that Russian laborers had to do the job. The State Department eventually gave in to the Russian demands, arguing that the United States could easily clean out any bugs the Soviets placed, and that Soviet labor would in the end be cheaper than U.S. labor. The Soviets soon got to work, and only a few dozen U.S. supervisors were allowed at the site.*

---

* Incidentally, the new structure was placed in a low-lying area near the Moskva River, a relatively poor place for intercepting local radio and microwave signals. Meanwhile, back in Washington, the Soviets were building a large new chancery building—on one of the highest, best SIGINT

As a result of all this, the CIA now had to spend substantial resources to evaluate the Soviets' placement of listening devices in the new building. One of its first steps was to ask the remote viewers to find out which rooms in the finished embassy would have listening devices, and where they would be.

The viewers went to work, trying to envision the embassy in the present and then a few months into the future, eventually moving forward, in six-month leaps, to the mid-1980s. At first they found numerous bugs in the prefabricated walls already at the site; some were real, some were nuts-and-bolts decoys, but in any case they were too numerous to count, much less to remove entirely. Joe McMoneagle even described steel girders and reinforcing rods that had been welded together in a such a way as to serve as a giant broadcasting antenna for some of the bugs. The Soviets seemed to have achieved a remarkable level of sophistication with their eavesdropping techniques. But the strangest thing, for Atwater, was that as he stepped the viewers forward in time, year after year, the data started to fly out in all directions. Eventually none of the remote viewers agreed on anything. Fernand Gauvin, asked to remote-view the embassy sometime in the mid-1980s, described a comfortable brownstone house, with a fire in the fireplace. Something was wrong with the target somehow. Was it too far out in the future? Had the remote viewers run into some kind of space-time barrier?

A year or two later, in 1983, a CIA/NSA team quietly brought a large X-ray machine to the construction site, to look inside the walls. The Soviets, when they realized what the U.S. team was doing, suddenly announced that they were walking off the job, in "protest" at this impolite intrusion into their work space. The game was up. The CIA

---

spots in Washington, with line-of-sight views to the Pentagon and other key buildings.

found that the structure was indeed riddled with thousands of bugs and metallic decoys; they would later find the girders welded together as antennas, as McMoneagle had described, in addition to bugs that were actually wired into the electrical system, and giant room-bugs that could be powered by microwaves beamed in from outside. Construction slowed to a stop. In Washington, reports were written and commissions were appointed to study the problem. By the late 1980s the consensus seemed to be that the building should be torn down. Only then would Atwater understand why the remote viewers had had so much trouble remote-viewing the future of the embassy building: The building had no future.*

Some of the unit's tasks, especially in the early years, involved domestic targets—mostly operations security targets—brought in by military officials anxious to see whether their secret programs could be penetrated by remote viewers. One day Scotty Watt handed Atwater a sealed envelope and told him to send the remote viewers against the target represented inside. Unknown to Atwater, the envelope contained a black-and-white photograph of an aircraft hangar at an undisclosed base. The Army had hidden an experimental XM-1 tank inside the hangar, hoping that the aircraft hangar surroundings might confuse the remote viewers into missing the target.

Atwater put McMoneagle on the target, and McMoneagle started to describe a keyboard-like instrument attached to some kind of computer. There was an optical

---

* Although President Reagan recommended that the building be torn down, it was later decided that a modification of the existing unfinished building would be cheaper than a completely new project. In late 1994 Congress approved $240 million for a planned "Top Hat" reconstruction project that would remove the top two floors and add four new "secure" floors. The project is scheduled for completion in 1999.

system involved, too. And there were large explosive shells. McMoneagle eventually moved his perception back a few paces and saw the tank. Though he had no prior knowledge of the XM-1's design, and apparently did not even know that he was perceiving the tank, he eventually produced a detailed engineer-style drawing, with a cutaway diagram of the laser-targeting system, the ammunition storage and feeder, the turret lockdowns, the main gun assembly, and the special high-tech armor. McMoneagle would later declare it to have been one of his best sessions ever. What the XM-1 project's security people thought was never recorded, but they never came back.

One of Mel Riley's best sessions also resulted from an opsec tasking. A security team from the Air Force approached Atwater one day and handed him a target envelope; it contained a blurry photograph of what could have been almost anything.

As he usually did when a tasking came in, Atwater assigned it to at least several viewers. After a session or two for each viewer, he evaluated the data, looking for details that more than one remote viewer had described. These details he considered the most reliable, and the remote viewers who had produced most of the reliable data were the ones he continued to send against the target.

McMoneagle, as usual, was a producer on this one. He described an aircraft crash, and saw a suspicious person picking up a piece of the wreckage and hiding it away. Atwater wondered if that was what the Air Force had been after.

But Atwater quickly became more interested in what Riley was producing. Riley, in his zone, described a strange batlike flying-wing shape, with a bulbous cockpit like a 747's. Stranger than that were his descriptions of the aircraft's control mechanisms. They looked to him like strings, yet when he looked down their length, all he saw was light. He wondered if he was remote-viewing some kind of toy. "This must be the screwiest thing I've ever seen in my life," he told Atwater.

Atwater later handed Riley's sharply detailed sketches and descriptions to the Air Force team. They looked at the material, and blanched. They told Atwater to give them back the blurry photograph they had provided, and to stop targeting it with remote viewers.

Atwater never heard from them again. But years later, he was at home watching television when the Air Force publicly rolled out its B-2 Stealth bomber for the first time. As he saw the bat-like flying-wing shape, he felt a shiver up his spine, and remembered Riley's session. Riley had remote-viewed his way into the heart of the Stealth program, which at the time had been one of the Pentagon's most secret projects. Atwater later found out why Riley had described "strings" with "light." To reduce the bomber's radar signature, the Air Force had decided to use fiber-optic control wires instead of traditional electromechanical or hydraulic lines.

Remote-viewing sessions as accurate and detailed as Riley's Stealth job, or McMoneagle's XM-1 tank job, didn't happen every day. Even for the best remote viewers, bad sessions—in which the data had relatively little relation to the target—came at least as often as good sessions. Yet Atwater was convinced that a good team of remote viewers, managed properly, could be accurate and reliable enough to represent a significant security threat. The question was, What could America do about it? To the extent that a foreign remote viewer could burrow noiselessly through time and space, what conceivably could be done to stop him?

Atwater bravely came up with a number of suggestions for psi countermeasures. One was inspired by a bizarre intelligence report about Soviet gift-giving to visiting Americans. The report indicated that such gifts were sometimes intended to serve as beacons for KGB and military remote viewers, to help them zero in on a target. Thus, for example, when Senator Junket returned from his fact-finding tour of Russia, he might proudly put his souvenir samovar, a gift from the Komsomol Youth League, on a shelf in his office. Soviet remote viewers, meanwhile, would be asked to find the samovar. When they did, the theory went, they would also sense what was going on in the room, perhaps something that directly shed light on sensitive U.S. policies, or something embarrassing that the KGB could use to blackmail the senator.

As a result of all this, Atwater actually wrote a report recommending that gifts brought from Communist countries should always be placed in innocuous locations, such as one's attic or basement, far away from any activity or materials that might interest the Soviets. He also made another more general suggestion about protecting targets against Soviet remote viewers. His reasoning went as follows: If a Soviet remote viewer was sent against a U.S. target and began to describe things that were radically, insanely incongruous with the target—say, a large Mickey Mouse balloon inside a missile silo—then whoever was monitoring his session or analyzing his data was likely to conclude that this remote viewer was having a bad day, and if this sort of thing kept up, he might even become a candidate for psychiatric treatment. Atwater suggested, delicately, that if U.S. officials were concerned about Soviet psi-spying activities, they should consider festooning sensitive sites with such strange objects.

Within the weird world of remote viewing, Atwater's proposal seemed perfectly logical. But most intelligence officials still lived outside that weird world; to them such proposals merely sounded crazy. To Atwater's knowledge, U.S. missile silos were never decorated with Mickey Mouse balloons.

The Grill Flame project itself, by its mere existence, already drew plenty of scorn from those who knew about it.

One day Skip Atwater was at a briefing for Major General William Odom, who had succeeded Ed Thompson as the Army's ACSI in 1981. In giving the general some examples of how good remote-viewing data could be, Atwater showed him some sessions on the U.S. Embassy building in Moscow, where McMoneagle had anticipated the later discovery of widespread bugs, girders welded into antennas, and so forth. Odom looked at the RV data, then said dismissively, "Yes, we know that already."

Odom, like many highly educated people inside and outside government, often seemed embarrassed that the Army was spending any money at all on the paranormal. He appeared to believe that, whether or not there was anything to it, it was something best left alone by the military. The precise reasons for such conclusions were sometimes elusive, although in many cases, the remote-viewing program's supporters thought they detected a whiff of churchly Inquisition. In 1980 President Carter's Defense R&D chief William Perry (later the secretary of defense in the Clinton administration) struck the funding for the Fort Meade unit from his R&D budget; Perry's reasoning was purely secular, but it was rumored that Perry had noticed the controversial unit only because a born-again-Christian staffer for a western senator had drawn his attention to it. Grill Flame managed to stay alive anyway, with funds pulled in from other Army projects, but it had been a close call, and it wouldn't be the last.

The keepers of Grill Flame, as they might have been called, were an eclectic group, scattered widely around the intelligence community. Many had been converted to support for the program after they had brought in their own targets, and the remote viewers had impressed them with a show of clairvoyant prowess. Some, like General Thompson at the Pentagon, and several officials at the CIA and DIA, had successfully taken turns as remote viewers themselves. Everyone seemed to know, however, that support for the program could vanish overnight, especially if there were a public revelation. Yet some promoters of the program were so convinced that they could not keep silent. For example, there was Congressman Charlie Rose, a North Carolina Democrat who chaired the House Intelligence Committee's Evaluation Subcommittee. Rose was briefed on Grill Flame in the late 1970s by General Thompson, and also by Grill Flame's overall manager, Jack Vorona, the head of the DIA's Scientific and Technical Intelligence Directorate. Accompanied by Vorona, Rose toured the remote-viewing facilities at both SRI and Fort Meade, chatting with remote viewers and witnessing practice sessions. He even discussed the program with President Carter.

Rose's constituents in North Carolina lay squarely in the Bible Belt, where dabbling in the paranormal was often construed as flirtation with the devil. Yet Rose became such a staunch supporter of the program that in 1979 he tossed political care to the winds—not to mention security concerns—in a revealing interview for *Omni* magazine. Condemning the skeptics and "publicity-shy" intelligence officials who regularly tried to snuff out Grill Flame, he made a strong pitch for the program, even referring to remote-viewing data he had seen on an unnamed Soviet target. "What these people 'saw,' " he said, referring to the remote viewers, "was confirmed by aerial photography. There's no way it could have been faked."

4

JOE OF ARC

The information he gave us was the *absolute* answer.

> —Former CIA official,
> commenting on a remote-viewing
> session by Joe McMoneagle

He's one of the best on the planet.

> —SRI researcher Ed May,
> on McMoneagle

OH-DARK-THIRTY, THEY CALLED IT IN THE ARMY. WAY BEFORE SUN-rise. The ringing of the phone snatched Mel Riley out of somewhere deep, as Brigitte stirred beside him.

Riley sleepily picked up the phone. It was Atwater, calling from the office. Riley was needed immediately.

Riley dressed and drove over to the office, parking next to two black, official-looking cars with Defense Department plates. Their occupants were inside with Watt and Atwater. They wore civilian clothes, and one of them carried a large envelope. No one was introduced. Atwater and Watt looked tired and serious. Watt signed for the envelope, and the two men left.

Riley went over to the ops building, and Atwater followed with the envelope. Riley lay down on the couch, packed his anxieties away in the imaginary suitcase, and drifted down to his zone. He was nearing the bottom, fighting sleep. Atwater wanted him to concentrate on something described in the envelope, to envision where it would be at a certain time two days in the future.

Riley drifted along and eventually sensed something heavy, big, dark, a vehicle. A tank. On a rail car somewhere. After he came out of the zone, he sketched it.

Atwater showed the session data to Watt, who raced out the door to his car and drove over to 4554, the INSCOM building, where he had access to a secure phone. He called the Defense Department men from the secure phone, and told them that Riley had described the tank on a rail car. It was what they had hoped to hear.

The Russian T-72 tank is nowadays considered somewhat old and second-rate, compared with the latest American models, but in the late 1970s, it was brand-new, and U.S. intelligence experts knew little about its capabilities. Ideally, they wanted their own T-72, to take apart, to "reverse-engineer." So they did it the American way: they went out and bought one.

The seller, dealing through an international arms merchant based in the Middle East, was an Eastern European general. Atwater remembers that he was Polish, Riley that he was Romanian.* Whichever he was, the mysterious general had no direct contact with the United States, only with

---

* In a 1994 article about secret U.S. purchases of Soviet arms via Eastern Europe, *The Washington Post* reporter Ben Weiser noted that the purchases began through Romania in the late 1970s, with the cooperation of the Romanian defense minister. Later, Poland became the main conduit. Weiser strongly implied that General Wojciech Jaruzelski of Poland, notorious for imposing martial law on his country in 1981, had known about and approved these transactions, although Jaruzelski denied this to Weiser in an interview. A former senior Pentagon official, who didn't want to be quoted or directly identified, told me that in his opinion, Jaruzelski had been a U.S. agent.

the representatives of the arms dealer, who in turn dealt with U.S. intelligence officials.

The U.S. officials running the operation were, naturally, nervous about the deal. Was it all a double cross, they wondered, a trap for American intelligence? Perhaps the remote viewers could help in the tracking of the tank as the operation progressed.

Not long after Scotty Watt came back from his phone call in building 4554, Hartleigh Trent, Ken Bell, and Joe McMoneagle arrived. Riley and Trent went over to the ops building with the envelope.* Trent, monitored by Riley, sank down into a relaxed state and tried to focus on the object described in the envelope—the tank—this time another few days into the future. Trent found himself on a ship at sea. Riley asked him to peer into the hold. Trent saw a tank and what looked like parts of an aircraft. McMoneagle and Bell described similar scenes. Everyone seemed to be "on" today.

The unit continued to monitor the arms merchant, and the voyage of the tank, over the next few days. But now they did it in "real-time," not in the future. They watched as the tank started in a rail yard, then moved to a port, and was loaded into the hold of a ship. The ship set sail, with what Riley believed was a Greek captain.

At one point, Joe McMoneagle remote-viewed the ship, monitored by Atwater. He sensed that wherever the ship was (presumably in the Black Sea or the Baltic) it was late at night. He also sensed that the ship was dead in the water.

---

* Riley believes that the targeting envelope, for the first day of the operation, contained cashier's checks destined for the payment of the tank's seller. But Atwater doesn't remember that part, and a Pentagon source with extensive experience in such operations told me that a simple transfer of cash or cashier's checks was "not how those transactions were ever done." More likely, he said, the money was wired to a Swiss bank account, for collection by the seller when the transaction had been completed successfully.

Whether he was seeing something that had just happened, or was about to happen, he didn't know, but it was certainly vivid. The first ship was boarded by men wearing black, as in some World War II commando movie. They had come from another large ship that stood nearby. The men held the captain at gunpoint. He had his hands in the air. The other ship pulled alongside, swung a crane over the hold, and winched up the container that held the tank. They were stealing the Pentagon's multimillion-dollar cargo, just like that.

McMoneagle began to concentrate on the first ship's captain, the one standing at gunpoint. He decided to try a "telepathic" interrogation. *What's going on here?* he asked the captain. To his surprise, the captain seemed unfazed by the commandos with guns. Everything was going as planned. The hijacking had merely been staged, presumably to cover the trail of the general who was selling the tank. Whether the hijackers were U.S. Special Forces soldiers, or the arms merchant's hired guns, or even Romanian or Polish sailors, Atwater and McMoneagle never found out.

But one thing they did find out: A few weeks later, a ship that had come from a Middle Eastern port cruised up Chesapeake Bay, and unloaded a special cargo at the Army's tank R&D center at Aberdeen Proving Grounds. It was a shiny new Soviet T-72.

Early in the program, Skip Atwater, Scotty Watt, and other officials recognized that Joe McMoneagle was simply the best all-around remote viewer in the unit. With his bull-neck build, he looked as if he should have been out playing football, or charging machine-gun nests. But genetics and circumstance had combined to turn him into a one-in-a-million psi savant, a shaman in Army boots.

An incident in McMoneagle's childhood recalls the legend of the French warrior-mystic "Joan of Arc." According to the legend, thirteen-year-old Joan was playing in an orchard one day with friends, then sat down, exhausted, by a tree. Suddenly the child world faded away, a strange globe of light settled down nearby, and an adult voice began to speak to her. Such voices, sometimes accompanied by angelic apparitions, went on to tell Joan that she would take up arms and lead beleaguered France to victory in its battles with the invading English army.

McMoneagle's own somewhat humbler version of this experience occurred when he was eleven years old, in 1957. He was camping with a group of friends next to an orange grove in his home state of Florida. One night he and his friends were all up late, in the grove, playing one of those primitive combat games that preadolescent boys seem to devise instinctively. One boy, designated "it," had to run and hide, while the others tried to find him. After a certain number of rounds, it was McMoneagle's turn to hide. He ran into the dark, climbed an orange tree, found a secure position, and relaxed. He had been playing the game for a few hours now, and was very tired. His eyes closed . . .

Someone tapped him. He opened his eyes. A strange, ghostlike woman was floating in space next to the tree. She gently took Joe's arm, and he floated along with her. The scenery changed. They were in a clearing somewhere, in a forest or a swamp; it felt special. The woman gently lectured Joe on the future. He would grow to be a strong boy. He would join the Army and be sent to a far-off war. Many would be killed there, but Joe would come back all right. The woman's survey of the future seemed to last an hour, unveiling detail after detail of Joe's life, up to about 1970, where the path of his future seemed to vanish into a dark wall.

Joe woke up in the tree. What a strange dream.

Eight years later he enlisted in the Army and soon entered the Army Security Agency. He was trained in special radio direction finding (RDF) techniques, used by the Army to determine, for example, the location of enemy radio transmitters and thus the location of the enemy himself. One of his first posts was on the island of Eleuthera in the Bahamas, where (under the cover of an air and sea rescue installation) his unit tried to spy electronically on Soviet and Cuban ships and submarines. Late one night in October 1965, as McMoneagle walked with a friend along a road on the island, the landscape suddenly lit up. McMoneagle looked overhead and saw a large, intensely bright disk-shaped UFO. It seemed to hover for a while, and then it skipped to a new position; it skipped six or seven times and then zoomed silently over the broad Atlantic horizon, and the night resumed. The next morning, McMoneagle and his friend felt sick. Like some other close encounter experiencers from the lore, their skin felt sunburned, their eyes felt oddly gritty, and they had flulike symptoms for several days. They didn't report the incident, for fear they would be transferred.

McMoneagle didn't want to be transferred, because he loved the Bahamas. He swam and snorkeled and fished, ate marvelously well, got a good tan, and even lived through a hurricane. Then in 1966 he was sent to a place called Vietnam.

Ever since joining the Army at age eighteen, McMoneagle had been having a recurring nightmare. In the nightmare, some kind of white light kept enveloping him, and McMoneagle always had the impression that the white light meant death. When it became clear that he was headed to a war zone, the nightmares intensified. But when his troop plane arrived at Bien Hoa air base outside Saigon, McMoneagle suddenly had a different vision: He saw himself leaving the war alive and intact. He was going to be all right. The only odd thing was—he saw himself leaving Vietnam in a *canary yellow* plane. When the vision ended, he told the guy standing next to him what he had seen. *This canary yellow plane . . .* The guy looked at him. Okay, Joe.

McMoneagle spent much of the war in the Vietnamese central highlands, south of the city of Da Nang. The borders of Laos and Cambodia were nearby, and the Vietcong and North Vietnamese Army criss-crossed them regularly. McMoneagle was stationed at a series of "firebase" outposts in the area. He had an old, beat-up lawn chair he would lie in when off duty. Sometimes, on a perfectly sunny day or a perfectly starry evening, a strange feeling would come over him, a sense of something about to happen, and he would pack up the lawn chair, put on his helmet and flak jacket, and head for his assigned bunker. Then mortar rounds would scream in from the surrounding forest, and all hell would break loose.

The other fellows started noticing how often Joe seemed to anticipate these attacks. It got so that whenever he would start packing up his lawn chair, some of the rest of them would put down what they were doing and head for their bunkers, too. Eventually, they began to mimic his most arbitrary and inconsequential actions. When Joe tied his boots a different way one day, looping the laces around the back, suddenly half a dozen of the others started tying their boots the same way. A soldier couldn't be too superstitious in a war like this.

McMoneagle would later be reluctant to talk about some of his experiences in the war, and not just because some of them were classified. Vietnam evoked the strongest emotions many young servicemen would ever encounter, and McMoneagle, despite his linebackerly gruffness, was probably more emotionally sensitive than the average soldier. It would be said that there were several particularly stressful stretches in his tour of which he had little or no memory.

But no bullet or mortar round ever found him, and despite a helicopter accident that left him with chronic back problems, he made it out on his own two feet. Walking onto the tarmac at the airport in Saigon, he saw the plane that would be taking him home. The Pentagon had set up a troop plane contract with Braniff Airlines, which had a fleet of passenger aircraft in various garish and pastel colors. Looking at the plane, McMoneagle had to smile. The plane was canary yellow.

In 1970, McMoneagle was posted in southern Germany, with a small electronic-intercept detachment in a forest near the Czech and Austrian borders. The detachment was out on the hairy edge of the Cold War. Every so often a Soviet bomber would steal across the Czech border, flying in at treetop level, trying to stay under the NATO radar. McMoneagle, if he was outside, would suddenly see a series of bright flashes and hear a strange *pop pop pop pop* noise as the bomber passed overhead. Configured for intelligence-gathering, the bomber had a series of high-powered flashguns in its bomb bay, synced to spy cameras, and these would go off as the plane went by. The plane flew so low, McMoneagle and the others in the detachment liked to say, that they could see the pilot's eyes.

One Sunday afternoon, McMoneagle and his wife and a friend were in a nearby Austrian village, having a leisurely lunch and washing it all down with rum concoctions. Whether it was the alcohol, or some arterial blockage, or both, McMoneagle suddenly collapsed, swallowed his tongue, stopped breathing, and went into cardiac arrest. He found himself standing upright, in some kind of out-of-body state, looking down at his actual, physical, dying body. His friend knelt over the body, performing CPR. With every compression of his chest, Joe felt a click, a stab of pain, and for a moment saw out of his physical eyes again—before switching back to his ghostly observer state. When the paramedics came and hauled the body into the ambulance, Joe's ghost flew alongside the vehicle, zooming in and out of the power lines by the road, following all the way into the emergency room. After the hospital staff started on his body with the defibrillator paddles, Joe began a "near-death experience" with all the usual motifs: He felt himself moving up through a tunnel; he was enveloped by a white Light, the same light from his recurring nightmares, but it wasn't death. It was God, radiating unconditional love. God told Joe to go back to physical reality; he wasn't going to die. Joe resisted—it felt just great where he was— but then the scene faded, and he sat upright in his hospital bed, crying, wishing he could go back.

There wasn't any evidence of serious damage on his brain scans, but McMoneagle increasingly seemed like a new person. He would be talking to someone, and it would seem as if he were conducting a two-track conversation, one auditory and the other telepathic. Were they just voices in his head? Was he going crazy? Reality and imagination seemed to be colliding everywhere. He would lie down on his living room couch for a nap and suddenly would find himself . . . relocated, with Technicolor clarity . . . to a beach on a southern ocean, or to a desert, or, once, to a temple in Japan, where he floated through the trees, mesmerized by the creaking sound from the wheel on a wheelbarrow being pushed down a dirt path.

Like many other near-death experiencers, McMoneagle found his worldview changing dramatically, in the direction of the mystical and spiritual. Past events took on a new significance. The glowing woman in the orange grove in 1957—had she been just a dream? His consciousness began to expand until it encompassed all life, all matter, all energy, the universe. His marriage, meanwhile, started to deteriorate.

Late in 1977, he was working for INSCOM at Arlington Hall when the Gondola Wish dragnet caught him up. He was suddenly hoisted into a strange new world, a world where all that had seemed crazy in his life was now appreciated and encouraged.

* * *

Among other things, McMoneagle's Celtic genes and Austrian near-death experience seemed to have given him a very useful ability—the ability to remain semialert while descending into a dreamlike state of consciousness. Most people achieved such a state, sometimes called "vivid dreaming," only once in a while, perhaps after a too-heavy meal, or during an illness. But McMoneagle seemed able to enter this magical zone almost at will.

As a result, his remote-viewing visions had a remarkable realism and narrative consistency. After a session down in his zone, he could often recall and sketch what he had seen down to the tiniest detail. Even during the session, he was occasionally able to describe scenes just as if he were watching a film in a theater. It could be that easy.

At times, however, certain strange perceptual distortions crept in that required subtle interpretation. One day in about 1980, a client in the intelligence community came to the Fort Meade unit with a special tasking. The client wanted the remote viewers to track the movements of a person, apparently a foreign agent based in Europe, at certain specific times—every twelve hours or so— over a period of several days in the recent past.

Atwater soon ran McMoneagle against the target. The target folder had the agent's photograph inside. On the outside were the specified dates and times when the client wanted to know what he had been doing. Atwater told McMoneagle the target was a person; his task was to describe the person and his surroundings at the times written on the envelope.

McMoneagle sank down into his zone, and began to run through the list of times. For one of the specified times, he sensed a road. It wound through hills. He realized that the target was the driver of a car on this road. He was male, dark-haired, neatly dressed, perhaps a businessman. McMoneagle described the road, and the hills, and the car, and then about five minutes into the session, something about the target changed. McMoneagle became confused. "The guy's going somewhere I can't go," he said. "What do you mean?" asked Atwater. "Well," said McMoneagle, "it's like I was looking at his picture and the picture turned sideways." The target had suddenly vanished.

Later, after delivering the session results to the client, Atwater learned that the man in the photograph had failed to appear for a meeting with his case officer. That was why the client had wanted to retrospectively track his movements. Some time after the remote viewers turned in their data, the client discovered that the man—at the point in time where Joe McMoneagle had remote-viewed him—had somehow lost control of his car on a winding road in Italy, and had plunged over a cliff to his death.

At CIA headquarters one day, Norm Everheart was telephoned by a man he knew from the FBI. The FBI man, who knew about Grill Flame, had a counterintelligence situation that he hoped the remote viewers could help him with. There was one hitch, however. The FBI man was unable to task the remote viewers himself. His boss, on religious or skeptical grounds, or both, refused to let him have any dealings at all with Grill Flame's psychics. Therefore the FBI man had come to Norm Everheart. Could Everheart handle this for him, under the table? Everheart, a relatively friendly, easygoing man in what was generally a cold and conniving business, said he would be happy to help.

The situation the FBI man was concerned about had come to his attention through sheer luck. On a recent morning, at about six, a local police officer somewhere in suburban Maryland had stopped a car that had gone too quickly past a stop sign. The police officer saw that the car had diplomatic plates. He walked up to the driver's-side window, and asked to see the driver's license and registration. The driver, as was clear from the documents, was a senior Soviet Embassy official. He was dressed in a business suit, and he was clearly annoyed at having been stopped. Across the backseat of his car, the officer noted, the embassy man had a fishing pole. The policeman's report soon landed at the FBI's Soviet counterintelligence office.

A fishing pole . . . What would a Soviet intelligence officer—assuming that that was what he was—have been doing dressed in a business suit at 6:00 A.M., driving in suburban Maryland with a fishing pole in his backseat?

Norm Everheart found it odd, too. And it wasn't the first such case he had heard of. Fishing poles seemed to be sprouting up all over the Soviet diplomatic corps. Either the Soviets were becoming avid fishermen, or the fishing poles concealed some kind of electronic gadget—perhaps a covert communications device or a SIGINT collection system.

Everheart knew of a recent case, in some other country, where the host intelligence service had noticed that a certain Soviet Embassy employee always went out to a certain lake to fish, while some local official—perhaps his agent—fished on the opposite side. Were they communicating hydrophonically, through the poles? An operation was mounted to find out, but nothing ever came of it.

Whatever was going on, the Soviets who possessed the poles seemed to regard them as incredibly sensitive and valuable. One day, somewhere in Scandinavia, a Soviet Embassy man had been involved in a serious auto accident. He had been lying in his car, bleeding and badly injured, as the paramedics worked on him, but he had loudly refused to be taken to the hospital. He had insisted upon waiting until his colleagues at the embassy arrived and took from him the things he clutched tightly in his hand—five of the mysterious fishing poles.

In some cases, the Soviets took pains to create the impression that they really did like to fish with those ubiquitous poles. In a certain capital city in Africa, a group of

Soviet Embassy officials—paired as husbands and wives—
had developed the habit of going out to a lake in a boat,
and sitting there with their fishing poles for hours, apparently fishing. CIA eavesdropping specialists had eventually
managed to plant a listening device in the boat, through
which they heard the wives complaining: *It was Olga's turn
to go this week. Why do I have to be here?* And so forth.
None of the Soviets said anything that was particularly in-
criminating, but they clearly regarded this as a duty, rather
than recreation. Everheart hoped that the remote viewers
would clear up the mystery once and for all.

Joe McMoneagle was one of the first to go after the
target. All he knew was that the target was a person whose
picture was in the target envelope, at some unstated location at some unstated time. He sank down into his zone
and saw a man driving his car, and being stopped by a
policeman. The man was dressed in a business suit. He
spoke Russian. He had a fishing pole in his backseat.
Atwater didn't even know the fishing pole was supposed to
be there; Norm Everheart, with his usual oblique targeting
method, hadn't told him. But now Atwater realized the
pole was important, and he directed McMoneagle to press
the attack. What was the significance of the fishing pole?
How did the man in the car intend to use it?

McMoneagle decided to ask the man in the car. *What
are you going to do with that fishing pole?* This was an especially strange use of the telepathic interrogation technique,
since the target was not only at a different place, but at a
different *time*, at least several days in the past.

Whatever was really happening, McMoneagle seemed to
interrogate the KGB man for a while, and then he followed
his journey in the car with the pole: The KGB man drove to
a wooded area at the edge of a sensitive military installation, which was surrounded by a high perimeter fence. At
one point the fence was interrupted by a tall building, and
about fifteen feet up the outer wall of the building there

was a loose piece of masonry. The KGB man walked up to the building and telescoped out his fishing pole. He used it to reach up and dislodge a small package that some Soviet-controlled American agent, presumably working at the installation, had wedged into the wall by the loose masonry.

When Everheart read the remote viewer's data, his heart sank. It just didn't seem right. In all the other cases in which the pole had made its appearance, it had seemed to harbor some kind of sophisticated electronic device. But according to the remote viewer, the pole was simply being used as a mechanical aid, to service what spies called a "dead-drop" site, a secret place where agents stashed film or other materials for collection by their case officers. Even so, Everheart passed the information on to the man at the FBI. Later he heard that the FBI had staked out the site by the military installation, and had seen the KGB officer using the pole to dislodge something from a chink high up in the side of the building.

McMoneagle had not only been incredibly accurate—he had helped to break an important case. Now Norm Everheart began to wonder about all the other fishing pole stories. Were the Soviets using the poles simply to hide and retrieve material at elevated and otherwise inaccessible dead-drops? Everheart never knew, but he was satisfied that he had found the answer in at least this one episode.

Like all remote viewers, McMoneagle had a series of three-digit "code numbers" randomly assigned to him. For any remote-viewing session, whether training or operational, he would use one of these to identify himself. It was a practice designed to protect the remote viewers from prying eyes outside the unit. Still, word of his abilities couldn't help spreading to certain members of the intelligence community, even if they knew him only as a number. During the Carter administration, the National Security Council knew him primarily as Viewer 518, thanks to a sensational series of sessions he did for them under that numerical *nom de guerre*.

The National Security Council staff in those years included a Navy lieutenant commander named Jake Stewart, an enthusiastic supporter of Grill Flame. One day in September 1979 Stewart brought Scotty Watt and Skip Atwater a series of photographs recently taken by a KH-9 spy satellite. The photographs depicted a large industrial facility on the edge of a body of water, somewhere in northern Russia. Atwater would later find out that the facility was at the port of Severodvinsk on the White Sea, just below the Arctic Circle.

Stewart pointed out to Atwater a particular building in the shipyard, Building 402, around which a certain amount of construction was evidently going on. The NSC, he told Atwater, wanted to know what was happening inside that building.

Atwater examined the photograph. The building looked to him like a gymnasium. Then he noticed how tiny everything else was around it; the building was actually more than a quarter of a mile long on each side.

In McMoneagle's first session against the target, Atwater gave him only the building's geographical coordinates, which obviously described a place close to the Arctic Circle. McMoneagle sensed himself in an unpleasantly cold place, on a hill or mountain stretching over a wide area. Atwater was not too impressed, but he gave the remote viewer another chance a day or so later. This time McMoneagle saw large buildings, smokestacks, and nearby a semi-frozen sea.

Atwater now decided to give McMoneagle feedback, to encourage him to go further. He showed him the satellite photo, and asked him to penetrate the building Jake Stewart had specified. McMoneagle went down into his trance, and was quickly inside the building. It was a noisy place. The interior seemed to be layered, with large slabs or scaffolds everywhere. There were girders, and flashing blue-white lights—the arcs of welding torches, he decided. After the session, sitting up awake, he sketched what he had seen.

A day or so later, Atwater put McMoneagle through a third session. This time, he saw more clearly what was inside the building. In one large area there was a submarine, apparently being repaired. In a second area there was a pile of construction materials. The third and largest area was what would interest the NSC the most. McMoneagle saw in it a very large submarine, still being constructed. "This sucker is big," he murmured, and now he realized that it was the largest object in the building.

McMoneagle described its tail, a very long and flat aft deck, a conning tower, and a line of paired missile tubes, unusually canted at angles away from vertical. "How many tubes do you see?" asked Atwater. But counting, or reading numbers or letters during remote viewing, was as hard as it was in dreams; it seemed to pull the mind out of its groove. Whenever McMoneagle tried to count like that, he would become lost after a few seconds. Instead, Atwater let him come out of his trance, and McMoneagle sketched what he had seen. He decided from his sketch that there had been either nine or ten pairs of tubes; in other words, the sub would carry eighteen or twenty missiles.

McMoneagle—along with Hartleigh Trent, who also accessed the target—went on to describe a new type of drive mechanism in the submarine, an unusual double hull, and details of the special welding techniques the Soviets were using.

Back at the National Security Council, there was a certain amount of scoffing over these results. Aside from the fact that they came from psychics, the data described what would be the largest submarine then in existence. It seemed unlikely that the intelligence community would have known nothing about it before now.

Still, Jake Stewart followed up his request by asking Atwater to find out when the big sub would be launched from its factory. Atwater went back to McMoneagle, and stepped him forward in time, month by month. It wasn't obvious how the Soviets would ever launch the sub, because the building where it was being constructed was actually inland a hundred yards or so. But as the months rolled by in McMoneagle's mind's eye, he saw a new type of construction taking place. The Soviets were dynamiting and bulldozing a path from the edge of the submarine factory to the sea. Sometime in month number four, the sub floated down this artificial channel, later proceeding to sea trials.

The new information was passed to Stewart and the NSC, and it turned out that McMoneagle's prediction hadn't been far from the mark at all. Satellite photos taken in January 1980, about four months from McMoneagle's last session, showed the massive new submarine—*Typhoon*, its class was soon dubbed by NATO—resting at dockside. It had twenty canted tubes for ballistic missiles and a large, flat aft deck. Next to it was the smaller submarine that had been in for repairs, an *Oscar* heavy attack sub.

The case sparked a lively debate inside the National Security Council, over the value of remote viewing. Some, like Robert Gates, a young Soviet analyst on loan from the CIA, were flatly skeptical, dismissing the data as sketchy or trivial, or unverifiable, or a lucky guess. Others, like Jake Stewart, were believers; as far as they were concerned, Joe McMoneagle—Viewer 518—was a valuable national asset, as close to the psychic "perfect spy" as America was likely to get.

5

BOUNCING OFF THE WALLS

There's a lot of work involved. It's very difficult. Quite often, especially when you're really onto the signal line—if you're really out there with the target—when you get done, you have a tingling throughout your body. It's like a high, only it's a natural high.

—Mel Riley

ANOTHER DAY, ANOTHER REMOTE-VIEWING SESSION. MEL RILEY walked out of one of the RV rooms in 2560. He had just had a long session; he felt as if part of him were still at the target. He walked down the corridor, to the open room at the end, and out the door, exiting the ops building. A couple of the others were outside and watched as he walked out into the parking lot.

Riley sometimes looked this way after a session— zonked, spaced out. On the other hand, he wasn't aimless. Somewhere down in his mind, he knew where he was going. He kept walking, apparently oblivious of everything but his own inner guidance system. He was headed for the big metal trash dumpster, the Dipsy Dumpster, they called it. It was over to one side of the parking lot, where they threw all their garbage. Riley walked up to the dumpster and lifted its metal lid. With his free hand he reached into one of his trouser pockets, took out his car keys, and threw them into the open maw of the dumpster. The keys disappeared with a little tinkling noise, sliding down amid the paper balls and tinfoil balls and dulled nail files and mostly-empty Pepsi cans and one or two Budweiser bottles and crushed lunch bags and old newspapers. Riley let the lid slam down, and then he turned toward building 2561.

The others were still watching him, and laughing. Poor Mel!

Gradually Riley's fog started to lift, until he noticed he was there in the parking lot, next to the Dipsy Dumpster, just having thrown his car keys in. The sun burned through, and it occurred to him that the last remote-viewing session perhaps had left him a little *too* spaced out. He had been a zombie. The business of the car keys had presumably been his subconscious's way of telling him to forget about trying to drive anywhere.

Remote viewing's aftereffects were more than a little bit like those of a hallucinogenic drug. Coming out of an intense session, walking outside, say, on a summer's day, you would see the sky as, somehow, bluer. The grass would be greener—impossibly, effervescently green. A couple of birds on a wire could sound like a rain forest full of toucans and warblers. In the words of that old hallucinophile, Aldous Huxley, the "doors of perception" would be open a bit wider than usual. All that concentration on one's inner, delicate, tenuous, semiconscious, barely perceptible experience—which was what remote viewing was—all of that forced the mind to focus harder. Afterwards, back in the real world, it would be as if the volume knobs on one's sensory systems had been turned up, all the way. The usual trickle of sensory data was now a flood. *The greenness of that grass* . . . In a sense, it was a symptom of mental fatigue, but it wasn't necessarily a bad feeling. It was like a perfectly mild dose of LSD. Everything was just bursting with gorgeous colors and sounds and tastes and smells and textures. If the preceding RV session had gone well, if you had nailed the target, then so much the better. You had that extra electric tingle throughout your body. And you stared, and stumbled, and giggled, and shed tears for no reason. You "bounced off the walls," as the remote viewers liked to say. The only experience Riley could compare it with was his first parachute jump in the Army; there had been so much adrenaline pumping in his system afterwards that even though he had come safely back to earth, and had been walking around, carrying his furled parachute, he almost hadn't felt his feet touch the ground.

This kind of effect, it was thought, was only temporary. An hour or so after an intense RV session, the viewer would be as good as new. On the other hand, it was just possible that having a fairly deep altered-state experience almost every day, during daylight hours, could make your mind more liable to slip into that state spontaneously, when you didn't want to be in it. Perhaps it could even lead to psychiatric problems. Perhaps you wouldn't be as good as new until you stopped remote viewing for a long period—and perhaps not even then.

It was this kind of concern that had moved the Army to categorize remote viewing in Grill Flame as human use experimentation. As part of the oversight process, which included a blizzard of consent forms and a medical review panel, the remote viewers had been introduced to Dr. Dick Hartsell, an INSCOM psychologist. Hartsell gave them some psychological tests, and interviewed them, ostensibly probing for any unsoundness of mind. But after that first round of interviews, early in 1978, Hartsell seemed to lose interest in the unit. Riley never saw him again. The rumor went around that Hartsell was simply spooked by the remote viewers, and wanted nothing more to do with them.

In early 1979, Islamic fundamentalists led by a gray-bearded cleric, the Ayatollah Ruhollah Khomeini, took over the government of Iran. The ousted Shah, Reza Pahlavi, who had made his country one of America's staunchest allies in the Middle East, fled to America. On November 4 of that year, an Iranian mob invaded the U.S. Embassy in downtown Tehran, took the occupants hostage, and demanded that the Shah be returned.

The Carter administration froze Iranian assets in the United States and cut off Iranian oil imports. The UN Security Council was mobilized to condemn the Iranian action and to demand the return of the hostages. The case was brought to the Court of International Justice, which also demanded the return of the hostages. The Shah, meanwhile, moved to an Air Force base in Texas, then to Panama, then to Egypt. No one seemed to want him, except for his former subjects, who seemed to want desperately to tear him limb from limb.

There were other crises facing U.S. foreign policy makers at the time. Russia was invading Afghanistan. Vietnam, having just consolidated its grip on Cambodia, was invaded by China. Russia threatened war with China if China didn't desist. Iraq, seeing opportunity in chaos, invaded Iran. Cuba decided to export tens of thousands of criminals in a massive boatlift to the United States. Yet the hostages in Iran seemed to obliterate all else on the radar screen of the American electorate. They were at once a national fixation, a symbol of further national humiliation in the wake of the Vietnam War, and above all, a symbol of the failure of the Carter presidency. Something had to be done.

The CIA apparently had an Iranian agent with some access to the embassy building and the hostages' placement, but so far the Agency had kept him largely dormant, fearing that any activity or dissemination of his information would endanger his life. The bottom line was that there was very little known about the situation in the U.S. intelligence community.

The remote viewers were therefore kept busy. In late

1979 and early 1980 they were tasked by the Pentagon and National Security Council, literally hundreds of times, to provide information on the hostages' whereabouts, their physical and mental states, the appearances and attitudes of their captors, and the layouts of the buildings where they were being held captive.

For Mel Riley and the others, it was gratifying to be part of such a key intelligence effort, but as they saw it, the Carter administration in its scramble to obtain information from remote viewers was going about it the wrong way. The remote-viewing taskings were relentless, with similar targets day after day. Remote viewers needed variety, to keep their minds from being cluttered with the same images. After a few weeks down in the zone with American hostages and ever-bearded Iranian guards—targets that were also constantly being depicted on TV at the time— Riley and others found it hard to see anything else, no matter what the target.

However, as winter turned to spring, Riley noticed that they were increasingly describing sites away from the hostages—urban buildings, sewer tunnels beneath the streets, government radio stations, and even remote desert locations. No one knew what any of this meant, other than that the administration still had Iran on its mind. An Air Force colonel now seemed to be the one providing the targets.

One day in April 1980, Riley ran Hartleigh Trent in a remote-viewing session, and Trent began to describe American soldiers rappelling out of helicopters in the desert. Trent and Riley guessed that the target had been somewhere in Iran, and that the rappelling soldiers were commandos on a mission to rescue the hostages. Presumably the soldiers weren't there yet, for it often happened that future or intended events drifted into remote-viewing data.

In any case, a few days later Scotty Watt gathered the six full- and part-time members of the unit together and told them to pack their bags. Within hours, they all had gathered at a motel in the town of Laurel, not far from Fort Meade. Most of one floor had been set aside for them. Each viewer had one room to sleep and work, and there was a large suite for unit meetings.

Watt came in and confirmed that a covert mission to rescue the hostages was under way. Henceforth they would be remote-viewing targets related to the mission. To protect the security of the mission, and to keep them all from being tainted by images of the hostages they might see on TV, they were discouraged from leaving the motel until it was all over.

To Mel Riley, it seemed like a strange setup. The motel was part of a major chain, new-smelling and nicely carpeted, just renovated in fact, but the structure itself was much older. And it was completely infested with mice. Riley could hear them in the ceilings and the walls, and beneath the floorboards. Squeaking ghosts. They were all over the place.

Not long after the unit's sequestration had begun, Riley went over to Hartleigh Trent's room, to monitor him for a session. He turned out the lights, and Trent lay down and quieted his brain. Minutes later, Trent was drifting along, watching the images flicker past, checking out the main radio station in Tehran, or whatever it was, and Riley was trying to monitor him, very quietly, very patiently, quiet questions, no sudden noises. And Riley began to notice that with the lights off, the mice had really come to life. They were dancing around in the ceiling, making all kinds of scurrying and scuffling noises. After a while, some of them were bold enough to venture out into the room. One of the mice hit Riley's shoe, and decided to climb it. Then he climbed up Riley's sock, the tiny claws digging into the cotton. Then the little fellow started up Riley's leg, inside his trousers. The mouse made it up to Riley's knee before Riley reached down and shook it out, and all the time, Riley—laid-back Riley—didn't let on, didn't make a sound, so that Hartleigh Trent could continue to float along to the noiseless rhythms of the ethereal zone.

To Riley, the mice were far from the worst things about the hostage rescue affair. The worst things were the monotony and the brutal pace of the remote viewing. Just as it had been in the months after the hostage crisis began, whoever was tasking them didn't seem to have a clue to how remote viewing worked. There had been operations in the past when a viewer had had to do two or three sessions per day on the same kind of target. That was trying enough, but to do more than that invited severe burnout. Now they were remote-viewing virtually non-stop, around the clock.

To the Air Force colonel running the taskings, the idea of becoming mentally burned out after lying on a couch in a semi-conscious state for an hour might have sounded absurd, like some crazy New Age form of malingering. But to the remote viewers, it was as real as anything they did. It was a barrier like the one long-distance runners sometimes hit. As you approached this barrier, Riley and the others believed, your RV data turned to garbage, and when you hit it, you were like someone who hadn't slept for days; the necessary neurotransmitters had dried up, burned up. You were apt to become emotionally fragile, and you acquired a certain vacant stare.

Attacking target after target, again and again, the remote viewers soon bounced off this wall, the parts of their minds that worked during RV slowly collapsing from exhaustion. Imagination flooded in. Making it all worse was the fact that they had no feedback. They had no idea how well, or how badly, they were doing. To Riley and some of the others, this was another guarantee of failure.

On the morning of April 25 word came in that President Carter was about to make a speech on television. The unit turned on the set in the meeting room, and there was Carter, ruefully spelling it out: the rendezvous site at Desert One, the mechanical failure of several helicopters, the collision of two aircraft in the desert, the eight deaths, the horrific injuries, the whole debacle.

A number of them swore quietly. The young INSCOM analyst Nancy Stern began to cry, unleashing a torrent of anger, fuck this, fuck that, fuck the mission planners, fuck Carter, fuck Fate. In the weeks that followed, she left the unit. Soon afterward Rhode Islander Fern Gauvin also left the unit, vowing never to remote-view again.

Jackie Keith, the INSCOM special ops man, had dropped out not long after being selected for the original Gondola Wish team. But he still came by now and then to task the remote viewers with targets related to his own operations. He was always running around somewhere or other in his sports car, a Datsun 280-Z, living what seemed to be a muted Army-civilian version of the James Bond life.

As 1980 wore on, Keith and the remote viewers became involved in the Carter administration's plans for a second hostage rescue mission in Iran. In the wake of the first rescue attempt, the hostages had now been dispersed; one of the main tasks now was to find where they all were.

One day Keith was in the control room in building 2560, listening in while Mel Riley ran Hartleigh Trent against some hostage-related target. Trent was drifting along in his zone. Riley had on headphones and was listening to Keith's instructions on what questions to ask. Suddenly Riley heard a heavy thud in the headphones. The thud also came through the wall, jolting Trent out of his trance. Both Trent and Riley went to the control room and found Jackie Keith sprawled on the floor. Heart attack—no pulse. Trent ran to get a phone, and Riley started CPR. McMoneagle came in and helped him until the paramedics arrived. They hit him with the defibrillators all the way to the hospital, but it was no use. Riley and the others could hardly believe it. Keith was only in his late thirties; he had just married, and his young widow was pregnant with his first child. It was a tragedy without an explanation. After the paramedics had left, Atwater carried Keith's briefcase into Watt's office. Keith had been headed to New York, on one of his many operations. In the briefcase was a several-thousand-dollar payoff for some now-orphaned secret agent.

President Carter, worried that intelligence on the hostages' locations was too unreliable, eventually decided not to make a second rescue attempt. In the final humiliation, the hostages were released the moment his presidency ended. The remote viewers received a slap in the face too when the Air Force colonel debriefed them on what their intense work had achieved. He told them, with what seemed to be deliberate ambiguity, that their data had been "no worse" than the intelligence collected by more conventional methods.

Military officers and enlisted personnel are generally expected to move from one posting to another every three years. By early 1981, a sea change was under way at the remote-viewing unit. The full-time military personnel—Watt, Atwater, Bell, McMoneagle, and Riley—all faced possible transfers elsewhere in the world. Even the unit's chief protector, Major General Thompson, was headed for a transfer out of his Pentagon office. Watt and Atwater meanwhile were searching for new recruits and were working with researchers out at SRI to develop improved techniques for psychic spying.

In the end, Grill Flame's managers managed to keep a nucleus of original members in place at the unit. Atwater was allowed to stay on. McMoneagle, the anchor of the remote-viewing team, was only a tour away from reaching twenty years' service—retirement time—and was also allowed to remain. Ken Bell arranged to stay, but would leave within a year to rejoin the regular Army career track. He would retire in the late 1980s as a lieutenant colonel.

Under different circumstances, Mel Riley would have

liked to stay at Fort Meade too. Remote viewing, and the activities surrounding it, were as near to his ideal occupation as he could imagine. When orders came in sending Riley to a posting near Wiesbaden, his old haunt and his wife's hometown, Atwater and officials higher up in the program could have easily changed them. But Riley didn't want them to. He saw that the unit was on relatively firm ground now, with an increasing budget and a new generation of recruits on the way. It wasn't going to disappear anytime soon, and Atwater made clear that he could come back whenever he wanted. Riley decided he would go to Germany for three years, back to warm beer and the real, live Cold War. And when his tour there ended, he promised himself, he would return.

Book Two

A LITTLE SIDE GAME

I had no intention of doing ESP research. I had no intention of making these spooky contacts. Nothing of the sort. This was just a little side game, as far as I was concerned. And what happened was, people showed up and said, "Hey, we're interested in this. We've been looking for potential contractors to do work in this area. And this seems the right kind of place, and you seem the right kind of person. Do you want a little contract to look into this?"

—Hal Puthoff

6
PUTHOFF

On summer days in the early 1950s, when junior high school was out, Hal Puthoff and his friends would take the bus over the causeway to Miami Beach. Starting at one of the public beaches, they would go a few yards out into the Atlantic and then swim along the seemingly endless strip of high-class hotels nearby. Unless you were a guest, you couldn't get to the hotels any other way. So they would swim to a hotel they hadn't tried in a while, and they would come ashore and hang around on its beach, looking at the girls, and after a while they would lounge in chairs by the hotel pool, ordering Cokes, pretending to be hotel guests, and when one of the hotel staff eventually got wise, they would run out onto the beach again, into the Atlantic, and then would swim on up to the next hotel. And the days passed like that, and in the evenings there was the band. It was a guitar band, mostly. On Friday nights they would play for Sears Roebuck, on a second-story veranda at the big Sears store downtown, at the corner of Fourteenth Street and Biscayne Boulevard. The band was a form of advertising, to draw in the evening shoppers, and Hal and the others were dressed in suits, with their hair slicked down—Hal's was a bushy pompadour, and hard to slick down—and the guitar music would carry through the tropical air . . . Nat King Cole, Buddy Holly, all the radio hits, but done with guitars. Hal and a couple of the other fellows played instruments known as "electric steel Hawaiian" guitars, made by the Gibson Company. They made a wonderful, loopy sound, evoking paradise right there in the humid night air of downtown Miami.

Hal Puthoff loved his electric steel Hawaiian guitar. He loved tinkering with electronic things like that, and building gadgets. He also had a ham radio set, and tapping away with his Morse code key, he talked to people all over the world with it—people in Cuba, Venezuela, New Mexico, Canada, the Caribbean, one time even Yugoslavia—all those dots and dashes in the ether. Other than that he was mostly shy and quiet, a short kid with a pompadour haircut and sad eyes, looking vaguely like the young Mick Jagger would look one day. Hal's father, a personnel manager for a string of trucking companies, had died a few years before, and Hal and his mother had moved from Warren, Ohio, down here to Miami to live with his aunt. They didn't have much money. Hal went to a vocational high school, and dreamed of becoming, someday, a radio deejay.

Two decades later, Hal Puthoff was a lecturer at Stanford University, in the electrical engineering department. He had a Stanford Ph.D., and a patent on a tunable infrared laser he'd invented, and he had just co-authored an influential textbook, *Fundamentals of Quantum Electronics*. At the age of thirty-three, he was a force to be reckoned with in the fast-growing field of laser physics and engineering.

And he was at another turning point in his life. His first

marriage was failing. He was bored with teaching. In fact, he was becoming bored with academia in general.

Puthoff had a reputation for being creative and energetic, rolling up his sleeves and sweating the details, getting things done one way or another, however long it took. But he didn't quite fit the gear-head engineer stereotype. In his quiet, shy way he was concerned about the meaning of it all, had been up to the Esalen Institute, had done some Gestalt psychology workshops, that kind of thing. There were phenomena, out there, that other scientists didn't seem interested in exploring. But he was interested.

In 1969 Puthoff separated from his wife, then met and moved in with a new girlfriend. Soon he left the Stanford electrical engineering department, and joined a nearby think tank, Stanford Research Institute. SRI, as it was known, was spread out on a leafy, grassy, modernistically quadrangled campus in the town of Menlo Park, only a few miles south of the university. It had close ties to Stanford, but it was mainly fuelled by about seventy million dollars in government contracts annually, many of them highly classified. Among scientific think-tanks only the Rand Corporation was larger or more prestigious.

SRI brought Puthoff on board to help out with a laser-related project for the government, but after a while the laser work began to tail off, and Puthoff had a new project in mind. He wanted to do some psi experiments, to see if they could shed light on some of the stranger reaches of quantum theory. After getting permission from his boss, Puthoff went out in search of funding for the project. He soon hooked up with a philanthropist friend from Texas— Bill Church, part owner of the Church's Fried Chicken restaurant chain, and an amateur scientist as well—who gave him ten thousand dollars.

Then, of all people, an artist in New York contacted him. The artist, Ingo Swann, had been working as a subject in psi experiments at the City College of New York and the

American Society for Psychical Research, and had seen Puthoff's proposal for funding. Swann told Puthoff about some of his reported feats, which included remotely altering the temperature of a graphite rod, and going "out of body" to view objects hidden in a laboratory.

After a few letters back and forth, Puthoff flew Swann out to SRI, to put him through some preliminary tests. He wasn't sure how Swann would fit into his plans. He mainly wanted to see what a real psychic looked like in action.

On June 6, 1972, two days after Swann had arrived in California, Puthoff brought him over to Stanford University, to a laboratory in the basement of the Varian Hall physics building. The laboratory housed a special, experimental magnetometer that had been built, with money from the Office of Naval Research, by a Stanford postdoctoral physics student, Arthur Hebard.

Hebard was hunting the subatomic particles known as quarks. His magnetometer was designed to measure, down in its protected measurement chamber, the extremely small magnetic field perturbations that passing quarks were expected to make.* To maintain this sensitivity, it had to keep from its inner sanctum all the electromagnetic noise of civilization, with barriers that included copper, aluminum, a special metal that confined magnetic fields, and a supercooled superconductor. Puthoff, who had heard about the device through friends, considered it a perfect challenge for a psychic, and had arranged the visit beforehand with Hebard. If Swann could somehow affect the output of this heavily shielded magnetometer, then he definitely should be taken seriously.

Down in Hebard's lab, Puthoff explained to Swann the basic workings of the magnetometer, and without further

---

* The magnetometer was the same one used, several years later, in the first reported experimental confirmation of the existence of quarks.

ado, asked him to alter the magnetometer's output. The magnetometer was mostly buried in a concrete well in the floor of the lab. Swann wasn't sure what to make of it. He had never done anything like this before. After a while he declared that he would first try to see clairvoyantly inside the magnetometer, to get a better psychic grip. As he did so, the magnetometer's steady output, printed on a nearby strip chart recorder, suddenly changed. Hebard and some of the other graduate students and staff who had gathered suspected that the disturbance was mundane—the result of some kind of coincidental noise in the magnetometer system. But to Puthoff, it seemed that the disturbances correlated closely with Swann's efforts to change the output. And when he and Swann eventually left the lab, the output returned to its baseline value.

Puthoff, it should be said, was an exceptionally, almost eerily mild-mannered man. And it was as if his calmness were deliberate, a guard against passions underneath, a recognition that he was now venturing in strange territory—career-wrecking territory—and the slightest emotional tremor could pitch him into the abyss. Still, the passions drove him onward. He was reasonably convinced that Ingo Swann had done something paranormal to Arthur He bard's magnetometer, and he wanted to investigate such phenomena in more detail.

Puthoff wrote up a short, dry, guarded description of the Varian Hall event, and circulated it, along with copies of the strip recorder output, to some more potential funding sources, including one or two government offices. Within several weeks, to his great surprise, the government was knocking on his door. Hal Puthoff had stumbled into one of the strangest arms races in modern history.

Governments have long dabbled with psi as an intelligence-gathering tool—probably as long as there have been people who claim to have psi abilities. The Israelites of the Old

Testament are said to have made military use of one of their prophets, Elisha. The Greeks had their oracles. The Elizabethan spy John Dee consulted psychics, and questioned all-seeing "angels" through his crystal ball. Even in the twentieth century, as psi became increasingly controversial scientifically, Western governments continued to employ it, here and there, in wartime.

In a campaign against Hungary in 1919, for example, a Czech officer set up a psychic spying unit consisting of two enlisted men under his command. Putting them in hypnotic trances, he would ask the men to report clairvoyantly on enemy positions. The Czech Army also used "dowsers" to search for traps, mines, and drinking water. Later, in World War II, the Soviet Union was said to have made use of a Polish-born psychic named Wolf Messing. Adolf Hitler, who put a price on Messing's head, employed his own astrologers and map-dowsers, the latter dangling pendulums over maps to try to detect Allied divisions and air units.

After the Cold War began, the United States and Soviet Union continued to dabble with psi, but never on a significant scale. Then something very strange occurred.

In February 1960 a sensational article appeared in a French magazine, *Science et Vie* (Science and Life). Titled "The Secret of the Nautilus," it reported that the U.S. government, in secret tests, had successfully employed telepathy to communicate with the crew of the *Nautilus,* its first nuclear submarine, while the sub had been underneath the Arctic ice cap. According to the story, the telepathy project had the special attention of President Eisenhower, and involved the Navy, the Air Force, Westinghouse, General Electric, Bell Laboratories, and the Rand Corporation.

The implications seemed enormous, for communicating with deeply submerged submarines had always been an extremely important research goal. If it stayed submerged, a submarine would normally be unable to transmit or receive information, since the seawater above it would block all but the very lowest and least useful radio frequencies. To communicate, the sub would have to surface and raise its radio antenna, thus exposing itself to enemy aircraft and spy satellites.

Telepathy seemed like the ideal solution, for it didn't appear to be stopped by seawater or any other earthly obstacle. In time, perhaps, with the development of the proper error-correcting algorithms, telepathy would revolutionize all of communications technology. Broadcast radio and secret codes would become obsolete.

The problem was, the *Nautilus* story seemed to evaporate the closer one got to it. An Air Force officer named in the story denied that any such incident had taken place, and the skipper of the *Nautilus* insisted that the sub had been in dry dock during the period it was said to have been conducting telepathy tests beneath the Arctic. Perhaps most suspiciously of all, the stated accuracy rate of the tests had been far higher than parapsychologists usually reported for telepathy experiments.

The *Nautilus* article had been written by a young *Science et Vie* staffer, Gerard Messadié. He in turn had been fed the story by a consulting editor named Jacques Bergier, who apparently had connections to French intelligence services. Bergier responded to skeptical queries by backpedalling from the story, and it soon began to seem that the whole thing had been fabricated—as Bergier's private fraud, or perhaps as some kind of disinformation ploy, designed to stir up valuable data about any American psi research, or to encourage Russia to undertake wasteful research on psi. Or both. Eventually, even Gerard Messadié would admit that he had probably been fooled.

But if the *Nautilus* story was declared a fake in the West, it had a very different reception in the East. The Soviets seemed to swallow it whole, and official American denials only served to confirm their suspicions that the entire episode had occurred just as reported, and had been a deep military secret.

Soviet psi research had been nearly extinct during the Stalin years, thanks to official ideological opposition to anything smacking of "idealism" or "superstition." Stalin's successor, Nikita Khrushchev, reportedly had opened the door somewhat, after witnessing the sensational displays of some Indian yogis during a state visit in 1955. But by 1960 no coordinated psi research program had yet developed.

The *Nautilus* story seemed to provide the necessary stimulus. Whether they believed it or not, a number of Soviet researchers eagerly cited the story as a confirmation of their own work, hinting that such work now needed much greater attention and funding. Leonid Vasiliev, chairman of the physiology department at the University of Leningrad, and a past winner of the Lenin Prize, would argue that "the discovery of the energy underlying ESP will be equivalent to the discovery of atomic energy." By the early sixties, Vasiliev was heading a well-funded parapsychology laboratory, and the establishment of numerous other psi research centers followed.

Vasiliev's work soon concentrated on "remote-influencing" experiments, for example in which a telepathic sender would try to put a distant receiver to sleep at a randomly selected time. Other researchers, like the electrical engineer I. M. Kogan, spent more of their efforts on ordinary telepathy experiments. Kogan, like most Soviet researchers, assumed that psi was just a low-frequency radio system built into human brains. He therefore tried to characterize it in terms familiar to communications specialists. He concluded from his experiments that psi data could be transmitted within a laboratory at about 0.1 "bit" of information per second on average—about one five-letter word every five minutes—while the rate decreased to 0.005 bits per second for psi data transmitted across six hundred miles.

The Czechs were also active in psi research, and in the mid-1960s, a researcher named Milan Ryzl conducted an experiment that seemed to confirm Kogan's communications-oriented approach. A 50-bit target sequence of ones and zeros was generated randomly. Ryzl, who did not know the sequence, then asked the psychic Pavel Stepanek to repeatedly guess each bit in the sequence, going back and forth (in an order unknown to Stepanek) through the sequence again and again. Ryzl combined Stepanek's guesses using a majority-vote error-correcting protocol, a technique like those used by telecommunications specialists to clean up signals on noisy transmission lines. After several days and twenty thousand guesses, Ryzl was confident that Stepanek had got the entire 50-bit sequence right. And he had.

Of course, with such a lengthy error-correcting protocol, the effective bit rate for the experiment turned out to be only about 0.0003 bps (one word per day), hardly a replacement for ordinary modes of telecommunication. But as a proof-of-concept experiment, it was impressive, suggesting that the *Nautilus* story might not have been so farfetched after all.

Indeed, if the Soviet parapsychologist Eduard Naumov could be believed, the *Nautilus* results were old hat. At a conference in Moscow in 1968, Naumov announced to Western researchers that the Red Navy had replicated the entire *Nautilus* experiment successfully, using one of its own submarines. Not only that, claimed Naumov, but Soviet military researchers had developed a method for telepathically *tapping into* other people's psychic communications.

Wild stories like Naumov's eventually made their way into a book called *Psychic Discoveries Behind the Iron Curtain*, published in the United States in 1970. Just after the acknowledgments page its authors, Sheila Ostrander and Lynn Schroeder, printed a table showing "some" of the

Eastern bloc cities where psi research was supposed to be taking place: Moscow, Leningrad, Novosibirsk, Nizhny Tagil, Irkutsk, Khabarovsk, Vladivostok, Tomsk, Omsk . . . forty cities in all. And it was a safe bet that in such cities as Moscow and Leningrad, there would be more than one such research center.

Ostrander and Schroeder portrayed a veritable frenzy of psychic research going on in the USSR, where investigators were apparently combing cities and villages, uncovering powerful natural clairvoyants, psychokinetic prodigies, and dowsers whose talents could presumably be employed against the West. There was some opposition to this kind of work, on ideological grounds, but it seemed generally to come from the older, more ideological wing of Soviet officialdom, a vestige of the dark past. In the USSR, it was the psi believers who now were wrapping themselves in the mantle of scientific and technological progress.

By the late 1960s the U.S. intelligence community was becoming aware of all this, by way of popular books, official studies, Pentagon and CIA translations of foreign psi research papers, and agent and émigré reports. The first big result was a curiously titled Defense Intelligence Agency report, *Controlled Offensive Behavior—USSR*, which appeared in 1972. It noted that "the major impetus behind the Soviet drive to harness the possible capabilities of telepathic communication, telekinetics, and bionics are said to come from the Soviet military and the KGB." The report went on to cite, with almost comical blandness, the various horrors that could one day be inflicted on America:

Soviet efforts in the field of psi research, sooner or later, might enable them to do some of the following: (a) Know the contents of top secret U.S. documents, the movements of our troops and ships and the location and nature of our military installations. (b) Mold the thoughts of key U.S. military and civilian leaders at a distance. (c) Cause the instant death of any U.S. official at a distance. (d) Disable, at a distance, U.S. military equipment of all types including spacecraft.

Thanks to the Soviet "head start" in psi research, argued the DIA report-writer, "Soviet knowledge in this field is superior to that of the West." In other words, the United States, which already had to worry about a possible missile gap—a Soviet numerical superiority in ICBMs—now faced the prospect of a devastating "psi gap."

Not everyone agreed with the DIA's fire-and-brimstone alarmism. To some at the CIA, for example, reports of Soviet and East European enthusiasm over psi only reinforced the notion that science in those countries was often heavily influenced by mystical beliefs. The parapsychologist Eduard Naumov, for example, was also into "Kirlian photography" of human "biofields," and believed that sunspots, by helping to shape a person's biofield at birth, thus shaped his destiny.

On the other hand, there were parapsychologists like I. M. Kogan, whose work seemed relatively serious. His work began to seem even more serious when it suddenly disappeared from public view in about 1969, coincident with reports that the KGB had begun to fund and direct his laboratory at the Popov Society.

Precisely how well the KGB and the military were really able to harness psi to nefarious purposes was anybody's guess, but they obviously were very interested, and there were reports of strange occurrences—perhaps mundane, but perhaps psi-related—that must have made a few American hairs stand on end. For example, near the end of his first term President Nixon made a very strange complaint to the CIA. According to testimony by CIA scientist Sidney Gottlieb at a congressional hearing in 1977, Nixon claimed that he and several members of his staff, including his personal physician, Walter Tkach, had exhibited unusual behavior, including "inappropriate tears and crying," during a visit to an unnamed "potentially hostile country" in the early 1970s. Nixon visited both China and the Soviet Union in 1972.

The end result of all this was that American intelligence agencies began to spend more time monitoring psi research around the world, including research in the United States itself. The CIA and the Pentagon, which during the 1950s and '60s had actually funded some low-key scientific investigations of possible psi applications, began to think about doing more research, covertly or overtly, to see whether the Soviets really were onto something. If U.S. researchers came up with nothing, then everyone could breathe a sigh of relief. If they produced something useful, then America would at least be able to stay in the race with the Russians.

But who would carry out this research? The low scientific status of psi meant that it attracted few investigators. Even fewer of these investigators had serious scientific credentials, and of those who did, most were wrapped up in abstract statistical pursuits, safely beyond the realm of real-world applications. Others had already done some work for the CIA and other agencies, but had come up with nothing of practical value. In addition, these were the turbulent, politicized early seventies, and quite a number of promising parapsychologists, despite their financial desperation, would have eschewed any kind of government involvement anyway. To them, psi was too important—and too pure and too beautiful—to leave to the generals.

The eyes of the intelligence community soon alighted on Hal Puthoff, after his report of the Varian Hall episode began to circulate. Puthoff seemed to have everything going for him. He was a respected mainstream researcher and engineer, he worked at a top-rank think tank which already did a great deal of defense and intelligence work, and he already had top-level clearances. Back in the early 1960s he had fulfilled his military service as a Navy officer at the National Security Agency at Fort Meade, later staying on as a civilian. He had earned a Pentagon commendation at NSA for his work towards a future generation of high-speed optical computers driven by light pulses rather than electrons. The bottom line was that Puthoff seemed like the perfect candidate to carry out secret, government-sponsored psi research.

In October of that year, 1972, Ingo Swann was back at SRI's offices in Menlo Park for a short visit. Puthoff told him that he had decided by this time that ESP experiments were more promising than psychokinesis. He ran Swann through some simple clairvoyance tests: Puthoff would leave an object inside a locked, thick-walled wooden box in a certain room, and Swann, accompanied by a second researcher, would enter the room and try to divine what was in the box.

One day two men from Washington, who had evidently been in touch with Puthoff, brought their own target and put it in the experiment box. They watched as Swann described the contents of the box as follows: "I see something small, brown, and irregular, sort of like a leaf, or something that resembles it, except that it seems very much alive, like it's even moving!" The target, which had been caught and placed in the box by one of the visitors, was in fact a large moth—brownish, leaflike, and very much alive.

A few weeks later, back in New York, Swann received a phone call from Puthoff. The two men with the moth had decided to give him $50,000 to fund eight months of further research. If he and Swann could come up with a repeatable psi phenomenon, then perhaps more money would follow.

The men, and their money, were from the Central Intelligence Agency.

7

THE COORDINATES

> Russell said, "Ingo, even if it did work, we could never publish a paper on it because we could never tell why coordinates are meaningful." And I said, "I'm here to try to find practical applications, not to please science, and we're going to do this, or I'm leaving right now, with the complaint that SRI did not live up to its contract!"
>
> —Ingo Swann

INGO DOUGLAS SWANN—BORN WITH JUST ONE *N*—WAS NOT FAR from the stereotypical image of the psychic. Growing up in Telluride, Colorado, he says, he had out-of-body experiences and premonitions, could see people's auras, and in his reveries encountered various supernatural beings. He was left-handed, intuitive, artistic, emotionally sensitive, curious about the unusual, and bored by the usual. He was considered odd, and had few friends at school. "I was doubly, triply, *quadruply* freaky," he would later remember, with bitter pride.

After college, he joined the Army, and served in Korea and later at a Nike missile base outside Boston. A photograph taken of him in Seoul in the mid-1950s shows a dapper, even rakish Radar O'Reilly, with a camouflage-patterned cravat enhancing his olive-drab uniform.

When he left the Army, Swann—"Douglas Swan"—

moved to New York City, to Greenwich Village, determined to become an artist. Nothing much sold, so he worked for the UN for a number of years, painting in his spare time, and then wrote pulp fiction for a while. By 1971 he was using his first name, Ingo, had added the second *n* to his surname on the advice of a numerologist, and had discovered that he seemed to have unusual psychic talents. He began earning his wages as a subject in parapsychology laboratories.

Swann arrived to begin his CIA contract at Stanford Research Institute a few days before Christmas 1972. He was a somewhat stout, soft-looking man, thirty-nine years old, with close-cropped brown hair and a broad Scandinavian face. Stepping off the plane in San Francisco, he wore a white jacket, white Levi's, and a white cowboy hat. By now something of a bon vivant in New York, he was accompanied by a large number of suitcases and trunks, containing his substantial and varied wardrobe. He seldom felt comfortable anywhere outside of Manhattan, but he had decided to give California a try.

Unfortunately, things didn't develop quite as Swann had expected, at least not at first. In experiment after experiment, his psi abilities seemed feeble. He became depressed, and had increasingly serious disagreements with Puthoff and his newly hired assistant, Russell Targ.

One of Swann's complaints had to do with Targ's ESP teaching machine. A special project Targ had brought with him to SRI, it was essentially a primitive computer that controlled the lightbulbs behind four small photographic slides of artworks. For each round, the computer would randomly illuminate one of the slides, and the subject had to try to guess which one beforehand. The results of each trial were automatically displayed, to give the subject feedback, and were automatically recorded, to prevent fraud. Targ called it an ESP "teaching" machine because, he argued, the feedback taught the subject, at some subconscious level, to do better next time.

Swann tried it out for a while, but he didn't do spectacularly well at it, and on the whole he disliked the little machine. To him the thing was a depressing remnant of old-time parapsychology, when psychics had been made to guess abstract symbols on cards again and again until they fled from boredom. The more he was pressured by Targ to work with the machine, the more he resented Targ.

Targ, like Puthoff, was a laser physicist. Until recently he had worked at the research laboratories of the Sylvania Corporation, which manufactured televisions and lightbulbs, among other things. The ivory tower atmosphere of SRI seemed to suit him better, for Targ was the very picture of the intense scientist, the thinker disengaged from prosaic reality. He had this amazing, frizzy and wavy mass of red-brown hair, and his deep, monotonal voice conveyed a sense of authority, of dispassionate gnosis. To complete the picture, he would squint down at you, from his height of six feet five, through extraordinarily thick, eye-magnifying glasses, goggles that seemed to protect him from the absurdities of the ordinary world. His sister had married the chess master Bobby Fischer, and it was easy to imagine, when you looked at Targ, that some of Fischer's neurotic cerebrality had somehow rubbed off on him. Another thing about Targ was that he had apparently been having spontaneous psychic experiences ever since he had been a child.

In any case, Swann had other experiments to contend with besides Targ's ESP machine. He was asked to guess, for example, whether a green argon laser in an adjacent room was turned on or off, and which of two identical canisters contained a promethium-147 radioactive source. Puthoff was trying to spice up the usual ESP routine, and he also knew that the psychic detection of, for example, radioactive material, would catch the eyes of intelligence officials.

Swann, who was trying to set up some psychic surveying work for petroleum companies, also arranged for experiments involving canisters filled with either water or oil.

But if Swann's results in these experiments occasionally poked up through the threshold of chance and random noise, they didn't set anyone's pulse racing. And when Swann went against a small SRI magnetometer, in order to replicate his apparent feat at Varian Hall, nothing happened at all. The SRI program was shaping up to be another dusty parapsychological dead end.

Ultimately, Swann knew, the CIA wanted to use psychics for long-distance spying. But in discussions with Puthoff and Targ, he had recognized a subtle problem with this. If someone said to him, "Ingo, please give me your psychic impressions of Ramenskoye Airfield, near Moscow," then whatever psychic impressions he might have of the airfield would probably be overwhelmed by his imagination—which would find it all too easy to conjure up scenes of massive runways and hangars. What he needed was a way to be directed to a target, precisely and economically, without actually being told what the target *was*.

According to Swann the answer came to him one evening in April 1973, as he lounged in a swimming pool, drinking scotch, at his apartment complex in nearby Mountain View. A voice in his head said, "Try coordinates." As in geographical coordinates. In other words, Puthoff and Targ, instead of telling him the target, could simply give him the target's precise latitude and longitude.

Swann arrived at the office the next morning and announced his proposal. Puthoff and Targ responded with thumbs down. As far as they were concerned, the idea of using geographical coordinates didn't even begin to make sense. In the first place, they pointed out, if they were to give Swann a set of coordinates and he ended up correctly describing what was there, it might only mean that he had seen the right map once, and had remembered everything on it, consciously or not. Psychologists called such a feat "eidetic" or "photographic" memory, or "cryptomnesia." Therefore no skeptic was ever going to believe Swann was using psi, regardless of whether coordinates seemed to work. Even the parapsychologists might not believe it. After all, coordinate systems were arbitrary human creations. There was no reason to suppose that they would lead someone's psi perception to a remote target. And if they did, they shouldn't work any better than telephone numbers or street addresses. The whole idea was just absurd.

But Swann persisted, and raised his voice, and threatened to leave SRI. His threats weren't necessarily idle. By this time he had already departed four or five times for short periods, sometimes to pursue other projects, but other times just to signal his annoyance at the way things were going.

Puthoff and Targ finally relented, agreeing to try Swann's coordinate clairvoyance scheme, unofficially and temporarily, during their late-afternoon coffee breaks. The experiment, they decided, would run for two workweeks, and each afternoon they would give Swann ten pairs of coordinates.

To obtain the coordinates, they would simply consult a large world map that hung on the wall of a nearby lab. They would then bring the coordinates to Swann, who would have one or two minutes to describe what was at each coordinate-pair. Afterwards his descriptions would be compared with what was actually shown on the map. If after two weeks there was no sign of success, then the experiment would be over.

The first run of ten targets was on April 23, and took only fifteen minutes, from 5:10 to 5:25 P.M. Puthoff and Targ started out by giving Swann the coordinate-pair of 30 degrees north latitude, 90 degrees west longitude, which indicated a point in the eastern suburbs of New Orleans.

Swann's description read in part: "Offshore . . . Island to west . . . Tropical." When informed of the actual target and, again, the coordinates, he complained: "Thought you said 9 degrees"—which would have made his description even less accurate, since 30° north, 9° west lies in the foothills of the Atlas Mountains, about 100 miles south-southwest of Marrakesh.

The second target was at 75° north, 45° west, which virtually anyone who had ever studied a world map would know was well within the Arctic Circle, somewhere around Greenland. Swann saw: "Ice." It went on like this for eight more coordinate-pairs, descriptions that were obviously wrong alternating with descriptions that were trivially correct. After five days and fifty coordinate-pairs, Swann's output remained more or less the same.

Puthoff and Targ were fairly sure that the experiment was headed for failure, and they communicated their lack of enthusiasm in various ways. One day Targ brought a phone into the testing room, in order to take calls if necessary. He didn't think he should be tied down incommunicado by Swann, even for twenty minutes. Swann walked in and saw this phone, this auditory bomb, waiting to detonate inside his central nervous system as soon as he began to concentrate on a target. When Targ declined to remove it, Swann in frustration reached down, grasped the phone, ripped it out of its jack on the wall, and hurled it, cord flailing, into the corridor.

Starting in the second week of the coffee break tests, Swann's responses seemed to increase in both accuracy and detail. When he was given the coordinates 41.5° north, 122° west, which described a place just east of California's Mount Shasta, he said: "Definitely see mountain to southwest, not far, also to east. Must also be a big valley." And the coordinates 64° north, 19° west, which described a point about 20 miles east of the volcano Mount Hekla in southern Iceland, prompted him to respond: "Volcano to southwest. I think I'm over ocean."

When Puthoff gave him the coordinates 2° south, 34° east—which Puthoff thought described the middle of Lake Victoria in Africa—Swann responded with: "Sense of speeding over water, landing on land. Lake to west, high elevation." It looked like a near miss, but Swann insisted he had been right on target, and persuaded Puthoff to go out to a bookstore and buy a proper atlas. The *Times Atlas of the World* showed that 2° south, 34° east marked a spot *not* in the middle of Lake Victoria, as Puthoff had supposed, but near the Tanzanian village of Ushashi, some thirty miles inland from Victoria's southeastern shore. Swann had indeed been right.

By the time ten days and one hundred coordinates had passed, Puthoff and Targ still found it hard to believe that Swann was actually using psi to obtain information on the places defined by the coordinates. But they did agree to further study, and they also tightened up the protocol. They arranged for their SRI division chief's secretary, Judy Schmickley, to select coordinates from maps. She would then hand the coordinates, without any accompanying description, to Puthoff and Targ, who would sit with Swann while he went into psychic mode. In this way Puthoff and Targ wouldn't know in advance what was at the coordinates, and thus couldn't inadvertently cue Swann to the right answer.

One day, May 29 to be precise, Puthoff was sufficiently impressed with the coordinate experiments that he placed a call to CIA headquarters, to the office of Richard Kennett.

Kennett was in his early thirties, with a wife and two young sons, and a house in the Virginia suburbs. He looked somewhat like the tennis player Jimmy Connors, though he and Connors didn't have much else in common. Within a decade, Kennett would be the assistant national intelligence officer* for chemical and biological warfare issues.

Here in the spring of 1973, Kennett was still only a few years into his CIA career, and served as an analyst in the Agency's Office of Scientific Intelligence. He had a Ph.D. in neurophysiology, was soon to complete his M.D., and spent much of his time preparing top-secret evaluations of the health of various foreign heads of state.

Kennett was a man of eclectic interests. The free world's greatest spy organization often attracted his type. Ordinary science, like ordinary life, all too often left him bored; he seemed more at home confronting the wild extremes of human behavior. Religion and mysticism in particular fascinated him. Appropriately, then, he spent some of his CIA time monitoring the fringes of medicine and psychology, watching trends, attending conferences, visiting laboratories, looking for things that, though unconventional, might be useful to one side or another in the great game of the Cold War.

One of the areas he kept an eye on was parapsychology, in particular the goings-on at SRI. Although the contract with SRI was being run by a different office from Kennett's,† the Agency had wanted him to make an independent evaluation of the work being done there, as part of an

---

* The NIO was the intelligence community's top analyst in a given subject, chairing interagency panels and writing annual reports on the subject.

† The CIA funding and contract management came to be handled jointly by two offices. The first was the Technical Services Division (TSD), in the Directorate of Operations, which had funded some low-level psi research during the 1960s. In the summer of 1973 TSD was transferred to the Directorate of Science and Technology, and became known as the Office of Technical Service (OTS). TSD/OTS was responsible for technical assistance to certain spying and covert-action operations, and was a bit like the gadget-strewn "Q Branch" in the old James Bond films. The second SRI psi-funding office, also under the Directorate of Science and Technology, was the more scientifically oriented Office of Research and Development (ORD).

overall assessment of the importance of parapsychological research in the United States and the Soviet Union. Unfortunately, little of the work at SRI had interested him so far, but now Hal Puthoff was phoning him with news of a possible breakthrough: Ingo Swann's coordinate-based clairvoyance scheme.

Kennett was open-minded about the phenomena of psi. He wanted to see Puthoff perform rigorous scientific experiments, and let the chips fall where they may. But the CIA analyst scoffed at the idea of coordinates, for the same reasons that Puthoff had first been dubious.

"All right," said Puthoff. "Why don't you give me the coordinates of a place that I don't know anything about?"

"Okay," said Kennett, "But I'll do you one better. I'll get you the coordinates of some place that even *I* don't know about."

Kennett put the phone down and walked out of his office into the hallway. He had passed seven or eight doorways when he ran into a colleague named Bill O'Donnell. "Bill, I want some coordinates of something that's on the East Coast," he told him. "Some place where, if I show you a drawing or a photograph later, you'll be able to say, 'Yes, that's what's at those coordinates.'" "Sure," said O'Donnell. "Give me a little while."

A few hours later, towards the end of the day, O'Donnell walked into Kennett's office with a pair of coordinates written on a small slip of paper. They were precise coordinates, written down to minutes and seconds of latitude and longitude. Had Kennett checked a map, he would have seen that they described a location somewhere in the Blue Ridge Mountains, a few hours west of Washington. Just what was there, only O'Donnell knew.

Kennett thanked O'Donnell, picked up the phone, and called Hal Puthoff at SRI.

* * *

A short time later, Swann sat at one end of a table in a conference room at SRI—smoking a cigar, as was his habit for most of his waking hours. Puthoff, sitting at the other end, read him the coordinates. The psychic wrote them down, and then, alternately closing his eyes, staring at the walls, and staring down at his writing paper, he began to sketch and to verbalize his impressions. The impressions seemed to arrive in brief, wavelike bursts of images and other sensory data: "This seems to be some sort of mounds or rolling hills . . . There is a city to the north; I can see taller buildings and some smog . . . This seems to be a strange place, somewhat like the lawns that one would find around a military base, but I get the impression that there are either some old bunkers around, or maybe this is a covered reservoir . . . There must be a flagpole, some highways to the west, possibly a river over to the far east, to the south more city." He drew a map showing a circular target surrounded by a road to the south, a road to the west, and a river to the east. To the north was a town. The session had taken six minutes.

The next morning, at his apartment in Mountain View, Swann had the impulse to do the site again. He worked on it between seven-thirty and eight, and brought in the following report to Puthoff:

Cliffs to the east, fence to the north. There's a circular building (a tower?), buildings to the south. Is this a former Nike base or something like that? This is about as far as I could go without feedback, and perhaps guidance as to what was wanted. There is something strange about this area, but since I don't know particularly what to look for within the scope of the cloudy ability, it is extremely difficult to make decisions on what is there and what is not. Imagination seems to get in the way. (For example, I seem to get the impression of something underground, but I'm not sure.) However, it is apparent that on first sighting the general location was correctly spotted.

Swann also had another more detailed map for Puthoff, depicting a broad, open space in a forested area. Lined by fences and a circular driveway, it contained a tall, flagpole-like object, and something large and circular. That was as far as Swann could go.

Puthoff didn't know how well the psychic had done, but he put Swann's report together and prepared to send it to Kennett. Before he could, Fate twisted, and a man named Patrick Price telephoned him.

Price was a graying, semi-retired, somewhat grizzled-looking fellow in his fifties who lived up at Lake Tahoe. He had a small building-contractor business, and also raised Christmas trees to sell in the Bay Area. He had met Puthoff at a lecture in Los Angeles a few years before, and Puthoff and Swann had run into him more recently, in late 1972, as he was selling Christmas trees from a lot in Mountain View.

Price considered himself a psychic. Back in the 1950s, for example, he had been a local councilman in Burbank, a suburb of L.A., and had briefly served as the town's police commissioner. Some difficult cases had arisen, and he believed he had developed important leads on them, thanks to information that had seemed to come to him spontaneously. At times, he claimed, he would even sit in the police dispatcher's office, trying to get psychic impressions of the places where criminals were hiding. By now, he said, he had psychic impressions about people and distant events almost every day.

"On impulse," Puthoff would say later, he decided to give Price the coordinates Richard Kennett had phoned in. It wasn't a very secure or scientific way of going about things, but Kennett hadn't said the coordinates were classified, and anyway there didn't seem to be much to lose. Price said he would give it a try.

That, according to Puthoff, was on the afternoon of the first of June. On the fourth, he received in the mail from Price an envelope, postmarked the second. It contained several pages of verbal descriptions and sketches. In those pages, Price had described more or less the same place that Swann had, but in much more detail, starting from high above the target and then moving down and around and within it.

Looked at general area from altitude of about 1500′ above highest terrain. On my left forward quadrant is a peak in a chain of mountains, elevation approximately 4996′ above sea level. Slopes are greyish slate covered with variety of broad leaf trees, vines, shrubbery, and undergrowth. I am facing about 3°–5° west of north. Looking down the mountain to the right (east) side is a roadway, freeway country style—curves around base of mountain from S.W.—swings north for a few miles, then heads E.N.E. to a fairly large city about 30–40 miles distant. This area was a battleground in civil war—low rolling hills, creeks, few lakes or reservoirs. There is a smaller town a little S.E. . . . Weather at this time is cloudy, rainy. Temperature at my altitude about 54°— high cumulo-nimbus clouds to about 25,000–30,000′. Clear area, but turbulent, between that level and some cirro-stratus at 46,000′. Air mass in that strip moving W.N.W. to S.E.

Perceived that peak area has large underground storage areas. Road comes up back side of mountains (west slopes), fairly well concealed, deliberately so. It's cut under trees where possible. Would be very hard to detect flying over area. Looks like former missile site—bases for launchers still there, but area now houses record storage area, microfilm, file cabinets; as you go into underground area through aluminum rolled-up doors, first areas filled with records, etc. Rooms about 100′ long, 4′ wide, 20′ ceilings with concrete supporting pilasters, flare-shaped. Temperature cool—fluorescent lighted. Personnel, Army 5th Corps engineers. M/Sgt Long on desk placard on grey steel desk—file cabinets security locked—combination locks, steel rods through eye bolts. Beyond these rooms, heading east, are several bays with computers, communications equipment, large maps, display type, overlays. Personnel, Army Signal Corps. Elevators.

Puthoff looked at all this and immediately telephoned Price. He asked him to try to pick up more detailed information from within the site, especially any secret codewords, if possible. The SRI physicist sensed that Price was dead on target, and he wanted to gather enough information to impress the CIA beyond a shadow of a doubt. A few days later, Price responded with some impressions from one of the underground offices he had psychically entered:

Top of desk had papers labelled:
    Flytrap
    Minerva

File cabinet on north wall labelled:
    Operation Pool (2nd word unreadable)
Folders inside cabinet labelled:
    Cueball
    14 Ball
    8 Ball
    Rackup

Name of site seems vaguely like Hayfork or Haystack

Personnel:

Col. R.J. Hamilton

Maj. Gen. George R. Nash

Major John C. Calhoun??

Puthoff sent it all in to Richard Kennett, who looked at the material, then handed it to Bill O'Donnell, the fellow CIA officer who had provided the coordinates.

"Rick, this isn't even close," said O'Donnell apologetically, once he had read the descriptions. "I gave you the coordinates of my summer cabin. I just took the maps out of my car, found out where my cabin was in the woods, and that's what I gave you. This"—he said, pointing to the descriptions by Swann and Price—"is bullshit."

Kennett was embarrassed, but he found it intriguing that both Swann and Price had described what seemed to be the same site. Was there something like that out in the Blue Ridge Mountains, near his friend's cabin?

The next weekend he took his wife and children for a drive into the countryside. A few miles from his friend's cabin he found a dirt road, a government No Trespassing sign, and some satellite antennas in the background. It was obviously some kind of secret military installation, and it seemed to match many of the SRI psychics' descriptions. It was as if Swann and Price, instead of focussing on the cabin in the woods, had simply found this place more interesting.

Monday morning, back at work, Kennett looked up an official who he thought might know about the strange military base out in West Virginia. He gave him the SRI psychics' descriptions. The official said he would check the information out.

Within a short time, a day or two, Richard Kennett found himself at the center of an intense and very hostile security investigation. Ingo Swann, and to a far greater extent Pat Price, had described details of a secret Pentagon facility in the hills near the West Virginia village of Sugar Grove. Ostensibly a U.S. Navy communications base, the site was manned by numerous military and civilian National Security Agency cryptographers, and it included large subterranean facilities tucked into the base of Reddish Knob Mountain, elevation 4,397 feet. Among its secret functions were the interception of international telephone communications, and the control of U.S. spy satellites. Much of it was underground, and nuclear-hardened, because it would be one of the first targets the Soviets hit if war broke out. Swann's and Price's remote-viewing data had been accurate enough to conjure up images, in Pentagon minds, of a massive and criminal leakage of top-secret, codeword-clearance information.

"How did you get inside?" they asked Kennett, now made to feel like some Soviet mole. "What the hell were you doing there?"

Kennett explained as best he could, but the Pentagon security officials didn't seem interested in stories about psychics. Hal Puthoff and Russell Targ were interrogated too, and soon learned that agents from the Defense Investigative Service were knocking on doors around their respective homes, asking neighbors whether Mr. Puthoff or Mr. Targ had ever been a Communist, or was spending too much money, or was otherwise behaving like a Soviet agent.

Failing to establish that anyone at SRI or Kennett's office had deliberately stolen or leaked classified information, the Pentagon investigators eventually left them alone. A few years later, the National Security Agency, which ran the Sugar Grove site, would itself become involved in tasking remote-viewers at SRI and Fort Meade.

In the meantime, in that summer of 1973, Pat Price extended the olive branch to NSA, the CIA, and Richard

Kennett, as only he could. He did some more clairvoyant snooping, and came up with a detailed description of a Soviet installation that performed functions similar to the NSA site's. Price pinpointed it at Mount Narodnaya in the remote northern Ural Mountains:

> Area site underground, reinforced concrete, doorways of steel of the roll-up type . . . I see some helipads, concrete. Light rail tracks run from pads to another set of rails that parallel the doors into the mountain. 30 miles north (5° west of north) of the site is a radar installation with 1 large (165') dish and two small fast-track dishes.

Price also noted the strange but potentially useful detail that at the time he viewed it—nighttime in the USSR—the base was staffed by an unusually high proportion of female workers.

The CIA soon confirmed that Price, again, was right.

8

THE SHAMANS

I remember one time before we went into the SRI cafeteria for lunch with some government people, and Hal said to Pat, "Don't tell them you can create clouds!"

—Ingo Swann, on his rival
Pat Price

THE STORY OF THE PSYCHIC SPIES SPREAD QUICKLY, AND IT WASN'T long before interested members of the intelligence community—high-ranking military officers, scientists and analysts, congressmen and staffers—began making pilgrimages from Washington to see the fabled wonder-workers of SRI. Can you find Soviet submarines? they would ask Swann and Price. Can you see into the future? Can you visit the past? Someone from the CIA even suggested that the two psychics should act as spirit mediums, transmitting the ethereal messages of foreign agents whose lives had been snuffed out before they had been able to deliver the goods to their American case officers.

But most of the requests, in the years that followed, were tailored to Swann's coordinate-based clairvoyance scheme, which he began to call scanning-by-coordinate, "Scanate" for short. Sometimes the coordinates would be mailed in, or telephoned in. More often they would be hand-carried from Washington, by officials who would ensure that the coordinates were presented to Price, and to Swann, only at the moment they began their psychic performances.

The arrangement was in the nature of a promotional offer: SRI's psychics would provide samples of their product free of charge, and their visitors—vetted to exclude mere curiosity seekers—would decide whether or not they wanted to pay for more of it.

Swann and Price didn't always know for whom they were demonstrating their psychic abilities, but they were always eager to perform well. They held out hope that their achievements would not be entombed in some obscure parapsychology journal, but instead would be used, ultimately, in support of the highest national goals. What with all the visitors from Washington, and top-secret target sites, they began to see themselves as super-spies, James Bonds of the Aquarian Age.

But the idea that they were now Cold Warriors was not the only thing energizing Swann and Price—for they were also competing against each other. This was natural, considering that they practiced such an individualistic and esoteric discipline. In fact, one could have argued that they were more individualistic and esoteric than any ordinary spy or soldier, for in their own minds, at least, they ventured alone and naked, savants with extraordinary powers, against the howling darkness of the ethereal realm. They were up there with the great magicians and medicine men, seers and healers, shamans and sorcerers.

Scholars often quarrel about how to define particular variants of the visionary or "shamanic" personality, but from the literature it seems clear that all these types share a relative proneness to altered states of consciousness. In many cases, this trance-proneness appears to have genetic causes. Shamanic behavior often runs in families, in primitive cultures as well as our own, and the shamanic person in early life may seem mentally unstable, "neurotic," or "labile," in extreme cases manifesting the symptoms of what we might now call epilepsy, hysteria, schizophrenia, or dissociative disorders.* He may suffer seizures under stress. Sudden trances and fugues may make him oblivious of his surroundings, and may leave him wandering alone and amnesic, far from home. He may hear voices, see visions, have unnerving out-of-body experiences and confrontations with supernatural entities. He may claim a range of ailments—headaches, stomachaches, fatigue, miscellaneous wounds—that are imagined, feigned, or self-induced.

In other cases, this neuropsychological lability may develop out of such things as hormonal imbalances, near-terminal diseases, severe head injuries, and of course psychological stresses. The historian Mircea Eliade, citing the anthropologist Knud Rasmussen, has even noted that one Eskimo shaman "obtained his power after being struck by a ball of fire." And the modern UFO lore contains numerous examples of people whose close encounters with "flying saucers" or other unidentified aerial phenomena appear to have bestowed upon them a trance-proneness similar to that seen in shamans.†

Ingo Swann had never had a close encounter with a ball

---

* Dissociative disorders include persistent or recurrent amnesias, fugue or trance states, feelings of unreality, spirit-possession syndromes, and the modern, medicalized version of spirit-possession, known as multiple personality disorder. These disorders are named for the psychiatric term *dissociation,* which refers (somewhat vaguely) to the splitting off of various mental processes from consciousness. For example, dissociative disorder sufferers often appear to be amnesic after dissociative episodes, as if their experience and behavior during those episodes were dissociated from normal consciousness and memory. They also can dissociate pain and other autonomic feedback mechanisms, and thus are capable of unusual physical feats—although the fantasy-proneness of many dissociative people also leads them to imagine or feign pain that isn't there.

† Some researchers have theorized that UFOs in such cases are geo-atmospheric phenomena associated with intense magnetic fields that can in-

of fire or a flying saucer, and had never been mentally ill. Puthoff and others at SRI regarded him as a witty and clever man with a daring, inquisitive mind. But there were otherworldly, vaguely shamanic themes running throughout his life story. Swann would say, for example, that a great-grandmother on his mother's side was a Sioux Indian medicine woman, and that his own childhood had been haunted by a variety of paranormal experiences. His general fascination with the occult had led him to an exploration of various alternative or New Ageish disciplines, and his worldview, despite a modern gloss, featured many exotic motifs. Swann considered himself an accomplished astrologer, believed that his soul had once belonged to an eighth-century European,* and was deeply interested in UFOs and the idea that aliens were visiting planet Earth.

To most of the government people visiting SRI, it probably seemed that there was nothing even remotely shamanic about Pat Price, except for his mysterious psychic abilities. Puthoff and Targ touted him as "a former police commissioner," a rock of conventionality. Now in semi-retirement, so the story went, he was just a businessman, an ordinary joe who liked to play poker and go fishing on the weekends.

In fact, Price was in some ways even more shamanic than Swann. Not only did he have out-of-body experiences and a history of alternative religious leanings, but he also claimed the ancient—and now somewhat quaint—shamanic power of being able to change the weather, creating

---

duce seizures, hallucinations, and even permanent neurological damage in nearby witnesses.

* Swann told an interviewer in early 1973: "I recall a time in the past when people with paranormal abilities were appreciated. I was an adviser to a conqueror in Europe who had a great deal of faith in such people, and employed them as advisers. At that time it was very easy for me to read people's minds. I would advise the conqueror or king what I felt were the true motivations of a person who came for an audience. I think that was in the eighth century."

or evaporating clouds at will. Furthermore, he believed that he could make traffic lights change through psychokinesis, and that his soul had once belonged to the American colonial orator Patrick Henry. Last but not least, he believed that an alien civilization flew its silvery saucers into bases on the moon and Mars—and also here on Earth, under the oceans and beneath great mountains. Not long after arriving at SRI, he reported to Puthoff that Alaska's Mount Hayes, the jewel of a glacial range northeast of Anchorage, housed one of the aliens' largest bases.

Paranormal competitions have always been a great pastime of shamanic types. Often waged like athletic bouts, they are found throughout the lore of religion and magic—for example, Moses's duels with the Pharaoh's sorcerers—as well as in more recent writings on the subject. The ethnologist Holger Kalweit gives an example from the Washo Indians of North America, among whom shamans stage competitions to see who has the greatest power. "One form of their competition consists in seeing who can knock over the greatest number of poles, which are tightly rammed into the earth in a line, merely by pointing at them." Another form of competition, presumably, is the telling of tall tales to wide-eyed ethnologists. But whether in legend or in reality, shamans have often seemed preoccupied with battling it out amongst themselves. Mircea Eliade refers to the "intense rivalry" of their contests.

A similar form of contest now seemed to take hold at SRI, the goal being to spy psychically upon targets in the most dramatic and convincing detail. For each session, Swann or Price would sit down at a table with a stack of blank paper and a pen. The psychic would begin by writing on his top sheet of paper the date, the time, and his special three-digit code number. Puthoff had introduced the code numbers. The idea was to help keep things as sanitized and anonymous as possible, not only for scientific and security reasons, but—perhaps in vain—to help dampen any personal rivalries among his psychics.

When given a set of coordinates, Swann or Price would write them down, and then would start talking, or writing, or sketching whatever came to mind. Puthoff or Targ, acting as the session monitor, would prompt with questions: What's that right there? Can you elaborate? What does this look like from up close? Eventually, the sketches and descriptions would be analyzed and summarized, and delivered to the prospective client.

In late July of 1973, Richard Kennett telephoned Hal Puthoff with the coordinates 49°20'S, 70°14'E. Puthoff walked into the "Scanate" room, sat down, and read them to Swann.

Swann's first impressions of the target left him confused. He seemed to be out in open ocean. Was it some kind of trick target? He wasn't sure what he should do.

"Is there anything nearby?" asked Puthoff.

Swann sensed a landmass nearby, and decided to go with that. "My initial response," he told Puthoff, "is that it's an island, maybe a mountain sticking up through a cloud cover. Terrain seems rocky. Must be some sort of small plants growing there. Cloud bank to the west. Very cold. I see some buildings rather mathematically laid out. One of them is orange. There is something like a radar antenna, a round disc . . . Two white cylindrical tanks, quite large. To the northwest, a small airstrip. Wind is blowing. Must be two or three trucks in front of building . . ."

Puthoff seemed happy with that, but Swann wanted to press on. His mind's eye was filled with coastal vistas, so much so that he felt he could map the island accurately. "If I look to the west, hills; to the north, flatlands, and I think, airstrip and ocean in the distance to the east; can't see anything to the south. I move to the coastline and follow it around . . ." He began to sketch the outline of the island on a blank sheet of paper, but it wasn't anything like conscious artistry. His autonomic nervous system had taken over, and it wanted more space. Swann's pen began to move around as if the paper weren't even there, and when it reached the edge of one sheet of paper Puthoff would hurriedly put down a new sheet so the pen could continue to trace. All the while Swann kept up a commentary about what he was sensing at that part of the coastline. One place there were birds everywhere, and bird dung, and the guano smell seemed to fill his nostrils. Another place there were rocks and breakers and the smell of sea spray. There were buildings, boats, a wharf, bays, mountains, promontories, and beaches.

After a while Swann had completed a rough drawing of the island, adding features according to his commentary. He and Puthoff Scotch-taped the sheets together and sent them to Kennett. The coordinates, it turned out, described a point within a small bay on the eastern side of remote Kerguelen Island in the southern Indian Ocean. Owned by France, Kerguelen was the site of a joint French-Soviet "upper atmospheric meteorological research facility," rumored to double, at least for the Soviets, as some kind of secret listening post or missile-tracking station. Swann had not only described its outline fairly accurately, he had accurately placed and described many other features not even available on the few maps of the island.

There were claps on the back for Swann, and Puthoff and Targ promoted the event in meetings with various intelligence officials in Washington. But Price didn't seem too impressed. One day, Puthoff handed him his own set of coordinates—"sexy" coordinates, as the classified ones would soon come to be known.

Price wasn't aware of it, but a month or so before, at CIA headquarters, Puthoff and Targ had briefed senior CIA officials on their research. The officials included Office of Technical Service chief John McMahon, and his boss, Deputy Director for Science and Technology Carl Duckett. The Agency officials had suggested that the time was ripe for psychic spying on more sensitive targets overseas.

The coordinates Price was given described the location of a mysterious Soviet military research facility at the southern edge of the Semipalatinsk nuclear test area in the Kazakh Republic. The target's CIA nickname was URDF-3—for "unidentified R&D facility" number 3. Air Force intelligence called it P-NUTS, for "probable nuclear underground test site." No one in the U.S. intelligence community really knew what went on there. The CIA officials who brought in the coordinates, an Office of Technical Service engineer, Ken Kress,* and a physicist named Peter Maris, told Puthoff and Targ that the site was "a research facility." That was about all Kress and Maris knew, too.

Price did the session from within an electrically shielded room on the second floor of SRI's Radio Physics Building.† Targ, serving as his monitor, turned on a tape recorder, said a few words in preamble, and then read Price the coordinates of the site, explaining that it was some kind of research facility. Price polished his glasses with a handkerchief, closed his eyes, and leaned back in his chair. After a minute or so, he said, "This reminds me of the old joke that starts with a guy in his penthouse looking up at the Third Avenue El." In his clairvoyant reverie, he explained, he was lying on his back, in warm sunshine, on the roof of a several-story building. But towering over him—straddling the building, in fact—was a large crane. "As I drift up in the air and look down, it seems to be riding on a track

---

* Kress had brought Puthoff the first CIA contract in 1972.

† Such rooms were normally used to protect sensitive computing and telephone equipment. The grounded metal shielding in the walls blocked most electromagnetic radiation the equipment might emit, thus helping to protect it from would-be eavesdroppers. Shielded rooms were occasionally used by Puthoff and Targ to bolster their argument that psi was not an electromagnetic phenomenon.

with one rail on each side of the building. I've never seen anything like that."

The wheeled crane, said Price, was being used to move large, heavy objects in and around a semi-underground facility. The wheels on the crane were each twice the height of a man. Near the crane were several other buildings, and a cluster of tall compressed-gas canisters.

Ken Kress and Peter Maris, when they first heard Price's description of the Semipalatinsk site, didn't know what to make of it. But back in Washington, they checked with colleagues and found a recent satellite photo of the site—and there was the crane on rails, and the building between the rails, just as Price had described them.

Meanwhile, guided by Puthoff and Targ, Price periodically returned to the site at Semipalatinsk, describing additional details. He sketched a layout of the site, with a river nearby to the north. Then he went inside the low building under the crane, into a room where large curved sections—"gores"—of steel were lying around. Workers were trying to weld them into sixty-foot-diameter spheres, said Price. But the steel was so thick that the workers were having difficulty welding them together, and were experimenting with new welding techniques.

At some point, within a week or so of his first session against the site, Price met directly with Kress and Maris. They now explained that they were from the CIA, and that his description of the crane was substantially accurate. Questioned by the two Agency officers, Price explored the site further. Two weeks after his initial session with Targ, he had filled several hours' worth of cassette tapes, plus a large sketchbook. It seemed from the data that the Semipalatinsk facility would soon be conducting controlled explosions of some kind. The metal spheres were to be used to contain the explosions.

Aside from the sketch of the crane, and the general layout of the site, there was little that Kress and Maris could confirm. But the sketch of the crane was on its own extremely impressive. The correspondence between it and the relevant satellite photo of the site was so close that merely by showing those two images side by side, in briefings for senior intelligence officials, Puthoff and Targ would ensure SRI's psi research funding for the next several years.

As for the large metal spheres, a U.S. satellite caught them out in the open, in completed form, sometime in late 1974 or early 1975. Photo analysts estimated them to be about sixty feet in diameter.

The existence of the spheres would touch off a wild debate within the American intelligence community. Air Force intelligence officials would argue that the spheres were to be used to contain low-yield nuclear explosions, which in turn would drive an advanced proton-beam weapon that could shoot down U.S. aircraft and missiles. This idea was eventually leaked to a reporter at the magazine *Aviation Week*, which in May 1977 ran an alarming, eight-thousand-word article on Semipalatinsk and other supposed beam-weapons sites:

SOVIETS PUSH FOR BEAM WEAPON

. . . The Semipalatinsk facility where beams weapons tests are taking place has been under observation by the US for about 10 years. The central building at the facility is believed by some officials to contain a collective accelerator, electron injectors, and power stores.

The building is 200 ft. wide and 700 ft. long, with walls of reinforced concrete 10-ft. thick. . . . [The test site] is surrounded by a series of security fences.

The US used high-resolution photographic reconnaissance satellites to watch as the Soviet technicians had four holes dug through solid granite formations not far from the main large building at the facility. Mine heads were constructed over each opening, and frames were built over the holes. As tons of rock were removed, a large underground chamber was built deep inside the rock formation.

In a nearby building, huge, extremely thick steel gores were manufactured. The building has since been removed. These steel segments were parts of a large sphere estimated to be about 18 meters (57.8 ft.) in diameter. Enough gores for two complete spheres were constructed. US officials believe the spheres are needed to capture and store energy from nuclear-driven explosives or pulse-power generators. The steel gores are believed by some officials to be among the earliest clues to what might be taking place at the facility.

The components were moved to the nearby mine heads and lowered into the chamber.

The Air Force hypothesis fell on deaf ears at the CIA, where in-house physicists and consultants scoffed at the beam-weapons idea, suggesting that the spheres might merely contain nuclear waste, or perhaps conventional explosions that would be used to experiment with advanced pulse-power technologies.* But both the CIA and the Air Force would agree that the spheres were there, and that the Soviets had devised an ingenious new "flux-welding" technique to put them together. On both those counts Pat Price had been right, and he had described the spheres and the special welding techniques before *anyone in the United States knew they existed.* To Puthoff and Targ, that made it just about the best test of psychic spying they could imagine.

---

* The Soviets never did develop a workable beam-weapon, either at the Semipalatinsk site or anywhere else. A former Air Force intelligence source admitted that, in retrospect, it appeared that the site had been used not for beam-weapons development but for basic pulse-power generation experiments, using low-yield nuclear explosions. A CIA scientist familiar with the debate still scoffed at the idea that the spheres could have contained nuclear explosions rather than conventional high explosives.

* * *

Pat Price was so good, it seemed, that he could do psychic spying virtually in his sleep, without coordinates, and without even being asked to look for anything. He would lie in bed at night and drift around the globe, his psi faculties primed for whatever big events were happening or about to happen. On one occasion, he told Puthoff he had seen a school of Russian submarines out in the Pacific, moving around in a strange parallelogram pattern. Puthoff made some phone calls, and soon confirmed Price's report. In the autumn of 1973, according to Puthoff, Price saw the Yom Kippur war coming, and saw it going, predicting the cease-fire date a few weeks in advance.

Another time, Price came into the office at SRI and declared that President Nixon had a device in his office that was going to make him suffer. Puthoff wondered what the hell this meant. Had the Russians smuggled something into the Oval Office—some awful toxin, or perhaps a mind-warping microwave source? Puthoff dutifully passed the information on to Ken Kress at the CIA. Whether Kress in turn passed it on to the White House, Puthoff never knew, but months later, as Watergate ground to its conclusion, he heard about Nixon's Oval Office tape recorder, and decided that that had probably been what Price had detected.

Price seldom knew how he did it. He just did it. Swann, on the other hand, was interested in how it all worked, and he liked to define and name the various parts and modes of psi functioning. *Scanate* was just one of the new terms he had invented; there was also *Scanex*, for *scan*ning-*ex*tended, which referred to the eyes-closed altered-state form of psychic spying that Price, for example, used in his nocturnal jaunts. The viewer in Scanex mode could perform an open search for anything interesting, as Price liked to do, or, like Swann, he could attempt to find the unknown location of some known target—for example hidden nuclear missiles, or some important person.

But if Swann was adept at providing insights into his psychic excursions, Price was simply a better psychic. He wasn't perfect—he had bad days like anyone else—but to Hal Puthoff and Richard Kennett and Ken Kress and the others he worked with, he seemed more accurate, more consistent, and more attuned to the technical details of target sites. On the whole, he could pick up more data. One of the most promising things about him was that he seemed able to pick up not only visual and other sensory data, but also alphanumeric data, words and numbers. Swann, by contrast, would be able to pull accurate alphanumeric information from a target only two or three times in his life, and always in visual rather than verbal form, not recognizing at first that the shapes he drew belonged to an alphabet. Swann, like Puthoff and Targ, took the view that if one tried psychically to recognize a number or a letter or a word, even while unconscious of the fact, the perceptual process tended to short-circuit. One would shift away from the deeper, more basic parts of the brain, where psi processing seemed to occur, and would engage the left cortex, where the bulk of the verbal and analytical apparatus resided. In other words the psi process, by its very attempt to recognize alphanumeric data, would shut itself off.

Well, to Pat Price that was a very interesting theory, and it sounded reasonable. But it didn't stop him at all. When he was going after a target, he could often read numbers or words on pieces of paper, or names on uniforms, as at the NSA site in West Virginia. It wasn't easy, and he wasn't always right, but it could be done. When it came to raw shamanic prowess, Price was in a league of his own.

There was another difference between Swann and Price, perhaps widened by Price's amazing feats in the psychic spying room. Swann's ego seemed more fragile, his demeanor more pedantic. He could be great fun one minute, the life of the party, but if the proper respect were not paid, if a word in jest went amiss, if an obstacle were placed in his path, he could quickly become ill tempered. Never completely at home in the world, ever beset by a confederacy of dunces, he was, to some, a perpetual storm waiting to break.

Price, by contrast, seemed an endless sunny day. He did not worry over the design of experiments. He did not mind the secrecy concerns that occasionally prevented him from knowing how well he had done. He ignored the inconveniences that might have sent other psychics into a stupor of resentment, and he never threatened to leave SRI, as Swann often did. His cheerful emotional resilience, his "rough and ready" demeanor, as Puthoff would later describe it, charmed just about everyone he met. To Puthoff and Targ and the CIA people, he seemed like the ideal psychic subject.

Pat Price did not, however, charm Ingo Swann, who came to regard him as a "manipulator," and treated him somewhat coolly—on the increasingly rare occasions that they were within speaking range. In fact, toward the end of his first eight-month contract at SRI, Swann was usually absent from Menlo Park, busy instead doing parapsychological experiments elsewhere, or trying to sell his psychic services to oil companies, or working on half a dozen other projects in New York and around the country. Swann must have been bitterly aware of the irony. He had succeeded dramatically in his task at SRI, turning around what might have been a dismal failure of a research program. He had isolated a psi phenomenon robust enough to be replicated, and perhaps even to be used operationally. Despite all this, he had already begun to slip into obsolescence. Pat Price, and not he, now seemed to be the favorite of both SRI and the sponsors in Washington.

When Swann's contract at SRI ended in mid-August of 1973, he was handed a small plaque, commemorating his contribution to the SRI research program. Puthoff, driving him to the airport, gave him a pep talk about all they had accomplished, and all they would accomplish in the future, once the money really started to roll in.

But Swann angrily vowed that he would never return to SRI.

9

The Trickster

There is something of the trickster in the character of the shaman and medicine-man. . . .

—Carl Jung, *Four Archetypes,*
1959

I would rather be an enigma than anything else.

—Uri Geller, in conversation

URI GELLER IS AT THE WHEEL OF THE CAR, DRIVING THROUGH A residential section near Menlo Park. He is wearing a blindfold. An *Apollo 14* astronaut, Edgar Mitchell, who walked on the moon only two years ago, is in the front passenger seat. It's not a dream. It's real, and Hal Puthoff is there in the backseat, bracing himself for a crash, and meanwhile Geller navigates, supposedly through ESP, and describes all the scenery just to let everyone know that, despite the blindfold, he's still in control.

That car that just passed us is red!

Okay, Uri . . .

Stop sign!

Uri, that's enough, now. . . .

There is a nice house over there.

You've shown us, Uri. . . .

Another car—a big one, white.

Okay, you got it, Uri. Now. . . .

And Puthoff is thinking that this is a hell of a way for
Geller to inaugurate a serious scientific investigation—with
the blindfolded-driving routine, an old stage-magician's
trick.

Uri Geller, just arrived from Israel and fast becoming an
international celebrity, had first visited SRI in the fall of
1972. Puthoff and Targ had wanted to test him. Ken Kress
and Richard Kennett and others at the CIA, looking quietly
over the SRI researchers' shoulders, had also wanted to get
a look at the controversial Israeli wonder-worker.

For the first full year of their psi research at SRI, Puthoff
and Targ therefore performed a kind of juggling act, coaxing the flamboyant Israeli into the lab when neither Price
nor Swann was there, trying—not very successfully, in the
case of Swann vs. Geller—to keep the rivalries and resent-
ments under control.

The first visit was arranged through Geller's minder, a
neurologist, inventor, and psi enthusiast named Andrija
Puharich. He warned Puthoff and his colleagues that studying the young Israeli wouldn't be too easy. Uri seemed
spooked by the prospect of being stuck in a laboratory
environment. He needed room to breathe, to move. According to Puharich, Geller also believed himself to be
some kind of space-age prophet; specifically, he claimed
that his powers came from a huge flying saucer–shaped
computer, "Spectra," somewhere out there in Earth's grav-
itational field. Spectra was in turn controlled by a distant,
bureaucratic entity named Hoova, a sort of ethereal governor of planet Earth.* Hey, whatever, shrugged Puthoff and
Targ.

So Geller came to SRI, and drove blindfolded. He bent

---

* Geller disavowed these beliefs years later, blaming them on regression
hypnosis sessions Puharich had performed on him.

or broke spoons and rings and various other metal items. He seemed to remotely reduce the weight of a one-gram object on an electronic scale. He described simple sketches locked in briefcases. He apparently scrambled the electronic innards of an SRI magnetometer's strip chart recorder, and somehow, from a distance of several feet, caused the image on a video screen to shift.

It should have been mind-blowing stuff, but Geller's style was so hyperkinetic, so chaotic, as if designed to misdirect the eye, that Puthoff and Targ usually suspected sleight of hand. The young Israeli was like a walking stage magician, and a very good one—although for some feats, the answer was almost too obvious, like that blindfolded-driving trick. Puthoff and Targ believed that Geller could have accomplished it simply by looking through the gap, which is always there, between blindfold and nose.

Geller was born on the winter solstice of 1946, in Tel Aviv, of Hungarian emigré parents. Playing in his parents' garden at the age of four, according to the Geller legend, he was visited by a strange luminous apparition—the Joan of Arc motif again—and thereafter began to manifest paranormal talents. Unlike Swann and Price, he did not have out-of-body experiences or premonitions; instead he is said to have been able to read minds, to visualize hidden objects and drawings clairvoyantly, and to bend small pieces of metal.

When Geller was ten, his parents separated, and he went to live with his mother on the island of Cyprus. At the age of seventeen, he returned to Israel, entered military service, joined the paratroops, and was wounded during the Six-Day War in 1967.

After he recuperated, he put his good looks to work, appearing as a model in advertisements for shaving cream and other consumer products. Encouraged by a friend named Shipi Strang, he put on his first public performance of mind reading and metal-bending in a Tel Aviv school hall in 1969. More public performances followed, and through the connections of a girlfriend who worked in advertising, he also became a performer at private parties throughout Israel. As time went by, the partygoers seemed to become more prestigious, and one day he found himself doing his routine for Prime Minister Golda Meir. Shortly thereafter, in response to a reporter's question about the future of Israel, Meir remarked, "I don't know—ask Uri Geller." Already moderately well known, Geller now became an Israeli household word.

By the middle of 1970 the reaction had begun, and skeptics in Israel were attacking him loudly. Some illustrated their arguments by apparently duplicating his feats with ordinary sleight-of-hand tricks. Others made specific allegations of cheating. But already, it seemed, Geller's celebrity was beyond the reach of the skeptics. He seemed to be moving in higher circles, where his supporters included key officials of the Israeli government. According to his own account, Geller one evening was invited to dinner at a steakhouse near Tel Aviv by General Moshe Dayan, hero of the Six-Day War. Dayan wanted to know whether the psychic was genuine. Geller obliged him, bending a key and doing some successful ESP demonstrations, even having Dayan act as a telepathic receiver of information. Later Dayan invited Geller to his house, and asked him to find a photograph he had hidden somewhere in his study. Geller eventually pointed out a book on a shelf, and described the photograph as the flag of Israel. Laughing, Dayan turned to page 201 of the book, and showed Geller the target: a photo of the main tower of Tel Aviv's Lod Airport, atop which the Israeli flag was flying. "You've proved yourself, Uri," Geller says Dayan remarked. "I don't want to see any more. There's no need for you to bend anything. Now, what can you do for Israel?"

Geller, so the story goes, went on to meet with military

intelligence chief Aharon Yariv,* as well as with officials of Mossad (roughly, the Israeli CIA) and Shin Bet (the Israeli FBI). He was tested by these agencies, and began to work for them. He became a modern-day version of the Israeli prophet Elisha, whose legendary exploits are recounted in the Old Testament:

> Then the king of Syria warred against Israel, and took counsel with his servants, saying, In such and such a place shall be my camp.
>
> And the man of God [Elisha] sent unto the king of Israel, saying, Beware that thou pass not such a place; for thither the Syrians are come down.
>
> And the king of Israel sent to the place which the man of God told him and warned him of, and saved himself there, not once nor twice.
>
> Therefore the heart of the king of Syria was sore troubled for this thing; and he called his servants, and said unto them, Will ye not shew me which of us is for the king of Israel?
>
> And one of his servants said, None, my lord, O king, but Elisha, the prophet that is in Israel, telleth the king of Israel the words that thou speakest in thy bedchamber.

Some things never change. Geller's attempted tasks allegedly included the clairvoyant viewing of intelligence targets in Syria and other countries in the Middle East, the prediction of hostile troop deployments, and even the telepathic influencing of various Arab figures. But to the chagrin of the Israeli government (he would later say) he decided that he would rather pursue a high-profile career as a stage performer than a zero-profile career as a psychic

---

* In an interview with science writer John Wilhelm in the mid-1970s, Yariv denied ever meeting or consulting with Geller (but then, he *would* say that, wouldn't he?)

warrior. In 1972, Geller was enticed to America by Andrija Puharich, who funded the visit with a grant from the Institute of Noetic Science, run by former astronaut Edgar Mitchell, a psi enthusiast.

Rumors soon spread that the Soviets were interested in Geller and his feats, and were actually following him around the United States. Whether or not the rumors were true, some CIA officials were certainly interested. They made clear to Puthoff that they wanted to know whether the Israeli psychic was for real, and if he was, how valuable an intelligence asset he could be, to whoever might employ him.

And if he *wasn't* for real, the Agency wanted to know how he managed to look real. There were wild surmises in the air. Perhaps Geller was some sort of bionic man, with magnetic implants that enabled him to stop watches, shift television screens, spin compasses, tickle magnetometers, and so forth. Perhaps he had radio receivers—for communicating with secret confederates—implanted in his inner ears, or in his teeth. Perhaps he was part of some Mossad disinformation project, designed to spook the Arabs into believing that Israel possessed a paranormal superman. Or perhaps Israeli intelligence wanted to use him to infiltrate SRI, to spy on America's most sensitive psychic research.*

To complicate the picture, several Israeli officials turned up at SRI one day in the summer of 1973. Puthoff had the impression that they were from Israeli military intelligence. Whoever they were, they proceeded to explain, in deliberately vague terms, that Geller had done some surprisingly

---

* Geller says that he met secretly, in hotel rooms in the United States, with a group of Israeli officials to brief them in detail about his experiences at SRI. According to Geller, the same officials warned him "not to do certain things" at SRI, things that Geller won't specify. Puthoff says he was never told by Geller about these contacts, but as Geller recalls, the SRI physicist did keep him from getting too close to the experiments with Swann and Price.

good work for them against Middle Eastern military targets. The officials said they wanted to know: Was this just amazing luck, or did Geller have actual psychic talents that could be verified by scientific experimentation? Perhaps Puthoff, as a reputable scientist performing controlled experiments, could help them determine what was what. But the Israelis and their questions only made Puthoff and his colleagues more paranoid.

In all, Geller made several visits to SRI. Some were high-profile, and some were never reported, but most followed the same pattern. In some tests, there seemed no room for doubt that his psi abilities were genuine, while in other tests, he seemed to do no more than a stage magician could.

His stay in August of 1973 was fairly typical. To start with, Geller was put in an electromagnetically shielded room. Sealed inside with a pen and blank paper, he was asked to reproduce drawings of objects chosen by Puthoff. The scientist would choose targets by arbitrarily selecting a page from a dictionary and finding the first drawable word. In the first test, Puthoff selected the word *fuse,* then had an SRI artist quietly sketch a fuse and firecracker. Puthoff taped the sketch to the wall outside the shielded room. Geller was told via intercom to start concentrating. Within a few seconds he said, "I see a cylinder with noise coming out of it," although none of his eventual sketches—which included a giraffe, a snare drum, and a long-necked human with a stringlike thing coming out of one ear—was absolutely on target. His next attempt, however, couldn't have been more accurate. The SRI artist drew a bunch of grapes—twenty-four, to be exact—and inside the shielded room Geller began to talk about "drops of water coming out of the picture," and "purple circles," before sketching a bunch of precisely twenty-four grapes, to the same scale as the SRI artist's drawing.

It went on like this for various types of experiment. Sometimes Geller would be tested for clairvoyance, the target drawing being left on an unattended computer screen, or on a computer disc, or sealed inside a shielded room. Sometimes the experiment would be set up to test telepathy, and the target drawing would be watched by someone such as Puthoff, or his SRI division chief, Bart Cox. Geller didn't always describe the targets perfectly, but he did so often enough to suggest to Puthoff and others at SRI that he had some genuine ability. "He was wonderful, not just all right," Ingo Swann would later say, in a rare concession to one of his great rivals.

With Geller's trademark talent, psychokinesis, the story was somewhat different. Puthoff and Targ would later seem to duplicate many of the psychic's metal-bending or machine-altering demonstrations with mundane magician's tricks. And Geller's psychokinetic displays never occurred under controlled conditions. He would stand for hours in a room, covered by video cameras from several angles, but it seemed that the spoons, bars, and rings over which he hovered would bend only when he was allowed to handle them over long periods, or when the monitoring cameras momentarily ran out of videotape. And when his only monitors were unaided humans, he seemed always in motion, keeping up a patter, using his voice and body language—his audience thought—to divert attention while his eyes looked patiently for the magician's enchanted window of opportunity. Outside the laboratory, at lunch in the SRI dining room for instance, one had only to turn one's attention from him for a second, and he would suddenly produce, bent into a loop, the fork that had just been nestling beside one's plate.

A story later made the rounds, to the effect that Geller had been videotaped performing a sleight-of-hand trick during a metal-bending attempt. Swann even claimed that he had urged the scrutiny of the tape that had revealed the trick. Puthoff and Targ denied the existence of any such smoking gun, but it was clear that they were on guard against magician's tricks. Once or twice, they put the experienced stage magician Milbourne Christopher into the laboratory during experiments, disguised as a camera-wielding lab technician. On a few other occasions, after Geller had left for the day, Puthoff and Targ searched the laboratory rafters and acoustic tiles for hidden audio or video bugs.

They never found anything.

And so the essential question persisted: Was Geller a psychic or wasn't he? He had come up with remarkable results in tests that seemed to have been reasonably well controlled. How could one reconcile such results with his tricksterish demeanor? Was he a shamanic savant, or a clever illusionist?

Or was such a strong distinction realistic? For the tales of shamans and other visionaries, throughout history and across cultures, contained a striking number of references to the development of sleight-of-hand skills, and to the manifestation of an incorrigibly childlike trickiness, all this intermingled with apparently "genuine" skills and beliefs. "The elementary mythology of shamanism," wrote Joseph Campbell in his *Historical Atlas of World Mythology*, "is neither of truth and falsehood nor of good and evil, but of degrees of power: power achieved by breaking through the walls of space and barriers of time to sources unavailable to others. Shamanic combat is but one manifestation of this interest. The use of magical tricks and deceptions to impress and intimidate the uninitiated represents another." Campbell gave as example an Eskimo shaman who had been interviewed in the 1920s by the anthropologist Knud Rasmussen:

Najagneq, for example, had frequently employed deceptions to protect himself from his neighbors by playing on their superstitions, and he was not afraid to admit that he had made an art of pulling their legs. But when Rasmussen asked if he really believed in all the powers to which he pretended, he replied: "Yes, a power that we call Sila, one that cannot be explained in so many words. . . ."

On occasion the leg-pulling of the shamans seemed to serve an even more interesting purpose, according to Campbell, who wrote that the effects of the shaman's "mystifications, theatrical scenes, and sleight-of-hand illusionism . . . turn back on the mind of the shaman himself and become the aids and generators of his own translation to ecstasy." Which was another way of saying that the shaman sometimes bootstrapped himself into an altered state with his own stage-magic tricks, as if his right brain didn't know what his left was doing.

In fact, tricksterish themes are found not just in shamanism, but throughout the psi lore, from mystics to mediums. The psychologist Carl Jung, remarking on this connection, named "the Trickster" one of the four great archetypes of the human psyche.

Whether he was a shamanic trickster or not, Geller was certainly an enigma to some, although most seem to have decided that he was completely genuine, or just a very skilled showman. Puthoff and Targ remained reasonably open-minded, but even so they eventually gave up on him; Geller simply attracted too much heat from skeptics inside and outside the think-tank. He didn't seem to be worth the trouble.

The Pentagon's Advanced Research Projects Agency, which sent a three-man team to look at Geller at SRI in early 1973, came to the same conclusion—although one member of the ARPA team, University of Virginia psychologist Robert Van de Castle, seemed reasonably impressed, and would have liked to see further investigations of the young Israeli.

As for the CIA, corporately it didn't seem to have an opinion. SRI was never given money explicitly for the purpose of studying Geller. And yet some at the Agency were deeply impressed by Geller, and would long remain puzzled by him.

One day, during one of Geller's visits to SRI, Puthoff telephoned Richard Kennett at his office at CIA headquarters, and they conducted an informal experiment. Kennett was to select a target, and Geller, standing beside Puthoff out at SRI, would try to describe it. All right, said Kennett, who went over to his bookshelf, took out *Gray's Anatomy*, and turned to a glossy overlay page depicting the architecture of the human brain. He told Puthoff he was ready, and Puthoff relayed the word to Geller. The psychic began to concentrate. He said he was having trouble with this one. "I don't know what to say . . . it's like a blob of scrambled eggs . . . or like a brain . . . or something to do with architecture."

Geller did even better on another occasion, a hot Saturday afternoon late in the summer of 1973. This time Kennett, working from his home in suburban Virginia, chose several numbers, sealed them in an envelope, put the envelope in his den, and then sat down by the phone to concentrate on them. Geller was on the other end of the line, while Puthoff stood by. Kennett had hardly begun to concentrate when Geller said, "Oh my God, something has happened! Rick, go find out what has happened!"

Kennett asked him what the hell this was all about, and Geller explained that something dramatic had just occurred in Kennett's house. "Rick, please believe me," he said, "I've got this terrible feeling of glass slivers and shards slicing through my body. I'm seeing this picture of this sea of green, smooth green. And in the middle of the green, there's a strange-looking dog with a square face. He's all white, but he's got blood on his neck and down his chin."

Kennett went back to his den and saw that his white bulldog, who wore a blood-red macramé collar with a tassel, had run into the room moments before, knocking over a tall lamp with a glass globe on top. The globe had shattered, and shards of white glass lay all over the green carpet.

A few years after Geller left SRI, when he was living in Mexico, members of the CIA's Mexico City station apparently made use of him, in return giving him favorable U.S. visa arrangements. According to Geller, he tried to psychically spy on local Soviet case officers, their agents, and the dead-drop sites they used. Through his social connections, he also apparently tried to convince senior Mexican officials to reduce the bloated KGB presence in the Soviets' Mexico City embassy.

Geller eventually left Mexico in a hurry, after a British tabloid linked him romantically (they were just friends, Geller protested) to the wife of Mexican President José Lopez-Portillo. Afterwards, Geller claimed, he did psychic detective work for the FBI in New York. He also continued his stage career, and did some apparently lucrative psychic tasks for oil and mining companies in South America and the western Pacific. In the 1980s, he would settle in England, in an enormous house on the banks of the Thames. When people asked him, "If you're so psychic, why aren't you rich?" he would laugh and say—"I *am* rich."

10

REMOTE VIEWING

10:00　Outbound experimenter leaves with 10 envelopes (containing target locations) and random number generator; begins half-hour drive.

10:10　Experimenters remaining with subject in the laboratory elicit from subject a description of where outbound experimenter will be from 10:45 to 11:00.

10:25　Subject response completed, at which time laboratory part of experiment is over.

10:30　Outbound experimenter obtains random number from a random number generator, counts down to associated envelope, and proceeds to target location indicated.

10:45　Outbound experimenter remains at target location for 15 minutes (10:45–11:00).

—Precognitive remote-viewing
protocol, SRI

WHEN URI GELLER HAD GONE, THERE WAS ONLY PAT PRICE, THE rough-and-ready leprechaun. For the moment, he was all SRI would need, and even twenty-three years later, in conversations with me, Hal Puthoff and former intelligence officials who had overseen the SRI program would shake their heads and swear that they had never seen another psychic as good as he.

I was shown a photograph taken after one of Price's many triumphs. The scene is a small airfield, the backdrop the coastal foothills of northern California. Close to the camera, Richard Kennett, Hal Puthoff, and Pat Price lean against a smoothly aerodynamic-looking glider.

That day, Kennett had wanted to test Price against a moving target. So while Price and Puthoff stayed on the ground, Kennett had gone up in the glider. In his shirt pocket he carried the target, a small piece of paper bearing a sequence of three numbers. The glider was towed aloft, soared around for a while, and then landed. Kennett got out and went over to Price.

No problem, said Price, and he showed Kennett the three numbers he had written down. They were the correct target numbers, and they were also in the right sequence. The only thing, indicated Price, was that the whole exercise had made him a bit queasy. He had been able to picture the numbers in his mind's eye, but behind them there had been this strange shape swinging back and forth. It had seemed to disorient his vestibular system, almost making him seasick. He drew the shape. It looked like an Egyptian cross, an "ankh." Kennett laughed, reached inside his shirt, and pulled out an ornamental silver ankh he kept on a cord around his neck. With the rolls and yaws of the sailplane, it had pendulated across his chest behind the numbers in his shirt pocket.

The photograph was taken just afterwards. Kennett is on the left, and Puthoff is on the right. Both grin happily in the low light of late afternoon, and between them, arms crossed, is Pat Price, with the slight, sure smile of the cat who has just eaten the canary.

Over the next year or so the CIA's Office of Technical Service and Office of Research and Development would pump about $150,000 into SRI's remote-viewing project. There were also two small contracts with the Navy and NASA, plus money left over from private grants for the Geller research.

By Washington standards, a few hundred thousand dollars spread over a few years was hardly even spare change. But psi research itself was very cheap to conduct, and SRI had enough to get by. Even so, it was made clear to Puthoff and Targ that major funding would come only when they began to publish some of their psi experiments in reputable scientific journals. Not only would this encourage senior intelligence officials to take them more seriously, but it also would boost their standing among ordinary scientists, who sat on government science advisory boards and grant review committees, and in general decided what was and wasn't "science."

But winning over the scientific community would prove to be a near-impossible task. Although Puthoff and Targ were soon writing hopefully that "many consider the study of these phenomena as only recently emerging from the realm of quasi-science," they had it backward. Psi research had once been considered "scientific," but since the late nineteenth century, scientific institutions had gradually been organizing it out of the picture.

Psi research in the modern era emerged from the same womb that modern psychiatry did. It began in the late 1700s with the study of the "Mesmeric trance," "magnetic sleep," and "artificial somnambulism"—all of which we now call "hypnosis." Dabblers in hypnosis quickly discovered that people who were very good at being hypnotized also seemed to be very good at "preternatural" skills like clairvoyance, psychokinesis, and even a kind of shamanic healing ability. Many of these talented "somnambules" and "clairvoyantes" were as celebrated as today's big-name psychics. By the 1840s, hypnosis-related psi abilities were so common that they had become a sort of parlor trick. English gentlemen would hypnotize their maidservants, showing off the girls' clairvoyant skills to dinner party guests.

The hypnosis craze soon gave way to a craze over a form of self-hypnosis—and theatrics—known as "spiritism" or "spiritualism." By the mid nineteenth century, thousands of spirit "mediums" were giving performances throughout America and Europe. These mediums supposedly spoke with the voices of entities from the supernatural world, levitated tables and other furniture, and transcribed—in trance, through "automatic writing"—the voluminous teachings of their familiar spirits. As such, they were a throwback to a much more ancient type of individual: the shaman, or the devotee of a possession cult, for whom "possession" by spirits, typically before an audience, was a form of social and psychological empowerment.

Most if not all nineteenth-century psi researchers seemed unaware of this ancient connection. To many of them, mediumship was new and mysterious, and deserved intense study. Even some who did not believe in or care for psi phenomena thought mediums worth investigation, realizing that their séance-room performances might at least shed light on the workings of the normally hidden subconscious. As a result, mediums became the focus of considerable psychological and psychiatric research,* at the same time that they and their séances helped spawn numerous organizations devoted to psi research.

The most famous psi research group of the era was the Society for Psychical Research, founded in London in 1882. The SPR's members included the psychologist Frederic Myers, the Cambridge philosopher Henry Sidgwick, the physiologist Charles Richet, the physicists Sir William Crookes and Sir Oliver Lodge, the poet William Butler Yeats, and the writer Sir Arthur Conan Doyle. An array of such luminaries would be hard for psi researchers to assemble today.

Yet despite their prestigious membership, and their pro-

---

* Carl Jung, for example, in his M.D. dissertation, spent much of his time discussing the case of a young spirit medium.

lific, high-profile, and sometimes hard-nosed investigations, the SPR and its cousins around the world were unable to establish psi firmly within the Western scientific worldview. The problem was, by the time psychical research began to come of age, the chaos and ferment that had characterized much of nineteenth-century science were already ending. Theories of nature—especially those regarding electromagnetism and the behavior of the atom—were hardening into laws of nature. And those laws, by most interpretations, just didn't admit that the human mind could span time and space unaided, remotely experiencing events and affecting matter. It became increasingly fashionable among scientists to portray psi as a primitive, retrograde fantasy which modernity was swiftly leaving behind.

In response to this worsening intellectual climate, psychical research began to transform itself into something more academic and mundane, the better to blend in with other scientific disciplines. The late J. B. Rhine is generally credited with this transformation.

Rhine was an eager young botanist, a natural scientist and a native of academia, when on an evening in Chicago in 1922 he heard Arthur Conan Doyle lecture enthusiastically about psychical research. Doyle seemed to strike some hidden chord inside the young scientist, and along with his wife Louisa, also a botanist, Rhine decided to embark on a new career.

Psychical research at the time was still dominated by the study of séance mediums, whose theatrical displays usually took place in the dark, under conditions that they themselves could substantially control. Rhine, by contrast, was used to working with much more compliant subjects of study, such as the leaves and stems and cells of plants. After sitting for a séance in Boston with the famous medium Mina "Margery" Crandon, he was infuriated. To him the entire thing had been a grotesque farce, an outrage against science.*

And so, wielding the tablets of scientific method, Rhine led psychical researchers into a promised land of university laboratories and experimental rigor, of dry statistics and subjects who did what they were told to do. Psychical research became "parapsychology," and at the Duke University Parapsychology Laboratory, which Rhine founded in 1930, mediumistic monkeying-about was banished. Research subjects instead took part in lengthy card-guessing or dice-throwing experiments, the object being to generate significant statistical evidence that the results were not merely due to the whims of chance.

Rhine and other parapsychologists produced a great deal of such evidence. Their methods were blessed by statisticians, and *Time* and *Reader's Digest* and *Scientific American* took an interest, and ripples of confusion and wonderment spread throughout the scientific community. By the 1960s and the Age of Aquarius, it seemed that psi research might even become an orthodox scientific discipline again. Everyone was talking about paradigm shifts and changes in consciousness. Popular belief in psi was sky-high. Surely scientific belief would follow. In 1969, after a rousing conference speech by the anthropologist Margaret Mead, the American Association for the Advancement of Science voted to admit psi researchers' main professional organization, the Parapsychological Association, to its ranks of approved disciplines.

But the paradigm failed to shift. The "laws" of nature, which had long endured the anomalies and paradoxes thrown up by such things as quantum physics, were not

---

* In one of Crandon's more sensational séance-room acts, she would remove her undergarments and emit "ectoplasm" from her navel. She is said to have had "affairs" with several of her more prominent supporters in the psychical research community.

about to be overturned by a few dozen dice throwers and card guessers in ill-funded laboratories.

Instead, an informal system of scientific apartheid was set up. Parapsychologists officially were allowed to call themselves scientists, but in practice were kept out of the scientific community. They found themselves ignored, ghettoized, forced to subsist on handouts from private philanthropists, forced to publish their work only in their own obscure and inconsequential journals.

It was relatively easy for the skeptics to get away with this, for somehow the parapsychologists never seemed to have anything to show for their work other than statistical evidence, usually marginal, in favor of whatever psi phenomenon they were studying. There was quite a discrepancy between these anesthetic tabulations on the one hand, and on the other the outrageous, seemingly boundless promise of psi. By caging psi in the laboratory, the parapsychologists seemed to have reduced it to an abstract curiosity. Where, the skeptics could ask tauntingly, were the machines, the technologies, that would run on psi? Where were the real-world applications? What was the *use* of it all?

Ironically, and frustratingly for Puthoff and Targ, that use was now highly classified. The most powerful weapon in psi's evidentiary arsenal—psychic spying on intelligence targets—could not be used to convince ordinary academic scientists.

Puthoff and Targ therefore decided that alongside their more hush-hush work with long-distance clairvoyance, they would experiment with an ESP technique that was related but had less obvious intelligence applications. The technique had the further advantage that it did not involve geographical coordinates. Puthoff and Targ still regarded the use of coordinates as scientifically and metaphysically dubious, even though it somehow seemed to work.

The new protocol relied on a person who would act as

an "outbound" experimenter, visiting the target site while the psychic, back at SRI, tried to visualize the experimenter's surroundings. After the session, the psychic himself could actually visit the target site, thus getting a richer feedback than was usually possible with classified coordinate targets—for which feedback was often no more than a smile and a pat on the back.

The first formal test of this "outbound" protocol occurred on the afternoon of October 4, 1973,* and went about as well as Puthoff and Targ could have hoped. Pat Price was taken by Russell Targ into an experiment room, and both men sat down at a table. At the same time Puthoff and his SRI branch chief, a man named Earle Jones, went over to the office of their division chief, Bart Cox. Cox had a long list of possible target sites in the San Francisco Bay Area. He generated a random number with his calculator, used it to select a target site from the list, pulled out the appropriate file with directions to the site, and handed it to Puthoff. Puthoff took the file, went with Jones to his car, opened the file, and followed the enclosed directions to the target, which was Hoover Tower on the Stanford University campus, in nearby Palo Alto.

Puthoff and Jones looked around, went up the tower to an observation deck, and generally tried to soak up sensations at the site, the better to serve as ESP "beacons" for Price. At an agreed-upon time, back at SRI, Price tried to visualize where Puthoff and Jones were standing. "I get them on a ridge or bluff overlooking the ocean," he said initially. "I would say they are about four hundred feet

---

* Puthoff, in recent public comments on the early history of remote viewing, has suggested that outbound experiments came first, before coordinate remote-viewing experiments. As I've established from an examination of the record and from conversations with him and with Ingo Swann, this isn't quite accurate. The first record of an outbound experiment is from October 1973, six months after Swann's first coordinate experiments.

above sea level. . . . I had a flash of being in a room with a Spanish-tile floor and a colonnade, about three miles south of here. Outside the colonnades I get the feeling that it's a library or a museum-type area with an exhibit there. I was just looking around. The area I have seems like it would be Hoover Tower. . . ."

It was soon clear to Puthoff that Price's results were going to be much more robust than the usual parapsychological fare. They represented a break with the past. And to underscore this break with the past, Puthoff decided to invent a new terminology for the kinds of psi phenomena Price was demonstrating. As far as Puthoff was concerned, the old terms such as *clairvoyance, ESP,* and *psychic perception* carried unwanted baggage, full of hysterical mediums, palm readers, and all those dead, dry card-guessing experiments at Duke University. Puthoff wanted something that sounded new and modern, technological and sober, something that would blend unobtrusively with the jargon of the hard sciences. Over the next few years he and Targ would use a variety of expressions to describe what was going on such as: "information transmission under conditions of sensory shielding," "a perceptual channel for information transfer over kilometer distances," "perceptual augmentation techniques," "remote perceptual abilities," and "remote perception." Eventually Puthoff came up with the punchier "remote viewing," and after a while, that name stuck.

Puthoff and Targ used modifiers to distinguish one remote-viewing technique from another. The outbound method became "outbound remote viewing." Swann's coordinate-based method was called "coordinate remote viewing" (CRV). Deeper altered-state methods, such as those favored by the unit at Fort Meade, would be given the term "extended remote viewing" (ERV).

In October 1973 Puthoff and Targ did nine outbound experiments with Price, involving nine separate target sites.

Afterwards a judge who hadn't participated in any of the previous experiments (a "blind" judge, in experimenter's parlance) went out to the sites with copies of Price's transcripts in hand, and tried to match each site to one of the transcripts. He matched transcripts to seven of the nine sites correctly. Had mere chance been at work, argued Puthoff and Targ, there should only have been about one correct match per judge. The odds that chance had produced seven correct matches, they said, were roughly one in 35,000.

Here and there Puthoff and Targ varied the variables. Sometimes they put Price in an electrically shielded "Faraday cage" for his outbound remote-viewing sessions, just to test the hypothesis that psi worked via some sort of radio waves. Most of the time they used an ordinary room at SRI. A couple of times they sat Price on a bench in a busy park. Or they used moving targets, as in the glider demonstration. It didn't seem to matter. Price blithely knocked off target after target.

Puthoff and Targ also tested Price for psychokinetic ability, and he did reasonably well. He seemed able to affect the swing rate of a brass clock pendulum, and also apparently perturbed—albeit marginally—a small SRI magnetometer that had defied Swann. In one bizarre demonstration, a researcher named Karlis Osis at the American Society for Psychical Research in New York set up a small copper box inside a locked room; within the box, a feather was monitored for the slightest motion by an infrared beam and photocell. When Price, a continent away, turned his attention to the target, the infrared sensor went off.

But most of Price's feats centered on remote viewing. There were some very strange episodes. One day Russell Targ and another SRI official named Hugh Crane were sitting with Price in the Faraday cage, waiting to do session number four of Price's celebrated nine-session run. Puthoff and his division chief Bart Cox were the outbound experimenters. Cox, still vaguely skeptical about remote viewing, decided on this day to change the protocol, to assure himself that Puthoff and Targ weren't somehow colluding with Price. Instead of going to the target selected for him at the lab, he would simply drive around, making turns according a pseudo-random algorithm that took into account the turns made by the cars in front of him. At the appointed time, he would stop somewhere and wait. He and Puthoff left at three in the afternoon.

At ten past three, back in the remote-viewing room with Price, Targ switched on the tape recorder, and went through the usual routine of naming the experimenters, the viewer, the date, the time, and when the outbound experimenters would arrive at their target site, which was three-thirty.

"We don't have to wait that long," interrupted Price, as Targ switched the recorder off. "I can tell you right now where they'll be." Targ switched the recorder back on. "What I'm looking at," Price continued, "is a little boat jetty or a little boat dock along the bay." He pointed to one of the walls of the shielded room. "In a direction about like that from here. Yeah, I see the little boats, some motor launches, some sailing ships, sails all furled, some with masts stepped and others are up. Little jetty or dock there . . ."

Puthoff and Cox ended up at the Redwood City Marina, in the direction Price had indicated, with the boats Price had described in view. But the really strange thing was, their aimless meanderings had not taken them to the marina until about five minutes after Price had described it. Price apparently had stretched his perception not only across space, but across time as well.

Puthoff and Targ were astounded by that, but it would eventually come to seem like a fairly tame example of a remote viewer slipping through time.

The last target in Price's nine-target series was a pair of

public swimming pools at Rinconada Park in Palo Alto. Price described the sizes and the shapes of the two pools accurately—one was round, one rectangular—and even detected a small concrete blockhouse nearby. But to Puthoff and Targ's dismay, he interpreted the site as a water-treatment plant, and added something that wasn't at the site at all: a set of two large elevated water tanks. Although Price's description was still easy for a judge to match to the site, Puthoff and Targ assumed that the water-treatment idea and the large tanks were figments of Price's imagination. Then one day, twenty-one and a half years later, Targ happened to read the 1995 annual report of the city of Palo Alto. In a discussion celebrating the city's hundredth year, the report mentioned: "In 1913 a new municipal water-works was built on the site of the present Rinconada Park." An accompanying photograph showed a tower with two water tanks, more or less in the place Price had described them.

Puthoff and Targ came to believe that Pat Price's feats, however mind-blowing, were merely extreme variants of an ability that everyone had to one degree or another. The two scientists even considered themselves moderately psychic; both had had spontaneous ESP experiences, precognitive dreams, and so on. And they would find, over the next decade, hundreds of other seemingly ordinary people who had strong psychic talents.

Initially, in late 1973 and early 1974, they focussed their research on four of these ordinary people, three of whom were SRI employees: a lab technician named Phyllis Cole; a mathematician named Marshall Pease; and a futurologist—an economic and cultural trend watcher—named Duane Elgin. Elgin did so well in remote-viewing tests that he moved on to other psi experiments, sitting for more than 7,000 trials on Targ's ESP teaching machine, and even trying his hand at psychokinesis.

The fourth ordinary person was Hella Hammid, a photographer friend of Russell Targ and his wife. The German-born Hella was in her early fifties, had somewhere left behind a husband and children, was temperamental, artistic, bisexual,* a social animal, an interesting character, but was not steeped in psi experiences as Swann and Price had been. She arrived on the scene in 1974, and turned out to have anything but ordinary psi abilities.

Puthoff and Targ put Hammid through a nine-site series of outbound remote-viewing trials, like Price's. The judge matched only five of her transcripts correctly. But for a given target, each transcript was "ranked" by the judge from one to nine, according to how well it corresponded to the target. Hammid's four "missed" sessions all were ranked second by the judge. (Price's two misses, by contrast, had been way off, ranked third and sixth.) The overall odds that Hammid's results had happened by chance, as Puthoff calculated it, were about 500,000 to one, which was actually far better than Price had done.†

All things considered, including coordinate remote viewing, Hammid wasn't quite as good as Price, but she was close, and she seemed able to keep up with him in a number of specific categories, such as precognitive remote viewing. One day Hammid was in the remote-viewing room with Russell Targ. Puthoff had just left to get a site from Earle Jones, their branch chief. Hammid for some

---

* I mention this only because sexual unorthodoxy seems unusually common (although certainly not universal) among people who come to be considered psychics. It is even mentioned in anthropological accounts of shamans and medicine men. The reasons may have to do with the genetics of the brain, and/or ordinary social psychology—perhaps being unorthodox in one way encourages a person to be unorthodox in other ways—but I don't know of any good research that sheds light on the question.

† These figures were later shown to be too high (though to Puthoff, still high enough), because the target set—like a deck of cards in which every card drawn alters the chances of drawing another—was not statistically independent.

reason was impatient to get the experiment over with, so she told Targ she already knew what the site was going to be. She proceeded to describe it, and then left. Her description had not only been accurate, but apparently had been made even before the site had been selected by random-number generator.

After one or two episodes like that, Puthoff and Targ developed a new protocol. Puthoff would drive around with a set of ten possible sites in sealed envelopes. Hammid would sit in the viewing room with Targ. At a prearranged time, Hammid would try to view the site precognitively. She would then go home. At a later prearranged time, Puthoff would take out his pocket calculator and, using the random-number function, would generate a number between zero and nine, selecting a site on this basis. He would then drive to the site, wait there for a specified time, and return. Hammid did four sites like this. Blind judging matched all her transcripts to the targets.

Puthoff and Targ tried just about everything in those early years at SRI. With the idea that psi information would often be too subtle to register consciously, they tried to augment ordinary telepathy with electroencephalograph (EEG) devices. The "sender" would sit in one room, blasted by a strobe light that would force his brain waves into a certain pattern. The "receiver" would sit in another, electrically shielded room, wired with an EEG to see if her own brain waves responded to the sender's. It was a souped-up version of the *Nautilus* story, the idea being to interest the CIA or the Navy in a possible telepathic system for long-distance communication, perhaps with submerged submarine crews.* Unfortunately, the experiment didn't

---

* A similar experiment, suggesting telepathic transfer between two out of fifteen tested pairs of identical twins, had been conducted by other U.S. researchers a few years previously.

seem to work as well as Puthoff and Targ had hoped. They tried six receivers, but only Hammid's EEG patterns seemed to change when the sender was trying to send psi information. Even then, the change wasn't useful. Her brain waves, instead of mimicking the sender's, merely showed slightly depressed "alpha" rhythms and slightly enhanced "beta" rhythms, indicating a mild and nonspecific response to a stimulus. Somewhere down in her mind the actual stimulus seemed to be seeping in, but at a level too deep to be reached by the EEG equipment.

Puthoff and Targ also tried a wide variety of remote-viewing experiments. They asked Pat Price to try to psychically distinguish envelopes with ordinary pencil drawings inside from those with drawings done in special CIA invisible inks (he did better than chance, but not perfectly).* They asked Price and other subjects to remote-view targets on computer disks, or the internal states of silicon chip random-number generators. They had them try to visualize objects in little boxes, or in arrays of cubbyholes, or in film canisters; Hella Hammid was the queen of remote viewers when it came to film canisters. They also did successful remote-viewing experiments in which the subjects sat in a deep-diving submersible off the southern California coast, and tried to visualize outbound sites in the San Francisco area. They even had Price and Hammid remote-view Puthoff when he was on vacation in Central America—and one day, when neither showed up, Targ himself stood in for them and nailed Puthoff's location on a small island air-

---

* "Secret writing" was a very common technique by which low-level foreign agents sent information to the spy agency employing them. The ability to find an envelope containing secret writing in a stack of ordinary mailroom envelopes would give an enormous counterintelligence advantage to whoever possessed it, for it would mean that enemy spies who communicated via secret writing could be tracked down relatively easily.

strip, where Puthoff had unexpectedly taken a short side trip.

They used technological targets, from photocopiers and power supplies to local sewage-treatment plants. They tried associative remote viewing (ARV) in which objects or geographic locations were used as surrogates for letters and numbers. They ran psychokinesis experiments with magnetometers and pendulums. They used Targ's ESP teaching machine to test a group of one hundred local schoolchildren.

And eventually they got some of this work published. In November 1974, amid much controversy, their first paper appeared in *Nature*, describing work with Geller, Price, Hammid, and the others. A year and a half later, they published an even longer paper in the prestigious electrical engineering society journal, *Proceedings of the IEEE*. The editor of the journal, Bell Labs scientist Robert Lucky, had initially been inclined to turn the paper down. But after Puthoff and Targ had visited Bell Labs to answer questions from skeptical scientists, Lucky was more impressed. Eventually he tried some of his own informal remote-viewing experiments, and decided that remote viewing was probably for real. A journalist would one day quote him as saying, "Psychic stuff is really not much more far-fetched than some of the physics behind the laser."

Puthoff and Targ were beginning to make progress.

11

You Can't Go Home Again

We tried to find him. We walked up and down the halls. But none of us had the balls to ask the hotel desk, "Hey, did you see that gray-suited, one-armed guy from space?"

—A source who didn't want his name used

At the same time that Puthoff and Targ were putting their psychic subjects through remote-viewing and psychokinesis and telepathy tests, they were running them through a battery of medical and psychological evaluations. Overseen by the Palo Alto Medical Clinic, the evaluations were designed to isolate any neurophysiological or personality features—mental hardware or software—that tended to coincide with good psychic abilities. The range of tests was bizarre; it was almost reminiscent of the testing regimen inflicted on the first astronaut candidates back in the 1960s, when so little had been known about what manned spaceflight would entail. But Puthoff and Targ and the CIA wanted to cast a wide net. If they could isolate any features related to psi ability, however unexpected those features might be, they might learn something about the way psi worked, and how it could be enhanced. In addition, they might be able to use such features as a kind of screening tool for selecting psychics from the general population.

The evaluations that Pat Price, Ingo Swann, and the others underwent included a complete medical history, eight blood tests, waking EEGs, sleeping EEGs, ear tests, eye tests, a brain magnetic imaging scan, a dynamometer grip strength test, the Groove Pegboard test, the Verbal Concept Attainment test, the Halstead-Wepman Aphasia Screening test, the Bender Gestalt Visual Motor test, the Buschke Memory test, the Benton Visual Memory test, the Knox Cube test, the Tactual Performance test, the Wechsler Adult Intelligence Scale, the Minnesota Multiphasic Personality Inventory, the Edwards Personality Preference Schedule, the Thematic Apperception Test—and the good old Rorschach inkblot test.

Alas, despite all of this neuropsychological poking and probing, there emerged no clear profile of what made a good psychic.* But there were, here and there, hints of distinguishing factors. There was some evidence to suggest, for example, that the most talented psychics in the population would also be relatively intuitive, non-judgmental, emotionally sensitive, and very intelligent. Being more prone to altered states and the visionary experiences that went with them, many would also exhibit some of the characteristics of people with dissociative disorders. Moreover, it seemed that the best psychics would be more likely to exhibit EEG "asynchronicities," or patterns of abnormally imbalanced electrical activity, between the two halves of the brain. One often found such EEG asynchronicities in individuals with minor seizure disorders or hyperactivity disorders. One also found them in people who could do certain things extraordinarily well, such as mentally calculating Pi to ten thousand places, or automatically naming the day of the week that, say, November 29, 2042 would fall on, or

---

* Swann and Price resisted taking or performed lackadaisically on some of these tests, declaring that they were "worthless."

playing a Mozart piano concerto flawlessly after hearing it only once.

To at least one scientist, what was most striking about the SRI psychics was that they managed to seem so ordinary, despite their different-ness. Some of them had had relatively intense dissociative experiences, had high IQs, and clearly didn't fit into the world the same way other people did.* And yet for the most part they were functional, emotionally healthy people—in some cases, much more functional and healthy than the average person. Joseph Campbell, in his studies of primitive religion, had noted that shamans shared some of the qualities of neurotics and schizophrenics, but Campbell had concluded that "the shamanistic crisis, when properly fostered, yields an adult not only of superior intelligence and refinement, but also of greater physical stamina and vitality of spirit than is normal to the members of the group." It must have been tempting to think that, like the great shamans of yore, the psychics at SRI walked on that exalted edge between boring ordinariness and the chaos of mental illness.

The relationship between psi and mental illness was never a major focus of research at SRI, and Puthoff and Targ never seriously discussed it in any of their published reports. But they did have occasion to confront it. One of their psi subjects was a patient in the Stanford University Medical Center psychiatric ward.

He had been admitted to the ward after claiming that his

---

* Swann and Price, in particular, had both bounced around a lot in their careers. Swann had been an Army clerk in Korea, an artist, a novelist, an astrologer, and an employee at the UN. Price, aside from being a local government official, a builder, and a Christmas tree salesman, had been a gold prospector in Alaska, a student pilot in World War II, the manager of an equipment-packing plant at Lockheed, and even—ironically enough— a security guard at Lockheed's celebrated Skunk Works during the development of the U-2 spy plane.

wife, and her secret lover, were out to get him. He could hear their voices, could see them plotting from afar . . . In short, he had classic symptoms of acute paranoid schizophrenia. But his claims about being able to read other people's thoughts and to see things happening in remote places were so insistent that one of the psychiatrists, knowing about the SRI research, approached Puthoff and asked if he had any interest in the case. Puthoff was skeptical. He suggested that the psychiatrist first do his own informal experiments, putting some playing cards in an envelope and seeing whether the patient could guess them.

The psychiatrist followed Puthoff's suggestion, and soon reported back that the patient had no trouble identifying cards hidden in envelopes. But that was true only if he was unmedicated. When he was given the antipsychotic drug Thorazine, his psi abilities were suppressed along with his psychoses. Puthoff eventually agreed to take a look at the man, and after running several tests found that he was indeed an extraordinary savant. But Puthoff also found that his subject was very disorganized mentally—in fact, "crazier than a loon"—and was almost impossible to work with. Puthoff sent him back to Stanford. He heard later from the psychiatrist that the man's voices had been right all along. After an extensive investigation the police had determined that the man's wife and her lover *had* been plotting to kill him.

Such cases suggested that psychiatric problems, perhaps by encouraging altered states of consciousness, might somehow activate or enable whatever it was in the brain that governed psi abilities. More worrisome was the possibility that the reverse could also be true: that practicing a lot of psi could cause psychiatric problems.

Already there were hints that this might be the case. In June 1973, at the invitation of a Czech researcher named Zdenek Rejdak, Puthoff and Swann had travelled to Prague for something called the First International Conference on

Psychotronic Research. "Psychotronic Research" was the Eastern Europeans' pseudo-technical term for psi research. In any case, at the conference Puthoff and Swann were virtually mobbed by Soviet and Eastern European psi researchers, who seemed most anxious to know one thing: How did SRI keep its psychic subjects mentally stable? Swann deduced from the questions that some of the Soviet bloc subjects had begun to have serious problems.

No one at SRI had descended into madness, but for those subjects who had been plucked out of a relatively psi-free life, such as Duane Elgin, it seemed that the sudden exposure to psi phenomena could have important effects on beliefs and behavior. Elgin had had quite a high-flying career as an SRI futurologist. He was considered creative but levelheaded, was making a substantial amount of money, and was respected by his peers and by the policy makers who read his reports. And then one day, according to the story, a statistician colleague at SRI began flipping a coin; Elgin, asked to guess heads or tails, did so correctly thirty-three times in a row. Puthoff soon heard about this and started running Elgin through some outbound remote-viewing experiments. Elgin also did some PK work, and one day when no one else was in the room, he claimed, he made a pendulum swing wildly, just by concentrating on it.

As Elgin's interest in psi phenomena intensified, it began to change his life. Before long he wrote up a very strange futurological report, and circulated it among his SRI colleagues. In the report, Elgin declared that if psi were not taken more seriously by mainstream science, there might soon be a "civil war" between psychics and non-psychics.

Elgin eventually left SRI, simultaneously taking up with a Tibetan guru who lived in San Francisco. He remained a sane and functional man, and would later become a successful author. But naturally some of his former colleagues at SRI found the sudden change in him disturbing. *What has my program done to this poor guy?* wondered Puthoff—

although in the end Puthoff reasoned that Elgin had probably always had a mystical streak that his psi experiences had simply brought to the surface.

Elgin himself considered his psi experiences at SRI to have been deeply transformative. He would tell a reporter for *New York* magazine in 1975: "Once you discover that space doesn't matter, or that time can be travelled through at will so that time doesn't matter, and that matter can be moved by consciousness so that matter doesn't matter—well, you can't go home again."

You can't go home again. You can't put the toothpaste back in the tube. Yet Elgin's life-changing experience with psi was a smooth ride compared with what happened to several employees of Lawrence Livermore Laboratory.

Livermore Lab was one of the two institutions—Los Alamos in New Mexico was the other—where most of America's nuclear weapons research and development took place. It occupied a square mile on the site of an old naval air station, next to the California town of Livermore, a few dozen miles inland from San Francisco Bay. The lab employed several thousand physicists and support personnel, and its security was among the highest of any facility in America.

By 1974 a number of Livermore personnel had heard about the experiments going on at nearby SRI, and, along with everyone else in America, had heard about the feats of Uri Geller. When Geller wasn't confounding the researchers at SRI, he was criss-crossing the continent, from talk show to stage show, bending spoons and stopping watches, and blowing minds.

It occurred to some of these Livermore personnel that Geller's feats, if they were genuine, represented a potentially serious security threat. If someone like Geller could really stop watches or interfere with television screens, what could he do to an ICBM's guidance computer? Or to the detonation trigger for a nuclear warhead? No one else seemed interested in looking at psychokinesis phenomena from a security standpoint, so a small group at Livermore decided to check it out themselves.

The group included a security officer named Ron Robertson, a physicist named Peter Crane, and about a half dozen other scientists and engineers. They worked on a variety of experiments with Geller during late 1974 and early 1975. Some were informal, and some were tightly controlled, but everything was done outside work hours, on a volunteer basis.

And since Geller was such a controversial figure, they kept him out of the actual Livermore facility. Instead they worked with him in a borrowed lab on an adjacent low-security facility, which had been carved out of the Livermore campus some years before, for the use of the University of California at Davis. The lab was in an old, wooden, World War II–built barracks structure, and the Livermore researchers brought Geller in on evenings and weekends when no one else was around.

The experiments were generally designed to test Geller's psychokinetic abilities. For example, he was asked to do his metal-bending feats on a variety of items while being videotaped from the side, from above, and even from underneath. Some objects were specially prepared with a coating of easily crushed "microspheres" which would betray any effort to bend the coated object by direct mechanical force. The group was relieved to find, just as Puthoff and Targ had found, that Geller apparently couldn't bend metal when he was prevented from actually touching it.

In other more delicate psychokinesis experiments, the group set up high-quality lasers and fired them at sensitive detector arrays to see if Geller could remotely deflect the beams. He couldn't. And when Geller was given a computer's magnetic program card, and was asked to erase it, he was unable to do so when the card was sealed inside a bottle. He was able to do it only when allowed to rub the card with his fingers. It seemed to the Livermore group that if Geller did have some kind of psychokinetic ability, it wasn't one that could work over long distances. America's nuclear weapons were probably safe.

On the other hand, Geller occasionally did do something outside the laboratory that was genuinely spooky. One day Ron Robertson was on the phone with him for some reason, and Geller suddenly stopped in mid-conversation. His voice changed slightly, and he said, "Ron, I see you involved with somebody with a large white dog. I see you very concerned over the health of an older man. I see trouble between two women close to you." Whereupon he resumed the conversation in a normal voice.

Four or five days later, on a Saturday morning, Robertson and his wife suddenly decided to go down to Pacific Grove, near Monterey, to visit an old friend. On arrival they discovered that their friend had recently acquired an enormous white German shepherd. A few minutes later Robertson's friend mentioned that an old acquaintance, a theater director for whom Robertson had worked back in the days when he was a stage lighting operator, was seriously ill and about to die. As Robertson sat there in his friend's house, wondering how the third prediction would come to pass, his wife somehow got into a disagreement with their host's daughter; the two women ended up in a virtual shouting match.

One day in the lab, several members of the Livermore group were monitoring Geller during a metal-bending session. They recorded him with audiotape, filmed him with videotape, and photographed him with a variety of still cameras, including one that was sensitive to thermal infrared radiation.

After the experiment they developed all the film and saw something very strange. The infrared camera had captured what seemed to be two diffuse patches of radiation on the upper part of one of the laboratory walls. It was as if someone had briefly shone two large heat sources, either from inside the lab or outside pointing in. The patches grew in intensity for a few frames, then over the next few frames diminished to nothing.

The Livermore Group were understandably puzzled over this, but it was only the beginning of the strangeness that would soon consume them. When they checked the audiotape they had made during the experiment, they found amid everything else a distinctive, metallic-sounding voice, unheard during the actual experiment but now clearly audible, if mostly unintelligible. All they could make out were a few apparently random words strung together.

If Geller could be believed, things like this had happened before. According to one story, on several occasions when his friend Andrija Puharich had put him under hypnosis,* audiotapes of the sessions had recorded similar strange voices. Another time, at a meeting with some Mossad officers, someone's tape recorder had suddenly seemed to start playing by itself, in full view of everyone.

In any case, Peter Crane and some of the others in the Livermore group quickly found themselves involved in more strangeness than they could handle. In the days and weeks that followed, they began to feel that they were collectively possessed by some kind of tormenting, teasing, hallucination-inducing spirit. They all would be in a laboratory together, setting up some experiment, or one of the fellows and his wife and children would be at home, just sitting around, when suddenly there in the middle of the room would be a weird, hovering, almost comically stereotypical image of a flying saucer. It was always about eight inches across, in a gray, fuzzy monochrome, as if it were

---

* Puharich, using Geller as a medium, was trying to communicate with the extraterrestrial entities that he believed controlled the young Israeli.

some kind of hologram. The thematic connection with Geller was obvious, when one remembered that Geller claimed to be controlled by a giant computerized flying saucer named Spectra.

On the other hand, the flying saucer wasn't the only form the Livermore visions took. There were sometimes animals—fantastic animals from the ecstatic lore of shamans—such as the large raven-like birds that were seen traipsing through the yards of several members of the group. One of them appeared briefly to a physicist named Mike Russo and his terrified wife. The two were lying around one morning when suddenly there was this giant bird staring at them from the foot of their bed.

After a few weeks of this, Russo and some of the others began seriously to wonder if they were losing their sanity. Peter Crane decided to call for help. He picked up the phone and called Richard Kennett.

Kennett had visited Livermore previously, in his capacity as a CIA analyst, to ask Crane and the others about their results with Geller. He had remained close-mouthed about the CIA's own psi research, but that had been expected. As far as Crane was concerned, Kennett was their best hope for a private, quiet solution to the problem. He had parapsychological experience, biomedical training, and high-level security access—an extremely rare set of qualifications.

On a Saturday morning not long thereafter, at the end of an otherwise unrelated trip to the San Francisco Bay Area, Kennett drove over and met with Crane in a coffee shop in the town of Livermore. Crane set out the situation for him, and soon Kennett was having long meetings with Russo and the others. They perspired, trembled, and even wept openly as they related some of the things that had happened to them. It was as if their world had collapsed around them. Nothing made sense anymore.

Kennett knew that if he took any of these stories to a regular psychiatrist, the diagnosis would be some kind of dissociative, hallucinatory, or otherwise delusional experience. Even when two or three people claimed to have shared a vision, it would almost certainly be dismissed as *folie à deux*, or *folie à trois*. Such terms were used to refer to rare group hallucinations, when one hallucinating or delusional individual had such a dominant personality that others came to believe they had seen or experienced the same thing.

Kennett didn't rule out such explanations, but he seemed fairly convinced that something else less pat and conventional was going on. For one thing, Crane, Russo, and the others had no history of involvement in the occult, and as far as Kennett could tell, their emotional situations immediately prior to these visionary experiences hadn't been particularly stressful or otherwise hallucinogenic. Moreover, they all had top-secret security clearances, which had required among other things that they be screened for psychological disorders.

Then there was the very strange business of the metallic voice on the audiotape. Among the few intelligible words it pronounced were two or three together which Kennett recognized as the code name of a very closely held government project. The project had nothing to do with psychic research, and neither it nor its code name was known to Crane or Russo or the others at Livermore. It was as if whoever or whatever had produced the code name on the tape had known that Kennett would soon arrive on the scene and had saved this special shiver down the spine just for him.

Kennett, going by the book, reported the code name incident to the security people at the CIA, muting the outlandish details only slightly. The security people filed it away, and wondered if Dr. Kennett might be getting a little too close to his subject matter.

*　*　*

The situation at Livermore eventually resolved itself, after Russo complained about a telephone call from the strange metallic voice. The voice demanded that the Livermore group cease its research activities with Geller. The group did, and within a month, the bizarre apparitions faded away.

One of the last such apparitions sprang itself upon a Livermore physicist named Don Curtis and his wife. They were sitting in their living room one evening, soberly, uneventfully, not talking about Geller or the paranormal, when suddenly there was this . . . arm . . . hovering holographically in the middle of the room.

The arm was clothed as if it belonged to a man wearing a plain gray suit. There was no bloody stump where it should have connected with a shoulder. It merely faded into clear space. But at the end of the arm where a hand should have been, there was no hand, only a hook. The hooked arm twisted around for a few seconds in front of Curtis and his wife, and then disappeared.

Curtis related the story to Kennett, and for some reason, it seemed to push the CIA officer over the edge. He telephoned Hal Puthoff and Russell Targ and demanded that they meet with him on their next trip to Washington. He didn't quite believe that they could have cooked all of this up, using their SRI lasers to make haunted-house holograms. But he suspected that with their own ample experiences of Geller and his associated phenomena, they would be able to shed some light on what was happening.

Within a few days, Puthoff and Targ arrived in Washington for a scheduled fund-raising tour of government offices. Kennett met them shortly after they had arrived at their hotel, and though it was close to midnight, he sat them down and told them the whole story, including the story of the floating arm.

"And so the goddamn arm—" said Kennett, winding up his story. "The thing was rotating, with this gray suit on, and it had a hook on it. It was a false arm. What do you think of that?"

And as Kennett pronounced the word *that,* there was a sharp, heavy pounding on the door to the hotel room, as if someone were intending to knock it down. Kennett had a mischievous streak. Was he playing some kind of practical joke here? Puthoff and Targ didn't think so. The pounding was so loud, it was frightening. After a moment, Targ went over to the window and hid behind the curtains. Puthoff stood inside the bathroom. Kennett went over to the door and opened it.

Standing in the doorway was a man who at first glance was remarkable only by his unremarkableness. He was nondescript and unthreatening, somewhere in middle age. He walked past Kennett very slowly, with a stiff gait, to the middle of the room, between the two beds. He turned around, and said in an oddly stilted voice, *"Oh! I guess . . . I must . . . be . . . in . . . the wrong . . . room."*

And with that he walked out, slowly, stiffly, giving all of them time to see that one sleeve of his gray suit, pinned to his side, was empty.

12

AN EIGHT-MARTINI EVENING

He was extraordinarily accurate, unbelievably accurate.

—a former CIA official, on a
series of remote viewings
by Pat Price

THANKFULLY, NO SUCH CRAZINESS SWIRLED IN THE WAKE OF PAT
Price, although the accuracy of his data shook people up
now and then.

One of Price's more startling psychic spying attempts
began on the afternoon of Tuesday, February 5, 1974. Hal
Puthoff was sitting at his desk when his branch chief Earle
Jones walked into his office bearing a message from the
Berkeley police: They wanted some paranormal assistance.

The night before, as everyone knew by now from the
radio and the TV news, the daughter of newspaper mag-
nate Randolph Hearst had been kidnapped. By whom, no
one yet knew, but Hearst's fortune pointed to a likely mo-
tive. The Berkeley police, having heard of the psychic feats
at SRI, wanted to see if Puthoff's remote viewers could help
them get a jump on the kidnappers.

Puthoff and Pat Price met the police that afternoon at
Patty Hearst's apartment, and Price had a chance to look

around the place and pick up impressions. He surprised everyone by saying immediately that he didn't feel the kidnapping was about money, but was more of a political, terroristic act designed to draw attention and sympathy.

Afterwards, they went over to the police station, and Price went through volume after volume of unlabeled mug shots—the usual suspects, plus some others. He picked out three. He pointed to one, of a young man, and told the police that the name Lobo came to him, *lobo* being Spanish for "wolf." This man Lobo, said Price, was something of a kindred spirit, shamanically speaking. He had extraordinary mental control. For instance, he had recently had his teeth pulled at the dentist without anesthesia, relying instead upon self-hypnosis.

Two days later police received the first of a series of "communiqués" from the kidnappers. As Price had predicted, they did not demand money; instead they demanded food for the poor. They called themselves the Symbionese Liberation Army. Eventually the police and FBI also determined that the three men Price had selected from the mug shot book were members of the group. The one Price had called Lobo was a Berkeley dropout named William Wolfe; "Willie the Wolf" was one of his nicknames. Police even confirmed the bizarre anecdote about Wolfe's anesthetic-free dental surgery.

It was all very encouraging, but Price's main task was to find Hearst's whereabouts. For this, Puthoff served as his Dr. Watson, following him around whenever he was working on the case, making tape recordings and notes of his comments, organizing his sketches, chauffeuring him to various locations. At first Price tried to find Hearst the direct way, by describing her surroundings in enough detail that the police could zero in on the precise address. But though he could vividly see her locked in a closet in someone's house—as she indeed was at the time—he was ultimately unable to move his psi perception smoothly outside and to the nearest corner, where he might have read the street names. He watched her daily, in helpless frustration.

In time Price began trying to find Patty Hearst indirectly, by triangulating her position. Puthoff would drive him to some spot in the Bay Area, and Price would sit and wait for an impression of the direction of her kidnappers' hideout. It was as if there were some kind of compass in his brain, with Patty Hearst at true north. When Price had an impression of Hearst's direction, Puthoff would plot their position along with the indicated direction on a map of the area, repeating the sequence for different positions around the Bay Area. The idea was that after several impressions from different places had been received, the lines would cross somewhere. Puthoff and Price would then go to the crossing area and triangulate further, and when they had circled close enough to their quarry, the lines would finally converge upon a given house, which police could then burst into and free the abducted heiress. That was the idea, anyway.

By early April, unfortunately, Hearst had begun to sound less like a damsel in distress than a crazed terrorist herself. The SLA released a tape-recorded statement in which she said she wanted to "stay and fight" with the group. She was soon photographed with other SLA members as they carried out a bank robbery in San Francisco. Nevertheless, Price doggedly stayed on the case, coming up with some new clue every week. One day in May, he told Puthoff he wanted to do one more scan of the Bay Area. He felt confident that they were going to find her this time. But the following day, before they had had a chance to set out, police cornered and killed a group of SLA members (including William Wolfe, who had become Hearst's lover) in a building in Los Angeles. Hearst, who was apparently elsewhere in Los Angeles at the time, stayed in hiding, moving around the country with her remaining SLA companions for another sixteen months. She was finally caught and arrested while living in an apartment in San Francisco's Mission District, long after Price had stopped looking for her.

Ingo Swann, back in New York, had also spent some time looking for Patty Hearst, at the suggestion of former astronaut Edgar Mitchell. In the end he'd had no more luck than Price, although he claimed afterwards to have sensed that "the big action will take place in Los Angeles."

Swann also worked on some other, lower-profile missing person cases, but soon gave up the practice. Most, he would say later, ended with the discovery that the missing person was dead. That could be hard on him—remote viewing amplified one's emotional sensitivity—and could be even harder on the missing person's family, whose members typically ended up distraught and confused, unsure whether to believe the psychic's grim news.

Swann sat for some parapsychological experiments, at the American Society for Psychical Research and the Maimonides Dream Laboratory, in New York, and at various other places in the psi research world. He also did some work for oil companies, helicoptering out to a rig in the Gulf of Mexico, and riding around Kentucky and Tennessee and Arkansas with a wildcatting team funded by Bill Keeler, the chairman of Phillips Petroleum. None of those relationships lasted very long, but Swann would earn enough money in this period to buy a four-story house in the Bowery section of lower Manhattan.

Swann tried his hand, or mind, at global prophecy, predicting in late 1973 and again in 1974 that mainstream science would soon come to accept psychic phenomena. He also remote-viewed Mars and Jupiter and Mercury in advance of American and Russian space probes, trying to see how far out his perception could go. Some of the data were interesting,* although skeptics like Carl Sagan later dismissed it all as a mixture of the predictable, the ambiguous, and—like the "lichen" Swann saw growing on the lead-melting surface of Mercury—the wildly incorrect.

One of Swann's most interesting projects was a novel, a strange half-philanthropic, half-misanthropic fantasy titled *Star Fire*. The main character was a youthful, handsome rock star with extraordinary psychic powers. He could remote-view anywhere in the universe, and could also remotely exert psychokinetic effects—scrambling computers and dissolving files and so forth. There was a secret arms race between the superpowers involving satellite-borne microwave death-beam weapons. A shady Dr. No–type character on some distant island also possessed one of the weapons. The rock star knew about all this, from his nightly remote viewings, and disapproved. He began to send anonymous letters to the White House and the Politburo, telling them to shut down their death-beam programs, or else. They came looking for him, so he cashed in all his millions, faked his own death, and resided in suspended animation in an obscure life-support facility. Meanwhile his consciousness roamed freely around the globe, tweaking the superpowers' noses. In the end the superpowers didn't accede to his demands swiftly enough, so he psychically hijacked the death-beam satellites and trained them on the countries that had built them. Goodbye, Omaha. Goodbye, Novosibirsk. Goodbye, Dr. No. The End.

Swann returned to SRI as a consultant in the autumn of 1974. Puthoff had offered him increased compensation, and relative freedom to develop further his coordinate

---

* Swann's data suggested (and space probes later confirmed) that Jupiter had a ring somewhat like the rings of Saturn.

remote-viewing technique. His arrival also was to correspond with the departure of Pat Price.

Price had no complaints about how SRI had treated him, but the fact remained that his renown had spread, and many people now regarded him not merely as a scientific curiosity, but as a sort of golden-egg-laying goose. That autumn he went to work for a coal company in Huntington, West Virginia. The company president, who wanted to take some time off, offered Price his job, a substantial salary, and shares of stock. Price's task, besides serving as president, was to use his psi talents to find rich veins of coal in the West Virginia hills. He told Hal Puthoff that he would spend only a year or so out on the East Coast, then would return to SRI with his presumed millions—which, he said, when properly invested, would ensure that the SRI psi research program was funded forever.

What he didn't tell Puthoff was that he was also going to work directly for the CIA.

Norm Everheart, meanwhile, was about to enter the remote-viewing scene for the first time.

Everheart was only forty-four, but he already had nearly a quarter century of service in the CIA behind him. In 1950, as a twenty-year-old television engineer with the military draft hanging over him, he had been recruited by the fledgling intelligence agency, and had quickly been sent to Greece. There he had been a clandestine radio operator, broadcasting propaganda to help prevent a Communist takeover of the country, living in the hills, on the run. Later he had put his technical skills to work for the Agency's Office of Communications, and then the Technical Services Division (later the Office of Technical Service). His last posting, aptly enough, had been as the chief of OTS's regional "tech base" in Athens.

When Everheart came home from Athens, he had a meeting with the head of OTS, a beefy CIA veteran named

John McMahon. McMahon told Everheart he was appointing him liaison to the Agency's cryptically named "Staff D," an office that specialized in small-scale signals-intelligence collection,* and often worked closely with OTS. Everheart's job, McMahon told him, was to keep Staff D and OTS informed of what each office was doing and how they might be able to help each other.

One day, in late 1974 or early 1975, Everheart received a call from a young, dark-haired OTS engineer, a man named Ken Kress. In some ways the father of America's remote-viewing program, Kress had given SRI its first psi research contract back in 1972, and now he was Pat Price's handler.

Kress handed Everheart a document which described some of the remote-viewing experiments that had been run out at SRI. Everheart, though he later became the CIA's chief liaison to Grill Flame, knew nothing about the subject at this point. But Kress urged him to consider whether there were any Staff D operations that might benefit from the assistance of remote viewers—in particular, Pat Price. Kress had already generated several other operational-type taskings from other offices at the Agency, but he wanted to know if Staff D was interested.

Everheart thought about the matter for a while, and eventually came up with what seemed to be a good target. Recent intelligence had suggested that the communications office in the Chinese Embassy in a certain foreign capital was in the basement of the building. To an ordinary citizen, this piece of information would have no significance at all, but to an intelligence officer whose job was to intercept the communications of foreign adversaries, it sounded like a golden opportunity. In every other Chinese embassy, the communications office was on the top floor, the hardest for outside spies to access. A ground floor or basement target was a piece of cake by comparison. For Everheart and Staff

---

* Staff D was later known as the Office of SIGINT Operations.

D, all that prevented an operation to penetrate the embassy's communications was a confirmation that the basement was indeed the communications office. So far they had no firm confirmation. The basement had once been a wine cellar; perhaps that was all it was now. It would be a disaster if they mounted a major break-in operation only to discover that they had penetrated the wrong room.

Everheart, after looking over some of the data Pat Price had generated, decided that if the psychic came up with a detailed description of code clerks and communications gear in the basement of the embassy in question, then the SIGINT penetration operation should proceed. He formally proposed that Price be asked to describe the embassy's basement.

The chief of Staff D, Ed Rogers, regarded Everheart's proposal with a good deal of skepticism. It seemed questionable enough, on operational grounds, but there were also political repercussions within the Agency to think about. Rogers could just imagine the laughter raining down on him should it become widely known that his office was consulting a psychic. Norm Everheart came to call that concern "the giggle factor."

Rogers eventually agreed to consider Price for the operation, but with a major condition. Price first had to succeed in three tests against similar targets—targets on which the Agency already had ample information.

Three paranormal tests . . . The idea had a strange, mythic resonance. It sounded almost like the twelve great labors of Hercules. Would Price be able to handle it? Everheart didn't know, but in consultation with Ed Rogers, he set about assembling the three tests.

A few days later, while Price was on a visit to the Washington area, Ken Kress and another CIA officer, Nick Clancy, came to his hotel room for the first test. After some small talk, Kress opened his briefcase and pulled out a black-and-white photograph of a building somewhere in the world. Unknown to Price, the building was the Chinese Embassy in a large city in Africa; the CIA knew the layout of the embassy down to tiny details.

Price looked at the photo and then sat down at the desk in the room, took out some paper and a pen, and started sketching. He sketched a rough outline of the continent of Africa, drew a line horizontally through it, to indicate the equator, and then marked a point where he believed the building was. Clancy, whose job for the last few years had been to conduct technical penetrations of such embassies in Africa, southern Europe, and the Middle East, could see that Price was dead on target.

"How far is this building from the ocean?" asked Clancy.

"One hundred fifty miles," said Price, getting it right again. Then Price looked at the photograph and pointed at the building. "Wait a minute . . . There are *three* buildings at this site, not just this one."

Kress and Clancy exchanged glances. Right again.

Now Price, down in his zone, went into the building depicted in the photograph. It was as if his ghost were actually in the building, walking through it, while his physical body delivered a sort of tour guide's monologue, and sketched out the embassy's floor plan. "Watch your step when you go down this hallway," he told the two CIA men. "The light is bad." And Clancy remembered that he had once gone down that very hallway, during an operation, and had almost lost his footing because of the bad light.

Price's train of thought was already jumping onto a new track. Holding the photo of the building, he turned to Clancy and said: "*You* developed this picture in the basement of a house about a mile down the road from this building." Clancy had to think about it for a moment, but he soon realized that Price was absolutely right.

After the session with Price was over, Clancy went out with Kress for a drink. Multiple drinks, actually—Clancy later described it to Norm Everheart as an "eight-martini evening." He had been that shaken up.

A day or so later, in the same hotel room, Pat Price faced his second test. Ken Kress and Nick Clancy handed him another black-and-white photo of a building, and Price quickly drew a map of Italy, marking Rome. Then he moved his pen down, across the Mediterranean Sea, to a North African capital. The building was in that city, he said. Right so far, thought Kress and Clancy.

After locating the building, Price walked in through its main entrance, into a large foyer. "What a magnificent staircase!" he remarked, but after gliding ethereally up its steps, he suddenly stopped. "You know, that's the most beds I've seen in any one place."

Kress and Clancy looked at him. *Beds?*

But Price was gliding through the building again. After some more description, he said, "There are a lot of people hurting in here."

Clancy realized now that something was wrong. There weren't a lot of beds in the embassy, as far as he knew. There weren't a lot of injured people. Price sounded as if he were describing a dormitory or a hospital, not an embassy. And when Clancy asked Price to describe his progress up to the front of the building—were there any obstructions?—Price just seemed to drift right up to the door. The large iron gate that blocked the main entrance in real life didn't seem to exist in Price's otherworldly tableau.

Price otherwise described the layout of the embassy accurately. But Clancy was perplexed by the information he knew wasn't true. What had Price been seeing? Clancy later did some checking, and found out that the embassy had been a girls' school dormitory in the years just before World War II, and then had been used as a hospital during the war. Back then there had been no iron gate. Price, without knowing it, had simply slipped through another one of his time warps.

For the third target, a Chinese consular building in Rome, Price redeemed himself, describing the layout accurately and in present time. He even described a mural on the ceiling of one of the embassy's more important rooms. Clancy knew only too well about the mural. Had it not been for the difficulty of concealing any holes they made in the mural—there were no Michelangelos at the CIA—he and his men would have planted bugs in that ceiling long before.

Norm Everheart eventually presented the results of these three tests to Staff D chief Ed Rogers. Everheart was confident that Price had passed the tests. Rogers, who perhaps had assumed that Price would fail miserably, seemed startled by the quality of the data. But the giggle factor still worried him; he just wasn't ready to rely on a psychic to guide such a high-stakes break-in. "It may be the only opportunity we ever have to find something at ground level," he told Everheart. "I'm not going to screw it up by reading tea leaves."

And that was that. The giggle factor had won out. In the end, Rogers approved a risky operation to check the targeted embassy's basement by close-up technical means. The operation resulted in the conclusion that the Chinese Embassy's basement was, after all, only a wine cellar.

13

EVIL RAYS

Frequently the chief object of a raiding party . . . was
to kill the medicine man of an opposing group.

—E. Lucas Bridges, *Uttermost
Part of the Earth: Indians of
Tierra del Fuego*

BY JULY 1975 PRICE HAD FINISHED HIS STINT WITH THE COAL COM-
pany in West Virginia. The job hadn't been a cover for his
CIA work. He had actually worked for the enterprise. Unfortunately it hadn't made him an enormous amount of
money, and it hadn't been very glamorous. One day, in a
burst of largesse, Price had offered to fly Ken Kress, Richard
Kennett, and some other CIA officials out to West Virginia,
using the corporate plane he said he had at his disposal.
The officials dutifully turned up at Dulles Airport outside
Washington, looking for a Learjet with Price's coal company's logo on the side. Instead they were directed to a
small propeller plane, apparently chartered for the occasion. Out in Huntington, at the coal company headquarters, they found a group of trailers on a muddy hillside.

Price himself bought some land out in West Virginia,
apparently having remote-viewed large coal deposits beneath. The land did turn out to be rich with coal, and if

Price didn't have enough money to fund the SRI program single-handedly, he at least had money to live on. He planned to move back to California, to rejoin the SRI program and to keep up his contacts with the CIA.

In mid-July of that year Price set out from Huntington on a several-week trip west. He stopped off first in Washington, then flew to Utah for a brief visit with his son. Then he went on to Las Vegas. He loved gambling in Vegas, and though he was never fortunate enough to clean out the house, it seemed that he usually ended up with at least a small pile of winnings. He planned to go on from Las Vegas, after a few days, to SRI and the Bay Area, and then to visit his wife, Ann, who was living down in Los Angeles and working as a nurse.*

In Los Angeles, Price had decided, he was finally going to get some serious medical attention. He had been feeling less and less healthy since he'd left SRI, and now he seemed to be getting much worse. During his medical evaluation at SRI, a year or so before, his electrocardiograms had suggested advanced coronary artery disease. The doctors at the Palo Alto Medical Clinic, along with Richard Kennett and Hal Puthoff and Ken Kress and others at SRI and CIA, had tried to get him to cut down on his eating and his drinking—and his smoking, which still amounted to two and a half packs of cigarettes a day. He had shrugged them off the way he often shrugged off adverse news, but now the attacks of angina pain were coming more frequently. He was only fifty-six years old, but he could easily have passed for seventy.

In Las Vegas Price was accompanied by an old friend named Bill Alvarez, and his wife, Judy. The three checked into the Stardust Hotel, rested, and went into the restaurant for dinner. At dinner Price complained that he wasn't feel-

---

* Some CIA officials who worked with Price were unaware that he was married.

ing good. According to a story Alvarez would later tell, Price now mentioned that at dinner in Washington the night before, someone had seemed to slip something into his coffee. He seemed serious about it.

Price soon felt so bad that he went upstairs to his room. He lay down, felt worse, and called the Alvarezes. They came to the room and found Price on the bed, in cardiac arrest. Alvarez called paramedics, who tried to resuscitate Price with defibrillator paddles. They couldn't, and Price was declared dead in the local hospital's emergency room.

From there the story became stranger. When Richard Kennett and others tried to find out what had happened, they learned that no autopsy had been performed. For deaths in the hospital from well-understood causes, autopsies were often waived—but for deaths outside the hospital, when the deceased was from out of town, autopsies were the norm. To Kennett, the lack of an autopsy raised questions. But inquirers were merely told that a friend of Price—not Alvarez—had turned up with a briefcase full of his medical records. These, and the statements of the emergency room physician, had apparently been enough to convince Las Vegas medical officials to waive an autopsy and declare Price dead of a heart attack. Kennett tried to track down this mysterious person with the briefcase, but never found out who he was, or whether he even existed.

Price's death gave birth to a flock of rumors and whispered questions. Was the man with the briefcase someone from the CIA? Why had he prevented an autopsy? What had he feared the pathologist would discover? Was Price even dead? Was he living somewhere under some new identity, as the perfect, untraceable spy?

Or had he been murdered by the Soviets? Price, like Swann, had long seemed concerned about this kind of thing, however paranoid such a concern might have seemed. Perhaps the man with the briefcase had wanted to prevent the pathologist from stumbling onto a KGB assassination plot, with all the furor that would entail. Or perhaps this man with the briefcase was merely the invention of the medical examiner, who was under orders from the FBI to leave Price's autopsy to a more specialized group of pathologists, trained to search for the most subtle toxins and poisons.*

Adding to this ripe stew of speculation was Bill Alvarez, who told everyone the story he said Price had told him, about the drug in Price's coffee in Washington. Then another friend of Price's stepped forward and said he'd had a vision, much more vivid than a dream, in which Price's ghost appeared to him, like the ghost of Hamlet's father, and complained that he'd been poisoned. Unfortunately, the remote viewer's ghost failed to point the finger at anyone.

For many who knew Pat Price, and were aware of his severe heart disease, there was no real mystery here. Yet in the decades to come, within the small community of the remote-viewing program, Price's untimely death would have, so to speak, a life of its own. Virtually every possible scenario, every reason for Price's suffering and demise, would be constructed and pondered. Theories would rise and fall. But in the end, few were willing to believe anything too strongly. As late as 1994, Russell Targ would tell me, "I don't know how Pat Price died."

Whatever had really happened to Price, it was clear that the Soviets were still competing intensely for the psychic high ground. They had dozens of facilities dedicated to psi re-

---

* More than a decade later, the novelist Larry Collins would make use of this KGB-assassination scenario in his potboiler *Maze*, about the U.S.-Soviet psi race. Incidentally, a CIA official who worked with Price told me that as far as he knew, the Agency had no connection with any of the events surrounding Price's death, including the (alleged) appearance of the mysterious man with the medical records.

search, many of them staffed by widely respected scientists. Leningrad University's Leonid Vasiliev had retired now, but his laboratory continued its work under a successor, Pavel Gulayev. A Dr. Lev Lupichev headed a psi research center called the Institute of Control Problems, attached to the USSR Academy of Sciences. In the vast, cold "Science City" in Novosibirsk, under the direction of a Navy colonel named Vitali Perov, there was reportedly something called Special Department No. 8, which carried out a secret program of military-oriented psi work. In Moscow, hush-hush psi research also went on in a well-guarded facility called the Institute for the Problems of Information Transmission (IPPI) and at a laboratory in the Pavlov "Institute of Higher Nervous Activity." And of course there was I. M. Kogan's old psi laboratory at the Popov Society, which was said to have moved to, and expanded in, a new and secret location. Kogan's employee Eduard Naumov, who had always seemed a bit too free with the psi research gossip, was sentenced to two years' hard labor in 1974, ostensibly because he had charged lecture fees without permission. Western psi researchers assumed that Soviet officials simply wanted to keep Naumov on a tighter leash.

By this time, the mid-1970s, the Soviets had apparently embarked upon a society-wide screening program for talented psychics, covering high schools, universities, and Red Army recruits. The KGB and the military intelligence agencies were after the best natural clairvoyants, the best psychokinetic savants, the best all-around visionaries and wonder-workers that the mystical races of the Russian Empire could produce.

And they got them, if one could believe the scattered reports filtering out from spies, defectors, émigrés, and the general rumor mill. There was talk, for example, of a Central Asian woman, a licensed physician, who was the Russian Empire's answer to Pat Price. It was said she could remote-view secret military installations in detail, from hundreds and presumably thousands of miles away.

There were stories of cosmonauts trained to use telepathy as an emergency communications system. There were tales of the "extrasensors" from IPPI who could psychically tap into otherwise secure communications links and into the minds of important foreigners. One savant on loan from IPPI reportedly enabled a Soviet Army unit, during military exercises, to anticipate its opponents' movements and lay a successful ambush.

The Czechs and Bulgarians were said to have similar, if smaller, programs. For example, a blind Bulgarian seeress named Vanga Dimitrova was openly employed by the state, and even had two secretaries.

Ironically, despite the rich esoteric traditions of the Slavonic world, theories for psi in these countries had to bow first to Communist ideology, which promoted "scientific materialism" and rejected any "idealism" or "superstition." As recently as 1956 the *Soviet Encyclopedia* had scowlingly defined ESP as "an anti-social idealist fiction about man's supernatural power to perceive phenomena which, considering the time and the place, cannot be perceived."

There were still some of those negative vibrations in the air during the Brezhnev era. One didn't want to get too far out of line. Brezhnev and the top ranks of the Soviet *nomenklatura* regularly availed themselves of the services of shapely Dzhuna Davitashvili, a Georgian healer, and sundry other seers and mystagogues. But outside the protected ranks of the *nomenklatura*, researchers had to be more careful. Their terminology was often deliberately anti-mystical. They spoke of *transmission* and *reception* of psi information. I. M. Kogan argued that telepathy was nothing more than communication via extremely-low-frequency (ELF) radio waves in the 10 Hz region.* This, he said, corresponded to the "alpha" brain wave frequency that was so prominent on electroencephalographs. Kogan hypothesized that these low-frequency signals were produced by the sender's brain and sensed by the receiver's brain. Other Russian researchers even spoke of "psi particles," as if psi, like electromagnetic phenomena, behaved with wave-particle duality.

It all sounded very dry and scientific. But if émigrés and the rumor mill could be believed, East bloc psi research was also very brutal and sinister. When one read of the things that some of these scientists were supposedly doing, one could almost see—in grainy black and white, with a chamber of horrors pipe organ playing in the background—the grinning faces of the Russian researchers and their hunchbacked henchmen, as they inflicted pain and suffering on their howling subjects, and plotted a hellish conquest of the world. One experiment, according to a story told by Eduard Naumov, involved a group of baby rabbits on board a submarine. Their mother, with electrodes planted deep in her brain, sat in a laboratory onshore. It was yet another *Nautilus*-style telepathy attempt, but this time with a sadistic twist. At a prearranged time researchers on the submarine killed the baby rabbits . . . snapping their necks, one by one . . . while onshore, researchers tried to detect any unusual activity in the mother rabbit's brain.

At Special Department No. 8, according to an émigré physicist named August Stern, the same sort of experiment was tried, but with a mother cat and her newborn kittens— which were tortured with electroshocks. It was said that even human subjects received brutal treatment, with over-

---

* One reason for this hypothesis was that at certain frequencies ELF electromagnetic waves could travel long distances with relatively little attenuation.

doses of stimulants like Adrenalin, and depressants like phenobarbitol, and electrical shocks, and high-strength magnetic fields, all in an effort to induce hypnotic or otherwise psi-conducive states. Rumor had it that some died, and others were brain-damaged.

Some of the reports of Soviet "remote-influencing" experiments made clear what the Russians intended to do with psi if they ever perfected it. A Leningrad woman named Nina Kulagina, for example, was reported to have remotely stopped the beating heart of a frog. As for her power over humans, it was said that she once used her psychokinetic "whammy" to induce tachycardia—an abnormally rapid heart rate—in a skeptical psychiatrist. Dread Nina, it was claimed, was also able to cause severe burning sensations in people, including at least one visiting Western researcher, just by touching them.

According to émigrés and intelligence reports, the KGB and GRU (military intelligence) had scoured the mystical eastern vastnesses of the Soviet Union in order to find the toughest Siberian shamans, the best-trained Tibetan priests, the most powerful Mongolian *chi gong* masters. At Special Department No. 8 in Siberia, according to August Stern, shamans tried to use their PK powers to make people fall off streetcars, or to kill small animals. An émigré parapsychologist named Larissa Vilenskaya claimed that at I.M. Kogan's lab she was once shown a film of a PK master listening to a foreign politician on the radio, and trying to send detrimental psi particles his way.

At IPPI one day, it was said, a group of Tibetans succeeded in breaking a human skull a few yards away, just by concentrating on it. Also at IPPI, and at a laboratory in Kazakhstan, shamans took madryushka dolls, hand-carved wooden spoons, souvenir models of Sputnik—the usual beriozka store trinkets—and zapped them with evil psi energies. The gifts now supposedly emitted debilitating rays, almost as if they had been impregnated with some kind of radioactive material; they were given to hapless foreign visitors, who would thereafter, it was believed, suffer neuralgia, depression, even nervous breakdowns. It was black magic, pure and simple, cloaked in the gray vernacular of psi particles and psi radiation and transmission and reception. Lev Lupichev, from the Institute of Control Problems, and a fellow named Boris Ivanov, at the "Laboratory of Bio-Information," even claimed to have perfected "batteries" that could store and discharge these negative vibrations— or negative particles, or whatever one was supposed to call them.

There were still wilder stories, all presumably apocryphal, such as the one about the medicine man someone had found who was incredibly powerful, could stop the heart of a small animal a mile away, yet, like a wild fastballer, had an occasional problem with control. They sent him against a rat in a cage and he ended up killing one of the researchers. And then there was the one about the fellow who was supposed to stop the heart of some poor human subject in the next room, a convicted criminal who had involuntarily donated his living body to science. The shaman or whoever he was wound up and sent his psi energies flying, and sure enough, the convict's heart stopped cold—but so did the shaman's.

Because Soviet researchers often thought of psi phenomena as being mediated by electromagnetic radiation, they eventually thought of building psi machines. One idea had to do with a remote-influencing, or "mind control," device built from a simple low-frequency radio transmitter that had been tuned to the proper nervous-system frequencies.

By the mid-1970s the CIA and DIA had begun to receive various reports of "psychotronic generators" being designed and built along these lines. There was one device that supposedly could cause strokes or heart attacks. Another gave people a sensation of anxiety, or of a disorienting blow to the head. Another made them aggressive, or drove them mad. Some reports credited a Russian scientist named Viktor Inyushin with the development of this technology. Others cited a Czech engineer named Robert Pavlita. An émigré named Nikolai Khokhlov, apparently a former KGB officer, claimed that his erstwhile employers had "tested" such generators against certain selected communities in North America.

Many in the U.S. intelligence community simply regarded these stories as evidence that the Russian psi program was spiraling off into insanity. "The greatest threat," one senior CIA official would later say, "was that they would *stop* wasting money on this!"

There seemed little chance of that; Soviet enthusiasm for far-fetched weaponry reached all the way to the top. In a strange speech delivered in June of 1975, according to *The New York Times:*

> Leonid I. Brezhnev, the Soviet leader, urged the United States to agree on a ban of research and development of new kinds of weapons "more terrible" than anything the world has known. American arms control negotiators have tried to find out from their Soviet counterparts what he had in mind, but they have not learned anything more than that he meant "some kind of rays," according to United States officials.

Aside from doing their own psi research, which seemed to be extensive and well funded, the Soviets tried to obtain information about American efforts in this area, including the work at SRI.

Puthoff and Targ and their friends in the government knew that the Soviets were interested in the SRI research, and were understandably concerned that the Soviets might recruit psychics to infiltrate the SRI program. But the grasping hand of Soviet espionage seemed less subtle than that. In early 1976, for example, after Puthoff and Targ had published a number of their experiments in *Proceedings of the IEEE,* they began a long wrangle with the editors of the journal's Soviet edition.

In the normal course of events, the Puthoff and Targ article would have appeared in the Soviet edition without much if any correspondence between authors and editors. However, in this case, the Soviet editors insisted that they wouldn't publish the article unless Puthoff and Targ provided further details of the SRI experiments. They sent the two researchers a long list of questions they wanted answered: How fine was the detail that remote viewers could perceive? How did SRI manage to find people who were good remote viewers? Did they use drugs, or hypnosis, or some other technique to bring about psi-conducive states of consciousness? Did they know of any way to shield targets from remote viewers? Puthoff and Targ refused to respond to the list of questions, and forwarded the list to their government sponsors in Washington. The article was eventually published anyway, but several years later, Soviet parapsychologist Larissa Vilenskaya emigrated to the United States and told Western researchers that the whole thing had indeed been a hamfisted KGB intelligence-gathering ploy. She knew, she said, because she had been the one forced to write the list of questions.

One day another Soviet request came in to SRI, this time from the Soviet Consulate in San Francisco. A cosmonaut named Vitali Sevastyanov was in town and wanted to talk to Puthoff and Targ about some psychic experiences he'd had. He would be accompanied by Soviet parapsychologist Lev Lupichev and by the local vice-consul, Oleg Sidorenko.

Puthoff and the rest of SRI officialdom accepted the request, but were warned by CIA and SRI security officials, in case they weren't already aware, that the visit probably wasn't as innocent as it sounded. The three Russians got no farther than the SRI dining room, but they still managed to pepper Puthoff and Targ with questions—more or less the same ones on the list from the Soviet *IEEE* editors. Puthoff and Targ fielded the questions as cleanly, or as uncleanly, as they could. Towards the end of the lunch they suggested that in the spirit of détente they should do an experiment: SRI's psychics would remote-view Lupichev's lab, and Lupichev's psychics could do the same to SRI. Lupichev seemed to like the idea, but Puthoff and Targ never heard from him again.

Of all Puthoff's encounters with the Soviets, the strangest had to have been the one in Prague in the summer of 1973, at the First International Congress on Psychotronic Research. A group of well-known Soviet researchers had been due to appear at the conference, but at the last minute they had cancelled. In their place had come some other Soviets who were unknown on the psi scene but who nevertheless claimed to be psi researchers.

There was just enough time to run the newcomers' names past the CIA before Puthoff, with Swann, took off for Prague. Word came back that the leader of the Soviet group was a KGB officer. But when Puthoff and Swann got to the conference, it hardly seemed to matter who was KGB and who wasn't. Almost everyone who came up to query them, whether Soviet or Eastern European, was reading off what seemed to be the same centrally prepared list of questions.

14

THE UNBELIEVERS

When it came up, I was embarrassed to mention to my
superiors that there were people in my part of the establishment who thought there was something to it.

> —Lieutenant General Daniel O.
> Graham, DIA director, 1975–76,
> recalling his agency's initial
> involvement in psi research

That data could have been [fabricated] by anybody, at
any place, at any time. . . . I think it was absolute non-
sense.

> —Sam Koslov, former scientific
> adviser to the secretary of the
> navy, explaining the reasoning
> behind his termination of an SRI
> contract in 1976

WHATEVER PSI HORRORS SOVIET BLOC RESEARCHERS PERPETRATED
or planned, at least they believed in psi, and could talk
about it freely with scientific colleagues. The same wasn't
true in the West. Although most American and European
scientists privately seemed open-minded about the possibility of psi (if questioned by poll takers), very few were
prepared to stand up for the paranormal before their breth-
ren. Psi might have been embraced by ordinary culture, but

it had mostly been expelled from scientific culture. In fact, the mainstream scientists who were really evangelical on the subject of psi tended to be the *un*believers, the skeptics—for whom parapsychology as a whole was not a legitimate area of research but a "pathological science," full of fraud and delusion and sloppy experimentation.

One such skeptic was a CIA employee named Laura Dickens. As reports came in, from Richard Kennett and Ken Kress and others, of miraculous remote-viewing results out at SRI, she decided to investigate for herself. She flew out from Washington, and told Puthoff, up front, that she had come to debunk his research.

Puthoff, in his measured, mild-mannered way, decided that he would convert Dickens to a more positive view of psi. It wouldn't be easy. He began by allowing her to observe while Duane Elgin did an outbound remote-viewing session. Afterwards, with the transcript of Elgin's comments in hand, Dickens, Elgin, Targ, and Puthoff went out to the site. Elgin's description clearly matched the site, but Dickens wasn't impressed. "It's got to be a trick," she told Puthoff.

The following day, so the story goes, Dickens and Puthoff were the outbound experimenters. They took randomly chosen site directions from Bart Cox, and went out to the site.

Now, the previous day, Dickens had suspected that a car or even a helicopter had followed the outbound experimenters and had secretly conveyed the site data back to Elgin at SRI. So on this day, Dickens waited with Puthoff for fifteen of the thirty minutes they were supposed to stay at the site. She guessed that the car or helicopter would be long gone by then. Then she said, "Okay, let's get into the car and go to another site." Puthoff complained that Dickens was tampering with their standard protocol, but she insisted, and they drove over to another site of her choosing. When the thirty minutes were up, they returned to SRI.

Elgin, they discovered, had still been on target. He had accurately described the first site, and had noted the fact that the experimenters were unexpectedly getting into a car in the middle of the session. He had then gone on to describe the second site. Laura Dickens said she wanted to think about this overnight.

While Dickens pondered her next move, Puthoff and Targ conferred on the matter. They agreed that Dickens was going to be a hard sell. The seeing-is-believing treatment hadn't worked. It looked as if they would have to try doing-is-believing.

The next morning Dickens arrived at SRI. Puthoff and Targ were in the remote-viewing room, which was otherwise empty. "Where's the remote viewer?" Dickens wanted to know.

"You are the remote viewer," explained Puthoff.

"You've got to be kidding," said Dickens. "I don't believe in this bullshit. I'm not going to do this."

Puthoff and Targ argued that whatever Dickens's beliefs might be, this would be an ideal way for her to experience the experimental protocol from the viewer's end. After further protests, Dickens finally agreed to try it out. Puthoff went to Cox, got the site, drove out to it, and waited there for the requisite half hour. Meanwhile Targ sat in the viewing room with Dickens.

"Close your eyes and tell me what you see," said Targ.

"Okay," said Dickens. "My eyes are closed. It's dark. I see the backs of my eyelids."

"Come on, use your imagination."

"All right, I've got a great imagination. I see a bridge by a stream. But that's just my imagination."

Puthoff came back after a while, and he and Targ took Dickens out to the site. It was a bridge over a little stream in a park on the SRI campus.

Dickens seemed slightly upset. But after a while she regained her composure. She decided that Targ, in the remote-viewing room beforehand, had somehow subliminally cued her about the site. She told Puthoff and Targ that she wanted to do the experiment again, but this time she didn't want Targ in the room with her.

All right, said Puthoff and Targ. They left her in the room, and taped the door shut behind them, to make sure she couldn't accuse them of lax protocols. Puthoff got the directions from Bart Cox and went out to the site. It was a place called Baylands Nature Preserve, in Palo Alto. After the requisite interval, he drove back. He and Targ untaped the door and opened the remote-viewing room.

Dickens was huddled in one corner, her hands over her ears and her notepad tucked up close to her chest, to foil whatever video surveillance cameras or subliminal-suggestion speakers might be hidden in the room.

Puthoff and Targ looked at what she had drawn, smiled, and then took her out to the nature preserve. Again it was obvious that Dickens had hit the site.

Dickens looked unhappy again, but fairly soon her core unbeliefs reasserted themselves, and she decided she knew how the trick had been done. Puthoff and Targ had simply looked at her sketch and then had taken her to the nearest place that matched it.

She told them she wanted to do another site. This time she wanted Puthoff and Targ to go to the site, come back, and tell her what the site was *before* she showed them her sketches.

All right, said Puthoff and Targ. They taped Dickens into the remote-viewing room again, got a new site assignment from Bart Cox, and drove out to it. The site was a children's playground, about two miles from SRI. There were a number of items there, but one of the most prominent was a spinning circular platform with looping bars, the kind of thing that kids hold on to, screaming, while they try to resist the centrifugal force. It was a kind of mini merry-go-round.

They went back afterwards, and gave Dickens the site directions. It turned out that Dickens had sketched something that looked very like the mini merry-go-round with its looping bars—although as remote viewers often did, she had erroneously analyzed her sketch, deciding it was a cupola that might fit atop a house. However, the visual correspondence between her sketch and the little merry-go-round was so striking that when Puthoff and Targ took Dickens out to the site, she pointed to the little merry-go-round and said, "That's it, isn't it?" And then: "My God, it really works!"

Dickens proved to be one of the best remote viewers SRI ever tested, and soon joined a small in-house informal group of the CIA's own psychic spies.

Puthoff and Targ chalked up another victory, but the battle raged on many fronts, and most skeptics kept themselves at a safe distance from remote-viewing experiments.

Ironically, the two researchers were probably criticized most severely by skeptics inside SRI, who thought their research unseemly and tried—but failed—to have it stopped. Outside SRI, they were portrayed by the science editor of *Time*, Leon Jaroff, as gullible and sloppy.* Even the editors of *Nature*, where Puthoff and Targ managed to get their first paper published, gave them a chilly reception. In an editorial accompanying the paper, *Nature*'s editors made clear that they didn't regard Puthoff's and Targ's work as particularly solid or convincing. They deconstructed the paper in advance by summarizing the negative

---

* According to former *Time* science writer John Wilhelm, Jaroff privately associated parapsychology with the occult beliefs that had helped give rise to fascism in Europe. Jaroff is said to have concluded that SRI's psi research should "be destroyed."

comments made by the paper's referees, comments that concerned relatively minor points, even though Puthoff and Targ had apparently addressed these in their final manuscript. This was, to say the least, rare treatment for scientists publishing in *Nature*.

Puthoff and Targ were kept on the defensive by other critics throughout the 1970s. Some clearly made valid arguments, and forced the SRI researchers to improve their data analysis techniques.*But no matter how dramatic the results the two men published, errors were always postulated, even if they couldn't be found, and the scientific consensus would always seem to be that remote viewing's existence was "unproved."

This popular scientific bias against psi made it easy for doubters to attack the SRI work on relatively non-scientific grounds. Some would even hint that there was a religious conspiracy afoot. As Leon Jaroff put it, in a *Time* cover story on psi in early 1974, Hal Puthoff and Ingo Swann were members of "the bizarre and controversial cult of Scientology."

It was true, although to be fair, both men had joined

---

* The most serious criticism involved the transcripts of outbound remote-viewing sessions, which judges carried around and tried to match to the list of target sites. It was pointed out that the transcript for a given target sometimes contained references to other targets in the series that already had been remote-viewed. Skeptics argued that this invalidated the experiments, because it enabled the judges to match transcripts to targets simply by looking for such non-psi-related clues in the transcripts. Puthoff and Targ, though admitting that they had erred, maintained that with the inadvertent clues to other targets removed from the transcripts, the rejudged data still suggested the existence of psi. They also pointed out that the compare-and-match procedure they had used, while it simplified the mathematics of the situation, grossly underestimated the real statistical significance of the remote-viewing results. For example, Pat Price had correctly *named* the Hoover Tower target; the actual odds against naming such a target purely by chance, they argued, had to be astronomical, if they were even calculable.

Scientology back in the sixties, a time when it had been much less controversial.* A Scientology "mission," in those days, would merely have seemed like one of many places where suitably inclined people could go to try to enrich their inner lives. Through a series of (expensive) courses, Scientology adherents were supposed to learn to get rid of phobias, repressed traumas, and other mental noise, freeing their minds and giving them irresistible confidence and power. Scientology seemed particularly attractive to people who were both spiritually and technically oriented, probably because it combined Eastern religious themes of reincarnation and introspection with Western themes of predestination, ethical rigor, and self-improvement through science and technology. It was, arguably, a severely mutated form of Protestantism, gone amok in the machine age.

Puthoff resigned his Scientology membership in the mid-1970s, and thereafter lent his support to a group of anti-Scientologists, who criticized the church for what they believed was indeed a conspiratorial, cult-like atmosphere. Swann would later resign from Scientology, too. Still, Scientology had a remarkably strong foothold among high-tech professionals on the West Coast. At SRI, there seemed

---

* Scientology was invented by L. Ron Hubbard, the meaty-faced son of a Nebraska farmer. In his early years Hubbard drifted from place to place, writing science fiction, spinning tall tales, performing outrageous occult rituals, and generally building a reputation as a ne'er-do-well. He eventually wrote a book, *Dianetics*, in which he argued, in effect, that most human ailments and inadequacies are psychological in nature. Suddenly, Hubbard was mobbed by followers who were eager to improve themselves by practicing Dianetics. In 1953, Hubbard turned his relatively loose Dianetics organization into a formal religion, the Church of Scientology. By the early 1970s, Scientology would be a major international operation, run by Hubbard from a ship called the *Apollo* which cruised international waters. By the late 1970s, the Church of Scientology had had various run-ins with the U.S. government, and was under attack from a variety of angry former Scientologists.

to be Scientologists everywhere. Pat Price, up to his death, had been deeply involved in Scientology. That was how Puthoff had known him; they had met at a Scientology course in Los Angeles. One of Puthoff's lab assistants was a Scientologist. Astronaut Edgar Mitchell, whose private foundation had funded some of SRI's work with Geller, had briefly taken an interest in Scientology. Even Pat Price's coal company deal had Scientology connections. A senior company official had recovered from a serious illness, he believed, through the help of Scientological techniques, and later he had tried to use those techniques to "cure" his company of its corporate problems. He had heard about Price on the Scientology grapevine.

One of the central doctrines of the Church of Scientology was that human beings have innate psi abilities. Thus the view circulated, among some psi critics, that Scientologists should never be trusted to conduct psi experiments impartially. Negative results were against their religion. Puthoff, backed up by Targ, who was not a Scientologist, emphasized that in the laboratory he was a scientist first and foremost. Within a year or two of the Leon Jaroff article, Puthoff left Scientology anyway. But some of the mud stuck, and even two decades later, observers of the remote-viewing scene would still whisper in disapproving tones about the Scientology connection.

The heaviest blow in those years had little to do with anyone's religious beliefs. And it came from the otherwise supportive CIA.

As Agency analyst Richard Kennett saw it, remote viewing was clearly a genuine phenomenon. He himself had served as a remote-viewing beacon for Pat Price several times, and could never be a complete skeptic again. Still, Kennett wasn't sure it was wise to continue funding the remote-viewing program, at least not in its present form. The problem, for Kennett, was that out of all the psychics evaluated at SRI and the CIA, only Pat Price had come close to being accurate and reliable enough for regular intelligence use, and even then, he had often been defeated by the giggle factor. In any case, as of the summer of 1975, Price was dead and gone.

Short of finding another super-psychic, Kennett believed, SRI would have to develop the remote-viewing phenomenon itself, making it more accurate and reliable even when used by relatively ordinary people. But he knew that getting to that magical point would require more than just a few years of off-the-cuff funding. The only thing he thought could be justified was a large-scale, long-term program, involving a lot of money, serious in-depth neuropsychological studies of psychics, and numerous, rigorous remote-viewing experiments.

As he knew, the CIA wasn't going to be able to handle that kind of program in the increasingly volatile political climate of the mid-1970s. Plans for large-scale experimentation on human subjects by the CIA, involving brain-wave monitoring and talk of ESP, would be on the front page of *The New York Times*, accompanied by howls of derision and protest, before SRI ever saw a dime of new funding.

The reason for this was simple. In the wake of the Watergate scandal, Congress had begun to exercise an unprecedented scrutiny over executive branch operations, particularly CIA operations. The CIA's "skeletons" were being dragged out of the closet, embarrassing the Agency with fantastically lurid revelations. For example, it emerged that in the 1950s and 1960s, under a group of about 200 projects collectively code-named MKULTRA,* the CIA had tried to devise—and in some cases had used—exotic assassination weapons, including chemical toxins, biological agents, and even radio-guided animals filled with bombs.

---

* MKULTRA subproject 136, oddly enough, had involved ESP research, under academic cover. Apparently it had been relatively inconsequential.

In addition, believing that the Soviets had secretly devised some kind of mind-control drug,* the Agency had done extensive experiments of its own with strong mind-altering substances, including LSD. One group of subjects was kept on LSD continuously for seventy-seven days to see if they could be brainwashed. An Army researcher named Frank Olson took LSD at an informal gathering with CIA and Army officials, and later underwent strong personality changes; he committed suicide a few weeks later, jumping to his death from a New York hotel room. It was rumored that a number of suspected Soviet double agents also died after being subjected, without their knowledge, to experimental drugs while in CIA custody.

MKULTRA had been run by the Agency's Technical Services Staff and its bureaucratic successor, the Technical Services Division (TSD)—later known as the Office of Technical Service. One of the key figures in these projects was Dr. Sidney Gottlieb, still the head of TSD in late 1972, when the division awarded Hal Puthoff his first psi research contract.

Though Gottlieb's MKULTRA work had been approved at the highest levels, he would come to be seen, in congressional hearings in the mid and late 1970s, as the personification of a CIA running out of control. He had been the one who put LSD in Frank Olson's drink. He also had travelled to Africa in 1960 to try to assassinate Congolese nationalist Patrice Lumumba with a biological agent, and had later tried to kill an Iraqi colonel by mailing him a handkerchief soaked with a powerful toxin (both men had died before Gottlieb's gifts reached them). Gottlieb had also

---

* At the Moscow show-trials of the late Stalin era, some celebrated defendants had behaved in such a way that CIA officials suspected they had been brainwashed and "re-programmed" to actually believe the false stories they were telling. Such fears inspired not only MKULTRA but also the famous novel and film *The Manchurian Candidate*.

been the scientist at the center of the CIA's attempts to kill Fidel Castro; the weapons he had devised for those ill-fated attempts included pills with botulinum toxin, a poison pen, a poison dart gun, and bacterial powder that was to have been sprayed into the Cuban leader's scuba-diving wet suit.

In the summer of 1973 TSD was transferred out of the Directorate for Operations and became OTS, under the Directorate for Science and Technology. Gottlieb took the opportunity to retire from the Agency (John McMahon took his place as the head of the new OTS), but the storm over the CIA's skeletons was just beginning to break. William Colby, who became the director of central intelligence a few months later, spent much of his time trying to cope with attacks on the Agency from Congress, and eventually ordered the CIA to get rid of as many politically sensitive projects as it could.

OTS was still involved in a number of highly sensitive projects, not just the remnants of MKULTRA but other projects which even now have not been exposed. John McMahon was relatively enthusiastic about the potential of remote viewing, but by the time Pat Price died, it was decided that funding remote-viewing research was one potential liability OTS would have to do without. There were no further contracts for SRI from the Agency, and the CIA's informal group of in-house remote viewers gradually broke up. When McMahon moved to another post in 1976, he was replaced at the helm of OTS by a man named Dave Brandwyne, who was not at all sympathetic towards remote viewing. Brandwyne came down hard on OTS engineer Ken Kress for his involvement in the program and his attempts to arrange a new contract for SRI. He made it clear to Kress, and to Hal Puthoff, that he was not about to let OTS get back into the remote-viewing business. "If I say no a hundred percent of the time," he told Puthoff, "I'll be right eighty percent of the time."

More sympathetic CIA officials, such as John McMahon,

Ken Kress, and Norm Everheart, managed to stay in touch with the SRI program, and later the Fort Meade unit. But in terms of political exposure, the CIA was to keep an increasingly low profile, encouraging other, less vulnerable agencies to take the lead in funding and promoting the espionage use of psi.

In late 1974, when the second and last CIA contract began to run out, Puthoff and Targ faced the prospect of a severe funding drought. They were forced to go on the road, giving presentation after presentation in Washington, displaying their results, virtually begging for funds. Sometimes their audience turned thumbs down on the spot. At other times they showed enthusiasm, made promises, but didn't have the political power to come through with actual budget allocations. And when they weren't doing presentations, it seemed, Puthoff and Targ were battling skeptics inside and outside SRI. Puthoff regularly worked eighty-hour weeks, and several times his (second) marriage nearly ended.

The two researchers also spent time collaborating on a book, a popular account of their work that they titled *Mind Reach*. Aside from the usual literary considerations, they hoped it would generate the large-scale funding interest that their presentations in Washington had not yet been able to do.

At one low point, word reached Puthoff and Targ, then in Washington, that their jobs at SRI were on the line. They had to return to Menlo Park with a promise of funding, or else.

Puthoff and Targ's literary agent was a woman named Roslyn Targ, who happened to be Russell's stepmother. She also represented Richard Bach, author of the best-seller *Jonathan Livingston Seagull*. She told the two scientists that Bach, whose book had been inspired by some unusual, out-of-body-ish experiences, might be interested in what they were doing at SRI. A meeting was arranged, and Puthoff and Targ flew down to Florida to meet Bach at his home.

It turned out that Bach had an amazing place, with model airplanes hanging everywhere from the ceiling so that one felt as if one were drifting with them through the atmosphere. Anyhow, Puthoff and Targ laid it out for him: They were doing some paradigm-smashing research, but just now money was tight. Could he spare some?

What Bach thought of this—two high-profile researchers from a respected think tank coming to him for a handout—is unrecorded, but in any case it seems he had a tender heart as well as deep pockets. He donated forty thousand dollars, stipulating only that he be allowed to participate as a remote viewer in an experiment. Puthoff and Targ, now reprieved from early retirement at SRI, agreed.

On his way to a speaking engagement in Hawaii, a few months afterwards, Bach touched his plane down in California and went over to SRI. He sat in the remote viewing room and did a passable job of remote-viewing Puthoff and his car in Palo Alto. Afterwards he made the by now common observation that whenever he had tried to analyze what he was seeing, he had tended to be wrong. For example, when Puthoff had walked into a church, Bach somehow, through some wild mixture of metaphor, had mistaken the altar for an airline ticket counter, and a gold cross on the wall had been perceived as "the logo of the company . . . it looks like a big gold fleur de lis."

When the session was over, Bach flew on to Hawaii, and Puthoff and Targ had their $40,000. That, and a few other similar sums from public and private sources, would be stretched to keep them going over the next couple of years.

One contract, for about $100,000, was sponsored by the Office of Naval Research and concentrated on further EEG-telepathy experiments, along with operational-type remote viewings of submarines and other foreign military targets. Puthoff and Targ and their Navy contract monitor, Lieutenant Commander James Foote, guessed that an obviously ESP-related project might trigger a bad reaction, so they cagily titled the contract "Sensing of Remote EM [electromagnetic] Sources (Physiological Correlates)."

One day in 1976 Sam Koslov, the scientific adviser to the Secretary of the Navy, was reviewing a group of contracts run by the Office of Naval Research when he saw the "Sensing of Remote EM Sources" contract. The title caught his attention. He read it again. *Sensing of Remote EM Sources . . .*

Koslov became angry. He suspected that "Sensing of Remote EM Sources (Physiological Correlates)" was someone's euphemistic way of describing an electromagnetic mind-control experiment, involving human subjects. The CIA's MKULTRA mind-control experiments were just beginning to explode into scandal. Koslov ordered a private briefing on the "Sensing of Remote EM Sources" project, to find out more about it.

When he got the briefing, he only became angrier. Although the good news was that the SRI experiments were not about mind control, the bad news was that they were about telepathy, with some operational-type remote viewing on the side. To Koslov, a decided psi unbeliever, it might as well have been called witchcraft. He ordered the contract cut off. And when it wasn't cut off as soon as he wanted, he ordered the Navy's inspector general to look into the matter.

Not long after the Navy contract was terminated,* Puthoff landed a small contract with Dale Graff, a physicist at the Air Force's Foreign Technology Division. Graff wanted to

---

* Employees at a Navy lab in San Diego, advised by Puthoff, soon started their own in-house project to experiment with remote viewing—as an

try to replicate the successful psi communications work that the Soviet Navy—in the wake of the *Nautilus* story—had reportedly done. He also wanted to explore the leading Soviet hypothesis regarding psi—namely, that it was transmitted via extremely-low-frequency (ELF) electromagnetic waves.

An opportunity to conduct experiments covering both of these areas arose in July 1977, thanks to Stephan Schwartz, a former Navy officer who was now a successful Los Angeles businessman and psi enthusiast. Schwartz wanted to see if he could use remote viewers to find previously undiscovered shipwrecks off the California coast. He persuaded Ingo Swann and Hella Hammid to serve as his remote viewers.

Swann and Hammid started by psychically scanning maps that Schwartz had provided, to try to find anything interesting. They settled on a relatively small area near Santa Catalina Island, thirty miles southwest of Los Angeles, and sketched various shipboard items they thought would be at the site.

For the next part of the venture Schwartz hired a submersible from the University of Southern California's marine lab. He wanted Swann and Hammid to go down in the submersible, to help him zero in on the wreck site. They agreed to do so and eventually found some debris that suggested they had hit the right wreck. But by arrangement with Schwartz, they also used the submersible to conduct some experiments for Graff's secret Air Force contract.

At a prearranged time, an outbound experiment team at SRI went to a randomly chosen target site in the San Francisco Bay Area. Hammid, in the cramped submersible 550 feet beneath the Pacific, tried to pick up impressions of the

---

underwater communications technique, and as a method for hunting Soviet submarines. That project was eventually shut down too.

site the team was visiting. "A very tall looming object," she said. "A very, very huge, tall tree and a lot of space behind them. There almost feels like there is a drop-off or a palisade or a cliff behind them."

At this point, the protocol diverged from the usual outbound experiment. Hammid, within the submersible, was handed a series of six envelopes, containing photographs of separate sites in the Bay Area. One was the target that the SRI team had just visited. Her task was to match her description to the correct target photograph. That turned out to be easy; she picked a photo of a giant oak on a hilltop in Portola Valley. Then she turned over the photograph; on the back, Puthoff or Targ had printed a simple submarine-type signalling message, such as "Surface immediately for satellite communication" or "Proceed to rendezvous A." The message wasn't meant to be acted upon; it was just a dummy message, meant to make the experiment seem more "real." The experiment was, in fact, a kind of associative remote-viewing exercise, in which the usual outbound target sites were associated with specific messages. The aim was to see whether such messages could be "transmitted" accurately through psi, just as in the *Nautilus* story two decades before.

Later Swann went down in the submersible, to a depth of about 250 feet, while the SRI team went to a new site. Swann described "flat stone flooring, walls, small pool, reddish stone walk, large doors, walking around, an enclosed space." Of the six possible targets, he chose a shopping mall with a pool of water in Mountain View, and copied down the dummy message on the back.

Despite the claustral confines of the submersible, and Hammid's seasickness, and a schedule of work they had quickly fallen behind on, both remote viewers had been right in their choices. America's first direct test of psi for submarine communication had worked perfectly.

After this initial round of experiments, a set of three

other remote viewers back at SRI tried to pull information in the other direction. At agreed-upon times, they tried to remote-view photographs contained in envelopes inside the submersible. The target envelopes had been selected by Hammid and Swann, down in the submersible, from a larger set they had brought with them. Back at SRI, the remote viewers tried to match their descriptions of the targets to photographs from the same set. In three tries they got two right.

Aside from pointing to the possibility of psi as an emergency communications system for submarine crews, the experiments had more or less disproved the leading Soviet theory of psi—namely, that it somehow involved extremely-low-frequency (ELF) electromagnetic radiation. At the submersible's depth during the experiments, the seawater should have reduced such ELF waves, at the expected frequencies (which were supposed to be in the same range as brain-wave frequencies), to less than 1 percent of their strength above the ocean. Had the ELF hypothesis been correct, Swann and Hammid should have noticed a major reduction in their remote-viewing accuracy. But their sessions were as quick and as accurate as any they had conducted at short ranges on land. The ELF hypothesis for psi was dead, as far as SRI and its military clients were concerned.

Hal Puthoff soon wrote up the results, and he and Dale Graff briefed them to an undersecretary of the navy, pushing the associative remote-viewing technique they had used as a possible emergency communications system for Navy submarine crews. It wasn't 100 percent reliable, they admitted, but perhaps it could be improved upon, and in any case, it would be very cheap to research and develop.

With the help of the undersecretary, a briefing was arranged at higher levels of the Navy. But before the briefing could be held, Puthoff received word that the Navy was most definitely *not* interested in discussing remote viewing or any other manifestation of the paranormal. Puthoff later heard that Sam Koslov, once again, had personally intervened to prevent any Navy involvement.*

Late in that summer of 1977 *The Washington Post* published an article by a science writer named John Wilhelm about the government's attempts to do psychic spying research. Wilhelm cited a few sources who believed in it all, but he included few details, and his tone was cautiously skeptical.

The next day, CIA director Stansfield Turner was asked about the subject at a previously scheduled meeting with reporters. Turner admitted that the intelligence community had done some research in the area, largely in response to reports of Soviet psi research. But he too downplayed the idea of psi, making it sound like an interesting though fruitless escapade. Turner, clearly referring to Pat Price, said that the CIA had once worked with a man who seemed to have some psychic ability. This man had been able to draw pictures of foreign targets he had otherwise never seen, but the drawings, though reasonably accurate, had (Turner claimed) been quite rudimentary. In any case, added Tur-

---

* The Navy went on to spend billions for the development of a simple, one-way submarine signalling system. Under the project names Sanguine and Seafarer, the system used giant ELF electromagnetic transmitters buried across large stretches of Michigan and Wisconsin. The ELF waves, which were a bit like small-scale seismic waves, could penetrate even to moderate ocean depths, halfway around the planet; their chief drawback was that their frequencies were too low to allow much data to be transmitted at any one time. (It seemed to Puthoff and Graff that much more information was transmissible in a quick remote-viewing session.) At best, the ELF system sent extremely simple messages to submarines, ordering them to surface at such and such a time and location, to pick up more detailed information from a satellite. And the system worked only one-way, from base to submarine. Still, it was probably much more reliable than an RV-based system would have been.

ner with a smirk, "he died, and we haven't heard from him since."

That seemed to end the matter, and from then on, for another decade and a half, little more was said of SRI and psychic spying. One might have guessed that the program had lived, briefly and strangely, like some flower in a mid-winter warm spell, but that the natural order of things had soon reasserted itself. One might have guessed that the proponents of psychic spying had been too far ahead of—or misguidedly behind—their time.

But the program lived still; it had merely become a deeper secret.

BOOK THREE

A NEW AGE

I will tell you for the record that there are structures underneath the surface of Mars. . . . I will also tell you that there are machines under the surface of Mars that you can look at. You can find out in detail, you can see what they are, where they are, who they are and a lot of detail about them . . . you can do that through remote viewing.

—Major General Albert
Stubblebine, U.S. Army,
commander of INSCOM,
1981–84

15

THE SUPER GOD IN THE SKY

She went into a trance. And while she was in a trance, she gave some latitude and longitude figures. We focussed our satellite cameras on that point and the plane was there.

—Former President Jimmy Carter

ON ONE OF THE FLOORS BELOW THE REMOTE-VIEWING LAB AT SRI, there was a metal-shielded "secure room" with a special fax machine protected by an encryption system. Occasionally a classified tasking would come through on the fax machine from Washington, and someone from the secure room would carry it up to Hal Puthoff.

One day in May 1978, Puthoff was handed a special classified fax from General Ed Thompson's office at the Pentagon. Apparently Thompson had sent it on behalf of the CIA. It was an urgent tasking concerning a Soviet Tupolev-22 bomber—a type code-named "Blinder" by NATO—that had been lost somewhere in Zaire. A day or so before, apparently on an intelligence-gathering mission over central Africa,* it had somehow crashed in the jungle. If the wreckage could be found by American spies before the Soviets reached it, it could be sifted through for valu-

---

* The bomber reportedly had been configured for the gathering of electronic and photographic intelligence.

able clues to Soviet intelligence targets and techniques. The Soviet Union's loss could be America's gain.

Unfortunately, though U.S. spy satellites had surveyed the area, looking for visual or infrared evidence of a downed craft, they had come up with nothing. The plane seemed to have been swallowed up by the jungle.

Puthoff by this time had perhaps a dozen remote viewers to choose from, including Ingo Swann, Hella Hammid, and a man named Gary Langford at SRI, plus a few free-lancers scattered around the country. He chose Langford for this mission. Langford was an SRI computer expert in his mid-thirties. Somehow it had been found that he had more than the average psi talent. He was tall and slim with a quiet, polite manner, and though he seemed in his element in front of a keyboard, he was not as eccentric as some of the other remote viewers. Down in his remote-viewing zone, he appeared to be particularly good against high-tech intelligence targets; his broad technical knowledge enabled him to describe the things he was psychically perceiving with a precision and an eye for detail unavailable to his more artistically oriented colleagues. He was also relatively good at using remote viewing to find things. There were times when he began to seem like a new Pat Price.

Puthoff walked with Langford into the RV room, which Ingo Swann had constructed a few years earlier. It was a soundproofed space with blank grayish white walls, a gray carpet, and a gray conference-type table. The lights were kept dim, to avoid any bright spots in the room. SRI's research had found that bright spots tended to leave after-images on the remote viewer's retinas, images that in turn could invade the remote viewer's data when the session began. With the lights dimmed, there were no such distractions. The room was a warm gray cocoon.

The two men sat at either end of the table. Before them lay pens and stacks of paper. Above them, like watchful bats, hung two black video cameras that were to record the session. Langford sat quietly for a few minutes, calming his mind, and then Puthoff turned on the cameras and placed the target envelope on the table. The target, he told Langford, was a lost aircraft.

Within ten minutes Langford was sensing a river in a jungle. The plane was there, but most of it was submerged. Langford sketched a battered tail section jutting up from the river's brown and turbulent surface. He also tried to sketch the surrounding area, with terrain and roads, but it wasn't clear whether there would be enough detail to isolate the location. Still, Puthoff was confident that the search should be concentrated along the rivers in the region of the crash.

Puthoff faxed the information back to the Pentagon, and then sat back and waited.

Air Force physicist Dale Graff was also considering the Zaire problem. Graff, at the Air Force's Foreign Technology Division at Wright-Patterson Air Force Base in Ohio, was a thin, absentminded professor type, with a long passion for psi. He liked to keep track of his dreams, and for a while in the late 1970s, had tried to communicate telepathically with a friend who lived across town. Each had scanned his or her dream content, to try to find material that had secretly been sent by the other. Graff taught a parapsychology course on the side, at a community college near Wright-Pat. A strong backer of Grill Flame, he was one of SRI's current funders; his contract tasked Puthoff and his associates with the duplication of some psi experiments the Soviets and Chinese were reported to have done.

Graff also had put together a small, informal group of remote viewers at Wright-Patterson, one of the best of whom was a woman named Frances Bryan, who seemed to have a special talent for finding things. When Graff heard about the downed Soviet plane in Zaire and the failure of efforts to find it, he sat Bryan down and gave her a photograph of a Tu-22. He told her that a similar plane had crashed somewhere in Africa.

Bryan's resulting sketch of the crashed plane wasn't as detailed as Langford's, but she produced a better overhead view of the crash site and the river, with numerous prominent terrain features. Graff matched the sketch to an area that turned out to be in the general region where the plane had gone down. A summary of Bryan's and Langford's data was sent via the Pentagon to the CIA's Europe and Africa Division in the Directorate of Operations, which cabled the information—not mentioning the bizarre source—to the Agency's station chief in Kinshasa.

The station chief wasn't too impressed. The area indicated in the cable was about seventy miles to the west of the area where his team now believed the plane had gone down. He cabled back to headquarters asking for more precise information, and meanwhile continued his search. The request went along the chain of command and eventually reached Graff at Wright-Patterson and Puthoff at SRI. They studied more maps of the area, and eventually Graff's office was able to match Fran Bryan's sketch to a specific spot along a particular river. The coordinates of the spot were quickly cabled to the station chief in Zaire.

By the time the coordinates arrived, the CIA's team was already well on its way into the jungle, headed for the area they believed the plane had crashed. As they passed near the other area, the one specified by the coordinates sent from headquarters, they noticed something very strange. Natives were emerging from the bush with strange pieces of metal—ragged parts of what appeared to be a downed aircraft. The jungle had already begun to digest its captured prey.

Shortly thereafter, the CIA's team found the main intact section of the downed plane. It was in the river Graff's office had indicated, within three miles of the given coordinates.

The wreckage was quickly brought out of Zaire, and information about the Soviet plane, and Soviet intelligence-gathering activities in Africa, began to flow into the knowledge banks of U.S. spy agencies. For the CIA, it was a nice, neat victory, and its director, Stansfield Turner, was pleased to inform President Carter of the successful recovery effort.

Yes, but how did you recover it so quickly? the President wanted to know.

Uncertain what the reaction would be, Turner mentioned the role the psychics had played. Carter didn't seem to mind at all. He knew about the SRI program from National Security Council staffer Jake Stewart, and Congressman Charlie Rose. He seemed to approve of the idea. Seventeen years later, still full of wonder over the Zaire incident, he would briefly recall it (with some erroneous details) to an audience of college students when asked about unusual events during his presidency.

Back in Menlo Park, Hal Puthoff was eventually shown a photograph of the wreckage site, and it was something that he too would never forget. The photo depicted a brown turbulent river and the jutting metal tail of the Soviet reconnaissance plane, so closely matched to Langford's first sketch that it was as if the remote viewer had been there before any of them, hovering like a ghost in the trees, quietly seeing what no mortal eye had yet seen.

The drought was over. The rains had come. By the time of the Zaire operation, SRI was receiving funds from half a dozen sources, including the DIA's Scientific and Technical Intelligence Directorate (known as DT), and Dale Graff's office out at Wright-Patterson. Soon General Thompson's remote-viewing unit at Fort Meade would join in.

But the rush of funders into the gap left by CIA had its downside. The lines of control were becoming tangled. The contract monitors from the different funding offices were starting to compete for influence over SRI researchers and remote viewers. Skip Atwater and Scotty Watt would travel out to SRI, and would be told peremptorily by, say, the DIA's contract monitor, Jim Salyer, that they couldn't see a particular person because that person just then was preoccupied with secret work for Salyer. It was the kind of interagency rivalry that often gave defense industry contractors headaches.

Eventually, an arrangement was made to reduce all the rivalry and the crossed signals. By the beginning of 1979 the funding and the work tasks were coordinated by the DIA, and the separate elements of the project became known by the collective code name Grill Flame. The integration of the project also provided attractive political cover for other agencies that might have been embarrassed to fund psychic spying directly. Atop this cover was a curly-haired former nuclear physicist, Jack Vorona, who headed the DIA's DT section. As one of the Pentagon's top scientists, Vorona was privy to some of the strangest, most secret research projects ever conceived. Grill Flame was just one. Another was code-named Sleeping Beauty; it was a Defense Department study of remote microwave mind-influencing techniques, spurred—as always—by fears that the Soviets were working on the same technology. Vorona was politically daring, but with a spreading network of support in the Pentagon and on Capitol Hill, he had the power to be daring. Ingo Swann would call him "the super god in the sky over us."

If Vorona was Grill Flame's super god in the sky, Pat Price was its Elvis. In one remote-viewing session at Fort Meade in the late 1970s, Skip Atwater targeted an unwitting Joe McMoneagle against Price, telling him only that the target was a person. McMoneagle, down in his zone, described a man who looked like Price in an underground location, secretly working for the government. A number of remote viewers came to believe that Price was indeed still alive. The rumor circulated that someone (Puthoff, according to one story, although he denies it) had actually encountered Price in the late 1970s, in a suburban Virginia shopping mall, and Price had walked quickly away, hiding his face. Ingo Swann might have been king of the hill now at SRI, but that hill was haunted.

Swann's territory at SRI took up much of the third floor of building 44, the Radio Physics building, where the more sensitive RV work was conducted. Along one corridor he had his windowless gray-cocoon remote-viewing chamber, with cameras and microphones and a table he had designed himself with special shelves underneath, where viewers could store paper and pens. To one side of the chamber was a monitoring room, also known as a "recovery room," where visitors could watch RV sessions on video screens, and where remote viewers could relax after their labors. The place had couches and chairs and tables, dictionaries and encyclopedias; it looked vaguely like a doctor's waiting room. On the opposite side of the RV chamber was Swann's office, cluttered with books and files and memoranda and magazine cuttings.

The budget for the program at SRI was now between $500,000 and $1 million per year (at least half went for SRI's "overhead" expenses), and about a dozen people were on the payroll. Russell Targ had his own small contract fiefdoms, and Puthoff had also hired a physicist and computer expert named Ed May, who formed a third locus of psi-related research. But Puthoff ran the overall program, was the only one briefed on the most sensitive operations, and served as a monitor for most operational RV sessions. The on-site government representative, DIA's Jim Salyer, was also trained as a monitor, and had his own office in a temporary trailer just outside the RV lab's building. When operational taskings came in, they came in through Salyer, usually by courier or by secure fax or telephone. He often played the role that Scotty Watt did at Fort Meade, interfacing with clients while Puthoff (like Skip Atwater) ran the remote viewers.

For operational tasks, especially when Ingo Swann was the viewer, there were "calibration" targets before and after the main session. The feedback on these practice targets was immediately available. Swann had the idea that he could roughly gauge, from his accuracy in the calibration sessions, what his accuracy had been in the operational session. Calibration targets were called Class C targets, operational targets were Class B, and pure practice targets Class A.

Class B targets were also known as "sexy" targets, but *sexy* was not always the most appropriate term. SRI's taskers were often people whose job it was to cover the strangest and potentially most horrible military technologies of the Cold War. During one session against a target inside the Soviet Union, Swann started describing a hallway inside a building. There were green tiles on the walls, and signs that appeared to be in Cyrillic. People wore hospital-type gowns. Swann decided it was a biological-weapons research facility. Another time he found himself in a forest in central Europe. A set of well-guarded buildings lay before him. It looked like a gulag-style prison camp. Swann went down into one of the buildings, and found more biological-weapons research going on, involving not only animals—dogs, pigs, monkeys—but also humans, prisoners taken from the camp. Swann was so distraught at all this that he began crying uncontrollably, and Puthoff had to end the session. Swann later went out and had a few drinks to steady his nerves. The dramatic description of the target was never confirmed by the Pentagon, and the presence of human subjects seems unlikely, but the description of the site did bear certain similarities to a biological research facility at Obolensk, in a pine forest south of Moscow—where, it was revealed years later, at least animals had been exposed to lethal germ agents.

Swann and others were targeted against biological research or production sites not only at Obolensk, but at Stepnogorsk, Berdsk, an island in the Aral Sea called Vozrozhdeniye, and the city of Sverdlovsk, where a military accident involving spores of the anthrax bacterium had killed hundreds of civilians in 1979. Although it may have had little to do with the data provided by remote viewers, the DIA and the CIA by the mid-1980s would assemble a lengthy list of these Soviet sites, each of which contravened a 1972 treaty banning research towards the offensive use of biological weapons.

The remote viewers at SRI—particularly Gary Langford—also contributed to a number of operations simultaneously tasked to the Army's remote viewers at Fort Meade. Langford's sketches and descriptions of the massive *Typhoon* submarine at Severodvinsk in 1979 substantially matched what Joe McMoneagle produced at Fort Meade, and helped convince Jake Stewart and others in the National Security Council to take the information seriously. Langford and Swann also remote-viewed the failed Chinese nuclear test that year; Langford accurately described an explosion but nothing nuclear—while Swann, alas, veered into a vivid but erroneous description of a premature nuclear blast that had killed thousands of Chinese scientists.

Langford, Swann, and the others targeted Soviet submarines while they were submerged and under way. Among other things, they were asked to spy on particular grooves in mountain ranges beneath the Atlantic, to find out whether Soviet "boomers"—ICBM-launching submarines—were hiding there. Swann and Langford were also asked to participate in the mysterious, urgent operation to recover a lost NATO nuclear weapon near Spain, around 1980.

* * *

One day early in 1979, Dale Graff at Wright-Patterson telephoned Hal Puthoff and told him about a possible opportunity that had arisen. The Air Force, he said, was backing a massive multibillion-dollar project. It was a project that depended entirely on security, but remote viewing was just the thing that might be able to defeat that security. If they could prove that, they might get some serious high-level attention. And RV might quickly be catapulted into the mainstream of intelligence-gathering technology.

The Air Force program involved a new intercontinental ballistic missile, known as MX. The plan was that the MX would be specially based, in such a way as to evade a nuclear Pearl Harbor, a Soviet "first strike" that would destroy the entire land-based U.S. missile force.

Older generations of land-based ICBMs in the United States had simply been based in silos dug into the ground and surrounded by yards of steel and concrete. If the Soviets sent a first strike, the old reasoning went, their missiles wouldn't be accurate enough to knock out all these hardened U.S. silos, and thus the United States would have a substantial "counterstrike" capability. But newer intelligence suggested that Soviet ICBMs were becoming much more accurate; American missiles based in fixed silos would soon be vulnerable to direct hits from a first strike. Air Force officials, who believed they had to plan for the worst possible scenario, began to argue that the United States needed a new missile, one mobile enough to evade a Soviet first strike, but not so mobile that it lost its own accuracy.*

By 1979 the Air Force was backing a kind of shell game scheme in which each MX missile would be shuttled along a special railroad corridor, roughly thirty miles long, with twenty-three "garages" along the way, spaced a mile and a

---

* Launching from a known, fixed site, for which the minute variations in gravity and other factors could be computed in advance, enabled Pentagon scientists to calculate a more exact trajectory for the warhead.

half apart. The MX's special covered carrier vehicle would constantly shuttle randomly from one garage to the other, inserting the missile in the garage, or seeming to do so. Soviet strike planners, to be sure of hitting the one missile along this track, would have to target all twenty-three garages, which in nuclear-war logic meant two first-strike warheads per garage, or forty-six Soviet warheads to kill one U.S. missile. And in all there would be 200 MX missiles, based on 200 of these linear shell game tracks, spread out in the deserts of Utah and Nevada, so the Soviets would have to use up at least 9,200 warheads just to be sure of wiping out the entire MX force. (And they would still have to deal somehow with American bomber- and submarine-based nuclear weapons.) This kind of math, the Air Force hoped, would deter the Soviets from making a first strike.

Aside from the enormous cost, and the huge political opposition from citizens in Utah and Nevada, the MX scheme seemed airtight. But the Air Force wanted to be sure. It had set up a team at Norton Air Force Base in California, tasked with finding if there was a way, however obscure, by which the Soviets might defeat the scheme.* Dale Graff suggested that Puthoff should brief the team at Norton about remote viewing.

Puthoff, it turned out, had just the experiment to brief them on. Charles Tart, a parapsychologist at the University of California at Davis, had recently done a mass psi-ability screening experiment, with funds from the SRI program. He had begun with a basic ESP-card test, screening 2,000 students, graduate students, and faculty for those who had high scores. After another round of screening with a com-

---

* One possibility the Norton team investigated had to do with cockroaches. Knowing that cockroaches might be attracted to some of the materials present in a missile, and might therefore migrate toward the garage holding an MX, the Norton team looked into possible schemes for tracking the movements of cockroaches from overhead satellites.

puter ESP test, Tart isolated the ten best subjects, and ran them through a lengthy, final experiment.

This final experiment essentially involved a computer simulation of a shell game, with ten shells to choose from. For each run the computer randomly rearranged the apparent order of the shells (keeping track of which shell was which), and the subject had to guess which one held the marble. After a number of guesses for the same (constantly rearranged) set of shells, it was hoped, a single shell number would emerge from the statistical noise as the one the subject had chosen most often—and therefore the one most likely to harbor the marble. It was an error-correction strategy, like those used by Czech and Soviet parapsychologists since the 1960s. It essentially took whatever statistical advantage had been bestowed by psi, and amplified it. Tart gave each subject twenty-five guesses per run.

If pure, random chance had been the only thing at work, then each subject would have guessed the correct shell only about 10 percent of the time. There would be no benefit from error correction, because there would be no statistical advantage to amplify. No matter how many runs and rearrangements were performed, the accuracy rate would always average out to 10 percent.

It turned out that Tart's best performer, a woman named Mary Long, was much better than chance would have predicted. For any given one-out-of-ten guess, she had not a 10 percent chance of being right but a *25* percent chance of being right. With his error-correction strategy, Tart was easily able to boost that advantage. Analyzing Mary Long's twenty-five guesses per run, he was able to determine the shell that held the marble each time, for twenty separate shell-game runs in a row. The odds against such a result happening by chance were absurdly large.

Puthoff took Tart's results and wrote them up in a lengthy report, redoing the math to fit the MX problem. He calculated that at Mary Long's average hit rate, she would

find the hidden MX—with an accuracy of 80 percent—
within only fifty guesses. In other words, it would take
Mary Long, or a small team of remote viewers as good as
she, only a few hours to defeat a scheme on which the
Pentagon was willing to spend many billions of taxpayers'
dollars.

At Norton Air Force Base there was a certain amount of
unease over Puthoff's report, and it was forwarded to the
MX project office at the Pentagon. But the Air Force, which
jealously guarded the MX shell-game scheme, seemed to
ignore the remote-viewing report. Still, Puthoff wasn't
ready to give up. With help from Dale Graff, he decided to
go around the Air Force, and briefed the MX results to Jake
Stewart at the National Security Council, who then circulated the report to other Carter administration officials.

Some officials simply refused to accept the idea that
psychics could have an impact in such weighty strategic
matters. Others were more impressed, though in the end,
the SRI report probably did not have a major influence on
the ultimate MX decision, which was left by President
Carter to his successor, Ronald Reagan.*

Even so, the remote-viewing proponents had left their
mark. Unfortunately, instead of attracting sympathy and
funding to the RV program, they had incurred the wrath of
the Air Force brass. In 1980, Dale Graff applied for and
won a fellowship for "exceptional analysts" within the intelligence community. The fellowship normally enabled a
recipient to spend two years conducting sabbatical-type research in other laboratories. Graff planned to spend the

---

* In 1983 Reagan decided to abandon the Air Force's shell-game scheme,
probably for budgetary and political reasons more than anything else. He
obtained funding from Congress for one hundred MX "Peacekeeper" missiles, and fifty were eventually built. Although the Bush administration
later considered basing the missiles in special rail cars on railroads around
the western United States, the missiles ended up in old, fixed Minuteman
ICBM silos at Warren AFB in Wyoming and Colorado.

two years at four labs: SRI in California, a psychokinesis-oriented research laboratory at Princeton University, a J. B. Rhine–affiliated psi lab in Durham, North Carolina, and even a Department of Energy lab where microwave weapons technologies were being studied. Graff was about to get on a plane to Washington, for the award ceremonies at CIA headquarters, when he received a phone call. He was told that he would not be receiving the fellowship, and would not be spending two years visiting psi laboratories. The office of the Air Force Chief of Staff had taken the apparently unprecedented step of revoking Graff's award.

Graff's career at Wright-Patterson was now clearly over. Fortunately he could turn to Jack Vorona, the super god in the sky. With Vorona's encouragement, he soon resigned from Wright-Pat, shook the dust of the Air Force from his feet, and joined Vorona's group at the DIA.

▲ Hal Puthoff, as a naval officer working at the National Security Agency in the early 1960s.

▲ Ingo Swann, who was Puthoff's first test subject.

▲ CIA scientist Sidney Gottlieb. His Technical Services Division gave Puthoff a $50,000 contract in late 1972. [AP/Wide World]

▲ Russell Targ and Hal Puthoff at SRI.

▲ Uri Geller, who perplexed SRI and CIA officials during 1972–74. [Geller Enterprises]

CIA scientist Richard Kennett (*l*) posing with Pat Price and Hal Puthoff, after a successful glider-to-ground remote-viewing experiment near Menlo Park. Smiles (and plaid trousers) all round.

Satellite dishes at the Pentagon/NSA facility near Sugar Grove, West Virginia, as it looks today. The underground facility described by SRI remote viewers is nearby.

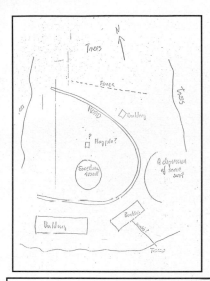

Weather at this time is cloudy, rainy. Temperature at my altitude about 54° - high cumulo nimbus clouds to about 25,000-30,000'. Clear area, but turbulent, between that level and some cirro stratus at 46,000' Air mass in that strip moving W.N.W. to S.E.

1318 - Perceived that peak area has large underground storage areas. Road comes up back side of mountains (west slopes), fairly well concealed, looks deliberately so. It's cut under trees where possible- would be very hard to detect flying over area. Looks like former missile site-bases for launchers still there, but area now houses record storage area, microfilm, file cabinets; as you go into underground area through aluminum rolled up doors, first areas filled with records, etc. Rooms about 100' long, 40' wide, 20' ceilings with concrete supporting pilasters, flare-shaped. Temperature cool- fluorescent lighted. Personnel, Army 5th Corps engineers. M/Sgt. Long on desk placard on grey steel desk-file cabinets security locked- combination locks, steel rods through eye bolts. Beyond these rooms, heading east, are several bays with computers, communication equipment, large maps, display type, overlays. Personnel, Army Signal Corps. Elevators.

"Top of desk had papers labeled:

    Flytrap

    Minerva

File cabinet on north wall labeled:

    Operation Pool ;-- (2nd word unreadable)

Folders inside cabinet labeled:

    Cueball

    14 Ball

    4 Ball

    8 Ball

    Backup

Some of the data generated by Ingo Swann and Pat Price on the Sugar Grove site in June 1973. They were accurate enough for the Pentagon to launch a security investigation. [CIA]

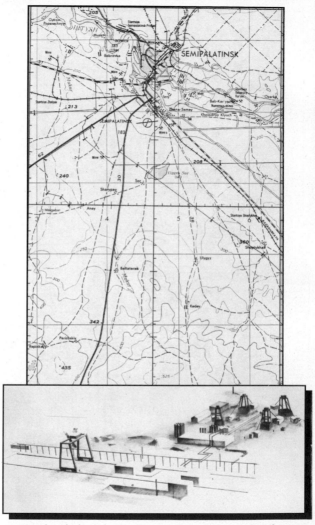

A CIA sketch, based on a spy satellite photograph, of a secret Soviet R&D facility south of Semipalatinsk. CIA officials brought the coordinates of this target to Pat Price at SRI in June 1974, and asked him to remote-view it. [map: DOD; sketch: CIA]

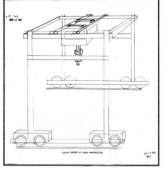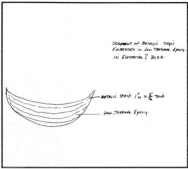

Price's lengthy description of the Semipalatinsk target included a sketch of an eight-wheeled crane (*l*) which closely matched the crane at the site. Price also described welding work on large steel spheres (*r*). The CIA didn't know about the spheres at the time, but later confirmed their existence with spy-satellite images. [CIA]

John McMahon, chief of the CIA's Office of Technical Service during 1974–76, and later the agency's deputy director. McMahon was a major supporter of the RV program, and kept an open mind about psi in general. At a party in 1983, he appeared to bend a spoon using psychokinesis. [Ronald Reagan Library]

"Norm Everheart," a technical operations specialist who was one of McMahon's key lieutenants. "Everheart" fed intelligence taskings to Pat Price during 1974–75, and later to the remote viewers at Fort Meade.

Dale Graff (*top r*) asked remote viewers to find a downed Soviet Tu-22 "Blinder" bomber (*top l*) in the jungles of Zaire. [Graff: ABC *Nightline*; Tu-22: DOD]

President Carter with (*l* to *r*) National Security Adviser Zbigniew Brzezinski, Vice President Walter Mondale, and CIA Director Stansfield Turner. Turner briefed an amazed Carter on the participation of remote viewers in the successful Tu-22 recovery. [White House]

▶ National Security Council aide Jake Stewart, who had direct access to President Carter and other top officials. Stewart telephoned SRI with a special task in July 1980. He needed a remote viewer to describe the whereabouts and mental state of a certain person of interest to the NSC. [U.S. Navy]

◀ Stewart's task was given to remote viewer Keith Harary (*l*). Harary described a thin, bearded man with a disabling neurological illness who was about to travel somewhere by plane. [Fortean Picture Library]

▲ The target was American hostage Richard Queen (*r*), then held by Islamic militants in Iran. Queen, who suffered from multiple sclerosis, was unexpectedly put on a plane by the Iranians two days later. Queen is shown here at a White House reception for the returned hostages in February 1981. [Ronald Reagan Library]

Buildings 2561 (*l*) and 2560 (*r*), where the Fort Meade remote-viewing unit was based from 1978 to 1995.

▼ An INSCOM memo from 1981 recounts some of the unit's early bureaucratic history. [U.S. Army]

Formalization of Project GRILL FLAME   IAOPS-H-P   10 Sep 1981
    DCG-I approve and sign proposed LOI implementing
first phase of assigning Project GRILL FLAME to USAOG   CPT Rittenburg/677-7807

ORIGIN OF ACTION: (U) ACSI orally tasked HQ INSCOM to evaluate Project GRILL FLAME in Oct
78. ADCSOPS-HUMINT established an ad hoc team, drawing personnel from in-house and
from other INSCOM elements in the Wash, D.C. and Fort Meade areas. Based on preliminary results and high level interest, INSCOM requested additional funds and 16 manpower
spaces in the HUMINT (PE 381321) GDIP input to the FY 82-86 and FY 83-87 POM's. These
resources were identified as being required to conduct GRILL FLAME operations on a continuing basis. Latest DA PBG authorized 5 spaces (2 civ, 2 off, and 1 EM) for INSCOM
as result of favorable Congressional action on the FY 82 Budget and Amendment, thereto.
Seven additional spaces (2 civ and 5 off) are included in the FY 83 PMRP and stand a
good chance of being approved. ACSI message of 11 Feb 81 (TAB A) formally transferred
GRILL FLAME Program management responsibility to INSCOM.

DISCUSSION:
    (U)
    a. The approved spaces are in the operational Overt HUMINT PE. They can not be
assigned to HQ INSCOM, an AMHA account. USAOG is the Overt HUMINT operational element
in CONUS and is the most suitable unit to eventually conduct the activity. However,
the limited manpower approved to date is insufficient to accomplish the mission. In
order to continue operations at the current level, personnel augmentation by outside
elements must continue, at least until receipt of the additional seven spaces (total
of 12) in FY 83.
    (U)
    b. USAOG has submitted TDA changes (TAB B) which will create an element, Det G,
                                                                    (See reverse)

DCSRM
USAOG   11Sep81
ADCSOPS-HUMINT

REGRADED UNCLASSIFIED
ON   6 Dec 95
BY CDR USAINSCOM F01/PO
AUTH Para 1-603 DOD 5200 1R

CHARLES F. SCANLON, COL, GS, DCSOPS
for   GARRETT
                SECRET NOFORN

REGRADED UNCLASSIFIED
WHEN SEPARATED FROM
CLASSIFIED ENCLOSURES

Major General Ed Thompson, Army Assistant Chief of Staff for Intelligence, 1977–81, and a key figure in the establishment of the Fort Meade unit. [U.S. Army]

INSCOM officer Skip Atwater, who first suggested the RV unit, and served as its operations officer from 1978 until his retirement in 1987.

Mel Riley, at Fort Meade, getting his sergeant first class stripes from Lieutenant Colonel Scotty Watt (*l*, in civilian clothes), and (*r*) Colonel Robert Keenan, the head of SED. [U.S. Army]

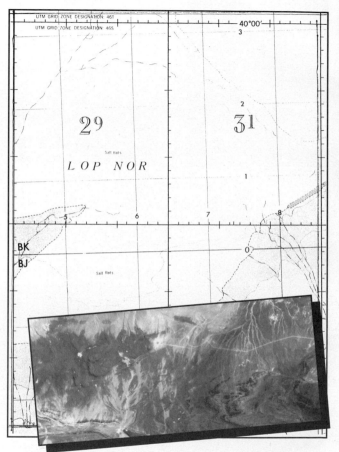

Chinese nuclear testing range at Lop Nor. In the summer of 1979, remote viewers at Fort Meade and SRI described a failed nuclear test here. [DOD map, CIA photo]

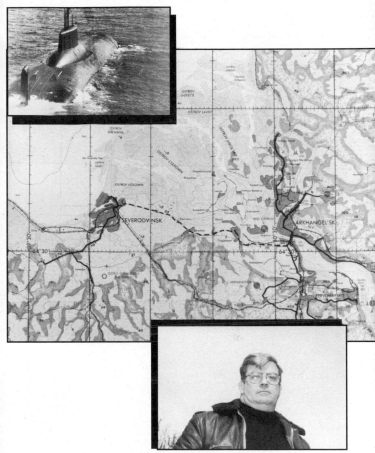

Fort Meade remote viewer Joe McMoneagle (*r*) peeked inside a building at Severodvinsk shipyard in 1979, and saw something the U.S. intelligence community had never seen before: a new Soviet "Typhoon"-class submarine, the largest in the world. [map, sub: DOD]

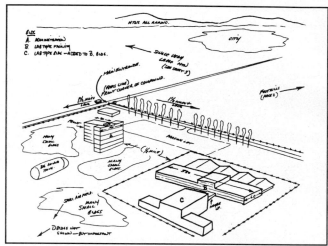

A sketch drawn by Joe McMoneagle in a remote-viewing session. Unknown to him, the target was Lawrence Livermore Laboratory. The sketch, which is generally accurate, shows the kind of detail that can be produced by some remote viewers. [DOD]

The Monroe Institute, in Virginia's Blue Ridge Mountains, where remote viewers and other INSCOM officers experimented with altered states.

▲ Major General Albert Stubblebine, INSCOM commander and paranormal enthusiast. [U.S. Army]

▲ Colonel John Alexander, holding a fork that a fellow officer apparently bent by psychokinesis at an INSCOM gathering in 1983. [Channel Four TV]

► Ed Dames, who joined the RV unit in 1983, and was trained by Ingo Swann.

◄ Remote viewer Paul Smith, one of Dame's classmates.

► Lyn Buchanan, hand-picked by General Stubblebine for his supposed skills at psychokinesis.

 Major General William Odom, who clashed with Stubblebine and eventually helped to force his resignation. [U.S. Army]

▼ The end of Stubblebine's reign at INSCOM was marked by memos like this one, curtailing the use of Monroe Institute "Hemi-Sync" tapes.

DEPARTMENT OF THE ARMY
UNITED STATES ARMY INTELLIGENCE AND SECURITY COMMAND
ARLINGTON HALL STATION
ARLINGTON, VIRGINIA 22212

REPLY TO
ATTENTION OF

IACS

6 JUL 1984

SUBJECT: Guidance Regarding Use of Hemi-Sync Tapes

SEE DISTRIBUTION

1. Reference:

a. Letter, IASJA, this Headquarters, dated 17 January 1984, Subject: High Performance Task Force Report (HPTF) Risk Assessment.

b. USAINSCOM Regulation 15-3, High Performance Review Procedures, dated 24 February 1984.

c. Message, IASP, this Headquarters (Fort Meade), DTG 270100Z APR 84, Subject: Discontinuation of Hemi-Sync Tapes.

2. Reference 1a directed that, pending further review of the potential risks involved in hemi-sync processes, the use of hemi-sync within the command be limited to those uses then ongoing and sponsored by CENTEX or the Staff Psychologist. Reference 1b established an INSCOM review process which resulted in subsequent review of several aspects of the hemi-sync technology by the INSCOM Human Technology Review Board (HTRB). Reference 1c advised addressees to cease further utilization of hemi-sync Catnapper and Sound Sleeper tapes until the protocol for their use had been reviewed and approved by the HTRB.

3. In addition to the above referenced hemi-sync experiences, some members of the INSCOM have participated in a hemi-sync workshop known as the "RAPT Program" at the Monroe Institute of Applied Sciences. Other persons have made private purchases of hemi-sync tapes and have attended hemi-sync workshops in a non-INSCOM sponsored capacity.

4. This letter is intended to provide INSCOM command and policy guidance as discussed in references 1a and 1c, and the command's policy position with respect to RAPT Program participation and non-sponsored activities involving hemi-sync.

5. Evidence to date regarding the efficacy of the hemi-sync process has not been sufficient, for a variety of reasons, to lend scientifically acceptable credence to proponency claims of human benefits. This is not to imply that the technology is without merit, rather it is to suggest that while testimonial-type comments may be favorable, medical claims and effects are not supported by scientifically acceptable studies. In this regard, a recent report issued by the Army Science Board, Ad Hoc Subgroup on Emerging Human Technologies, concluded with respect to hemi-sync that a "number of unanswered questions remain that require scientifically validated results."

▶ Major General Harry Soyster, an Odom ally and an opponent of the remote-viewing program. He succeeded Stubblebine as head of INSCOM, and kicked the remote viewers out. They landed safely at the DIA, but a few years later, they were doomed again when Soyster received a third star and became DIA's chief. [U.S. Army]

Other opponents of the remote-viewing unit included the CIA's Bob Gates (*far l*), and Defense Secretary Frank Carlucci (*next to Reagan*) who unleashed his inspector general on the Fort Meade remote viewers in 1988. [Ronald Reagan Library] But with the help of five powerful senators (*below*), the RV program managed to stay alive until the mid-1990s.

Robert Byrd (D-W.Va.)

Daniel Inouye (D-Hawaii)

John Glenn (D-Ohio)

William Cohen (R-Maine)

Ted Stevens (R-Alaska)

Ed Dames, on Rodeo Drive in Beverly Hills. [Channel Four TV]

Skip Atwater, on the job at the Monroe Institute.

Mel Riley, taking it easy in Wisconsin.

16

AOL

During a fever after another childhood illness, the boy [Nabokov] experienced a rush of clairvoyance: in bed, he saw his mother taking a sleigh to the Nevsky and watched her enter a store to buy a pencil that was then wrapped and taken out to the sleigh by the footman. He could not understand why she did not carry something as small as a pencil herself—until she stepped out of his vision and through his bedroom door, bearing a four-foot-long Faber display pencil she thought he might have coveted.

—Brian Boyd, *Vladimir Nabokov: The Russian Years*

By the close of the Carter administration the SRI program was reaching its peak. Operational targets flowed in, remote-viewing data flowed out, and operations-oriented experiments continued.

These experiments were by now increasingly esoteric. There were tests to see how accurately remote viewers could pinpoint events in time. Ingo Swann, for example, was once given the coordinates of a facility at a U.S. Air Force base, and was told that a rocket motor would be test-fired at the facility sometime during a particular half-hour period. His job was to determine when the event began.

"Wow!" he said at one point, sitting up in his chair in

the remote-viewing room. "I think it happened a few seconds ago." He was right. A similar test was run against a planned underground nuclear explosion at a U.S. government facility in Nevada. Swann's job in this case was to determine if the test had occurred at all, in a given time window. The blast happened, and Swann detected it.

There were studies of precognitive remote viewing, in which the chances of a given target's being selected by a computer were varied. Thus target one might have a 67 percent chance of being selected, and target two, 33 percent—or target one, 99 percent and target two, 1 percent. Puthoff and his colleagues wanted to know whether a remote viewer would be equally good at precognizing each target or whether the rarer targets—like unexpected events in real life—would be harder to foresee even with psi. (The data suggested that remote viewers tended to see the *probable* future rather than the actual future; perhaps this explained why lottery numbers and other low-probability targets were so hard to precognize.)

There were long-distance outbound remote-viewing experiments, spanning thousands of miles. There were simulations in which remote viewers tried to find kidnap victims or bombs hidden by terrorists. Much work was done against technical targets—nuclear power plants, aircraft-manufacturing facilities, and so forth—to tune the remote viewers' minds to the subtleties of military technologies.

The remote viewers' minds themselves were the subjects of study. As in the early days of the CIA-sponsored research, the viewers were given numerous standard and experimental personality tests that analyzed their thinking habits, their mood ranges and belief systems, their responses to stress, and other variables. They were given neurological tests, were wired to electroencephalographs, and even travelled to Los Alamos National Laboratory for deep brain-wave scans with superconducting *magneto*encephalographs. Puthoff and his government clients sought the region of the brain where psi functioning originated. The temporal lobes seemed to be involved, but as with so much of neuroscience, it was hard to penetrate the mystery much further.

There were tests of Joe McMoneagle's out-of-body experiences, in which the Army remote viewer was asked to lie down and travel astrally along a hallway and into a locked room, later to describe the target Puthoff had placed there. Puthoff had to give McMoneagle directions to the target room beforehand, so his astral body wouldn't lose its way.

During one remote-viewing experiment with McMoneagle, a computer near the viewing room suddenly crashed. McMoneagle was asked to try to crash the computer again deliberately. Unfortunately most of his psychokinetic successes (if they were not coincidences) were inadvertent. But Puthoff and Targ would obliquely refer to such incidents in a paper they presented at an American Association for the Advancement of Science meeting in 1979, noting the existence of "low-level perturbation of equipment observable during remote-viewing."

In the early 1980s there was even a study of the possible connection between remote-viewing success and the state of the Earth's magnetic field. This all began after Puthoff read a paper by Michael Persinger, an experimental psychologist at Laurentian University in Ontario.

Persinger, following Russian researchers like Kogan and Vasiliev, suspected that psi was at least mediated by extremely-low-frequency (ELF) electromagnetic radiation. In one of his forays in search of evidence for this, he had collected from the parapsychological literature the dates of hundreds of reported spontaneous ESP experiences. Then he had tried to find correlations between these data and several other variables, including the activity of the Earth's magnetic field, which was known to fluctuate from day to day. He came up with a moderate correlation showing that

ESP experiences tended to happen more often on days of quiet magnetic activity; this suggested in turn that intense magnetic storms could somehow interfere with psi. Persinger's finding seemed to support the ELF theory since magnetic "noise" in the atmosphere, in the ELF range, would naturally make it more difficult for psi-type ELF signals to be detected and processed by a remote viewer's brain. It would be like trying to listen to a weak AM radio station during a thunderstorm.

On the other hand, as Puthoff and others who disagreed with the ELF theory reasoned, magnetic noise in the atmosphere might interfere with psi in some other way, perhaps by causing subtle changes in remote viewers' brains, making it more difficult for them to access their psi function and perhaps other more prosaic functions as well.

In any case, Puthoff and his colleagues decided to investigate the magnetic field link themselves. If geomagnetic storms interfered with psi, for whatever reason, then they should be taken into account, especially for operational remote viewing. Puthoff ended up building his own geomagnetic field meter, with the help of a former Stanford University researcher, Marcia Adams, who had done similar work building low-frequency receivers for the Army. The literature suggested, oddly enough, that trees made very good and obviously very cheap ELF antennas, so Puthoff and Adams hooked a small ELF signal amplifier to a big oak tree outside their building at SRI and then ran the receiver output into a computer, which produced ELF field readings every minute.

In the end they found, as Persinger had, a correlation between low geomagnetic activity in the ELF range and successful psi experiments. But though parapsychologists would become considerably excited by such geomagnetic data over the next decade, Puthoff considered it too small a correlation to bother about, and neither proton showers nor X-ray flares nor full-blown geomagnetic storms kept

SRI's psychics from their appointed rounds through time and space.

As it had been almost from the beginning, a separate category of experimentation at SRI was reserved for the attempted replication of Soviet, East European, and Chinese research. In 1982 Puthoff heard about an odd Chinese experiment that worked as follows: A series of Chinese characters written on rice paper was placed on top of a strip of highly sensitive film. Electro-optical detectors were also focussed on the characters and the film, to independently detect any bursts of light. The entire apparatus was sealed inside a light-tight box. Then a psychic (or an "EHBF subject," since some Chinese researchers termed psi an "extraordinary human biological function") was asked to remote-view the characters on the rice paper inside the box. When the psychic began to remote-view, the Chinese experimenters claimed, the detectors inside the box began to register substantial light pulses in visible and infrared frequencies, while the sensitive film, when taken out and developed, was exposed in the shape of the Chinese characters—but only for those characters that the psychic had correctly remote-viewed!

This connection between remote viewing and remote physical effects was an attractive idea for Puthoff. In the very first psi experiment he had run while at SRI, he had asked Ingo Swann to affect the output of the Stanford magnetometer, and Swann had seemed to do so only when he was trying to remote-view its insides. Then there had been the computer crashes during RV experiments with McMoneagle.

Puthoff and his colleagues tried their best to replicate what the Chinese said they had done. Using double-blind procedures, they placed randomly selected photographic transparencies of target sites in front of a sensitive photomultiplier tube, then asked remote viewers to try to visualize the sites from another room. Calculating the accuracy and reliability of the remote-viewing sessions, they then tried to find correlations between these and any light pulses recorded by the photomultiplier. They did find a significant correlation, but unfortunately it was much weaker than what the Chinese had found, and they noted that the photomultiplier recorded transient pulses all the time, regardless of whether a remote viewer was operating nearby. The results, in short, didn't seem to justify further experimentation along these lines.

Ingo Swann kept himself apart from most of these experiments, believing that his own work was the most urgent and important. He saw as his primary task the development of a more accurate and reliable remote-viewing technique. Jack Vorona and General Ed Thompson and others in the intelligence community were already impressed by what remote viewing seemed able to accomplish, but they saw much room for improvement.

It had long been clear to everyone involved in the program that the main problem with remote viewing—really, the main problem with all forms of extrasensory perception—was a signal-to-noise problem. The "signal," meaning accurate target-related information, was too sparse, too weak, and too inconsistent. The "noise," meaning imagination and whatever else was *un*related to the target, was too great. It really was like listening to a weak AM radio in the middle of a thunderstorm, except that with remote viewing, the distortions of the signal were even worse. Hal Puthoff had calculated in the late 1970s that on average only about two-thirds of ordinary remote-viewing data—whether coordinate remote viewing, extended remote viewing, or outbound RV—were clearly and usefully related to the target. The rest could be considered noise. Others found those figures optimistic. On occasion, of course, a remote-viewing session unrolled with breathtaking clarity and accuracy. But one knew this only in hindsight. Even with the use of calibration sessions fore and aft of an operational session, it was difficult to know how much, if any, of a viewer's data could be trusted.*

To remedy this, it was thought, one had either to boost the psi signal or to reduce the noise. One could, for example, run different viewers against the same target, until the consistencies in their data—presumably the signal—stood clearly above the inconsistent "noise." One also could try to tap more directly into the signal, by having the remote viewer descend into a deep altered state, or by using "autonomic," subconscious-driven sketches of targets rather than verbal reports.

Some experimenters tried to boost the signal at an even deeper level. Anecdotal reports suggested that ESP often worked better when the target was a living thing that was undergoing some kind of dramatic, stressful event. Tales of the mother who clairvoyantly sees her son's death in battle were practically a cliché within the parapsychological lore. Soviet researchers took this logic to its experimental extreme, by inflicting fatal trauma on baby rabbits and other small animals, and then looking for a psi response in the brains of their mothers.

Other techniques focussed on reducing the noise—for example, the visualization ritual that many of the Fort Meade viewers used, in which they imagined locking up all their cares in suitcases. The Soviets apparently also experimented with drugs or other altered-state techniques in an effort to quiet the non-psi activities of the brain.

---

* The remote viewers at Fort Meade considered calibration sessions worthless. They noted the wide variations in accuracy that seemed to occur from one target to the next, the disabling fatigue that a pre-operational calibration session could bring about, and the fact that the prospect of an "operational" sexy target could boost (or lower) performance unpredictably.

By the late 1970s Swann had decided that he wanted to pursue neither the signal-boost nor the noise-reduction approach, at least not in their usual forms. What he wanted to do instead, first and foremost, was to teach the viewer how to *distinguish*, consciously, between signal and noise.

One could usually organize the information generated in a remote-viewing session along a spectrum with two extremes. At one extreme was what one might call "raw" data, in the form of very rough, unlabeled sketches of the target site, and basic, disconnected verbal descriptions such as "dry," "steep," "sharp," "low throbbing sound," and so on. At the other end lay more analytical, inductive, information-packed data, such as detailed drawings of target objects and precise verbal descriptions: "tennis court," "nuclear reactor," "looks like it could be Hoover Tower."

Puthoff's wife, Adrienne, a schoolteacher who was well read in the psychology of learning, had examined some of the remote-viewing data her husband had been bringing home since the early 1970s. She had noted that the more complex and analytical data, though they occasionally amounted to an exact description of the target, were more often simply wrong. Richard Bach's description of a Methodist church as an airline ticket counter and a gold cross on the wall as "the logo of the company . . . like a big gold fleur-de-lis" was a classic example. In fact, users of remote-viewing data, such as the CIA's Norm Everheart, had already learned to treat the remote viewers' *own* analyses of their data with considerable skepticism.

It eventually became clear that others who had experimented with RV-type extrasensory perception in the past had noticed its proneness to this type of error. A good example was the writer Upton Sinclair, a part-time psi enthusiast who had experimented in the 1920s with his wife, Mary Craig Sinclair, and other apparently talented psychics. In his book *Mental Radio,* Sinclair noted of "Craig":

Frequently she will make a good drawing of an object, but name it badly. . . . I drew a hoe [as a target], and she got the shape of it, but wrote: "May be scissors, may be spectacles with long stems to ears."

Also in the same series [were] reindeer horns, which she calls "holly leaves." It is psychologically interesting to note that reindeers and holly leaves were both associated with Christmas in Craig's childhood.

To Puthoff's wife, Adrienne, such observations were indeed psychologically interesting. She knew that the left cortex of the brain, very roughly speaking, tends to specialize in verbal, mathematical, and analytical data. It therefore seemed clear to her that remote viewing, which was seldom accurate or complete for alphanumeric or analytical information, primarily involved other, more primitive parts of the brain, such as those that specialize in visual, spatial, and basic sensory data.

Neuroscientists and psychologists whom Hal Puthoff consulted on the RV program backed up this observation. To them, a persistent failure to recognize alphanumeric data, and an inability to put accurate labels on drawings that were otherwise correct, were typical characteristics of patients with left-hemispheric damage—i.e., those who were forced, like remote viewers, into using other parts of their brains.*

But there was another aspect to all this. When a remote viewer mis-described a target—for example, as "a holly tree" when it was actually a pair of antlers—there was often something meaningful about the error. "Holly tree" and "antler" both were linked not only by their overall tree-like

---

* Remote viewers, like left-brain–damaged patients, also tended to make mistakes about "right" and "left." The sketches and diagrams they drew were sometimes mirror images of the correct targets.

form—their Gestalt, as Swann called it*—but also by their conceptual connection to Christmas. It was as if the psi data drifting up from somewhere in the remote viewer's brain were so sketchy that only the most basic perceptions and associations could be drawn from it. Mary Craig Sinclair's brain, straining to come up with a match between incomplete data (tree-like, Christmas-related) and objects stored in memory, had settled on "holly tree." It was close, but not close enough.

Swann and Puthoff incorporated these ideas into their evolving theory of remote viewing. As Swann put it in an internal SRI memorandum around this time, "It seems reasonable to assume that we are dealing with automatic analytical functions of some sort, and that, hypothetically, these are the source of the diluted or erroneous response." In other words, the associations generated by the brain in its attempt to make sense of the trickle of remote-viewing data constituted some, if not all, of the "noise." Swann, a great lover of neologisms, termed this noise analytical overlay—Aol for short—and set out to find ways of identifying it during a session. If he succeeded, then most, if not all, noisy data could simply be labeled as such, marked with the symbol *Aol* and treated accordingly.

Puthoff was confident that this was the right approach, and he even included a short essay by Swann in a then-classified report to his CIA sponsors in 1975. The essay read in part: "Enough data about this [signal-to-noise] difficulty has been gathered to establish that it is not necessarily a perceptual problem but in all probability [is] a process problem concerned with converting the signal of the psi-field matrix into a correct analytical sequence. . . . [C]ould the process difficulties be resolved, then the analyt-

---

* *Gestalt,* from a German word for "form," was a psychological term defined as a "perceived organized whole that is greater than the sum of its parts."

ical overlay would convert into a positive adjunct of the conversion process, rather than working against it." It was an example of the difficult, academic-sounding prose for which Swann would become known, but the process he had in mind was essentially simple. He would structure remote-viewing sessions in such a way that more analytical information would be ignored at the beginning, when it was most likely to be wrong, but would be taken into account later, when it was more likely to be right. In other words, he would teach the brain the correct way to process psi.

Around this time Hal Puthoff went to a parapsychology conference and listened to a paper read by a young British graduate student named Serena Roney-Dougal. Roney-Dougal's thesis adviser was a well-known psychologist, Norman Dixon, who had written a recent book on the phenomenon of subliminal perception. Roney-Dougal argued in her paper that ESP was a bit like subliminal perception. Puthoff recognized this as a major insight, and brought it back to SRI with him.

Subliminal perception was so called because it described perception that took place below ("sub-") the "limen," the lower threshold of consciousness. All mental activities—the remembering of a face, the tasting of chocolate, the hearing of distant thunder, the fearing of tomorrow—had to have a certain strength and duration to rise above the liminal threshold and produce a conscious perception. Those that fell below tended to manifest in less direct ways. For example, if a young man were given a fraction of a second exposure to a photograph of a beautiful nude woman, he might have no conscious understanding of what he had seen, yet at the same time, according to biomedical measurements, he might display various unambiguous signs of sexual arousal. Another example is probably more familiar: If a subject were shown a subliminally brief film clip of a person drinking a bottle of Coke, she might suddenly experience—not knowing why—an urge to get something to drink. Concerns over the use of these techniques by advertisers, for example within films at the cinema, led to a brief public scare over "subliminal seduction" in the mid-1970s.

In any case, Puthoff and Swann and the others at SRI began to notice now that remote-viewing data resembled the kinds of data generated by test subjects who had been exposed to subliminal stimuli. They did freehand, autonomous sketches that they often were unable to label accurately. They reported very rough sense perceptions and emotions such as "red" or "makes me sad." They gave out error-prone high-level descriptions—"like a gold fleur-de-lis"—as their minds desperately tried to make analytical sense of the subliminally faint stimulus.

It became clear to Puthoff and the others that remote viewing was largely a form of subliminal perception. How psi information came into the brain in the first place was still unknown, but it seemed to come in tenuously, in fragments, as if the remote viewer were continually being transported to his target, alighting there for the briefest of moments, and then being hauled back again. It began to seem that the remote-viewing faculty was like any other sensory faculty—taste, smell, touch, sight, hearing—only much, much weaker, unable in ordinary circumstances to make it across the liminal threshold. This implied that, short of some revolution in our understanding of the mind and our ability to manipulate it, remote-viewing perception would *always* be extremely noise-prone for most people. There was really no way to get rid of the noise; one could only try to recognize it and separate it from the signal. And that was precisely what Ingo Swann hoped to do.

Puthoff and Swann eventually showed some of their remote-viewing data to Norman Dixon, and he was so impressed by the apparent link between RV and subliminal perception that he wrote a short paper on the subject for a parapsychology journal, a paper that, of course, his colleagues in academic psychology ignored completely.

By 1980 Swann had begun to develop a remote-viewing technique that would separate the psi signal from noisy analytical overlay. His major insight here was to notice that when analytical overlay appeared in a remote-viewing session, it almost always did so in the form of "like a . . ." or "it seems to be a . . ." or "it reminds me of a. . . ." Any such qualifier, especially "like," became to Swann a cue that analytical overlay was about to follow. In his own sessions, he began to label all such information "Aol," afterwards immediately putting his pen down and trying to clear the presumably erroneous data from his mind. Later, in the analysis of the session, the Aol-labeled data—if it had appeared relatively early in the session—would be ignored or treated as having, at best, some kind of weak Gestalt-level association with the target.

But if the Aol data had appeared relatively late in the session, Swann might not discard them so easily. He believed that Aol data, if the session was handled properly, tended to converge on the target as the session wore on, just as a person's analysis of a subliminal stimulus grew clearer the longer the person was exposed to the stimulus.

If the target was, say, one of the great pyramids in Egypt, initial Aols, like "skyscraper," might be unhelpful. But later Aols, Swann believed, would tend to be more helpful: "like a tomb," "like a tent," "reminds me of the Nile." It became clear to Swann that remote viewers should postpone the more information-rich Aol-type data until the end of the session and should start the session by accepting only the more raw and basic data. Swann later spoke of the psi signal, or the "signal line," as a flow of information through an "aperture." At the outset, the aperture was tiny and the flow was merely a trickle, but as the session wore on, the aperture widened and the trickle grew to a flood.

Remote viewing, in other words, had a natural structure. The artist from New York therefore increasingly saw himself as a psychological engineer, charged with designing a technique that would keep remote viewers rigidly within that structure. In the terminology he later deployed for his training course, a remote viewer could stay "on the signal line" only if he stayed "in structure."

The very start of this structure Swann had no desire to change. He liked the discipline in which the viewer sat down, wrote his name on the paper, and waited silently, pen poised, for coordinates to be read. (Swann focussed his attention only on the coordinate technique he had devised.)

But what should the viewer do when he wrote down the coordinates? Should he begin by trying to focus on rough sense data, such as "smell of grass," or "green," or "quiet," or other unhewn thoughts that poked above his liminal threshold? Or should he begin with autonomic, unlabeled sketches that channelled the visual material below the threshold? What, in short, was the most basic and Aol-free type of information to start with?

At this point Swann turned to a book by the critic and painter Rudolf Arnheim, titled *Art and Visual Perception*. In its discussions of the psychology of seeing, the complexification of perception as one beholds an object, and the evolution of perception and artistic skill in children, Arnheim's classic probably served as the single greatest influence on Swann the remote-viewing engineer. Certainly it was the prime source for what Swann came to call Stage One of his remote-viewing system.

In the book Arnheim talked about subliminal and other forms of low-stimulus perception. He made the point that for an image glimpsed just briefly, only the most essential features of the image were perceived correctly. In other words, only the visual Gestalt came through; everything else was likely to be the product of the imagination.

Swann was determined that what worked for ordinary subliminal perception should work for remote viewing. He therefore decided that capturing the visual Gestalt of a given remote-viewing target should be the goal of Stage One.

In designing a method to do this, Swann took inspiration from Arnheim's description of the way people see things. "[I]n looking at an object," Arnheim had written, "we reach out for it. With an invisible finger we move through the space around us, go out to the distant places where things are found, touch them, scan them, scan their surfaces, trace their borders, explore their texture." Thus, for example, to look at the columns of the Parthenon was in a very real sense to feel oneself soaring vertically up, then down, then up, then down, and so on along the row, all the time feeling the smooth hardness of the marble, and the jaggedness where time and circumstance had gnawed that smoothness away.

Observing his and others' remote-viewing sessions, Swann decided that the kind of information Arnheim was talking about was available to a remote viewer in an almost instantaneous burst at the start of a session—in fact, the moment the coordinates had been read. But the strange thing was, this information wasn't available in visual form so much as in an autonomic, kinesthetic form. Swann would feel his writing hand making motions to describe the basic feature of a target—say, a rapid diagonal up, diagonal down for a mountain—just as his eyes might have scanned their way around the target had he been seeing it in real life. Swann's hand seemed to want to sketch this information automatically; in some cases, as Hal Puthoff pointed out to him, Swann even doodled with his pen in the air, above the paper.

As he experimented with these initial sketches—which

usually took only a second or two—Swann decided that they did often contain the basic visual and kinesthetic elements of the targets he was after. If the target was a mountain, the initial sketch was often like an inverted V. If the target was a place in the desert, the sketch tended to consist mainly of flat lines. If it was a building, the sketch might contain right angles, which rarely occurred in anything that was not man-made.

As his hand rapidly formed these images, Swann also tried to sense the basic kinesthetic and textural features of the target, the ups and downs, the hardness or softness. He called the images "ideograms," and the textural-kinesthetic descriptions "feeling motion."

Swann was, of course, simply taking Arnheim's idea about visual perception and imposing it on remote viewing, trying to make it work. But he was convinced that it did work, and he convinced Puthoff and others at SRI.

Thereafter, as soon as a remote viewer under Swann's tutelage wrote down the coordinates of the target site—in fact, even before he had raised his pen from the paper—the viewer would coax his hand to make a rapid sketch of whatever kinesthetic sensation occurred to his nervous system, following that with a verbal notation of the feeling motion, and perhaps an interpretation of what target Gestalt this indicated. If the target was a random place in mid-ocean, then ideally the remote viewer would rapidly sketch a flattish, wavy line, feeling a soft waviness as he did so. He would then write "wavy, soft," interpreting this as "water."

Swann saw this several-second burst of structured psi perception as the key to successful remote viewing—or, to use a different metaphor, as a noise-free foundation for the rest of the remote-viewing session. Swann would later rank his development of Stage One among his life's greatest achievements.

* * *

Swann practiced with ideograms for many months. When he began a session and thought that his ideogram was incorrect, or when his pen failed to form any ideogram at all, he simply declared a "miss," took a several-second break, and then wrote the coordinate down again, giving the kinesthetic burst from the signal line another chance to tremble through his arm and onto the paper. This might go on for several minutes, until his ideograms began to conform to a consistent shape. Once they did, and he recognized their meaning, they often shifted to something very different, describing a new aspect of the target—as if to say, "It's time to move on." Swann himself vocalized his thoughts during sessions, speaking every word he wrote down, and also writing down everything he spoke, believing that this would keep both halves of his brain, via his eyes and his ears, fully apprised of what was going on.

Ideograms and their interpretation formed Stage One. Stage Two came more naturally. Swann found that once he had the ideogram out of the way, basic sense perceptions would begin to surge above his liminal threshold and into consciousness: "hard," "gray," "roaring sound," "white," "steep," "motion," "smell of water." If a much more complex image or word, such as "fountain," came up, he would say out loud, "Aol break, fountain," writing "Aol brk" and beneath it "fountain"; he would then set down his pen and take a break of a few seconds to try to clear his mind of the noisy information.

After a string of Stage Two perceptions, Swann often began to feel certain aesthetic sensations, such as "breathtaking." Because these could sometimes come into consciousness quite strongly, generating Aol associations of their own, Swann learned to take quick aesthetic impact (Ai) breaks after them too, writing "Ai brk."

Related to Ai's in Swann's scheme, but subtly different, were "emotional impacts" (Ei); these could be emotions that others actually at the site were experiencing, or would normally experience while there. Thus he might write something down such as "Ei brk, routine—I feel bored."

After Stage Two had run for a minute or so, the data often switched to what Swann called "dimensionals"—perceptions such as "large," "expansive," "thick," "heavy." He defined this as the transition to Stage Three, and at this point the viewer often got the strong urge to start making relatively large autonomic sketches. Their meaning might not immediately—or ever—be clear, but as they progressed, sometimes for page after page, they might begin to suggest something about the target. For example, if the target was a hydroelectric dam, Swann might sketch several steeply angled lines across the page, with a line running horizontally connecting their tops, and another curved line beneath.

At this point, Aols would become more frequent, as the mind automatically tried to decide what the sketch represented. Swann might have to write down a string of Aol breaks—"Aol brk, wall," "Aol brk, mountain slope"—discarding all such information as probable noise.

For a long time Stage Three was as far as Swann could develop his remote-viewing technique. He considered it progress, but he wanted to go much further. He realized he was still missing a technique for pulling out more complex but noise-free information from a target, information that described its function or purpose.

Such a technique formed the basis for Stage Four. After more than a year of tinkering and experimentation, Swann decided simply to write a sequence of general headings across the top of a blank sheet of paper, going from left to right, placing his pen beneath each column and prompting for the desired information. The headings covered the usual early-stage information—Stage Two sense perceptions, dimensionals, Ai's, Ei's, and Aols—but also now included "tangibles" and "intangibles." Tangibles (things like "concrete," "steel," "machines," "cables," "energy") were relatively physical, material objects at the target, while intangibles ("public," "practical," "necessary") referred to associated concepts or functions. Both categories could be relatively noisy, but Swann believed that by this point in the RV session the subliminal mind would have been in intermittent contact with the signal over three stages and at least several minutes, enabling it to assemble analytical information much more accurately than at the beginning.

The prompting and vocalizing and writing would go on, across and down the page, and occasionally Swann felt the urge to break for a new sketch, then went back to start a new matrix or to finish the old one. Eventually, if all went well, the last bits of verbal and graphic information would come through, and Swann could make a final "analytical sketch" which brought together all the major elements of the target and allowed it to be identified.

An example of a four-stage CRV session follows:

STAGE ONE

40° 46' 16" N
73° 59' 43" W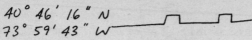

A. angles
B. buildings

STAGE TWO

cold
gray
concrete feel
can noises
water near
tall

Aol brk
cathedral

BREAK

STAGE ONE

40° 46' 16" N
73° 59' 43" W

A. angle
B. building

STAGE TWO

quiet
cool
metal smell
closed - in

Ai brk

claustrophobic
—as if no windows

BREAK

STAGE THREE

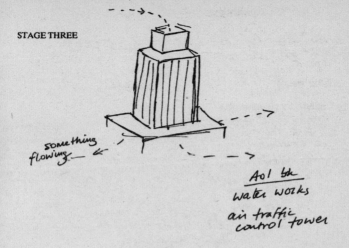

something
flowing

Aol bth
water works

air traffic
control tower

?

52   D   Ai/Ei   T   I   Ao1

quiet
motion

sounds of
many voices
—but somehow
not "real" voices

tall
verticals

many small
spaces

very busy—
many small
things happening
at once

metal, wires
electronics
machines
computers
fans/coolers
microwaves
antennas

automated
processing
"switching"
connecting

communications—
related

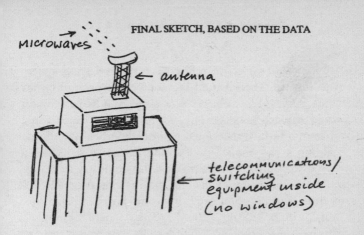

FINAL SKETCH, BASED ON THE DATA

microwaves

← antenna

← telecommunications/
switching
equipment inside
(no windows)

target: telephone switching center, 10th Ave. and 53rd St.,
Manhattan.

* * *

Swann would go on to refine his remote-viewing system even further. There would be methods of prompting for detail from specific objects at a target site, which Swann would explore in Stage Five. In Stage Six Swann would move into three-dimensional representations of the object, building a clay model, and noting further insights on a "Stage Six Matrix." In Stage Seven, he would try to dredge up the actual name of the site, taking a deep breath and uttering short "phonetics" until he began to zero in: "Vah," "huh," "dah," "huh"; "vah," "dah," "muh"— "Hoover dam." One or two of his students would seem to do very well at it,* although Swann himself eventually abandoned phonetics as too noise-prone.

Swann also discovered and named a couple of interesting remote-viewer pitfalls. There was the dread *Aol drive*, for example, which occurred when an Aol was so strong that the viewer couldn't get it out of his head, and it ended up "driving" the rest of the data in the session. To avoid Aol drive, the viewer might have to abandon the session for a day or so, or in some cases forever.

There was *peacocking*, which happened when one Aol led to another in a colorful spiral away from the actual target. There was *burnout* and *overtraining*, from too much remote viewing. There was a *too much break* for remote viewers overwhelmed by data within a session, and there was even a *confusion break* for viewers who sensed that data were coming in but somehow couldn't put them down on the page.

There was also the very strange phenomenon of "telepathic overlay." Sometimes the remote viewer reproduced in his RV session erroneous data that some other viewer

---

* Joe McMoneagle was probably the best at getting names from sites, although it usually happened spontaneously, and he never learned Swann's technique.

had come up with or data in the mind of the monitor. It was the kind of thing that had been reported since the early days of mesmerism and hypnosis, and there didn't seem to be much one could do about it, aside from keeping the monitors blind to the targets in operational sessions. Unfortunately, the existence of this overlay meant that two remote-viewing sessions, by two different remote viewers, might not be as "independent" as one might suppose.

Related to telepathic overlay was the phenomenon of "remote-viewing your feedback," in which the viewer, instead of remote-viewing the actual target described by coordinates, remote-viewed the feedback photograph in the target folder, reproducing it accurately even though it might contain elements no longer at the target site.

As destructive as these phenomena seemed, Swann and Puthoff were nevertheless satisfied that they seldom occurred, especially for experienced viewers. In any case, by the early 1980s Swann's new technique was attracting strong interest among Grill Flame's clients in Washington, while at SRI, Puthoff and others began to speak the new Swannian vernacular: "That was a big Aol"; "I'm in drive here"; "Whoa! That Ai blew me away"; "I've lost the signal line"; "I can't get the aperture open"; "Hey, that was a great Stage Two site."

Swann's remote-viewing scheme might have seemed arbitrary and bizarre, but in fact many of his insights had been made before by other psi researchers, despite their absence from the modern parapsychological literature. Upton Sinclair, for example, had not only noticed what Swann called analytical overlay but had even described telepathic overlay. In *Mental Radio*, Sinclair wrote that his wife's drawings "sometimes contain things which are not in [the target drawings], but which were in my mind while I was making them, or while she was 'concentrating.'"

And then there was René Warcollier, a French parapsychologist who had done psi experiments back in Sinclair's day. Sometime around 1982, Puthoff came across a secondhand English translation of a book by Warcollier, titled *Mind to Mind*, which had been put out just after the Second World War by an obscure and now-defunct publishing house. The book was essentially an edited version of a lecture Warcollier had given at the Sorbonne in the summer of 1946. Puthoff read through the book and was amazed to find that Warcollier, even more than Sinclair, had anticipated Swann's observations about remote viewing.

Trained as a chemical engineer, Warcollier had made his fortune in the early part of the twentieth century with the invention, strangely enough, of a chemical process for turning fish scales into artificial jewelry. Thus funded, he had begun to experiment with telepathy in about 1909, and had continued to do so, with breaks for two world wars, for most of the rest of his life. When Puthoff finished Warcollier's book, he sent a copy of it with a letter to Swann, who had just returned from a trip away from Menlo Park. The letter read in part:

Dear Ingo—

I believe that this is the book you've been waiting for. He [Warcollier] discusses everything you've come up with—analytical overlay (he calls it secondary elaboration); telepathic overlay (mental contagion); the fact that it is the dynamic or kinesthetic element that comes through most readily rather than the static image; drawing [is] better than words because telepathic data [are] processed at a pre-language level of organization; etc., etc. And he ties it all together on the basis of what perceptual psychologists know about the beginnings of *ordinary* perception in children and primitives . . . he is our kind of man talking our kind of language.

* * *

In the early 1980s Swann began to train others in his evolving technique, to gain insights into the workings of remote viewing, and to establish the feasibility of a formal training program that could be sold to Grill Flame managers in the DIA and the Army.

At Swann's direction, pictures and descriptions of test targets, designed to encourage a wide range of psi perceptions, were cut from old *National Geographic* magazines by Martha Thompson, a young woman who served as the RV lab's secretary. She would find the geographical coordinates of the targets on an atlas or on more precise Pentagon-provided maps. For each such target she would prepare a manila file folder with a short handwritten description of the target on the tab, and the coordinates written in large letters across the side. The viewer would start with the coordinates, and after the session was over, would get to see the pictures of the target inside the folder.

In all there were about a dozen volunteers trained by Swann at SRI from 1980 to 1982. Most were SRI employees who otherwise worked on psi-unrelated projects. A few were friends of Swann's, hired temporarily by SRI.

Jacques Vallée was one of the trainees. Although rapidly gaining renown as a writer about UFOs, he was also a computer scientist and an SRI consultant who had done, and was still doing, some of the pioneering development of computer network technology. Vallée became enthusiastic about remote viewing and even arranged for joint RV sessions among computer network users, although he seemed to have difficulty with Swann's scheme.

Hal Puthoff was another trainee, at least briefly. He had served as a monitor for many of Swann's RV sessions, particularly the operational ones, and in the early 1980s, Swann's urging and his own natural curiosity finally got the better of him. He turned out to be a reasonably good remote viewer. One training target was a waterfall in Brazil, which Puthoff, being particularly sensitive to the humid smells of the tropics, nicely sketched and described. Another target was a Union Carbide chemical plant; Puthoff sensed smoke and stacks and flames, smelled pungent chemical odors, and generated the unsurprising Aol of "oil refinery."

Gary Langford and Hella Hammid were also trainees, and Swann made sure to give them a bizarre range of targets. In May 1980 he gave them the coordinates of the erupting Mount St. Helens, which included the perplexing sensory juxtaposition of both fire and ice. Another time a trainee was given a site and felt that it was bleak, cold, and dangerous. "Men come here, and they leave," he noted on his session sheet. The coordinates he had been given, it turned out, were not terrestrial. They described Tranquillity Base, where the *Apollo 11* astronauts had landed on the moon. Like Mount St. Helens, it was a good Stage Two site, as Swann liked to say, because its basic sensory associations were intense and dramatic.

Stage Three sites were those with obvious and distinctive features that could be sketched easily, like the tall and narrow Washington Monument or the domed Taj Mahal. Stage Four sites were those with a clearly defined purpose, something that would pop right out in the intangibles column, like "generating power." Then there were Stage One sites. Swann in later years often told the story of a target he once gave Hella Hammid. The coordinates precisely described a precipice over the Khyber Pass, and the vertiginous kinesthetics of the site were apparently so strong that Hammid's hand, forming the initial ideogram, went sharply down, off the paper, and off the table.

17

BLUE

The situation at SRI was one of warring political factions. It was extremely stressful. It was, you know, pressures about funding, and then pressures within little groups and things that I don't want to get into. But it was not a pleasant place to work. . . . It was horrible; it was a nightmare; it was god-awful; it was a tragedy. It was the worst.

—Keith "Blue" Harary

THE STABLE OF SRI'S REGULAR REMOTE VIEWERS EXPANDED WITH THE addition of a young man named Keith Harary early in 1980. Harary was good enough that during the Iran hostage crisis that year, Jake Stewart at the National Security Council decided to task him with a special, high-priority target. Harary seemed to be particularly good at remote-viewing people, and in this case, the NSC was interested in an American hostage named Richard Queen, who was believed to be suffering from the early stages of multiple sclerosis. Stewart and the NSC wanted to know how he was bearing up.

Stewart told Puthoff only that he had a "target personality" he wanted remote-viewed. In other words, no one even at SRI knew what the target was. Monitored by Targ, Harary sat down at the table in the RV room for a series of sessions one afternoon. His style was more like extended remote viewing (ERV) than Ingo's CRV. He sat back quietly in his chair, very relaxed, often with his eyes closed, mostly verbalizing his impressions rather than sketching them. He described a thin, bearded man in spartan, cold surroundings. The man had health problems, including severe nausea and nerve damage that had nearly immobilized one side of his body. There were people around the man, and Harary described them too. The remote viewer also sensed that his target was about to travel; it seemed that he would be on an airplane within two or three days.

After the session was over and the results had been sent back to Stewart at the NSC, Harary discussed his results with Puthoff and Targ. They suspected that the target had been some head of state—but who?

Back at the NSC, Stewart was impressed by Harary's data. The description seemed clearly to be that of Richard Queen. The prediction about the airplane was puzzling, however. Were the Iranians up to something? Were they about to release Queen? The NSC began to prepare for that eventuality, and two days later the Iranians, evidently not wanting Queen to die in their custody, put him on a plane home. A U.S. medical team confirmed the things that Harary had said about his declining health. Later, Queen himself was debriefed, and some of Harary's data were read to him, without mention of the source. Queen became angry, concluding that one of his Iranian captors must have been an American spy all along—for how else could U.S. officials have known about his experiences in such detail?

Harary, still only in his late twenties, was the youngest remote viewer at SRI. Not very tall, he had dark, curly hair, a beard and a mustache, and an exotic bloodline that came from the small community of Jews in Egypt—though Harary himself was born on Long Island.

A series of intense out-of-body experiences in his teenage years had brought him to the American Society for Psychical Research in New York, where for a time he had worked alongside Ingo Swann. Swann and others knew Harary then as "Blue"—a nickname that Keith's friends had given him in childhood, and which he kept until the early 1980s.*

Later, as an undergraduate psychology major at Duke University, Harary sat for experiments with psi researchers at the school's electrical engineering department. One of these experiments is now legendary. Harary, accompanied by a researcher who monitored his condition, lay down on a bed in one building, and at a randomly selected time, was asked to enter a trance and have an out-of-body experience. When he reached that state, he tried to move his out-of-body self to a special room in another building. In that special room, arranged with a checkerboard pattern of black-and-white floor tiles, sat Harary's cat, "Spirit." Video monitors recorded Spirit's movements and noises, which seemed ordinary—until Harary, his physical self lying on a bed hundreds of yards away, reached his OBE state. At that point the cat became significantly calmer,† as if staring at something. When Harary came out of his trance, the cat went back to normal. The experiment had been almost spookily successful, although for some reason Harary and the Duke researchers had never really been able to repeat it. In any case, Harary's renown was such that after meeting Puthoff in late 1979, the young psychic had been invited to join the team at SRI.

Harary was an articulate and intelligent young man, with an intense, almost lawyerly love for precision and logic. He had some definite opinions about psi and remote viewing,

---

* Harary wouldn't tell me the exact origin of the name; perhaps "Blue Harary" was merely a bad pun on the Elvis Presley film *Blue Hawaii*.
† The cat's movements during the session were recorded by video camera; the rate of activity was checked for correlations with the period of Harary's OBE.

and preferred to be thought of as a researcher or a consultant; he came to detest the label *psychic*. He was therefore in many ways like Ingo Swann. Unsurprisingly, given their strong personalities, the two didn't get along very well.

Harary found Swann's professorial posture the hardest to take. The young remote viewer felt that he was about as good as, and perhaps in some senses better than, the older fellow teaching him. He was comfortable enough with his own remote-viewing insights and methods, and was far from being convinced that Swann's new multi-stage scheme was the one true technique that suited everyone.

To be convinced of such an argument, Harary reasoned, he would have to see some well-controlled studies comparing, say, remote viewers using Ingo's technique with the same remote viewers using their own varied techniques. He didn't see any serious efforts being made to gather such data.

Moreover, Harary believed that many of Swann's insights weren't original, having been made already by René Warcollier and Upton Sinclair. And those insights, he felt, could have been packaged into a remote-viewing scheme in any number of ways. To Harary, Swann didn't have a magic formula; he merely had strong opinions, and a certain protectiveness about anything he had invented himself.

A classic example of this protectiveness, as Harary saw it, was Swann's insistence on using geographical coordinates. It seemed that Swann liked coordinates because they were his idea, and he had charmed Jack Vorona and his contract monitor, Jim Salyer, and the money was flowing, and no one really thought to question it anymore.

But as far as Harary could tell, the use of coordinates only seemed to hurt the overall technique. When Harary heard a set of coordinates at the start of a session, his mind couldn't help trying to calculate where the target was. If the coordinates were something like 5° S, 30° E, AoI images of humid African jungle would immediately start to flash into his mind, though the target might be something significantly different. Geographical coordinates, Harary believed, were a tragic flaw in the procedure. Even when they seemed to work, they made remote viewing look bad.

At times, Puthoff seemed sympathetic to this view. Still, he didn't protest when the DIA sent funds for Swann's coordinate remote-viewing contract. In his ever-cautious, low-key manner, Puthoff merely suggested that alternative targeting methods should continue to be explored alongside coordinates.

But to Harary, the work at SRI already had provided evidence to suggest that alternative techniques worked just as well. There were all the experiments SRI had done without coordinates, such as outbound remote viewing, and remote viewing of objects in boxes and in canisters and on microdots. Eventually they tried putting objects in a matrix of cubbyholes, the matrix columns lettered A–G and the rows numbered 1–7. Thus, instead of a geographical coordinate scheme, there was a very basic letter/number coordinate scheme. Puthoff would sit down at the RV table and say, "B-seven," and Harary, or Hammid, or whoever was the viewer, would try to describe what he or she saw there. There was no obvious difference in accuracy between these tests and Swann's CRV scheme.

Nor did remote-viewing accuracy seem to suffer when Puthoff scrambled the geographical coordinates of the target with an encryption algorithm, and gave them to the viewer. Nor did accuracy suffer when Puthoff gave encrypted coordinates to viewers who *didn't even know* that the coordinates were encrypted; in other words, the numbers they had were random as far as they knew. Finally, one day, Puthoff was in the remote-viewing room with Harary, about to start a session, and Harary in exasperation said, "Why don't you just say 'target'?"

"Okay," said Puthoff. "Target."

Both remember that Harary nailed the site.

* * *

The infighting at SRI in those days may not have been extraordinary for a program of that size, but to some it did seem dismayingly unique. There were conflicts over space, over lab resources, over contract money, over research methods, and sometimes over nothing more than personality differences. Anyone expecting an enlightened environment of researchers pulling together, to advance the beleaguered cause of psi, would have been quickly brought down to earth after a brief exposure to the internal politics of SRI's remote-viewing lab.

There was, just for example, the clash between Hella Hammid and Keith Harary. In Harary's opinion, Hammid had begun to see herself as some kind of superpsychic or demi-goddess. The day after Harary and his wife Darlene were married, Hammid solemnly told the newlyweds that she had had an unfortunate psychic impression: Their marriage would never work. "Don't feel bad," she commiserated, "it will be a learning experience." (At the time of writing, fourteen years later, their marriage is still intact.)

The turf battles within SRI were much worse. There were battles between the DIA's Jim Salyer and SRI researchers, and there were battles between the researchers and consultants like Swann. Swann effectively oversaw a substantial part of the program, and perhaps understandably, guarded his domain with vigilance. As he would later paint the scene, his day-to-day work at SRI was a never-ending battle against encroachments by others in the program. Swann would later remember one episode in which, allegedly, he chased Targ and Puthoff out of some room at SRI—a room they had been trying to take over for another project—ran after them down a hall, and threw a hammer at them as they entered an elevator.

Ed May was a physicist who had been brought into the program in 1976. Short, bearded, a bit breathless, he struggled to set up his own contractual fiefdoms at SRI. In try-

ing to get funding for one of his projects, he ran afoul of
Swann, and the two men fell out. Swann would later say, "I
regret to this day that I didn't look at Ed May's horoscope
first."

Hal Puthoff stood in the middle, trying to exert a calming
influence, trying to keep all these centrifugal forces from
flinging the SRI program apart. For a while he succeeded.
But then, finally, everything seemed to come loose. Sometime in 1982 Harary and Hammid began to press for their
own project, which would be run by Targ and kept separate
from Swann's project. They didn't want to work with
Swann anymore.

Targ supported the idea. Memoranda were written. One,
pro Harary and Hammid and contra Swann, was written by
Gary Langford. Swann consequently demanded that all
three remote viewers be expelled from his domain. Puthoff
and Targ and Jim Salyer argued with Swann over this, but
when the dust had cleared, Harary and Hammid were gone
from SRI, and Langford, though he would stay on at the
lab, was gone from Swann's project. Swann stood atop the
rubble, triumphant again.*

Next to go was Targ, but this time Swann had little to do
with it.

As of 1982, Targ was one of the four or five best-known
figures in parapsychology, not just in America but in the
world. Yet Targ had been busy making enemies within Grill
Flame, and Swann wasn't the only one.

During 1981 and early 1982 Targ was supposed to have
been working on a study comparing different RV prompting techniques, including geographical coordinates, encrypted coordinates, the word "target," and the outbound

---

* Langford continued to do occasional operational RV sessions. During
the mid and late 1980s, as a freelancer, Harary was also given a few
operational targets by contacts developed in his SRI days.

remote-viewing protocol. When he finished his report, early in the spring of 1982, he put it on Salyer's desk.

Hal Puthoff had been away in China on a research trip. When he returned, he had a crisis on his hands. Salyer and other DIA officials had complained loudly that Targ's targeting studies report had been very sloppy, with problems ranging from faulty statistics to incorrect captions on graphs and photos. The DIA was now talking about kicking Targ off the project. Puthoff and Ed May spent some time correcting the report, and Puthoff sent Targ a stern memorandum, concluding ominously that the study's flaws "can lead people who assess your work to feel that there are legitimate reasons to question your professional competence as a Senior Research Physicist."

Targ promised to do better next time. But there would not be a next time. The DIA soon announced that Targ's salary would no longer be paid through Grill Flame funds.

In accordance with SRI rules for employees who suddenly are left without outside sponsorship, Targ was given a small office, and his salary was paid out of SRI's "overhead" account. But the clock was ticking. He had eight months in which to find an outside contract or to graft himself onto an ongoing SRI project. He didn't even try, and after the eight months had passed, in early 1983, Targ left SRI for good.

He let it be known that he had departed for high moral reasons. He had been sorely dismayed—shocked, *shocked,* he might have said—by the emphasis on military applications of remote viewing. Since SRI had not publicized the real reasons for Targ's ouster, this alternative explanation managed to survive without serious challenge.

For a while Targ teamed up with Keith Harary, and went for a tour of the Soviet Union. The two travelled to Bratislava, Moscow, Leningrad, Yerevan, meeting with psi researchers, giving lectures, swapping stories. The prospect of

Soviet intelligence officers getting their hands on Targ, who knew some of the most intimate details of one of the Pentagon's most sensitive programs, naturally raised concerns at SRI and the DIA. As one member of the program said later, "We had a very tight policy at SRI about not talking about sponsorship, not talking about details of experiments, unless given specific permission by the sponsor. In general, Russell seemed to have a little less regard for those constraints than everyone else. And once he was completely away from SRI, he probably felt constrained even less. It was always something to think about."

By the end of 1984 Targ had made three visits to the Soviet Union, and claimed to be working with remote-viewing researchers at the Institute of Theoretical Problems in Moscow. "We're looking for the physical correlates that relate psychic functioning to the rest of physics," he told the British magazine *New Scientist,* insisting that the work was pure science, far removed from military applications.

Back in California, in fact before Targ officially left SRI, he and Harary and a businessman named Tony White founded a company called Delphi Associates. Their first venture involved an ESP game that they tried to sell to the computer game maker Atari. Unfortunately Atari itself folded before anything substantial came of the idea.

Delphi's second venture involved the use of associative remote viewing to play the silver futures market. It worked like this: On a Sunday afternoon, for example, from a pool of several dozen Bay Area target sites, Targ would select two. One—say, the dramatic Transamerica skyscraper in San Francisco—would signify "market up on Monday." The other—say, Fisherman's Wharf—would signify "market down on Monday." Harary would not know about either of these sites. He would simply be asked to remote-view, precognitively, the site to which Targ would take him the following afternoon, after the market had closed. Targ, of course, would take him to the site—either Fisherman's

Wharf or the Transamerica building—that corresponded to the market's movement.

Thus, if Harary, on Sunday evening, descended into his zone and smelled ocean air and fish, and heard the cries of seagulls, Targ would assume that he was describing Fisherman's Wharf, and would instruct their broker to bet on a down market for Monday. If Harary felt vertigo and sensed that he was soaring above a city, Targ would assume that he was describing the Transamerica building and would bet on an upward market.

It started as an experiment, but after Harary had made two successful predictions of the daily market for a particular silver-futures option, an investor jumped in, betting real money, and Harary had seven more "hits." Targ began to calculate how long it would take them, at this rate, to become masters of the financial universe. But then, after a break of several weeks, the project suffered two "misses" in a row, and the investor bailed out of the project. Targ blamed Harary for losing his nerve. Harary blamed Targ for mis-analyzing his remote-viewing data. The blame-throwing broke out in public a few months later, during a lecture by Harary (with interruptions by Targ) at a conference at the Esalen Institute. Afterward Harary slapped Targ with a $1.5 million lawsuit, which was settled only after three years of further acrimony and countersuit. As late as the autumn of 1992, the two were still exchanging angry correspondence in parapsychology journals.

18

SPOONBENDER

It scared the hell out of him, quite frankly. . . . He put the fork down and said, "I wish that hadn't happened."

—Former INSCOM staff officer
Colonel John Alexander, recalling
an Army colleague's fork-
bending experience

ACROSS THE CONTINENT, AND ACROSS THE ATLANTIC, ON AN INSCOM base in Augsburg, West Germany, lived a soft-spoken, easygoing Texan, Sergeant Leonard "Lyn" Buchanan. He spoke Russian, and worked on computers. One day, early in 1984, he was asked to demonstrate a piece of software that helped integrate Army intelligence computers all over his sector of NATO. A group of officers assembled to watch. They were in a room with a large screen on the wall, displaying a map of the border area, with symbols for various NATO and Warsaw Pact military units and installations.

Buchanan started his program, which among other things should have modified the information on the large wall screen. But nothing happened. The screen remained obstinately unchanged. As Buchanan could see from the computer monitor he was working from, his program had crashed. "Did you mess with my program?" he asked a colleague, Stan Snyder, who often did just that. "Just one small change," admitted Snyder. And at that moment, as Buchanan's anger rose, the big screen on the wall went blank. Buchanan didn't know it—he would, soon enough—but hundreds of other computers on the network were crashing, too. They shouldn't have been affected by Buchanan's own flawed software, but they crashed just the same—the entire network—through every fail-safe mechanism written into the code. Getting it all back on-line took hours.

Buchanan had his own theory for why the network had gone down. He believed that similar things had happened to him as a child. For instance, he had once seemed to knock another boy, a neighborhood bully, off a bike—just by looking at the boy and willing it to happen. He had thought all that had been drummed out of him, years before, by the fundamentalist preachers of his East Texas youth, who had no truck with such devilish displays. But for some reason, Buchanan believed, his strange ability had suddenly returned, here in a moment of rage in Augsburg.

A month or so later, a new commander was installed at the Augsburg base. The two-star general who now headed INSCOM came over for the ceremony. His name was Major General Albert N. Stubblebine III.

Stubblebine was the spitting image of the actor Lee Marvin, and he didn't seem to mind the comparison; some at INSCOM actually believed that the two men were brothers. Marvin had been in that World War II film, *The Dirty Dozen,* in which he commands a group of death row convicts on a suicide mission. It seemed as if the same character were now in charge of INSCOM, and he was as gung-ho as ever. Intelligence and covert-action budgets were booming, in the wake of the perceived espionage failures of the Carter administration. Morale at INSCOM was high; the men and women there seemed genuinely to love their commander.

On the day of the ceremony installing the new base chief at Augsburg, Lyn Buchanan's department head ordered him to go home and put on his dress uniform. Buchanan guessed he was going to be asked to cater for a lunch or a cocktail party associated with the ceremonies. But his boss told him to report to the commander's office. "I don't know what you've done this time, Buchanan, but the general wants to see you."

Several hours later, Buchanan sat in the reception area of the Augsburg commander's office. When the ceremonics outside ended, the new commander walked in with General Stubblebine. Stubblebine's face was a bit softer than Lee Marvin's, and his voice was a husky Oklahoma tenor, not a gravel-bottomed baritone like the actor's. Still, he was an impressive figure, a man who knew he was in command. Stubblebine turned to the new base commander and said, pointing to Sergeant Buchanan, "I want to talk to him in private." Stubblebine then ushered Buchanan into the commander's new office, and closed the door behind them.

Buchanan had no idea why he was there. Had he done something wrong? Stubblebine stood facing him, looking him over, watching his eyes for any sign of guile. Finally, frowning, he challenged the confused sergeant. "Did you crash my computers?"

Buchanan thought about it a few seconds, then replied, "Yes, sir, I did."

A grin stole slowly across the general's face. "Far fucking *out!*"

It happened that one of Stubblebine's aides had been at Augsburg when the computer network had crashed. He had heard some of the other officers talking about the incident, and had wondered, like Buchanan, whether the incident might be paranormal in nature. The aide knew that Stubblebine was looking for soldiers with psi abilities, especially those with psychokinetic—PK—abilities. The general believed that the remote-viewing program should be augmented with a PK program; Buchanan seemed to be an excellent recruit.

"Would you consider being in a special project?" Stubblebine now asked Buchanan. "Something that would let you make use of your abilities?" "Absolutely, sir," said Buchanan, seeing that a whole new world had opened up for him. A month later, the current commander of the Fort Meade remote-viewing unit, Lieutenant Colonel Brian Busby, came out from Washington with Joe McMoneagle. They discussed the project with Buchanan in general terms. Among other things, they noted that if he joined the project, he would be exposed to psychic phenomena at a level and with a frequency that most people had never experienced before. As a result, he might change in certain ways. Ultimately, no harm should come to him, but he might have a new perspective on himself, his work, his marriage, the universe. In a sense, he might become a new man, and a new husband. Busby took Buchanan and his wife, Linda, out to dinner one night, and made sure Linda got the message, too. She might not be ready for a new husband, he said. She and Lyn should talk this over before they made the final commitment to go to Fort Meade.

So Linda and Lyn talked it over. Linda surprised her husband by saying that his unusual abilities had always been apparent to her. He was the kind of man who always seemed to know who was on the other end of the phone when it rang, or even before it rang. She didn't think he would change that much, but if he did, she would try to be ready.

A few months later, Lyn Buchanan joined the remote-viewing program, and never looked back.

In the halls of the U.S. government in those years, it really was as if a New Age were dawning. The things that were happening seldom made it into the media, and when they did, they somehow lacked resonance. No one seemed to care. And yet, had someone suddenly taken off in a time machine, travelling from Washington in the 1950s to Washington in the early 1980s, he might have wondered if he had the right planet. Here are some examples:

Jim Wright, an influential Democratic congressman from Texas who would soon be House Speaker, was attending lectures on prophecy given by a Virginia psychic named Anne Gehman. She later said that she had evaluated Wright and had found him to have significant psychic powers.

Charlie Rose, Democrat from North Carolina and a friend of Ingo Swann and Jack Vorona, reportedly stood in the gallery of the House one day with a philanthropist named Judy Skutch* and a group of psychics, beaming various telepathic pleas at House Speaker Tip O'Neill. They tried to get O'Neill to turn his head one way, then another. Later they psychically asked him to smile upon some projects that had been proposed in Rose's district. Another time, it is said, Rose supported a group of inventors trying to sell the Pentagon an electronic "paranoia inducer." Rose even had the device tested on himself, and concluded somehow that it worked, although the Pentagon apparently was unconvinced and never bought the device.

Rose was also unabashed about his support for the RV program. "I've seen some incredible examples of remote viewing," he told one journalist, "so much so that I think we ought to pay close attention to developments in this field, and especially to what the Soviets are doing." The Soviets, he said, "are up to their asses in this stuff."

Senator John Tower of Texas, ranking minority member of the Armed Services Committee, was said to be another supporter of the RV program, as was Claiborne Pell (D-RI). Pell by the early eighties was famously New Ageish; he consulted not only psychics but spirit mediums. The kindly Rhode Island senator used a medium to try to communi-

---

* Skutch had funded some of SRI's research with Uri Geller.

cate with dead Soviet leaders, to encourage them to communicate, in turn, with current Soviet leaders and convince them of the need for peace. Pell didn't even try to conceal his interest; he hired a full-time staffer, a former Navy intelligence officer named C. B. "Scott" Jones, just to keep track of paranormal matters for him.

This enthusiasm for psi and other far-out areas was embodied by more than just a loose network of interested individuals; it was increasingly a collective, corporate enthusiasm. Congressional committees now regularly signed off on budget requests for the Fort Meade and SRI units, and small groups of congressional enthusiasts occasionally met with Hal Puthoff, Jack Vorona, General Stubblebine, and others involved in managing the program. In the summer of 1981, the House Science and Technology Committee issued a report, surveying science and technology "present and future," which declared: "Recent experiments in remote-viewing and other studies in parapsychology suggest that there is an 'interconnectedness' of the human mind with other minds and with matter. . . . The implication of these experiments is that the human mind may be able to obtain information independent of geography and time. . . . Given the potentially powerful and far-reaching implications of knowledge in this field, and given that the Soviet Union is widely acknowledged to be supporting such research at a far higher and more official level, Congress may wish to undertake a serious assessment of research in this country."

The FBI also seemed open to the idea of psychic information gathering. In early 1981, a psychic named Noreen Renier lectured at the Bureau's training center in Quantico, Virginia, and predicted—accurately, it turned out—that someone would attempt to assassinate President Reagan in the spring. The FBI later set up a network of references linking interested local police departments to psychics who might be able to help them with difficult cases.

The White House itself seemed to be cheering on these efforts. Nancy Reagan often consulted the astrologer Joan Quigley, and White House insiders knew that the President himself approved; in fact, he had been consulting astrologers ever since his days as governor of California. Claiborne Pell's staffer Scott Jones would later quote an administration source as telling him, "This is a very psychic White House."

Grill Flame had its own stables of psychics, at SRI and Fort Meade, but increasingly there seemed to be a robust market for freelance psi spying. Scott Jones was in touch with a ring of psychics around the United States, whom he occasionally put in touch with various intelligence officials on operational matters. One was a freelance psychic named Alex Tannous. In 1984, a few months after the terrorist kidnapping of William Buckley, the CIA's station chief in Beirut, the Agency's Directorate of Operations asked Tannous if he could visualize Buckley's condition in captivity. Tannous described the route Buckley's kidnappers had taken, from the abduction point to the place he was interrogated; he concluded that Buckley had already been tortured to death. The Agency officials hadn't wanted to hear that, but they later found out it was all true. The psychics in Jones's ring also tried to track a potential Reagan assassin, nicknamed "Cat," for the Secret Service.

Rumors would circulate about crystal ball gazers, palm-readers, and other storefront psychics whom CIA and Navy officials occasionally tasked with high-level intelligence targets. At least one of the rumors had truth in it. Sometime in 1980 or so, a young CIA employee, Donald Ebsen, on a lark with his wife, went to see an elderly palm-reader who worked from an office near Tyson's Corner, Virginia. The palm-reader, Jean MacArthur, had hardly begun to inspect Ebsen's palm before she looked up at him and said, "You work for the CIA."

Ebsen gulped, and the woman continued: "You should tell someone at the CIA that saboteurs are going to plant bombs on an oil-drilling platform in the North Sea. It's going to blow up, and a lot of people are going to die."

Ebsen and his wife thanked Mrs. MacArthur, and left. Ebsen wasn't about to mention the incident to anyone. Then, about a week and a half later, he saw on the news that a large Norwegian oil-drilling platform in the North Sea had capsized in a storm, with great loss of life. It had seemed that the platform's design should have enabled it to withstand the storm. Had Mrs. MacArthur been right all along? Ebsen decided to tell his boss about the incident, and eventually he was told to contact Norm Everheart. Everheart was now a technical adviser to the deputy director of operations, John McMahon, and served as the CIA's primary liaison to the psychic spies of Grill Flame.

Everheart listened to Ebsen's story, and sent a level-headed operations officer he knew, Walt Jerome, to check out Mrs. MacArthur. He instructed Jerome to act just like an ordinary customer, paying Mrs. MacArthur's ordinary rates. But Jerome had barely made it through the door before Mrs. MacArthur said, "I know who you are! I know why you're here!" Norm Everheart was impressed enough by this to send a query through official channels to the Norwegians. How had the platform actually been destroyed? he wanted to know. Why do you want to know that? came the response. Everheart never found out the truth about the tragedy, and the official Norwegian investigation into the possibility of sabotage was "inconclusive."

Through Walt Jerome, Norm Everheart encouraged Mrs. MacArthur to stay in contact, reporting anything that seemed urgent or otherwise interesting. Mrs. MacArthur complied, but she also began to put pressure on Jerome and Everheart to hire her as a full-time CIA employee. She was getting on in years, had health problems, and desperately needed the insurance benefits that would come with government employment. Apparently to encourage the CIA to hire her, she told Jerome that the Israelis had already been consulting her, had given her numerous taskings, and at one point had even flown her over to Israel, to have her do a close-up psychic spying job in the Golan Heights. Neither Jerome nor Everheart knew whether any of this was true. In any case, they couldn't make her an official employee, and the relationship soon tailed off.

But Everheart and Jerome would always remember her strange predictions. One time, in the summer of 1980, just after the failure of the mission to rescue the U.S. hostages in Iran, Mrs. MacArthur had called up Jerome to request an urgent meeting. Jerome drove over to her office near Tysons Corner, and she explained what was bothering her: She wanted to let him know, she said, that she knew the Pentagon was planning a second rescue mission. The operation would swoop in from the west, at such a latitude and such a longitude, and it would involve tanks, planes, and paratroops. Some of the paratroops would land in the water.

A month or so later, at the latitude and longitude Mrs. MacArthur had specified, Iran was indeed invaded by tanks, planes, and paratroops. Some of the paratroops missed their targets and landed in the water. The only thing was, these invaders were not from the United States. They were the army of Iraq, firing some of the opening shots in a brutal war that was to last a decade.

The sun of a New Age shone on Washington in those years, but nowhere did it shine more brightly than on the U.S. Army. General Ed Thompson might have been a supporter of investigations into the paranormal, but the new INSCOM commander, General Stubblebine, seemed to be a true believer, an evangelist.

Stubblebine was a West Point man, with a master's degree in chemical engineering from Columbia University. He had a reputation not only for intelligence but for creativity, for lateral thinking, for viewing problems from unusual angles. His last command before INSCOM had been at the Army's intelligence school at Fort Huachuca, Arizona. It was there that things had begun to go beyond lateral thinking. Never a religious man, he had started to read books on the paranormal, and had cultivated friendships with others who were interested in these realms.

Not long after Stubblebine reached INSCOM in 1981, Army intelligence began to blossom under his influence with alternative, New Age–style thinking. A "High Performance Task Force" was set up to promote new projects in these alternative areas. There were motivational training exercises for generals and staff colonels, using "neuro-linguistic programming." Taught by the self-help guru Tony Robbins, dozens of these senior officers even walked over beds of hot coals, to demonstrate their supposed hidden potentials. *Think cold ice! cold ice! cold ice!*

Altered-state and visualization techniques were used to try to enhance learning and boost performance among marksmen and linguists. Meanwhile, INSCOM staff officers were sent to a place called the Monroe Institute, a retreat center in the Blue Ridge Mountains, where they lay in darkened cubicles, listened to altered-state–inducing tapes, and tried to have out-of-body experiences.

An INSCOM staff colonel named John Alexander oversaw many of these projects for Stubblebine. Alexander was a slender Texan with Special Forces training. He had seen combat during the Vietnam War, but since then had felt himself drawn to the alternative realm. After he hooked up with Stubblebine, his career took off. Most officers involved with remote viewing or other paranormal subjects worried that the association would hurt their chances for quick promotions. Not Alexander. He often commented that in his case the reverse was true.

Before arriving at INSCOM, Alexander wrote an unusual article for *Military Review,* a respected Army journal. Titled "The New Mental Battlefield," the piece promoted remote viewing, and suggested that effective mind-influencing devices were already a "lethal" reality, presumably in Soviet and Eastern European hands. Over the next few years, a number of other stories like these came out of the military woodwork. Charles Wallach, science editor for the *Journal of Defense and Diplomacy,* wrote an article calling for a "psychic service corps." Army Captain Richard Groller, in *Military Intelligence,* worried that "the Soviet psychotronic program is equivalent to roughly seven Manhattan projects." A retired lieutenant colonel and consultant named Tom Bearden actually obtained Army contracts for studies of "hyperspatial howitzers," alleged Soviet "photonic barrier modulators"—which he blamed for everything from UFOs to Legionnaires' disease—and other absurd-sounding weaponry. Even the Army's partly classified *Fire Support Mission Area Analysis* of 1981 talked about "cryptomental" technologies—"the relatively unexplored, unexploited human technologies in such areas as influence, communications, thinking, learning, and stress reduction. Discussions in this area represent an excursion into a largely unknown realm which appears to possess significant military application."

Taxpayer dollars were also lavished on something called Task Force Delta, an Army War College project whose mission was to investigate alternative philosophic realms for anything militarily useful. A Lieutenant Colonel Jim Channon and several other like-minded officers from the task force soon came up with an idea for something called the "First Earth Battalion," an eco-friendly politically correct warrior-monk vision of the future soldier. Before long, Channon and the others were into role-playing games, acting out this New Age fantasy. In a 1982 report of a Task Force Delta meeting, a Colonel Mike Malone wrote:

I am one of the tribal elders . . . my name is "The Mullet Man." I am known as the one who casts nets. And I try to tell people that of all those who cast nets, most should be concerned with the catching, but some, at least, should focus more on the casting than the catching. I live with, fish for, and push the cause of the mullet, because he is a "low-class" fish. He is simple. He is honest. He moves around in great formations and columns. He does damn near all the work. . . .

Next to Task Force Delta, the things Stubblebine was doing at INSCOM seemed hard-nosed. And although Stubblebine himself, behind closed doors, was arguably as starry-eyed as anyone in the Army, he did have his operational justifications for all the strange projects he supported. Aside from improving performance in specific hands-on skills, he wanted to shake his people up, wanted to get them thinking laterally, like him. He wanted them intellectually prepared for whatever exotic military technologies the Soviets or anyone else might throw at them.

That, at any rate, was how the general often talked about spoonbending.

Uri Geller had popularized the *idea* of spoonbending with his stage act in the early 1970s, but a decade later the actual manifestation of the phenomenon was being popularized, too. A defense consultant on the West Coast, Jack Houck, was throwing "spoonbending parties," at which people stood around with spoons—in fact, almost any piece of cutlery would do—and concentrated on them, waiting for a psychokinetic bend to begin. Some people tried to jump-start the effect by bending their spoons manually. At any rate, spoons would bend and stories would spread. Before long, Stubblebine, Houck, John Alexander and others were throwing spoonbending parties in the Washington area.

Occasionally, celebrities from the intelligence world

came to these parties. One party, around 1983, was hosted by Stubblebine and Alexander and a female psychic they knew. John McMahon, now deputy director of the CIA, was there, along with General Thompson, now a directorate chief at the DIA. When it came time for the main event, there was a short lecture from someone on how to bring about psychokinetic spoonbending, and then the partygoers stood around and concentrated on their spoons and forks. They concentrated, and they concentrated some more. Finally someone's child, a boy of twelve or so, shouted that his spoon was bending. Suddenly a lot of other spoons were bending. General Thompson watched as his own spoon began to curve down at the point he was holding it, down and around as if it were melting in his hands. John McMahon's spoon bent, too; by the time all the psychokinesis had stopped, the deputy director's spoon looked vaguely like a corkscrew. He went into CIA headquarters the next day and told some of his friends and aides about it. He even showed them the spoon, and let Norm Everheart take it home—where it resides today.

That had been just a private party, a bit of entertainment. But for Stubblebine, spoonbending had an important role to play in the management of military intelligence. One weekend a "retreat" was held for senior INSCOM staff officers, at a Xerox-run conference facility near Leesburg, Virginia. Part of the retreat included a cutlery-bending demonstration. Someone handed out spoons and forks, and Stubblebine gave a short talk on how it was done, and then twenty-five to thirty colonels and generals stood around holding these eating utensils and staring at them, waiting for something to happen.

At one point, a somewhat skeptical colonel turned his head to say something to a colleague, and as he did, his fork suddenly drooped into a ninety-degree angle. Everyone looked at him and his fork, at which point the fork bent back up, then down again, and finally settled into an angle of about forty-five degrees. The colonel whose fork it was put the thing down, shaking his head, evidently unsettled. He was a Christian, and later would denounce the entire thing as the trickery of the devil. Alexander kept the fork.

Though some in Grill Flame considered it a mixed blessing, General Stubblebine was also enthusiastic about remote viewing. His support was important, for in 1981, the Army's greatest proponent and protector of remote viewing, Major General Thompson, had departed his post as the assistant chief of staff for intelligence. Thompson's successor, an up-and-coming major general named William Odom, was far less optimistic about the military use of the paranormal.

The center of control over the remote-viewing program therefore shifted from the ACSI's office, now occupied by Odom, to INSCOM, run by Stubblebine. Under Stubblebine, the remote-viewing unit was first turned into a formal detachment—Detachment G, or Det-G—within INSCOM's Operations Group. Then, in 1983, the unit received its own code name, "Center Lane," and shifted from the Operations Group to the more direct control of Stubblebine's office at INSCOM headquarters. The unit now became known as ICLP—for "INSCOM Center Lane Project."

Scotty Watt, his tour over, was replaced by a Lieutenant Colonel Jachim in 1982, and he in turn was replaced in 1983 by Lieutenant Colonel Brian Busby. Busby was reasonably well liked, and was seen by the unit as a highflier, a man with a good career ahead of him. Busby and Skip Atwater regularly briefed senior Army and DIA officials on the program, and at times even went up to Capitol Hill to discuss the remote-viewing unit's work with sympathetic senators and representatives.

Despite all the high-level attention and support, the

Stubblebine years were an unsettling interlude for the unit. The first generation of viewers was fading away, and as it did, the unit was metamorphosing into something else, something whose ultimate shape was still unclear.

In the first phase of its existence, the unit had relied on more or less freestyle techniques for remote viewing. But in this new phase, a shift was beginning toward a more complex, standardized, and apparently "improved" style of remote viewing, based on Ingo Swann's work at SRI.

Atwater, Watt, and later Jachim searched the pool of talent coming out of the Army's advanced intelligence course at Fort Huachuca, and by early 1982, the remote-viewing unit had two new members, Captain Tom Nance and Captain Rob Cowart. The two began travelling out to SRI every few weeks for training. Swann was still developing his remote-viewing technique, and hadn't yet made it past Stage Three. He considered Nance and Cowart experimental prototypes of his eventual trainees, and warned INSCOM that their instruction in the fine arts of psi spying could take a long, long time.

While Nance and Cowart were in training, almost all of the operational RV work at Fort Meade was done by the unit's old-timers—Joe McMoneagle, Ken Bell, and Hartleigh Trent. But as the old-timers kept things running, they increasingly resented being treated as old-timers. Like Keith Harary and Gary Langford at SRI, they had doubts about the complex technique being pushed by Ingo Swann. They agreed with—even preached themselves—some of Swann's insights. But they believed that the specific "technique" a remote viewer used wasn't nearly as important as the viewer's own, natural psi ability. They didn't see enough evidence of strong natural ability in the newcomers. Convinced that the program was headed downhill, managerially and philosophically, Bell left the remote-viewing unit in 1982 for a more conventional intelligence posting.

McMoneagle, now only two years from retirement,

stayed on, but continued to argue against the direction the program was taking. At the same time, ironically, he took on an increasing share of the work at the unit, and when health problems began to sideline Rob Cowart and Hartleigh Trent in 1982, McMoneagle became the sole viewer for almost every operational project that came in.

One of the first big remote-viewing operations of the Stubblebine era began very strangely, a week or so before Christmas 1981. The target was the international terrorist known as "Carlos." There were concerns, in some intelligence circles, that he might be planning an assassination attempt on President Reagan.

Reagan, of course, had already narrowly missed being assassinated in March 1981, when John Hinckley shot him on a Washington sidewalk.* In the months following the incident, it had become clear that assassination and terrorism were now major intelligence problems. In May, Pope John Paul II was shot and almost killed by a Turkish man with Bulgarian ties. In October, Egypt's President Anwar el-Sadat was assassinated in a massive assault by Islamic extremists. By the end of the year, threats by Libya's Muammar Qaddafi against President Reagan's life, and rumors of Libyan "hit squads" sent around the world to kill various American personnel, had created near hysteria in U.S. intelligence agencies. As a result, President Reagan began to travel around Washington in an unmarked limousine convoy, while decoy convoys roamed elsewhere. The Secret Service began to assign security guards to the children of some White House staffers, and advised the Reagans not to venture outdoors for the National Christmas Tree lighting ceremony, asking them instead to light the

---

* According to one story, the FBI collected and destroyed Reagan's bloody clothes after the assassination attempt, to avoid the use of the material, voodoo-style, by enemy psychics.

tree from indoors. And in case someone tried to get at the Reagans within the White House, say, by crashing a plane into the building, there were now a pair of heat-seeking surface-to-air missiles installed on the roof.

Like the rest of the intelligence community, the remote viewers at SRI and Fort Meade were caught up in this tide of worry. For the next several years, suspected terrorists and their sponsors were frequent targets of RV operations.

For the Carlos operation, Puthoff at SRI and Atwater at Fort Meade were asked to use the remote viewers to find out whether Carlos had entered the United States, and if so, where he was. One day, Gary Langford was in the remote-viewing room at SRI, attempting to come to psychic grips with Carlos, when Hal Puthoff heard him describe something completely unlike all the Carlos sessions that had gone before. Yet Langford was as sure of this as anything.

Langford saw a blue van, with odd white markings on the side. A group of Mediterranean-looking kidnappers were driving the van. In a large trunk in the back of the van, bound and gagged, was their captive—a high-ranking U.S. official. Langford even sketched the trunk, labelling its dimensions. He sensed that this was all taking place a few days in the future. He also sensed that it was somehow inevitable. Nothing that he or any other remote viewer did would prevent it, or would end it once it had happened.

Puthoff knew it was still worth a try. Via Jim Salyer, the DIA's contract representative at SRI, Langford's data quickly landed on the desks of FBI and DIA counterterrorist officers. An alert was secretly issued to certain federal offices, warning of a possible kidnapping attempt against a senior U.S. official, perhaps in the Washington area.

Several days later, at the time Langford had predicted, Red Brigades terrorists in the city of Verona, Italy, seven thousand miles away from Menlo Park, broke into the apartment of Brigadier General James Dozier, a senior officer in the U.S. Army's European Command and NATO's

Southern European command. Leaving Dozier's wife bound and gagged in the apartment, the terrorists bundled the general into a trunk, put the trunk in their blue van—which had distinctive white markings on the side—and sped away.

Where they were now holding Dozier, no one knew. What everyone did know was that, three years earlier, the Red Brigades had carried out a similar kidnapping of the Christian Democratic leader Aldo Moro; eventually Moro's bullet-riddled body had been found in the back of an abandoned car.

U.S. authorities were determined to get Dozier back, and the kidnapping sparked a massive and international intelligence operation, with different U.S. agencies and military branches vying for control in Washington.

Stubblebine and INSCOM were relatively minor players, although Dale Graff, now at the DIA after his falling-out with the Air Force, managed to keep a line open to the remote viewers. Gary Langford, after his inadvertent success in describing the kidnappers' blue van, was flown to the Pentagon. He impressed officials there with further, precise descriptions of the kidnapping scene; he even noted, correctly, that one of Mrs. Dozier's earrings had ended up in a certain place on the floor of the apartment.

But of course, Pentagon officials wanted information they didn't already know; they wanted to know where Dozier was being held. Langford went on to provide details of where he thought the kidnappers' hideout was located, and with his data in hand, an Army officer flew to Europe to share the new intelligence with the Italians, who were running the day-to-day searches. Unfortunately, the officer soon found that Langford's leads on Dozier's whereabouts didn't appear to be accurate, or at any rate didn't provide enough information to find the kidnapped general.

Even worse, for SRI and Fort Meade, the Dozier case by this time was becoming overwhelmed by information from other psychics, most of them freelancers contacted by various military officials. At the urging of one DIA official, a Navy captain, a freelance psychic was flown out to the Dozier case operations center in Vicenza, Italy, to try to provide leads at close range. The psychic, Ted Wheatley, immediately began demanding special treatment, and kept U.S. and Italian officials busy with various dietary and lodging requirements. Finally, he told them where he thought Dozier was: "I see a small house, made of stone. It is surrounded by a stone wall and a few trees. It has a tile roof and there is a road junction nearby and mountains in the background." Wheatley's information, vague as it was, convinced the Italians that Dozier was being held in a specific house in a semirural area near Padua. They mounted an operation to free the general, and one morning, at dawn, a large team of Italian carabinieri sealed off the house from its surrounding neighborhood and then charged through the doors. Inside, they found an innocent—and presumably traumatized—Italian family.

Back at Fort Meade, Joe McMoneagle worked hard on the Dozier problem and eventually described a room on the second floor of a different building in Padua. He sketched a radiator on one wall, and a distinctive facade for the small store that he believed comprised the building's ground floor. The description seemed detailed enough to identify the location, but by this time, Pentagon planners were tiring of psychic data—there seemed to be no end of it—and McMoneagle's efforts didn't make it up the chain of command in time.

Dozier was eventually found in Padua, thanks in part to an extensive SIGINT operation by U.S. special-operations teams, which enabled the roundup of two dozen Red Brigades members in the area. One of the terrorists, who was either arrested or turned himself in for fear of imminent capture, gave Italian officials details of the hideout where Dozier was being kept. When Dozier was freed, he was in the second-story room McMoneagle had described, with the radiator on the wall and the store with the distinctive facade below.

Terrorism became a major focus again for the U.S. intelligence community in 1983, after the United States tried to establish a peacekeeping presence among warring Christian and Islamic militias in Lebanon. First a car bomb destroyed the U.S. Embassy, and a few months later another one demolished a barracks housing several hundred U.S. Marines. The bombings were carried out by the Hezbollah group of Shiite Muslim militants, sponsored by Iran and Syria and led by a cleric named Muhammad Hussein Fadlallah.

In response to the bombings, the Pentagon and the CIA wanted to strike Syrian military positions in Lebanon as well as Fadlallah himself. Concentrated on this effort were numerous intelligence assets, including reconnaissance satellites and aircraft, electronic intercepts, CIA-controlled Lebanese agents, and U.S. Army covert action squads. Fadlallah's house in southern Beirut was soon pinpointed and photographed, and Fort Meade and SRI remote viewers were asked to "go inside" and describe what they saw. They did, detailing floor plans, the positions of doors, windows, and locks, and who was normally in the house. Some of the information was later confirmed, but the operation to strike Fadlallah was abandoned by the Pentagon, ostensibly for fear of killing too many innocent bystanders. The operation may simply have been left to the Lebanese, for in early 1985, a Beirut militia group with CIA ties set off an enormous car bomb in front of Fadlallah's house, killing eighty people. Fadlallah, alas, was not among them.

One operation from the Stubblebine era was originated by Stubblebine himself. Part of an INSCOM project codenamed "Landbroker," it was aimed at Panamanian dictator Manuel Noriega.

The U.S. Army, with its huge Southern Command based in Panama, had a strange relationship with Noriega. He was on the one hand its host, and an occasional source of information, while on the other hand he was increasingly its adversary: He appeared to be running guns to leftist rebels in Central and South America, high-tech American goods to Moscow, and drugs to the United States; it was thought he had even managed to penetrate the U.S. Army with his own agents.

After INSCOM commander Stubblebine came back from one trip to Panama in 1983, angrily convinced that his room had been bugged by the dictator, he decided to set up Landbroker, an operation to spy directly on Noriega using an INSCOM special-operations squad called the Quick Reaction Team (QRT). One target was a villa where Noriega occasionally stayed in Panama City. QRT agents rented an apartment nearby, photographed the villa from several angles, and memorized the layout of the grounds. The photographs were sent back to Fort Meade, where they ended up, among other places, in sealed envelopes in building 2560. As Atwater held the envelopes and monitored the sessions, Joe McMoneagle tried to describe the inside layout of the house. He even tried to figure out what Noriega was saying and thinking at times when he was in the villa. Using the data provided by McMoneagle, two QRT agents went over the wall of the villa one night and attempted to break inside, to plant their own listening devices. Unfortunately they alerted two guard dogs, whose jaws just missed the feet of the agents as they quickly hoisted themselves back over the wall. Shortly afterwards, citing this and other security lapses by the QRT agents, INSCOM officials closed the operation down.

Sometime in 1983, with no more ceremony than a pat on the back and a handshake from Skip Atwater and Brian

Busby, Joe McMoneagle completed his thousandth remote-viewing session at Fort Meade.

It was a bittersweet moment, because for McMoneagle, remote viewing had become an increasingly lonely business. By the middle of 1983, he and Tom Nance were the only ones left at the unit, and Nance was often away in training at SRI. Even when Nance was at Fort Meade, he often kept his distance from McMoneagle. Nance enjoyed the training at SRI, but McMoneagle often argued with him about it, insisting that Nance had to free himself from the Ingo Swann technique, if he really wanted to become a good remote viewer. Brian Busby eventually told McMoneagle, in essence, to shut up and remote-view.

Nance was the only trainee in the system now. Rob Cowart's training had been cut short by illness. He had developed a cancerous tumor in his upper back, and though he eventually recovered, the long radiation treatment he received damaged his spinal cord and left him paralyzed from the waist down. He soon left the Army with a medical discharge.

Hartleigh Trent, meanwhile, had had a pain in one of his hips since about 1980. It had become steadily worse, and he had gone through various diagnoses and treatments. One day Trent was in the hospital for surgery that doctors believed would correct the problem. It was thought that he had a damaged disk in his spine. Then the doctors found that Trent was running a low-grade fever, with no obvious origin, so they investigated, and found a cancerous mass in his leg. He was belatedly diagnosed with Hodgkin's disease. His incredulous colleagues—even Riley was in touch from Germany—tried to keep up his spirits as he went through months of chemotherapy and radiation treatments. He worked full-time for a while, then only a few days per week, and then not at all. He died at Walter Reed Army Hospital, with his wife and Joe McMoneagle at his bedside.

Four new recruits were selected for the program by

Atwater and Busby in late 1983, and soon they began training at SRI. In early 1984, General Stubblebine unexpectedly handpicked three more recruits, including Lyn Buchanan. McMoneagle saw it was time to go, and began to arrange his retirement. The new guard would have to take over now, he thought; God help them.

19

OBI SWANN

The potential is there, just like Obi-Wan Kenobi said it
was.

—Ingo Swann

AT THE TIME HE JOINED THE REMOTE-VIEWING UNIT IN 1984, ED
Dames was thirty-five years old, but he seemed at least a
decade younger. He was tow-haired and short, about five
feet five, and he spoke with the accent of his native San
Diego. He looked as if he should have had a skateboard or a
surfboard tucked under his arm.

After graduating from high school, Dames had joined
the Army. He had ended up in the intelligence corps, had
learned Chinese, and had been sent to a National Security
Agency listening post on Taiwan. His job was, for the most
part, to eavesdrop on sensitive military communications
within mainland China.

On Taiwan, Dames fell in love with an attractive woman
from Taipei, divorced his high-school sweetheart from California, and at the ripe age of twenty, embarked on his
second marriage. Unfortunately, being married to a foreign
citizen disqualified Dames from his listening post job,

which required special-access signals-intelligence clearances. After working in less interesting positions for a while, he left the Army. He earned a degree in Chinese, considered studying engineering and working as a civilian, but eventually realized that civilian life bored him. He went back to the Army, this time as an officer. By the early 1980s he was at Fort Meade, as part of INSCOM's Systems Exploitation Detachment. Dames considered his branch of SED, which was concerned with analyzing certain high-tech Soviet weapons projects, to be an elite unit of creative thinkers who didn't care about the rule book. He was proud to be there.

The posting seemed to suit him, too, for Dames was intelligent and creative, and brimmed with a restless energy, an impulsiveness that could have doomed him in a more orthodox military setting. Growing up in California, he would later reminisce, he had been something of an excitable boy, "burning woods down, vandalizing graveyards, any number of things," just for fun—"If it hadn't been for corporal punishment, I'd be in a penitentiary now."

He ran on the cross-country team in high school, and would always be intensely athletic, running and weight lifting, anything to soak up the excess energy. He made his first parachute jump from an airplane when he was sixteen. He was also philosophically restless; as a boy he was captivated by stories of UFOs, Bigfoot, the paranormal in general. He wanted to know what it was all about. At Berkeley, where he studied for a few years after leaving Taiwan, he experimented with Zen meditation, and once had an out-of-body experience. Unfortunately, like many first-timers, he had a bad trip, becoming briefly terrified by the thought that he wouldn't be able to get back into his body. After that, he vowed never to have an OBE again.

Still, his interest in the occult continued. While at Fort Meade, he heard about the remote-viewing unit, and soon became a regular visitor to the unit's tree-shaded buildings. He began to send the unit intelligence targets from his office at SED, and when results came back, he took them seriously. He was as enthusiastic as anyone about remote viewing's potential; he saw it as a revolution in intelligence-collection technology.

Dames also took an interest in the remote-viewing training program out at SRI. He saw that Rob Cowart and Tom Nance, who had already begun their training, were Army captains like him, fresh from the advanced intelligence course at Fort Huachuca. They were no more "natural" psychics than he was. Indeed, in the wake of the debacle with Harary and Langford and Hammid, Swann had told the program's managers that he didn't want natural psychics. He wanted intelligent Army officers with a willingness to learn his new technique. That technique, Swann seemed to be promising, would give them plenty of talent, making them better than the best natural psychics.

It wasn't long before Dames was sounding out Skip Atwater, asking him if he might be able to join the training program himself. The more he thought about it, the less he wanted to do anything else with his Army career. The idea of it was like some fantastic dream: training at the feet of the great Ingo Swann, and then doing battle in the etheric heavens with the evil Russian "extrasensors," as they were being called. He was, he said, a good man for the job.

By late 1983, it was clear that the unit's budget would pay for the sending of four more officers to SRI. Swann would train these four INSCOM personnel, and afterward his remote-viewing technology would be deemed to have been transferred to the U.S. government. In other words, Swann's trainees could go on to train their own students in the same techniques. And no one else would ever sit at the feet of the master.

Dames eventually convinced Skip Atwater and Brian Busby to take him in. Alas, they did not plan to turn him

into a remote viewer—Atwater and Busby felt they had
enough of those—but instead into a remote-viewing monitor and analyst. Nevertheless, it was believed that as an
analyst, he would benefit from the same training received
by actual remote viewers. General Stubblebine signed off
on Dames's inclusion, and the young officer was accepted
as one of the final four.

At some point, Ed Dames was introduced to his fellow
students. One was Captain Bill Ray, a counterintelligence
officer, originally from Anaheim, California. Six feet one, in
his late thirties, he had graying dark hair, a mustache, an
athletic build, and chronic back problems from an old
parachuting accident. Ray was a staunch Irish Catholic,
liked being a soldier, liked his beer, liked to sing sentimen-
tal Irish songs off key, and always seemed to be smoking or
chewing on an old pipe.

Captain Paul Smith, an Arabic speaker, had come from
an INSCOM operations unit in Germany. He was stout and
friendly, with thick glasses and thinning hair. He liked
heavy metal music, but was also a devout Mormon.

The last member of the team was Charlene Cavanaugh,
a civilian analyst in her late thirties who worked for IN-
SCOM. Slim, dark-haired, pretty, and outgoing, she knew
Stubblebine, and was said to have performed quite well at
some of his spoonbending parties. Others at INSCOM
liked the way she carried herself. To Ed Dames, however,
the fact that Cavanaugh was female, and a civilian—two
qualities frequently regarded with disdain by male military
officers—slightly deflated the grandeur of the collective experience they were about to undergo.*

But never mind, the dream was about to begin. It
quickly became clear that it would proceed through stages,

---

* Dames in an interview said he did eventually soften his views in this
area.

through trials to be overcome, like the Hero's Journey that is ubiquitous in mythology. With each trial, Dames and the others would find their lives being altered further. At the end, they hoped, though few put it this way, there would be the final, transformed products—four trained shamans with special-access clearances.

The first stage on this path was reached on a Saturday late in 1983, when Dames and the others drove down to the Monroe Institute. The institute was two hours south of Washington, nestled in the Blue Ridge Mountains. Dames and his fellow trainees, along with a dozen other officers from INSCOM headquarters, were to spend six days there, practicing deeper and deeper altered states with the help of the Monroe audio technology.

Normally, for private clients who came to Monroe, the course was called "Gateway Voyage." But INSCOM needed to justify the course, in its budget request, as something that would contribute to the professional development of its officers. Thus, within the Army, the course was given the evocative acronym RAPT—for "Rapid Advanced Personal Training." Although Dames and the others were now essentially committed to the remote-viewing program for a three-year tour, they believed that the Monroe course was meant to help prepare them, broadening their minds for what was to come. Either that, or it would make clear to them, and to those running the RV program, that their minds lacked the requisite broadness.

Oddly enough, the Monroe Institute owed its involvement with the Army to Skip Atwater's mother. Learning of her son's involvement in psi matters in the mid-1970s, she had referred him to the institute, which friends of hers had attended. The institute was then on an old farm near Charlottesville, Virginia; by the early 1980s it had moved a dozen or so miles away, and comprised a set of modern buildings on a remote hilltop. A man named Bob Monroe had started it all.

Monroe had been a successful radio producer back in the 1950s, when one day in 1958 he had begun to suffer from severe insomnia, and then had begun to have out-of-body experiences. No one then seemed to know anything about such experiences. Doctors told him he was probably having a nervous breakdown of some sort. Monroe didn't think so, and he began to experiment, setting up a small laboratory in his radio production facility, with a special darkened booth for OBE subjects to lie in. To keep subjects from falling asleep in the booth, he played music through headphones. Somewhere around this time Monroe decided that sound was an excellent tool for manipulating states of consciousness, in ways that had never been tried before.

Altered states such as those in which OBEs occurred were, to a certain extent, physiologically measurable. Using electroencephalographs and other scanning devices, one could clearly see the changes in brain waves and brain-activity patterns. After a certain amount of tinkering and theorizing, Bob Monroe came up with the following idea for controlling those patterns: One could play sound with frequencies that matched the brain-wave frequencies, because the brain had a tendency to *mimic* the frequencies presented to it that way. Monroe decided, however, to present this mind-bending sound pattern in an indirect manner. He knew that when one frequency was presented to one ear, and a separate frequency to the other ear, the *difference* between those frequencies (e.g., 8,000 Hz minus 7,990 Hz equals 10 Hz) was also perceptible to the mind. It was what communications engineers called the "beat frequency." Monroe decided to present the altered-state-mimicking sound patterns as beat frequencies—i.e., one set of frequencies in one ear, and a slightly different set in the other ear, in such a way that the mixture would produce the desired waveform pattern. It seemed to work so well that Monroe patented it, and called it the "Hemi-Sync" method. Soon he had tapes to promote a variety of deeper and deeper altered states, including those that seemed to favor OBEs.

Skip Atwater visited the institute one day in 1977, privately, and explained to Bob Monroe that he had his own history of OBEs. Monroe put him on a small cot in a darkened room, and placed headphones on his ears. Then he turned on a Hemi-Sync tape.

What the—? Atwater felt the table lifting into the air. Was Monroe trying to jump-start the out-of-body process by jacking up the bed? Whatever Monroe was doing, it worked. Atwater floated around strange landscapes for a while, and then heard Monroe's voice on the tape, commanding him to come back into his body, back to "physical matter reality." After the session, with the lights on, Atwater got up from the bed and looked beneath it, expecting to see some kind of hydraulic lifting apparatus. There was none.

Atwater became a regular visitor to the institute, as did Joe McMoneagle, and Colonel John Alexander, and even Major General Stubblebine. They began sharing Hemi-Sync tapes with others at INSCOM or in Grill Flame, to help them cool down before remote-viewing sessions, or to cure insomnia or jet lag.

By the early 1980s the Monroe Institute was offering guided courses with the tapes. In the picturesque setting of the misty Blue Ridge Mountains, people could explore the strangest reaches of their inner space. Students in the main course, Gateway Voyage, would lie in small, darkened cubicles—"Controlled Holistic Environmental Chambers"—for several hours a day, for five straight days. They lay semi- or completely naked, under blankets, listening to Hemi-Sync tapes and experiencing weird visual phenomena, or disembodied voices, or vivid memory flashbacks, or full-blown OBEs, or simply their own meandering streams of consciousness. Afterward they would sit around informally and discuss their experiences with everyone else in the group, often with little inhibition and great emotion.

Stubblebine enjoyed the experience so much he began to send dozens of INSCOM officers there. An Army bus would leave Arlington Hall (where INSCOM headquarters was located) on Fridays, just to take people down. Some loved it, and came back with stories of strange altered-state excursions. Lyn Buchanan had his first OBE experience there. Lying in his chamber one afternoon, listening to one of the Monroe tapes, he tried to scratch an annoying itch on his chin, but suddenly felt as if his hand were wearing a glove. Holding his arm before his eyes, he saw that it was now glowing and translucent; his other, physical arm was still down by his side. He experimented with his new, ghostly arm, putting it through the wall of the chamber, and into the bed. When he put it back into his ordinary arm, the two suddenly melded together, and the strange experience ended. But it left him with the conviction— deeper than any the Bible had ever given him—that his spirit was somehow more real than his physical body.

Not everyone had such experiences; in fact, not everyone understood how altered states at the Monroe Institute contributed to the mission of Army intelligence. Some considered the institute's work an outrage, brainwashing, hysteria, even satanic. Others wondered how the group-therapy atmosphere at Monroe, in which people sat around in casual clothes, emoting and hugging each other, could ever really be compatible with rank-and-file military culture.

But for Dames, Ray, Smith, and Cavanaugh, as for most if not all of the remote viewers before them, the Monroe experience was all right. It was the start of their heroic journey. None of them had OBEs while in the course, but some of the tapes seemed fairly intense, mind-stretching. Dames would lie in his darkened cubicle—Paul Smith, his roommate, had his own cubicle a few yards away—and would put headphones on. He would wait as a Monroe staff person in a nearby control room put in a tape. The first time it happened, he was almost ecstatic with anticipation. He felt that his life would never again be the same.

For a typical visitor to Monroe, lying naked in his or her cubicle, the experience began with a prelude sequence featuring gently crashing waves—*shhhhhhhhhhh*—of synthesized noise. Then Bob Monroe's voice drifted in through the headphones, guiding the visitor through various exercises, preparatory visualizations, and subtly, behind everything, there were the Hemi-Sync tones.

The visitor now began to drift through the strange upside-down subterrain mapped by Bob Monroe . . . through gentle "Focus 10," where his arms and legs and torso stilled and slept . . . through higher-pitched, narcotic "Focus 12" . . . through portentous "Focus 15," where the sense of time was left behind . . . then up and up, the tones rising madly, though multicolored cloud layers, through the cloud-tops, incredible, tingling, muscles tensing, temporal lobes seizing, manic, orgasmic, hallucinogenic "Focus 21" . . . an alternate reality, indescribable—

—and then gently back down again, through the clouds, the Hemi-Sync tones singing quietly beneath the evocatively synthesized surf, beneath Bob Monroe's hypnotic voice.

As the week wore on, participants in the course found themselves going deeper and deeper into altered states, and more easily each time. They found that living in altered states in the daytime, focusing on those drifting, dreamlike experiences, was like living in another world. They were more relaxed, more introspective, more attuned to the hidden potentials that were always being talked about. They were effectively allowed only several hours of sleep per night—a sleep punctuated by wildly vivid, intense dreams—but that was all right, too; they seemed to get plenty of rest during the day, listening to the Hemi-Sync tapes.

Between the tapes and the group meetings they could walk out the ground-floor door of the Monroe building, near the meeting room, and it was as if they were walking out into space almost. A broad lawn stretched down in front of them into a valley, which rose up steeply again into a range of hills, with trees and fields, and someone's llama farm over there somewhere. After a particularly deep tape—"Freeflow Focus 12" worked wonders for some people—those trees and fields and hills could take on an amazing, floating, LSD-trip vividness. One look and the candidate remote viewers could see why Bob Monroe had chosen this spot to build his institute, his inner-space launch pad.

Bob Monroe was all right, too. His ideas might have seemed a bit exotic, but somehow they went down more easily because Monroe himself possessed such a worldly gravity. He was a kindly, gray-haired man in his sixties, with a mellow, southern-tinted accent, a lingual amalgam of all the places he had lived. The only hints of his otherworldly intercourse were two rather severe dark circles under his eyes; his sleep patterns had been permanently altered a quarter century before, at the start of his own journey, and he now slept only a few hours at a time.

When candidates in the remote-viewing program visited the Monroe Institute, they did so in the company of other INSCOM personnel, not ordinary civilians. But even in this somewhat secretive military environment, where no one asked too many questions about what a fellow student did back in Washington, there was a special inner circle of experiment and experience, consisting of those who were part of the remote-viewing program.

Monroe and his staff, for example, had a small research project that focused on Joe McMoneagle. In their research building, they had a special altered-state chamber, soundproofed, utterly dark, with a half-filled water bed set to human skin temperature. McMoneagle, wearing headphones, would sink into the bed and float down through his inner space. Monroe and his staff would sit in a control room outside, monitoring McMoneagle's state of consciousness via a number of electrical leads taped to his body. One set measured the electrical resistance of his skin; another the voltage between his head and his toes. When the values reached a certain level, it meant that Joe had gone into his zone.

They experimented for months with special Hemi-Sync tones and tapes, trying to boost McMoneagle's RV performance. (They only succeeded in shortening his cool-down time.) They taught the beefy warrant officer to have OBEs almost at will, and found that when he did so, the voltage between his head and his toes suddenly *reversed*. Why that should have been, no one seemed to know.

Down at Monroe, on the Gateway Course, Ed Dames and his fellow trainees heard the stories about McMoneagle's OBEs—plus some stranger ones. One time, for example, Bob Monroe had given Joe McMoneagle a target to remote-view, and McMoneagle had described an evolution-promoting energy being who had somehow come to Earth many years ago. The target, it turned out, was Jesus Christ. Another, less well-known entity, "Miranon," from somewhere else in space and time, seemed actually to possess Bob Monroe one day in the early 1980s, speaking through him like a spirit through a medium. In effect, Monroe's OBE session had turned into a "channelling" session. At the time Dames and the others first visited the institute, Miranon still possessed Bob fairly often. Bob had even given his guest's name to the pleasant lake down in the valley, Lake Miranon, where Monroe students swam naked on summer afternoons, cleansing themselves for their next dark adventures.

But the strangest story was the one about Bob Monroe's

encounter with the mysterious Inga Arnyet. Monroe had gone out of body one day, had been out in space, in some sparsely populated nether zone, when suddenly he had sensed a human presence. A woman. A foreign woman. The name "Inga Arnyet" came to him, and Monroe had the impression that she was a KGB "extrasensor," one of the Soviet counterparts of America's remote viewers. She had been trying to psychically zero in on America's remote-viewing program somehow, yet for some reason the only landing zone open to her had been in the alternate reality then inhabited by Bob Monroe. She hovered, watching him, sensing him, inside this weird and timeless OBE tableau. She seemed pleasant and unthreatening, but who could tell what she was up to? Was she reading his mind? Trying to read U.S. military secrets? Monroe quietly mentioned the incident to Skip Atwater, and suggested he look for an Inga Arnyet on the Pentagon's list of known Soviet intelligence personnel.

Atwater checked it out, but never found the name anywhere. Even so, the story spread among the Fort Meade initiates, and grew wings; it was a nice shamanic tale to get them on their way. After the Cold War was over, Ed Dames would claim to have heard more or less the same story, a story about Soviet extrasensors invading the mind of some elderly American gentleman, from a former KGB officer he met on the New Age conference circuit.

Ingo Swann would later say that he had not wanted to start the training program when he did. By the autumn of 1982, he had only reached Stage Three of his complex technique. But the DIA's Jack Vorona and Jim Salyer, and the Army, had put the pressure on, had made clear that it was now or never. Perhaps they had foreseen the climate shift that was about to occur.

In any case, Swann finally gave in. The first students, Tom Nance and Rob Cowart, arrived that November. Each month thereafter, more or less, they spent two weeks at SRI in training, and the other two back at Fort Meade. Soon Rob was forced to withdraw, after his cancer diagnosis. Later came two civilians from the National Security Agency—a woman named Debbie Norfeld, who was to be trained as a remote viewer, and a man named Richard Henderson, who was to be trained as her RV monitor and analyst. Unfortunately, after they had made a few visits, NSA suddenly backed out of the program. It turned out that Norfeld and Henderson's office apparently hadn't received the proper authorization for their participation in the strange training program at SRI. The higher-ups at NSA clamped down, and Swann never heard from Norfeld or Henderson again. Some time later, their training interleaved with Nance's, there were two trainees from another secretive agency. Finally, there were the four from INSCOM.

If Swann had begun his training program under pressure, at short notice, it wasn't evident by the time Ed Dames and the other three arrived at SRI in the spring of 1984. Swann was now in the didactic mode he seemed to like best. He made the rules, taught what he wanted, and his pupils obeyed and listened, or they were gone.

First there were lectures, given by Swann from the head of the RV table. Dames and the others would sit around the table and take notes, and afterwards—and overnight for homework—they would have to write essays on what Swann had said. Swann put great emphasis on the precise definition of certain key words, words like "structure," "matrix," "ideogram," "cognitron," "signal line," "feeling-motion," "aperture," "mind-dynamic process." Lectures were by far the least enjoyable part of the experience.

Even practice sessions were arduous, especially in the early months, with the focus on Stage One, and ideograms. Ideograms were the big trial of remote viewing, the wilderness one had to cross before one could achieve apotheosis. For hours and days, Swann called out the geographical co-ordinates of various easy targets, and Dames let his pen shake across the paper, and more often than not, Swann responded with a stony silence. Swann said he did not believe in negative reinforcement, in saying, "That's incorrect." To him, this only promoted despair, and thus damaged the neural-rewiring process of learning. When he wanted to signify failure, he said nothing. Dames and the others soon came to dread these nothings.

Eventually, after weeks of lectures and one-on-one practice sessions, Dames found that his ideograms were beginning to resemble the shapes that Swann said they should. Then he would do quick sessions, running from ideograms to Stage Two basic sensory perceptions, to dimensionals and rough, Stage Three sketches, vocalizing as he worked, "rolling" . . . "wavy" . . . "terrain" . . . "sandy" . . . "dry" . . . "hot" . . . "expansive" . . . and if it was a good day Swann would curtly respond "correct" . . . "correct" . . . "correct" to almost every bit of information as the session unfurled.* And finally Swann would say, "Okay, let's end the session," and putting his cigar down for a moment, he would hand Dames the target folder, and Dames would open it the way one might open a Christmas present, full of expectation and wonder, and there would be a clipping from *National Geographic*, with dramatic orange-brown dunes of the Sahara, a high sea of sand—sandy, dry, hot, expansive—and Dames would beam, barely able to contain his grin. "Pat yourself on the back," Swann

---

* Swann gave constant feedback throughout such sessions, in the same way a piano teacher might provide a running commentary as a student played. As a learning-reinforcement technique, it made sense, but of course it removed any experimental value the session results might have had. For rigorous experiments, no such feedback would be given, and the monitor himself would be blind to the actual target.

would say, for he did believe in positive reinforcement. On the other hand, he often made a student who had finished a good session "rest" for several hours, or even quit for the day, when all the student wanted to do was more remote viewing. Swann was constantly worried about "overtraining," overstretching the synapses until the developing structure collapsed.

For all Swann's prickliness and idiosyncrasies, Dames and the others began to love him, the way one begins to love, as retrospect nears, a stern drill sergeant or a tough but skillful schoolteacher. Some of them even likened Swann to those *Star Wars* characters, old Yoda and bearded Obi-Wan Kenobi, the wise instructors on Luke Skywalker's path to Jedi knighthood. Swann seemed to welcome the comparison.

Had remote-viewing training produced no new talents in the group from INSCOM, their sentiments toward Swann would have been far different. But all did well enough to be convinced, at a deep level, that it was all real, that they were developing a fantastic skill that could be useful. Some of them, at times during sessions, experienced a phenomenon that Swann came to call *bilocation*. Although CRV sessions normally proceeded with the viewer in a relatively awake, unaltered state of consciousness, a bilocation was a brief moment of total hallucination, a visionary flash in which the viewer had a deep, dreamlike awareness of the target. He suddenly lost touch with his surroundings, and was, as far as he could tell, *at* the target site, experiencing it with raw, sometimes overpowering emotional and sensory force—before he just as quickly snapped back again to the real world. When a bilocation happened, Swann made the viewer say and write "bilo break," and often terminated the session. Remote viewers who had experienced bilocations never forgot them. Paul

Smith would experience one during training, switching rapidly between a multi-sensory vision of Kwajalein atoll in the South Pacific, and the city streets where he was actually walking.

Dames and the others came to Swann for training two weeks every month or so, through the spring and summer of 1984. In Menlo Park, the four stayed in a local hotel, and when they were not in lectures, or waiting in the "recovery room" for their next RV session, they could loiter at pool-side, or go to the beach, or take in a movie. For a while, as part of the program, they underwent personality and neurological tests, but that didn't take long, and as training progressed, they had a remarkable amount of freedom. Weekends were the best, for Swann forbade drinking at all other times. Friday afternoon would come, and Swann would set down his pen and cigar for the day, and Dames might open his briefcase and take out a six-pack he'd stashed away, and when the group had consumed those, they would go out for more drinks, and dinner. Swann would often go with them—now fun-loving, amusingly voluble Ingo. Then Monday would dawn, one or two of the fellows nursing hangovers, and training would resume.

Ingo liked the four of them, liked to socialize with them, and liked the training program generally. But he didn't like Menlo Park; his heart had always been in New York City, where he still managed, with trips here and there, to spend a large part of his time. By prior arrangement with IN-SCOM, he moved his training school back to Manhattan in the summer of 1984. SRI had an office in midtown, where Swann set up an RV room and a control room like the one in California. Dames and the others now merely had to take a short flight up from Washington, and could go home on weekends. Common was the sight, that summer, of bearded, graying Ingo, leading three younger men and a woman around Manhattan landmarks, inviting them to experience the feeling-motion of a skyscraper, or the Stage Two texture of a lonely, soot-dusted tree.

Over a few beers, or otherwise running around Manhattan or the San Francisco Bay Area having a good time, Ed Dames seemed to consider himself one of the guys. But in his heart of hearts, he held himself apart. He believed that he alone understood the historical crest they all were riding; he believed that he alone was a true student of remote viewing, ready to take it back to the Army, to study it, to expand it, to make it better. He thought of himself as Ingo's one true protégé, his Luke Skywalker, groomed to become, in his words, "caretaker of the technology."

Swann, however, took a slightly different view. He liked Dames; he considered the young officer intelligent, and highly motivated. But Dames wasn't really meant to be a remote viewer, just a monitor and analyst. Swann considered his true protégé to be Tom Nance. The dark-haired Army captain, in Swann's view, was the formal prototype for the CRV-trained military remote viewer, the best that could be achieved. Dames and his classmates would train over several months, but Nance's training, begun in late 1982, would not really end until Swann's contract with INSCOM expired two years later.

Nance had jet-black hair and a mustache, and his face was handsome, vaguely impish. He brought a certain patience and precision to his RV work—but he also had, like Dames, a fierce independent spirit. He owned a motorcycle, and loved to travel long distances on the open road, *Easy Rider* style. Some of the others wondered what he was doing in the Army.

Nance became closer to Swann than any other student had been, and by most accounts, he was the best ever to emerge from Swann's training program. His sessions might start slow, with a few pages to get Stage One right—declaring "miss break" after each attempt, and taking the coordinates again—but by the end it would often seem that he had grasped the signal line as tightly as anyone ever could. In May 1984, near the close of his formal training program (he would return later for refresher work), Swann put him through a valedictory series of sessions, designed to showcase his talents. The results were bound into a red folder and shown to Army and DIA officials.*

One of the targets was Grand Coulee Dam. Nance had not only drawn it accurately, describing it as a dam, but had also made a Stage Six model in white clay, depicting the dam, and a small attached building near the riverbank. Later an SRI photographer had been sent out to take a picture of the dam from the same angle; the photo now lies next to the photo of Nance's almost identical clay model.

Another target was a certain site in Tulsa, Oklahoma, architecturally a zoo of geometries—globes and pyramids and cubes. The site reminded Nance of the Vatican, and of Disneyland; it was churchlike, school-like, and also a quiet place, "funereal." The strange geometric shapes began to appear on the session paper, first alone and then organized together. By Stage Four, Nance had identified the place as a university. At the end he had actually named the site, Oral Roberts University.

There was Bunker Hill National Monument, in Boston, which Nance sketched—with tourists—and named. There was Grant's Tomb in New York, named and drawn in neat detail. There was also a site in Mexico somewhere, gradually taking shape as the session wore on, a disused place, grand, overlooking the sea, a temple to forgotten gods. Nance tried Stage Seven phonics: "Tuh" "too" "luh" "loo"—"Tulum."

Six years later, following Nance's divorce, master and protégé would travel to the Yucatán together, among other

---

* Swann apparently was not blinded to these targets, and may have provided some feedback to Nance during the sessions.

things visiting the ancient temple at Tulum. And Nance would experience, as remote viewers often do when they encounter their targets in the real world, a certain strange thrill that told him he had already been there.

20

FLAMEOUT

> He was in the cubicle with his headphones on, and then
> he came out, naked. He went after a nurse. . . . They
> had to take him away in a straitjacket.
>
> —Ed Dames, on the Lieutenant
> Pemberton incident

AFTER LEAVING FORT MEADE IN 1981, MEL RILEY ENDED UP BACK
at his old aerial reconnaissance unit in Germany, and once
more became a conventional Cold Warrior, peeking under
the clouds at Warsaw Pact secrets. But he continued to
remote-view on occasion, informally, just to keep in
psychic shape. And he maintained contact with Atwater
and the others back at Fort Meade, monitoring the situation.

As he neared the end of his tour in Germany, he decided
that he wanted to become a professional remote viewer
again. The program was expanding with the SRI training
contract. Operational taskings were still coming in. It
sounded as if good things were happening.

Riley applied for transfer back to the unit, and his application was accepted. In the summer of 1984, he and his
wife Brigitte sold their house in Germany and packed their
bags for the trip home. In five more years Riley would be
eligible for retirement with full benefits. He intended to

finish those years as a remote viewer, and there seemed to be nothing to stop him.

Then one day, not long before he was to leave for the United States, he received a phone call from Brian Busby at Fort Meade. Busby was apologetic but blunt. Riley's destination, the remote-viewing unit, was about to become extinct. "Sorry, guy," said Busby. "You're fucked."

The crisis had been brewing since 1981, when Ed Thompson departed as the assistant chief of staff for intelligence. The ACSI was in a sense the top slot in Army intelligence, but the office then carried the same rank—major general— as the office of INSCOM commander. For Army intelligence to run smoothly, the ACSI and the INSCOM commander therefore had to get along relatively well. During Thompson's tour as ACSI that had been the case. Thompson and the INSCOM commander, William Rolya, had seen eye to eye on most issues, including the delicate issue of the remote-viewing program.

Then in 1981 the guard changed. Thompson was replaced by William Odom, and Rolya by Bert Stubblebine. Odom (who would go on to head the National Security Agency a few years later) emphatically did not share Stubblebine's interest in paranormal and mystical matters, and on the whole the two men did not get along. It was clear by the middle of 1984 that Stubblebine, now derisively nicknamed "General Spoonbender," was becoming increasingly marginalized in the running of Army intelligence. A number of INSCOM staff officers had begun, in effect, to take orders from Odom instead.

Even in the remote-viewing program, where support for Stubblebine might have been strongest, the general was thought to have gone too far in his enthusiasms. By promoting a series of questionable projects in the alternative realm, he was giving one that seemed to be worth something—remote viewing—a bad name.

The general was also starting to interfere directly with the remote-viewing program. Around 1983, he befriended freelance psychic Alex Tannous, and seemed to be thinking about giving him official psychic spying assignments, presumably on some kind of contract basis. Skip Atwater saw this and realized that it was time for damage control. On his advice, Brian Busby raised the matter with Stubblebine, respectfully making the point that Tannous should work through the Fort Meade remote-viewing unit, or should keep away from Army intelligence altogether. The unit, said Busby, would be happy to give him a tryout. Stubblebine eventually agreed.

One evening, not long afterwards, Tannous was at a party somewhere in the D.C. area when he was informed that General Stubblebine had a car and driver waiting outside for him. He went outside, got into the car, and was taken to Fort Meade. The driver pulled up in front of two isolated wooden buildings numbered 2560 and 2561.

Inside, Tannous was met by Atwater, Busby, and several remote viewers. He was suitably impressed by the cloak-and-dagger aura of it all. He was also wearing makeup and eyeliner, and seemed to conform all too well to the stereotype of the flaky, self-absorbed psychic. He seemed to be expecting this sort of special treatment.

After signing a nondisclosure form, Tannous was briefly told about the unit, now code-named Center Lane, and was then ushered into building 2560, into one of the RV rooms. Atwater gave him an operational target, related to a crisis then going on somewhere in the world. Tannous, instead of describing the target, began to ask questions about it. *Is it like this? Is it like that?* He seemed to need considerable "front-loading." In the end he produced no information of value. The tryout was over. Stubblebine backed down.

But Stubblebine still managed to handpick recruits, as long as he stayed within INSCOM's ranks. That kind of interference was also resented by Atwater, Busby, and the remote viewers. The program was meant to select people with reliable, well-tested psychic abilities as well as other attributes such as discipline and intelligence. Stubblebine didn't seem as interested in those criteria when he selected people. It was hit or miss. Lyn Buchanan, though a nice enough fellow, hadn't even been selected for his remote-viewing potential. Essentially he had been selected because Stubblebine was fascinated by spoonbending and other supposed PK manifestations, and had heard the story of the computer network crash at Augsburg—an incident that, of course, might have had a completely mundane explanation. Whether or not Buchanan had any real PK abilities, there was just no use for them in the program. Such phenomena were considered far less robust than remote viewing. Buchanan had therefore been squeezed into the role of remote viewer instead.*

In the end, Buchanan didn't perform badly, and he was also respected as a good monitor and a teacher of RV techniques. But a short time after he joined the unit, another Stubblebine recruit appeared on the scene—a blonde corporal from an INSCOM base in Greece, named Dawn Lutz. She was known to her friends as a palm-reader, and that seemed to have been good enough for Stubblebine to send her to Fort Meade. Unfortunately, she wasn't interested in learning the more formal remote-viewing techniques now being used by the unit. (There was no money in the budget to send Stubblebine's recruits to SRI, but they were expected to learn the Swann technique from others at Fort Meade who had been taught it.) Lutz, like Alex Tannous, didn't seem able to produce good data. Feeling unwelcome, she soon transferred out of the unit.

---

* The Army's Personnel Command (PERSCOM) briefly rescinded Buchanan's orders to transfer to the RV unit, advising him that the move was unjustified and could hurt his career. Stubblebine contacted PERSCOM and demanded that the orders be restored. They were.

* * *

It eventually became the perception, from the remote viewers on up to senior levels in the Pentagon, that Major General Stubblebine had begun to focus too intensely on the paranormal. It was as if he had embarked on some kind of spiritual quest, and were trying to take the Army along for the ride. Nothing symbolized this more than his visits to the Monroe Institute.

The Monroe Institute held its five-day Gateway Voyage/RAPT courses for INSCOM personnel every few weeks. In late 1983 and early 1984 Stubblebine managed to make his way down for most of the courses, to ride the waves of Bob Monroe's Hemi-Sync tapes. Once or twice he stayed for the entire five days, but mostly he came down only for the final day. He was there when Ed Dames and Paul Smith and the other Swann trainees took their course in December 1983, and he was there in the spring of 1984 when Lyn Buchanan and Dawn Lutz—and Colonel John Alexander, and even Stubblebine's own office secretary—went down for their own Hemi-Sync treatment.

Already by the winter of 1983, in the group discussions at the course, Stubblebine was telling his INSCOM officers the following story: One day, on a walk near the Monroe buildings, down the road towards Lake Miranon, he had seen a little yellow-orange salamander cross his path. It was just a salamander, yet—it seemed significant somehow. It symbolized the . . . *rightness* . . . of what he, Major General Stubblebine, was doing at INSCOM, the *wisdom* of his alternative approach to the management of military intelligence.

Now, the perception of hypersignificance in what would otherwise seem to be a random event was a classic aspect of altered-state behavior, probably most familiar to hallucinogen users. Sometimes it was the only kind of logic one heard down at Monroe, where people spent several hours in trance each day, straining to have some kind of mystical, transcendental experience. It seemed to some that the general was obsessed with the idea of having an OBE, and was compensating for his failure with the overblown salamander story. As such, it was all part of the Monroe experience, not to be taken too seriously.

But the story of the general and his salamander soon spread throughout INSCOM, and higher. Senior Army officials became worried about what was going on in Stubblebine's INSCOM. General Ed Thompson and a colleague went to see Stubblebine, and expressed their concerns. It didn't seem to make any difference. One general, a close friend of Stubblebine's from their days at West Point, would later describe Stubblebine as having gone "overboard." Stubblebine's critics would also use the term "loss of perspective."

Matters were made especially bad for Stubblebine by the brewing "Yellow Fruit" scandal, in which some of INSCOM's covert-action squads had used the blackness of their budgets to buy or rent expensive cars, prostitutes, and other things which were obviously not essential to their missions. Although Stubblebine was never accused of involvement, and in fact played an important part in exposing the scandal, the impression spread that INSCOM was out of control. Stubblebine's career seemed to be teetering on the edge of a precipice.

Back in 1982 or 1983, Richard Kennett at the CIA had been asked to consult with the Army on its involvement with the Monroe Institute. Kennett had declined any involvement, citing concerns over the "human use" implications. He believed that by promoting altered states, one made the brain more unstable, more prone to spontaneous hallucinations and delusions. He could see no reason at all why the Army should be involved with Monroe, and could see many reasons why it should not.

One of Kennett's reasons, though unstated in his comments to the Army, was that he had once had his own OBE, using some tips he had picked up from one of Bob Monroe's books. He had felt himself separating from his prone, sleeping form, like a crab molting from its old shell. Then he was free. He walked across the room—but now there were other beings in the room. There were monsters. Some kind of goblin hobbled up, put its nose right in his face, stared at him. *Jesus!* Kennett went back over to his bed, and tried to get back inside his body. He wasn't sure he could do it. The goblin—

Kennett made it back all right, but he would recommend, to anyone who asked, that out-of-body experiences be avoided like the plague. He suspected that the effects on the emotions, and on the nervous system in general, could result in heart attacks, psychological trauma, and even psychotic breaks in people who were already unstable.

Kennett's recommendations seemed to go unheard. Then one day in 1984, a young INSCOM lieutenant, Doug Pemberton, decided to go down to Monroe for the Gateway course. Pemberton, the son of a general, was the kind who would do two hundred push-ups before breakfast, and then would practice martial arts. In any case, he went down to the Monroe Institute on the INSCOM bus, and was assigned a Hemi-Sync cubicle. He began listening to the tapes, and sitting in on group discussion sessions. A day or so into the course, there was the perception that he was harassing one of the female trainers. The disturbance seemed to pass, but things still didn't seem quite right with Pemberton. At one point, around the third day of the course, Pemberton and the other students were in their cubicles, drifting along on those mellifluously synthesized waves of Hemi-Sync sound. Fifteen or twenty minutes into the tape, a Monroe staffer noticed Pemberton in one of the hallways near his room. Doug Pemberton had been riding those Hemi-Sync waves all right, but had gone a bit too far with them. He was naked and incoherent. He was taken away to a psychiatric ward at Walter Reed Army Medical Center.

It was revealed later that Lieutenant Pemberton (who soon recovered) had a history of psychiatric treatment that he had kept out of his Army records and had never admitted in the Monroe screening questionnaire.* Had this been known, it was said, Pemberton would never have been allowed into the Gateway course in the first place. But it was too late. The toothpaste was forever out of the tube. After William Odom, the ACSI, began to use the incident against Stubblebine at high levels, the INSCOM commander "fell on his sword," in a colleague's words, and resigned. He would later become an executive at the BDM Corporation, a defense contractor in suburban Virginia.

Stubblebine's replacement was Major General Harry Soyster, sent by higher-ups at the Pentagon to clean house at INSCOM. Like Odom, Soyster took a relatively dim view of the paranormal. But even before Soyster arrived at INSCOM, it was clear that Stubblebine's apparent excesses, and the growing opposition from Odom, spelled the end of the alternative, fringeish programs in the Army. Without support from somewhere else, the Fort Meade remote-viewing unit was doomed.

One day in 1984, around the time that Stubblebine's demise was becoming inevitable, Richard Kennett was asked to attend a briefing on the remote-viewing program. The briefing was primarily for CIA director William Casey and his top deputies; but as a senior analyst who had been read onto the program years before, and had written a number

---

* Oddly, the same was said to have been true of the famous MKULTRA casualty Frank Olson (see p. 202), who apparently had a history of suicidal tendencies for several years prior to his fateful acid test with CIA scientist Sidney Gottlieb.

of reports and recommendations on it, Kennett was invited as well.

Kennett now was only a year away from leaving the Agency for a job in private industry; meanwhile he was preoccupied with relatively mundane matters, especially the development of chemical and biological weapons by the Soviet Union and some of its client states and allies. His involvement with Pat Price and others at SRI was a distant memory. But he was anxious to see how the program had progressed under the DIA's and the Army's sponsorship.

Others were less anxious. Robert Gates, now the head of the Directorate of Intelligence, walked out of the room in disgust when he heard what the briefing was about. He simply refused to take any remote-viewing stories seriously. In any case, he had enough controversy on his hands already; the CIA was just then running a small war in Central America, funneling arms to the Nicaraguan contras and harassing the Sandinistas, and trying to keep Congress from shutting the whole operation down.

The briefing on the remote-viewing program was run by Jack Vorona from the DIA. He discussed the history of the program and some examples of recent operational and experimental sessions. Ostensibly, the briefing was meant to keep Casey and his top officials informed of what was going on.

But imparting information wasn't the only point of the briefing. Vorona was apparently also hoping for some support from the CIA. If only he could get a senior official from the Agency, someone at Gates's level, or even a rung lower, to say a few kind words about the program to the intelligence committees on Capitol Hill. A few kind words to keep the budget flowing. The supporters of the program in the DIA knew that John McMahon, at least privately, was still relatively enthusiastic about remote viewing. But McMahon, now at a fairly lofty stage in his career, had begun to seem more worried about the "giggle factor," and had been distancing himself from the program.

McMahon's boss, Casey, was more daring; in fact, he was one of the most politically fearless directors the Agency had ever seen. As nominal head of the U.S. intelligence community, he probably could have killed the remote-viewing program if he had wanted to, but he didn't. If anything, he seemed impressed and interested with what Vorona presented. He asked to be kept posted on further developments. Still, Casey reacted that way to a lot of things, and nothing really came of the briefing. Richard Kennett had the impression that no one at the Agency—no one the intelligence committees would take seriously—was about to stick his neck out for the RV program.

Kennett himself was disappointed by the briefing. The remote-viewing data he saw on Vorona's viewgraphs seemed to him like the same material he had seen ten years earlier. The remote viewers, for all their vaunted training at SRI, didn't seem to be getting any better. And still no one had figured out a way to tell when a remote viewer was *on*, as opposed to when he was off. The only way was to try to verify the information with other sources, but as Kennett saw it, the psi information wasn't consistently accurate or detailed enough in the first place to justify that kind of diversion of intelligence resources. Some of the data remote viewers provided were amazingly good, but other data were embarrassingly bad. (Kennett might not have known it, but around this time, one of the remote viewers out at SRI had spontaneously "foreseen" a deadly terrorist attack on Washington, D.C. The plot involved a vehicle with a nuclear device parked outside the U.S. Capitol on the night President Reagan was to give his annual State of the Union address. The FBI had been alerted, but no such vehicle had been found and no bomb had gone off. The entire thing had been an "Aol.")

Seeing that nothing much had changed in ten years,

Kennett was convinced that remote viewing's signal-to-noise ratio was just too low. There was no way, in his opinion, that it was ready to become a regular, everyday intelligence-gathering technology. The term *PSI-INT* would probably have to wait until the next millennium.

It looked as if Ed Dames's heroic journey to Jedi knighthood had hit a dead end. He was sent back to his old office at SED. Bill Ray and Paul Smith and Charlene Cavanaugh went into similar holding patterns. Others already at the remote-viewing unit began thinking about where else they might like to go.

The remote-viewing program nevertheless managed to survive. Jack Vorona, the super god in the sky, somehow worked it out with his budgeters and his friends in Congress, and arranged for a transfer of the men and women of the Fort Meade unit to his Scientific and Technical Intelligence Directorate at the DIA. The plan was that the unit would stay in its old offices at Fort Meade. When Army funding ran out, at the end of 1985, DIA funding would begin. In the meantime the unit would be in a kind of limbo; there would be no operations, only day after day of training. Lieutenant Colonel Brian Busby left for another post, and Bill Ray, now a major, was appointed as the unit's temporary commander.

Morale in the unit declined rapidly, and by the end of 1985 Tom Nance was gone. Nance had been something of a legend for the cool, technical perfection of his CRV sessions. He had been the living embodiment of the Swannian principles of remote viewing. He hadn't been perfect; he had had his bad days, and the rigid structure of his CRV technique had often prevented him from really getting to the heart of his targets. But he had been the best of the unit's second generation, and his departure was seen as a further blow to the program. He left, he said, to get back to ordinary life. His marriage and his Army career had suffered from his remote-viewing work. He took a post some-where overseas.

Shortly after Nance left, one of the remote viewers in the unit wrote up a series of memoranda, making light of the unit's predicament, and the hostility that continued to be directed at it by General Odom. One read:

THE CONTINUING SAGA OF THE PSI-FORCE 5
This week's thriller:
IMPENDING ODOOM
As we rejoin our heroes, we find that disaster has taken its toll among the ranks of the Psi-Force 5. The loss of their comrade, Tom, has seriously affected their ability to save the world from the encroaching mundanity of those dreaded enemies of forward thinkers everywhere, the Odomites. . . .

As our story opens, Bill, the fast-talking, take-charge commander of *The Force*, is briefing the crew on the training schedule:

"I know you all want to get on with fighting the Odomites, and saving humanity everywhere, but we are strategically prevented from working right now, and this is a good time for training. Like my idol, General Custer, used to say, 'Proper training and good leadership! That's what wins battles!'" . . .

The SRI program ended up faring better. During 1984 and into 1985, Vorona and Hal Puthoff lobbied Congress and various military and civilian intelligence offices for funding, while continuing to take occasional operational tasks to the remaining SRI viewers. Briefings and remote-viewing demonstrations were held for members of Congress, the White House, the Navy, the Air Force, the National Security Council, the Joint Chiefs of Staff, the CIA, the NSA, the FBI, the Secret Service, the Drug Enforcement Administration, the Customs Service, the Coast Guard, the

Defense Advanced Research Projects Agency, and various Pentagon task forces concerned with drug interdiction. Even President Reagan's science adviser, George Keyworth, received a briefing.

Eventually SRI won key support from one of these agencies—a Pentagon-affiliated agency which no one wants to identify—and a five-year, $10 million R&D contract was arranged, one of its purposes being the investigation of the neurophysiology of remote viewing and other forms of psi. An enviable assortment of scientific and medical review panels was set up. Hal Puthoff was satisfied that the SRI program would be safe for a while.

Especially now, in the post-Stubblebine climate, Puthoff knew he had to be very guarded in his enthusiasm for remote viewing when he spoke before congressmen or intelligence officials. But in private he seemed extraordinarily confident about the technique's potential. Since the mid and late 1970s he had been using remote viewing on jaunts to Las Vegas. He and his wife and friends would sit in their hotel room before going down to the casino. The plan was that they would go into the casino at a certain time, would walk over to one of the roulette wheels, and would start to bet immediately after the roulette ball landed on one of the green 00 markers. Up in the room beforehand, they would try to guess—precognitively—on the results of a stretch of, say, ten roulette spins following the 00, using a combined-result error-correcting technique like the one Charles Tart had used in the shell-game study. When Puthoff was satisfied that their guesses had converged on a particular sequence of blacks and reds, the party would go down to the casino, wait for the 00 signal, and place their bets. On many of these occasions, he said later, he and his friends won back the cost of their trip, and then some.

Towards the mid-1980s, Puthoff and his wife, Adrienne, became involved with the founding of a new private school in the Menlo Park area. A key investor backed out at the last minute, and the board was faced with a twenty-five-thousand-dollar shortfall, several weeks before the school year began. With nothing else left to do but fold the school and send teachers and students elsewhere, Puthoff proposed a variant of Targ and Harary's silver-futures scheme. The board warily backed the idea. Puthoff and his wife soon assembled a small team of board members and quickly trained them in associative remote viewing. On each day of silver-futures trading, they tried to view precognitively an unspecified object they would be shown the following day. Puthoff, running the operation, secretly selected two objects—say, a hat and a bicycle—one of which signified "market up," the other "market down." If the responses from the viewers were reasonably unambiguous on any given day, Puthoff would direct his broker to make a trade, buying or selling as appropriate. Unlike Targ and Harary's story, this one had a happy ending. After a month, these first-time remote viewers had made the twenty-five thousand dollars they needed. The school was saved.

But Puthoff's career was about to swerve onto a new track.

Puthoff knew that funding for SRI's remote-viewing research would continue until the end of the decade. But he could see the clouds that were building over the program, and he was beginning to grow bored with the management of it all. To add to his headaches, there were the internal politics at SRI, which seemed only to have gotten worse after the departure of Targ and Harary. Jim Salyer was starting to micromanage the program, and seemed to be playing favorites with certain remote viewers. He and Puthoff were increasingly at odds.

While all this was pressing in on him, Puthoff suddenly saw an opportunity elsewhere, an opportunity of suitable grandness for a man so used to working on the secret edge of things.

Since the early 1970s Puthoff had served as a part-time paid consultant to Bill Church, his philanthropist friend from Texas. Church, who had then been bothered by OPEC's stranglehold on world oil, wanted advice on alternative energy sources. Puthoff hadn't spent a lot of time researching the problem, but from the early 1980s he had become increasingly interested in a phenomenon known as "zero-point energy," or "vacuum energy," a background field of electromagnetic energy throughout the universe (which was different from, and much stronger than, the cosmic microwave background from the Big Bang). Though postulated for decades by quantum physicists, zero-point energy had generally been considered too obscure and difficult a subject for deep exploration. Puthoff nevertheless believed that he could conceivably tap into this energy, thus providing a truly ultimate power source, better even than nuclear fusion.

At Puthoff's urging, Church started a small company to try to develop zero-point-energy-tapping technology. By the late autumn of 1984, Puthoff was encouraged enough by preliminary engineering work that he made the decision to join the venture, Jupiter Technologies, full-time.

For months, while SRI's big remote-viewing contract was being negotiated through the DIA, Puthoff told no one of his decision to leave, for fear of jeopardizing the deal. Then, in the early summer of 1985, on the day the contract came through, he suddenly announced his resignation. Two weeks later, he was gone.

Joe McMoneagle had retired from the Army in September 1984. He had been in "retirement mode," as it was called, for a while, and his life had been changing. His second wife, Peggy, had become increasingly annoyed by his long hours at the RV unit, and by his long trips to SRI and the Monroe Institute. Joe and Peggy had grown apart, and then had separated, and then had agreed to divorce.

Throughout this time the Monroe Institute had become a kind of second home for McMoneagle. He loved working at the institute, with Bob Monroe and his staff; the atmosphere there was much more congenial than at Fort Meade. McMoneagle also had fallen in love with one of Bob Monroe's stepdaughters, Nancy Honeycutt, and hoped to marry her.

Aside from all that, there was something about the central Virginia hills that attracted McMoneagle. He had gone there to calm his soul after returning from Vietnam a decade and a half before. Now he went to those hills to get away from the bustle and clutter of the Washington, D.C., area. The city had been getting on his nerves. He suspected that years of remote viewing had left him too open to other people's mental noise. Up in the glorious hills, there was a lot less of that.

For the last year or so of his work at Fort Meade, McMoneagle spent his weekends down at Monroe, commuting up to Washington on Mondays and back on Fridays. After he retired, he and Nancy built a house near the institute. He signed on at SRI as a consultant, and did research and occasional operational work with Ed May, who was running the program after Puthoff's departure. Joe and Nancy also started their own company, Intuitive Intelligence Applications, catering to police departments or intelligence agencies or just ordinary people who felt they needed psychic assistance. He did a lot of work over the fax machine. A client could put a target in an envelope and place it on a desk in California, and McMoneagle could remote-view it, no problem, from his house in the hills three thousand miles away. His remote-viewing skills seemed undiminished despite all the years, and although he was disappointed at the way things had turned out at Fort Meade, he didn't feel burned out. He felt that he still had a lot of remote viewing left in him.

As McMoneagle knew, some of the others associated

with the program hadn't fared so well. In fact it was a bit unsettling that so many of them had seemed to die before their time. Had they been living too far out on the shamanic edge of things? Did the act of remote viewing, or even being near a remote viewer, produce some kind of hazardous effect on the human nervous system, or the immune system? McMoneagle didn't know, but the numbers seemed too high to ignore. There were Pat Price and Jackie Keith, who both had died of heart attacks. (Alex Tannous would later die of a heart attack too.) Rob Cowart and Hartleigh Trent had developed serious cases of cancer; Cowart had been severely disabled and Trent had died. Cancer was currently gnawing at Jim Salyer and Hella Hammid, neither of whom would live through the decade. Even the lab secretary at SRI, young and attractive Martha Thompson, was about to die from melanoma. The thought crossed McMoneagle's mind more than once—when am I going to go? Still, with his near-death experience in Europe and all the altered-state adventures since then, he had become convinced that beyond death was just another phase of existence. He had been there and done that, or at any rate closely enough not to be too afraid anymore.

One afternoon in June 1985, around the time that Puthoff abruptly departed SRI, McMoneagle and Nancy Honeycutt went out on Lake Miranon, in the small hollow below the Monroe Institute. There was a raft out in the middle of the lake, and they rowed a boat out to it and put down their towels and a jug of iced tea. They were lying on the raft, floating in Monroe heaven there in the Blue Ridge Mountains, when Joe felt a dull pain in his upper abdomen, as if someone had kicked him. Nancy rowed him back to shore, and drove him to the nearest hospital. As they pulled up in front of the emergency room, McMoneagle passed out. The doctors tried to stabilize him with various drugs—he was having a massive heart attack—and he drifted in and out of consciousness, in and out of exotic, alternate realities. After a week down in these shifting zones, he was sent by ambulance to a larger hospital at Charlottesville for emergency triple-bypass surgery. The doctors sawed open his rib cage, and put him on a heart-lung machine, and he watched them do it, hovering near the ceiling. Then he drifted somewhere else, somewhere that was better.

When he finally awoke, after the surgery, he had a breathing tube down his throat. He motioned to a nurse to bring him a pen and paper. The stuff he had seen—the light . . . the strange, godlike entities—somehow he had to get it all written down.

21

THE WITCHES

. . . Here, said she,
Is your card, the drowned Phoenician Sailor,
(Those are pearls that were his eyes. Look!)
Here is Belladonna, the Lady of the Rocks,
The Lady of situations.

—T. S. Eliot, *The Waste Land*

DULL METAL AND BLOOD GLEAMED IN THE SUNSHINE, AND THE sound of a melee filled Mel Riley's ears. Rocks, sticks, axes, arrows whizzed past his head. Dust was everywhere, almost choking him. He was in the middle of some kind of battle, on a hillside in a strange place, at a strange time, down in the most magical, frightening part of the zone, and he was physically ducking the arrows, hunching down in his chair to shield himself, and coughing from the dust. . . . And then Ed Dames's voice rose and pulled him out of it, and the bilocation was over and Mel Riley was back, at Fort Meade, in the CRV room in building 2560. Dames, now chuckling from across the table, handed Riley the feedback folder; it was a training target, some five-hundred-year-old battle in Cornwall.

Yes, Mel Riley was back, after all these years.

In the summer of 1984, stranded in Germany without a posting, he had abruptly been assigned to the Pentagon's

Rapid Deployment Force (RDF). It was based in Savannah, Georgia, and that was where Riley went to live for the next few years. They were difficult years. The RDF was conducting a number of politically sensitive operations in Central America at the time, mostly from Honduras, one of the bases for U.S. operations against Sandinista-controlled Nicaragua. Riley's battalion ran reconnaissance missions with an odd-looking Army propeller plane called the Mohawk; it carried a massive side-looking radar pod, to track the movements of vehicles and personnel through the steamy jungles of the region.

Within the battalion Riley was first sergeant for a company of about forty men and women. He had to get up every morning at four-thirty to lead all the enlisted personnel through a several-mile run and intensive calisthenics; he usually didn't finish his work until well into the evening. He was starting to feel too old for that kind of thing. Other soldiers in the unit were starting to feel the pressure too; Riley once had to disarm a staff sergeant who waved around a 9 mm handgun and threatened to kill the company commander.

In 1985 Mel and Brigitte finally divorced; she got custody of their daughters, and moved to Texas. Not long afterwards Riley met another German-born woman, Edith, ex-wife of an RDF soldier. Edith had had some psychic experiences herself, as a child, and didn't seem to mind at all that Mel had been, and hoped to be again, a remote viewer. So life wasn't all bad. They were married later that year.

When the situation at Fort Meade had stabilized, and it was clear that the DIA would keep the remote-viewing unit alive, Skip Atwater arranged a transfer for Riley. It wasn't easy; the Army's Personnel Command, which wanted to keep Riley at the RDF, had to be overridden by Jack Vorona's office at the DIA. But the deal was done, and in the summer of 1986, after a five-year absence, Riley finally arrived back at Fort Meade, ready to serve out the remainder of his Army career in the two wooden buildings under the trees on Llewellyn Street.

The unit meanwhile had undergone yet another name change. As part of the Scientific and Technical Intelligence Directorate at DIA, it had the unit prefix DT. Its specific unit designation was S, for "special," and so it was known as DT-S. The unit's old Army code name, Center Lane, had been replaced by a new DIA code name, Sun Streak.

The only faces Riley recognized at the unit now were Atwater's and Fern Gauvin's. Back in 1981, after the Iran hostage rescue debacle, Gauvin had sworn he would never professionally remote-view again. He had kept that oath, more or less, for he had now been hired back only as a monitor and analyst.

The unit commander—or "branch chief," as he was known within the DIA's bureaucracy—was Bill Ray. Under him worked the operations officer, still Skip Atwater, who in turn ran three assistant operations officers, who served as monitors and analysts for RV sessions. The assistant operations officers were Ed Dames, Fern Gauvin, and a burly, mustachioed Army warrant officer named Gene Kincaid. When a tasking came in, Dames, Gauvin, and Kincaid each would be assigned a different team of remote viewers to run against the target. Remote viewers themselves were now often referred to as "sources," to play up the analogy with ordinary secret agents controlled by case officers.

To Riley, it seemed that the unit was full of interesting characters. There was Ed Dames, who always seemed to be bouncing on the balls of his feet, restlessly planning some new psychic conquest of foreign adversaries' secrets. There was Paul Smith, the gentle Mormon with his heavy metal music. And there was Gene Kincaid, who had had a sensationally interesting Army career.

Like the late Jackie Keith, Kincaid had been an INSCOM

covert operative. Among his many operations, curiously enough, had been the purchase of the Soviet T-72 tank, six or seven years before. After helping set up the deal, Kincaid had been taken off the case because he had been just a warrant officer; only senior DIA or CIA or National Security Council officials had been included in the operation's final stages. Kincaid had always wondered how the deal had turned out. Atwater showed him: He opened the files and pulled out Joe McMoneagle's and Hartleigh Trent's and Mel Riley's RV sessions, which provided a psychic's-eye view of the operation from start to finish.

Kincaid was a wonderful storyteller, and was best known for his account of his near death in Vietnam. He had been a HUMINT specialist, running agents and working with the CIA. One time he was riding in a helicopter, near a small skirmish that was under way, when the copter began to take ground fire. He and the pilot were hit; Kincaid caught a bullet in the leg and in the stomach. The helicopter crash-landed, and Kincaid tumbled bloodily out. By the time the fire zone was secure and a medic found him, he was so far gone that he was virtually left for dead. There didn't seem to be any point in evacuating him ahead of the others who had a better chance. Eventually, after everyone else had been evacuated, he was picked up and put inside a medevac helicopter. He had lost a tremendous amount of blood; he felt his life slipping away. He felt like sleeping, but for some reason he decided that if he closed his eyes, he would die. *Gotta stay awake*, he kept telling himself. The helicopter brought him to an Army hospital, where he found himself in a room with several other badly wounded soldiers. The doctor looked at Kincaid, shook his head, and then a priest came in and gave him last rites while the doctor went to work on the others. *Gotta stay awake . . .* Finally the doctor finished with the others and came over. Kincaid let go and closed his eyes, but instead of falling asleep, he drifted out of his body. He floated down the hall to another operating room where doctors were working over a young Marine with badly wounded legs. He heard the doctors conferring over the Marine, and he found himself caught up in the drama of the operation. Eventually, Kincaid drifted out of the operating room, into an intensely bright light, and he was enveloped by love, and in the end he woke up with tubes sticking out of him in his own hospital bed. He checked with the hospital staff, and found that the details about the young Marine and his operation were accurate. Later, Kincaid told a priest about the experience; the priest assured him that it was the kind of thing that sometimes happened to people *in extremis,* and was nothing to worry about.

Kincaid and Riley and others who arrived after the end of Ingo Swann's training program now trained in CRV with those who had been trained by Swann. Some in the unit would still use deeper altered-state methods (ERV), but most would be able to do either. Atwater often employed viewers in CRV mode to acquire a target, and then ran some of them in ERV mode for the more in-depth work.

Swann had ordered his trainees always to use geographical coordinates, insisting that that method would always be superior to others. But when they went on RV duty back at Fort Meade, the trainees quickly abandoned the geographical coordinate scheme. Wherever they might have written down a target's latitude and longitude in a session, they now used two four-digit *random* numbers instead. To placate Swann a bit, and perhaps to make remote viewing seem less arbitrary and bizarre, they called these random numbers "encrypted coordinates," as if they had some relationship to actual geographical coordinates, although they didn't. They still referred to the technique as CRV.

Now freed from the constraints of physical geography, these random numbers were like addresses in the ethereal Matrix. They could be used to refer to anything—locations, people, possible events, objects. Swann shook his head and muttered apocalyptic warnings about this violation of his teaching, but no one took much notice. As Hal Puthoff had found at SRI when he tried abandoning geographical coordinates, there was no apparent decline in the quality of the data, at least not against ordinary targets. In fact, like Keith Harary and Gary Langford out at SRI, the remote viewers at DT-S found that geographical coordinates were apt to generate analytical overlay, spurring them to wonder where the coordinates had put them on the globe. With only random numbers to go by, there were no such distractions.

In April 1986, just before Riley arrived for his second tour, DT-S was given a target relating to a planned U.S. air raid on Libya and Muammar Qaddafi. The raid was meant by the Reagan administration as revenge for the bombing death of an American G.I. in Berlin, and as a general deterrent to Libya's increasingly bold sponsorship of international terrorism. In a nighttime strike, dozens of sites in Tripoli, Benghazi, and surrounding areas would be attacked by U.S. Navy and Air Force jets. The targets would include government buildings, suspected chemical weapons plants, terrorist training camps, and the nerve center of the Libyan armed forces—Qaddafi himself. DT-S was asked to help track Qaddafi, as he jumped from safe house to bunker to desert tent, nervously aware that the American military wanted to put him in its sights.

The unit worked long hours on the job, sketching various buildings and encampments. Later, after the raid, some of the photographs and diagrams of Qaddafi's hideaways would appear in the newspaper, and there would seem to be similarities to what some of the remote viewers had described. But as the remote viewers worked the target, they were faced with a serious problem: Even if they were perfectly accurate, and they weren't, they couldn't get their information up the chain of command before Qaddafi moved somewhere else. Eventually, they tried to describe

Qaddafi's location a certain number of hours or days in the future, to compensate for the delay. But they never had the impression that their data had made a difference. It seemed that Qaddafi's final location was plotted—and in the end, almost pinpointed—by a combination of human agents in Tripoli, overhead reconnaissance photos, and signals intelligence intercepts. On the night of the raid, the Bedouin-style camp where Qaddafi was hiding out was hit by several bombs; they missed their prime target by only a few hundred yards.

After the raid, a U.S. F-111 long-range bomber went down offshore; the remote-viewing unit was at work trying to find it when Ken Bell, now at another, unrelated posting, telephoned. He had remote-viewed the F-111 from his home, and believed he knew where it was on the bottom of the Gulf of Sidra. It would later turn out that Bell's information was reasonably accurate, but again, it didn't seem to have been used.

A few years later, in December 1989, a similar RV operation would be mounted against Manuel Noriega in Panama. In the wake of the American invasion of that country, Noriega went into hiding, and DT-S was asked to help find him. For several days of intense work the unit described a variety of locations. As with the Libya raid, some of the remote viewers' information in retrospect would seem to have been accurate, but it was never precise enough, or consistent enough. At one point Lyn Buchanan told his session monitor he had received a powerful impulse regarding Noriega's location. The impulse was telling him that the location was somehow known to the young American television actress Kristy McNichol. "Ask Kristy McNichol," he kept writing on his session paper. "Ask Kristy McNichol." But no one checked with Kristy McNichol, and the U.S. government never "caught" Noriega. He surfaced on his own, inside the Vatican embassy, and was later imprisoned in the United States and convicted of drug trafficking.

* * *

Other operations in the Sun Streak years involved suspected high-tech weapons sites in the Soviet Union. Many of these were tasked by Dale Graff, who now ran something called the Advanced Concepts Office within Jack Vorona's Scientific and Technical Intelligence Directorate. One target, brought in early in 1987, was a satellite-tracking and communications facility at Dushanbe in the USSR, with large lasers pointed skyward. Mel Riley, Paul Smith, and other remote viewers using the CRV technique described lasers and, eight to nine months in the future, large igloos or domes—which in fact did begin to be constructed, six months later.

DT-S was also involved in the lengthy Lebanon hostage crisis, and tried to track the locations and the health of Terry Anderson, Terry Waite, and other Western captives. In some cases they reviewed video footage taken on reconnaissance flights by remotely piloted vehicles, and tried, albeit unsuccessfully, to point out buildings where they thought hostages were being held. Riley, Smith, and others also provided data on Iranian weapons emplacements—especially Chinese-made Silkworm anti-ship missiles—along the Persian Gulf during the later stages of the Iran-Iraq War.

One category of tasking that expanded in the late 1980s had to do with counter-narcotics operations. The U.S. Customs Service, the Coast Guard, the Drug Enforcement Administration, and various Pentagon anti-drug offices and task forces became occasional customers of DT-S. The viewers were asked to peek inside suspected drug-smuggling vessels on the high seas, or to track the activities of certain drug cartel members south of the border. In a few cases in 1988 and 1989, the unit provided information on the whereabouts of suspected drug ships that was later confirmed to have been broadly accurate.

* * *

Probably the most clear-cut success for the unit, in the Sun Streak years, was an operation tasked by Brigadier General James Shufelt, a former deputy commander of INSCOM who had moved to a senior position at the DIA. Shufelt was already well known to those in the program, having married remote viewer Charlene Cavanaugh in 1986 (in a ceremony attended by many of those in the program, including Ingo Swann). One day, later that year, Shufelt and his new wife invited Skip Atwater over for dinner, and Shufelt told him about the tasking he'd just received. The Pentagon was getting pressure from veterans' groups, via Congress, to investigate the widespread stories about American POWs still being held captive in Vietnam. The stories were mostly tenuous, but they had raised enormous hopes in the veterans community. A small grass-roots movement had begun, supported by influential political and business figures such as Ross Perot. The Pentagon was now telling Shufelt to check the stories out and report his findings to Congress. Shufelt had the resources of the DIA at his disposal: satellite pictures, communications intercepts, the works. He wanted Atwater's remote viewers to help out, too.

Atwater suggested that Shufelt task the operation as a kind of controlled experiment. He should provide the unit with two sets of photos—one of buildings in Vietnam where it was rumored that POWs were being held, and the other of buildings in Vietnam where it was known for certain that there were *no* POWs. Neither Atwater nor anyone else in the remote-viewing unit would be told which photograph belonged to which category. That way, Shufelt would at least have some way of judging how reliable the RV information was likely to be.

Shufelt sent the photos over—there were several dozen of them in all—and Atwater put them all into target envelopes. Then he set up two RV teams, one headed by Ed Dames and the other by Gene Kincaid. Neither Dames nor Kincaid knew that the photographs were from Vietnam, or knew what the operation was about. Kincaid, running viewers in ERV mode, would show the photos to some of them as front-loading, but Dames gave his viewers only the random-number "coordinates" that had been assigned to the photos.

Atwater spread the operation out over several months, to keep the remote viewers from burning out or generating AoI from too many related targets. When all the data were in, he analyzed them and wrote a final report. His conclusion was straightforward: The remote viewers had found no POWs anywhere.

Atwater forwarded the report to Shufelt, who read it with genuine dismay. "That's just sad; that's just awful," he told Atwater. In the end, his other sources pointed towards the same conclusion. Shufelt told Congress he had come up empty-handed.

The POWs-in-Vietnam operation was one of the last big ones for Atwater. At the time it began, he was already in retirement mode, and had begun to transfer his duties to Fern Gauvin.

Back in 1982, Atwater had purchased some land near the Monroe Institute. Since then, with one of his teenage sons, he had been spending weekends down at his property, building a house. The house grew up slowly; it seemed to evolve out of the Blue Ridge ground. After five years, in late 1987, it was ready to be occupied, and Atwater was ready to retire. On his last day at Fort Meade, there was a small gathering, and he was ceremoniously given a coffee cup. There was some standard novelty-shop message on it; something about not having anyone to boss around now that he was retired. He thanked everyone, then cleaned out his desk, and went home. He and his wife Joan and their children moved down to the new house near the Monroe Institute. Bob Monroe made him director of research at the institute, and in an office looking out over the hills, Atwater studied brain waves, created new Hemi-Sync tapes, and generally tried to enjoy life.

When Mel Riley arrived at Fort Meade in the summer of 1986, he was overjoyed to be back. But it was soon clear to him, as it had been to others, that the unit had entered a decline. It seemed to have been discredited forever, in some eyes, by its expulsion from the Army.

Matters became worse in 1988, when Major General Harry Soyster, who had taken over INSCOM after Stubblebine and had favored the RV unit's expulsion, was promoted to lieutenant general and appointed to head the DIA. Soyster didn't want the remote-viewing program at DIA any more than he had wanted it at INSCOM. He wasn't completely opposed to the idea that remote viewing was a genuine phenomenon, but for the present, RV data just seemed to him to be too flaky to use in military situations. He worried about the giggle factor.

Remarkably, despite the opposition of Soyster and some of his top deputies, Jack Vorona was able to keep the unit afloat. He and Dale Graff maintained a network of supportive intelligence officials in the Pentagon, the DEA, the CIA, and other agencies; these officials could task DT-S on a low-key, experimental, cost-free basis, and could use the results as they saw fit. A number of the remote viewers travelled around the country, giving demonstrations to potential customers. In one case, Paul Smith, monitored by Lyn Buchanan, did a successful demonstration for officials of the Pentagon's anti-drug Joint Task Force Four in Key West, Florida.

There were also demonstrations for key people from Congress. Smith and a young Army civilian named Gabrielle Peters were sent to Capitol Hill one day. Peters, a former member of INSCOM's SED group, and a former tasker of the remote-viewing unit, was now a remote viewer herself, and apparently a talented one. She and Smith were greeted on the Hill by four supportive senators from the Intelligence Committee—William Cohen (R-Maine), Daniel Inouye (D-Hawaii), Ted Stevens (R-Alaska), and former astronaut John Glenn (D-Ohio). Dick D'Amato, an aide who handled intelligence-budget issues for Senate Majority Leader Robert Byrd, was there, too. In a room in the Russell Senate Office Building, D'Amato and the senators handed Smith two four-digit random numbers, indicating a site somewhere in the world. Smith read the numbers to Peters, who worked the target. It turned out to be a terrorism-related facility in Libya, and Peters did well enough to earn surprised looks and warm congratulations from the assembled legislators.

Demonstrations such as these might not have amounted to hard-nosed proof of the day-to-day usefulness of remote viewing, but they tended to shake people up, impressing them with the reality of the paranormal so much that they didn't want to see the program die. With support from Cohen and Inouye and D'Amato and the others, the program stayed alive. And through the informal networks Vorona and Graff had set up, DT-S was occasionally able to bypass the DIA's skeptical leadership, getting its results into the hands of those who could make use of them.

The problem, of course, was that no program could last long operating in such a furtive manner. As part of the DIA, which was primarily an analytical agency, the unit wasn't really supposed to be running operations anyway. And officially, almost no one in Congress or the intelligence community now wanted to be seen sanctioning the use of remote viewers for anything more than "experimentation." Even if a remote viewing of a specific target proved to have been accurate and useful, its user, afraid of the giggle factor, could almost never acknowledge the fact. Officers at Joint Task Force Four in Key West, for example, were relatively enthusiastic about remote viewing's potential, and believed that some of the data they had received had been operationally useful, but they employed remote viewers only a few times, semi-officially, afraid that their association with DT-S might get them in trouble with their superiors.

As the unit's bureaucratic marginalization increased, it also seemed to decay in other ways. Its clients were now increasingly interested in search problems—searches for drug-carrying ships, and terrorists, and fugitives like Noriega. Desperate for support, the unit's managers didn't want to turn taskings down. And yet search problems had always been the most difficult for remote viewers: The more search problems they did, the more their overall success rate fell.

The unit seemed to be well past its prime anyway, in terms of raw remote-viewing ability. For all the enthusiasm over Swann's multi-stage CRV technique, it seemed that there was no one in the unit with the consistency and the clarity of the great "naturals" like Pat Price, Joe McMoneagle, and Ken Bell. The last two, McMoneagle and Bell, were now working as civilians for SRI, and had largely supplanted Swann there. Going through samples of some of the DT-S operational data one day in 1989, out at SRI, McMoneagle would find a recent session against the same Severodvinsk shipyard he had been targeted against by the National Security Council in 1979. As he leafed through the session sheets, it seemed to him that the sketches were the same ones *he* had made a decade before, against the *Typhoon* submarine. He became convinced that someone at DT-S had spruced up his old session and put a new date and viewer number on it, to make it look like original data. The analysis of the session suggested that the Soviets were building a new high-tech sub at Severodvinsk. It was one of the apparently successful sessions that the RV program managers were using in briefings around the intelligence community. McMoneagle wondered how things could have become so bad at Fort Meade.

* * *

Fern Gauvin had seemed a good choice when he replaced Skip Atwater as operations officer in 1987, and became DT-S's branch chief a year later. Gauvin had more experience than anyone else at the unit, and had worked as both a monitor and a viewer.

But in the years of Gauvin's reign, the unit's decline worsened. There were rivalries, accusations of mismanagement, and operational failures. To hear some remote viewers tell it, the unit was slipping into paranormal chaos—a dark place, infested by madness and mischievous sprites, as in one of those paintings by Hieronymus Bosch. When it was over, as Lyn Buchanan would say later, "we didn't have any customers left."

Gauvin, in an interview years later, would reject suggestions that he had spent too much time out there in the Matrix—had flown too high in the paranormal sky. But in discussing the potential dangers of remote viewing, he conveyed a worldview very different from that of the average DIA branch chief.

The biggest concern is—will I be invaded by evil spirits? Maybe, but I can protect myself . . . Some other people call it, Okay, "cover yourself with the white light," and so on. All that is good intention. And if I have good intention—I don't care if you [a seductive evil spirit] are a whore on Fourteenth Street, I don't want anything to do with you—then you don't stand a chance, I don't care what the price. It's because I don't want to. I think that goes a long way in this line of work.

I've seen intrusions, temporary intrusions, but you know, nothing that could affect anybody or anything if they didn't want to be bothered. That's speaking broadly. It was never a huge problem.

In general, Gauvin preached pluralism when it came to remote-viewing styles: Whatever technique someone liked to use, he or she should use. He respected CRV and the accomplishments of Ingo Swann, but he felt that CRV was now somehow too intellectual, too concerned with method rather than results. Skip Atwater had also been relatively pluralistic, but he had come to believe that a certain amount of standardization of techniques was necessary. He and Bill Ray had effectively restricted remote viewers to two basic styles, ERV and CRV. Under Gauvin, however, these restrictions were off. Other, more exotic styles were introduced. And the sprites came out to play.

Angela Dellafiora, a raven-haired woman in her forties, had joined the unit early in 1986. Prior to that she had been an INSCOM civilian, a Latin American analyst. She had seemed dissatisfied with her job, and had felt drawn to the paranormal realm instead. She had attended a private psychic training institute in Washington, D.C., and somehow Stubblebine, then still at INSCOM, had heard about her. She had become the third (after Lyn Buchanan and Dawn Lutz) of his handpicked recruits for the remote-viewing unit. Because of the near death of the unit in 1984, her transfer had been delayed, and she had arrived only when the unit was transferred to DIA control.

While Atwater was operations officer, Dellafiora almost always worked with ERV, and, though she disliked the technique, she also trained briefly in CRV with Paul Smith (who did lectures) and Ed Dames and Lyn Buchanan (who ran practice sessions). At times she seemed to have some talent, but she didn't seem exceptional.

In the Fern Gauvin era, and evidently with Gauvin's encouragement, Dellafiora began to use a different technique to access targets. She would go into one of the RV rooms, would relax into a trance, and then after a while would announce the presence of an outside entity that had supposedly possessed her body. "Maurice" was her most common possessor. There was also "George," and a character who called himself "Dr. Einstein."

These entities tended to manifest themselves not vocally, but through what is known as "automatic writing." They would seize control of Angela's writing hand, and use it to set down their comments on a given target. Gauvin, who often served as monitor for these sessions, would sit across the table, asking the entity questions: *What is the health of the hostage Terry Waite?*

HE IS HUNGRY AND WEAK AND FRIGHTENED, BUT OTHERWISE ALL RIGHT, might come the response.

Later, Angela would emerge from her trance to find a few dozen sheets of data before her, neatly filled out in her familiar spirit's handwriting.

Angela's form of remote viewing came to be known as written-RV, or WRV, although it was essentially a form of spirit mediumship—in modern parlance, "channelling."

Channellers, such as the séance-room performer Mina "Margery" Crandon, had brought much discredit upon psychic research a century or so before. Now the theatrical practice was rearing its head again. And yet Angela, freed to channel, suddenly seemed to become one of the most accurate and reliable sources in the unit.

In the spring of 1989, the U.S. Customs Service asked DT-S to help find a former Customs officer, Charles Jordan, who was wanted for various crimes and was believed to be hiding out in the Caribbean. The CRVers described him in a variety of places including the Caribbean, South Florida, and even Central America. It seemed that they were zeroing in on him, but Angela, seized by one of her spirits, located Jordan somewhere else—in northern Wyoming, near the town of Lovell and also not far from an old Indian burial ground. The Customs Service decided to ignore all this conflicting information, but not long thereafter, Jordan was spotted by a ranger at Yellowstone National

Park—a few dozen miles from Lovell, Wyoming—and was arrested. Under interrogation, Jordan admitted to having been near Lovell around the time Angela had psychically placed him there.

In another case in 1989, Angela was asked how Muammar Qaddafi was reacting to recent U.S. charges that Libya was fabricating chemical weapons in the town of Rabta. She announced that a ship, the "Patua" or "Potua," would arrive at Tripoli to transport chemical weapons materials from Rabta to a different town, via the eastern Libyan port of Ras al Anuf. She seemed to have been close: A ship named the *Batato* did dock at Tripoli four days later, loaded an unknown cargo, and sailed for the eastern Libyan port of Benghazi.

Later that year, in mid-July, Angela spontaneously predicted that a U.S. passenger aircraft would be hijacked from Rome or Athens in a few weeks. And within three weeks, U.S. intelligence heard from other sources that just such an attack, though ultimately cancelled, was being planned by Islamic terrorists. A few months later, during the search for Noriega in Panama, Angela's RV sessions seemed so good that they were the only ones actually sent "downtown" to DT-S's friends in the Pentagon.

The male remote viewers in the unit didn't know whether to laugh or to cry. A channeller—*a channeller*—was taking over the U.S. government's psychic spying program. Dames and Riley and the others began to refer to Angela's possessing entities as "the boys," or "The Three Stooges." But while they joked about it, they also hoped that those at the upper levels of the program would come to their senses. They, the Jedi knights of CRV, had been trained by Swann or by Swann's trainees, and had been taught to regard the multi-stage CRV system as a quantum leap over all the old psychic methods. Now with Angela and her entities, they lamented, the unit was regressing from Ingo Swann's high-tech wizardry back to archaic and vaguely feminist witchery.

Some of the CRVers were willing to believe that Angela did have real, natural talent. That much they conceded. But most thought that she was prone to wild errors, and that with proper management, a team of CRVers could beat her every time. The Higgins operation, they liked to say, was a good example.

In February 1988, a senior U.S. Marine officer, Lieutenant Colonel William Higgins, was kidnapped from Beirut by the Islamic terrorist group Hezbollah. DT-S was asked to try to find him. Ed Dames, running a team of CRVers, came up with a description of a house where it seemed that Higgins was being held in South Lebanon. Angela Dellafiora, front-loaded with reconnaissance photographs of the area and monitored by Fern Gauvin, picked out instead a certain field near a road; she believed that Higgins was being held underground there, somehow. Several days later, the CRVers began to report that Higgins was dead. Angela reported that he was alive, and would soon be released. Both sets of data were sent downtown, but of course they conflicted, and were probably ignored.

Higgins's body was soon found, tortured to death, and it turned out that he had probably been in a house in South Lebanon, perhaps like the one the CRVers had described. Angela had been wrong. Dames bitterly criticized the "vitiation" of the CRV data by Angela's channelling.

Even when Angela seemed to have been successful in her channelling, the CRVers sometimes suggested that her performance hadn't been entirely paranormal. At the meeting with Joint Task Force Four officials in Key West, where Smith and Buchanan did a demonstration target, Angela was also present, and was given her own target—a person. Angela, according to the story, began by asking whether the target person was male.

Informed by the base officials that the target person was

not male, but was in fact female, Angela suggested that this female person nevertheless had male tendencies. The session went on like this, Angela getting closer and closer to the target and Smith and Buchanan getting more and more disgusted, until Angela began to describe the target relatively accurately. The base officials seemed impressed. But Smith and Buchanan concluded that Angela, despite a genuine psi ability, was too often inadvertently coached towards targets by her customers' questions and answers.

As time went on, and the rivalry intensified, some of the CRVers began to allege that, whether Angela meant it or not, she had a mesmerizing influence over one or two of the program's managers. There was something about a woman in an exotic altered state of consciousness, it seemed, that couldn't help stirring a man's deepest emotions. In any case, the CRVers would talk about how Gauvin would disappear with Angela into the ops building now and then, each time returning an hour or so later, his eyes bright and dreamy, as if he had just heard some blissful revelation. No one ever seriously suggested that Gauvin (or anyone else in the program) had a sexual relationship with Dellafiora; instead, they believed that Gauvin was going in for private readings, and was simply becoming emotionally dependent on them. Eventually, Gauvin confided to Riley that he had indeed been consulting Angela on various private matters, such as the Maryland horse farm he had long wanted to buy.

By late 1988, Jack Vorona himself was driving up from DIA headquarters, sometimes accompanied by a friendly congressman or staffer, to do occasional sessions with Angela. Vorona would later assert that these visits had been entirely for professional reasons. In other words, all the targets he brought had been operations-related—Angela was said to be especially good against human targets—or at least had served as some kind of legitimate test of her ability. Still, the CRVers were perplexed and annoyed that the same targets were never given to them, especially when they had so much time on their hands. After all the effort that had gone into the development of CRV, the managers of the program seemed to be discarding it.

In 1988 a young woman named Robin Dahlgren arrived at the unit. She had been among fifty or so DIA employees tested with a computer psi-ability analyzer that Ed May had developed out at SRI. Apparently she had done well, although for some reason she had declined to take any of the usual personality tests that went with it.

Dahlgren was in her late twenties, slim, attractive, dark haired, a chain-smoker. She had a cackling laugh, and a certain T-shirt she sometimes wore, one of those things you see at the seashore resorts; across her chest it read: "90% bitch, 10% angel."

Ed Dames, who drew the task of training Dahlgren in CRV, wondered where to find the 10 percent angel. Dahlgren made clear that she despised the complexities and rigidities of the technique, and one day, when Dames spoke to her sharply about some mistake she had made, she simply burst into tears and refused to go on. Later, when her training was finished, she vowed never to use CRV. She preferred a free-form, ERV-type style, she said. Encouraged by Angela's example, she also began to experiment with more archaic techniques. She began to work with tarot cards, and even began to practice channelling.

Unfortunately, as the CRVers saw it, Dahlgren's psi abilities were insignificant no matter what technique she used. In one long session against a certain operational target, she was able to determine only that "there is blue at the site." Another time, she pinpointed the location of an unknown object in the middle of the Arizona desert. The target, it turned out, was a drug-smuggling ship being tracked in the Atlantic by the Coast Guard. Paul Smith, before leaving the unit in the early 1990s, would perform a statistical evaluation of several RVers' performances against a selected group of operational targets, and would conclude that Dahlgren was the only one whose data had no significant correlation with the targets.

Dahlgren nevertheless seemed to do as she liked within the unit. Some wondered whether it had anything to do with her relationship to Dick D'Amato.

D'Amato, the senior aide to Senator Robert Byrd, was one of those men who are seldom in the public eye, yet have enormous, world-class power. As one of Byrd's key lieutenants on the Senate Appropriations Committee, he was in charge of intelligence and black-projects appropriations, and had a long list of special-access clearances. He was one of the few people with the effective authority to determine what stayed in, and what came out of, the annual intelligence budget. One of the aims he had in wielding that power was, evidently, to keep the Fort Meade remote-viewing unit alive.

Over at the CIA, there was growing skepticism about the entire remote-viewing program. Ron Pandolfi, a CIA scientist who had been tasked with monitoring new and exotic technologies, including remote viewing, had been battling for years with Jack Vorona and Dale Graff over access to Sun Streak. But Vorona and Graff managed to keep him off the clearance list; Pandolfi, in their opinion, only wanted to shut the program down forever.

Thwarted by the DIA, Pandolfi turned to Capitol Hill. In visits to staffers on the intelligence committees, he would ask why they had signed off on the Sun Streak budget request. Did they know what that million or so dollars was for? Every time, he would receive the same answer: Dick D'Amato, carrying the sceptre of Senate Majority Leader Robert Byrd, had himself inserted Sun Streak into the DIA's budget. The head of the DIA, Harry Soyster, apparently did not even want the project, but D'Amato had marked it up in the DIA's part of the intelligence appropriations bill anyway. Why, Pandolfi wanted to know, did the staffers not question this? The response said a lot about the politics of espionage: "Well, you know, Ron, if we did that, then every time *we* came up with a markup, he'd just shoot us down."

The relationship between the attractive tarot-card reader and the powerful Senate staffer was relatively out in the open. Everyone in the program seemed to know about it, from the remote viewers on up to senior DIA officials. When several unit members took a trip to Israel to see if RV could work better at close range to Middle Eastern targets, D'Amato came along, too, and disappeared with Dahlgren for several days. One DIA official figured that D'Amato had simply "lost sight of logic."

In one obvious sense, the D'Amato/Dahlgren connection appeared to be a boon for the unit. However scrupulously D'Amato might have separated work and play—and perhaps he did*—members of the remote-viewing unit suspected that the unit owed its continued existence to D'Amato's amatory inducement.

Yet every silver lining has its cloud. To the managers of the program, it appeared that Robin Dahlgren could not be fired, and could not be given instructions or orders as if she were any other remote viewer. It was believed that if anyone seriously crossed her, then D'Amato would respond by forcing the removal of managers from their positions, or even shutting down the unit altogether. "If I said something to her in the afternoon," one former manager would later remember, "I would hear about it the next morning from [DIA] headquarters."

---

* D'Amato, in an interview about the RV program with a reporter for *The Washington Post* in December 1995, stated that his activities in support of the RV program had been at the request of senators who wanted the program kept alive.

In any case, D'Amato did exert a substantial influence on the unit, not just where Dahlgren was concerned. As time went on, the view spread that he was "micromanaging" the program—and perhaps in this he was guided by the advice of Dahlgren, who in turn was informed by her magical cards.

22

A Haunted House

We thrived on adventure. You get men of action; we're not satisfied with sitting around and twiddling our thumbs year after year. Unless something happens, you're going to lose our interest. But there was enough happening in there to hold our interest.

—Ed Dames

As THE PROGRAM DRIFTED IN THE MARGINS OF THE INTELLIGENCE community, and the rate of operational taskings dwindled, the remote viewers tried, not always successfully, to keep busy. Paul Smith read parapsychology books, and wrote analyses of the unit's work. Lyn Buchanan set up a computer database of remote-viewing session data. Robin Dahlgren read her tarot cards. Angela Dellafiora pored over books full of logic puzzles: *Joe is married to Bob's sister. Bob is John's cousin. John's daughter is Catherine's niece. What is Catherine's relationship to Joe?*

There was one member of the unit who seemed almost to personify the fate of the program. He was a thirty-four-year-old Army captain, David Morehouse, and he arrived in the summer of 1988. Though Morehouse had never seen combat, he had commanded a Ranger company and had later, briefly, been a member of a secret special-operations squad known as Intelligence Support Activity (ISA). Morehouse was intelligent, a smooth talker, and his career seemed to be on a fast track. Even taking into account the enormous exaggerations that go into military performance reports, it was clear from Morehouse's that he was a cut above most officers.

Morehouse heard about the remote-viewing unit while he was at ISA. He had no history of psychic experiences, but he had a casual interest in the paranormal, and the idea of being transformed from an ordinary Army officer into a shaman-spy attracted him, as it had so many others. Paul Smith, charged with evaluating potential recruits, thought Morehouse—who like Smith was a Mormon—would make a good candidate.

After arriving at the unit and training with Smith and Dames and Lyn Buchanan, Morehouse began to participate in DT-S's day-to-day activities. He seemed reasonably enthusiastic about remote viewing—he wanted to be a Jedi knight like the rest of them—and there were occasions when it seemed that he did have some talent. As time went by, however, and DT-S was increasingly separated from operational military reality, Morehouse responded much the way the others did: by finding other things to do. He had a small home-improvement business, House Tech, that he was already running on the side; after a few months at Fort Meade, he began to spend most of his time attending to it. He would get in late, and leave early, and even while he was at the office, he often seemed to the others to be preoccupied with his House Tech paperwork. Eventually he began turning up at the office only one or two days per week.

The decline of the remote-viewing unit seemed to wear hardest on Ed Dames. He angrily blamed it on "the witches" and their wiles, and on what he saw as the mismanagement of the program by Gauvin and Graff and Vorona and D'Amato.

Dames might have responded by sitting back, relaxing,

and waiting for his next tour of duty, as most of the others seemed to be doing. Instead he intensified his involvement with remote viewing. He generated his own "operational" targets, selected from current events of interest to the Pentagon, and ran CRVers against them under the guise of advanced training. He targeted the mysterious crash of an Army transport plane at Gander, Newfoundland. He targeted suspected chemical and biological weapons facilities in the Soviet Union, the Far East, and the Middle East. His pride and joy was his penetration—he believed—of the Soviet Defense Council, the holy grail for a U.S. Army intelligence officer. He tried to send out the results through his own private channels, "under the table," urging his friends in the intelligence community to act on the information. Although most if not all of the information he generated this way was impossible to verify, Dames often seemed to assume that verification was unnecessary. Ingo Swann had promised him, and others, that CRV could be highly accurate as long as one "stayed in structure." Dames often reminded his colleagues of this promise. By the early 1990s, he would be claiming that CRV enabled virtually infallible "direct knowledge" of almost anything out there in the space-time Matrix.

Some "advanced training" targets were non-military, and were instead chosen for their maximum extrasensory impact on the viewer—a fifteenth-century brawl in Cornwall, the surface of an asteroid, the nuclear reactor meltdown at Chernobyl, a vertigo-inducing spot a mile above Grand Canyon. One time, Dames gave Riley a target, and Riley had a bilocation-type episode for a short period. He was in a kind of hypnotic, deep-ERV trance, murmuring descriptions of what he saw: He saw a stadium, and oddly dressed people going in to see a football game. He went inside the stadium, and a roar rose up from around him, shrieking, boisterous, a familiar sound, but there was no football being played here. He saw the lions—this was the Colosseum, in Rome, circa 100 A.D.—and Dames pulled him out of there, and Riley was in something of a zombie mood afterward, bouncing off the walls.

As the targets became more and more exotic, a small band of advanced training aficionados formed. Initially it included Dames, Riley, and Paul Smith; later, Dave Morehouse occasionally joined in. Dames decided that the purpose of the group should be to use remote viewing to investigate all manner of anomalous incidents and paranormal phenomena. In other words, while the Pentagon prevented them from using RV to answer military questions, they would push on to more important, transcendent questions. Dames would later refer to the resulting corpus of work as "The Enigma Files."

For a given enigma-oriented operation, Dames would select a target and run the viewers in the group against it. Ostensibly, he was letting the viewers produce the information, but it seemed to some of them that Dames, in his enthusiasm, was apt to inadvertently coach them towards the answers he happened to favor. On occasion, he would even exchange roles with the remote viewer in the middle of a session, and would start remote-viewing the target himself.

Dames tasked his viewers with the Loch Ness monster, and determined that it was merely a dinosaur's ghost. He had his team remote-view Fatima, Medjugorje, and other reputed sightings of the Virgin Mary. He decided that long-lost Atlantis was actually at the bottom of Lake Titicaca in Peru. In search of angels and demons and out-of-body shamanic adventures, he and his enigma-hunting colleagues went into deep, Hemi-Sync–assisted trances.

Christine Dames now saw that her husband's tremendous, restless energy had been channelled largely into his self-generated remote viewing work. He would go to Fort Meade at seven or eight in the morning and wouldn't come home for another twelve hours. After dinner and some time spent with their two boys, he would closet himself in his small study to do more remote viewing. After a few hours' sleep, he would then get up and go to work again. On the increasingly rare occasions when Ed and Christine had conversations, he would tell her about the frightening spirits he had encountered, the great, age-old enigmas he was solving. Christine worried that he was becoming obsessed, but Ed seemed to shrug off such concerns. He had found a cause, a high adventure. If Christine couldn't keep up, she remembers being told, then that was her problem.

Dames and some of the others often talked about the phenomenology of the Matrix, the strange things that happened there. They liked to say, for instance, that remote viewing was like switching on a beacon within the Matrix. It attracted strange things, the way a porch light attracts bugs on a hot summer night. They all knew the story of what had happened to Gene Kincaid, one afternoon back in 1987. Kincaid had been in one of the RV rooms, running Angela Dellafiora against a target. This was before all the channelling began, and Angela was in ERV mode. She was going through her routine, murmuring impressions from down in her zone, when suddenly Kincaid looked up and saw his dead father, standing there in the RV room, looking at him.

Kincaid had clearly been frightened by the experience, but Dames had only so much sympathy for him. He believed that those were the kinds of things that happened out there. You had to face them; you had to wrestle with them. In Dames's opinion, Kincaid was one of those devout Irishmen, always afraid of ghosts and goblins. Bill Ray was the same. Ray had been in one of the RV rooms, by himself, one morning somewhere around the transition to DIA control. As the unit's branch chief, he probably shouldn't have been indulging in altered states anymore, but he liked to keep in psychic shape with an occasional remote-viewing session. On this morning, he was doing a solo session, in

ERV mode. Though trained in CRV by Swann, he now preferred ERV because he could lie down, taking the strain off his bad back. He lay down on the ERV couch and went into his zone, into the Matrix, and at some point, he suddenly felt a hand grab him. It was very palpable. He rose from the ERV couch and saw . . . no one. Had it been some kind of tactile hallucination? Was it possible to hallucinate something so convincing? He wasn't sure. He returned to his office, thoroughly shaken. Thereafter, it was said, he tended to stay away from the ops building, and if he remote-viewed, he did so at home, with his wife nearby.

On another occasion, relatively early in the Sun Streak years, Ed Dames conducted a training session with Angela Dellafiora in ERV mode. She went into an altered state, and began to visualize the target. Something was a bit strange about the target site. It seemed too cold; everything was red. Eventually, Dames showed her the target folder. The target was a certain region on Mars known as Cydonia. Dames believed that an ancient humanoid civilization had lived there. Perhaps the Cydonian civilization was distantly related to modern Earth civilization. . . . Dellafiora promptly complained to Atwater and the unit's other managers about this bizarre targeting, and Dames was told to cease and desist.

From his boyhood, Ed Dames had always shown an interest in UFO sightings, the possibility of life on other planets, and other extraterrestrial-related subjects. As far as he was concerned, these were among the most important mysteries in human experience. Even in training at SRI, he had begun to think that remote viewing was a valuable tool for probing these mysteries. As long as he stayed in structure, he reasoned, the answers should come out right. In his hotel rooms in Menlo Park and Manhattan during training, Dames had even secretly tried to remote-view UFO-related targets he had assigned to himself. A few years later, with the advent of his "advanced training" at DT-S, he had moved his pursuit of extraterrestrials into high gear.

Such a pursuit might have seemed absurd, like trying to explain one magic trick with another. But remote viewing and ETs did appear to have some kind of weird attachment, not just for Dames but for many others involved in the program. Sooner or later, they were always seen together.

Even at senior management levels, those who supported the remote-viewing program seemed to have relatively strong beliefs in other areas of the paranormal and unexplained—especially when the subject had to do with extraterrestrials. SRI's Hal Puthoff, the CIA's Richard Kennett, the Army's General Bert Stubblebine, Senate staffer Dick D'Amato, and the DIA's Dale Graff all had an interest in the UFO lore. Some of them took great interest in stories that the Pentagon had secretly recovered a crashed flying saucer in New Mexico in 1947. In fact, when Dick D'Amato's power and influence were at their peak in the late 1980s and early 1990s, he allegedly embarked on a behind-the-scenes crusade to uncover the crashed saucer story. (D'Amato "has gone into official agencies with his list of crazy questions on [this] his stuff," said one former CIA official. "And memoranda get written, and basically what the analysts write is this guy asked me a bunch of crazy questions and I told him I didn't know the answers and he left in a huff.")

Even the head of the Sun Streak medical oversight board, a Navy captain named Paul Tyler, was a frequent visitor to UFO conferences. In 1993, he would tell an audience of UFO enthusiasts that flying saucers were probably piloted by "intelligent beings capable of doing things we can't."

Remote viewers themselves seemed just as captivated by the subject. And when they targeted UFOs in their remote viewings, strange things could happen. One of the strangest things was that they almost never failed to detect the UFO.

It could have been argued that this was part of a more general aspect of remote viewing. For example, among the practice targets generated at SRI and Fort Meade over the years, some were always easier than others to perceive psychically. This wasn't necessarily for straightforward aesthetic reasons. A visually striking building, simple to sketch and describe in real life, might be perpetually clouded by fog in the RV world, while a crumbling ruin, overgrown in a distant jungle, might shine like a lighthouse.

This area of remote-viewing phenomenology would always remain confusing, but in at least some cases, the characteristics of a target that made it "RV-friendly" were obvious: If a target had some religious or supernatural or paranormal significance, or was otherwise tinged with strangeness, remote viewers seemed to home in on it relatively rapidly. Or perhaps (though they tended to resist this explanation) they merely homed in on the strangeness, prompting flights of imagination which only obscured the real, mundane target.

One day back in 1976, during a formal series of long-distance outbound remote-viewing experiments at SRI, Gary Langford was asked to perceive the location of Russell Targ, then standing outside the New Orleans Superdome, two thousand miles away. Hal Puthoff, acting as the monitor, sat in the RV room with Langford. He could see Langford hesitating. The remote viewer was perceiving something, but didn't want to say what it was. Finally he told Puthoff he was seeing something that looked "like a flying saucer in the middle of a city," and he sketched out just that, modifying it later into a large domed building. Ironically, it turned out that Targ, standing by the Superdome and describing the scene around him into a tape recorder, had also compared the building to a flying saucer.

On several other occasions, remote viewers suddenly interrupted their sessions against a particular target to describe a flying saucer that they perceived to be in the vicinity. During a session at Fort Meade in June 1980, Joe McMoneagle was targeted against a site somewhere in the world, but found his attention drawn to an object over the site: He perceived a flat, discoidal, metallic craft at an altitude of 14,000 feet. Its outer edges were rotating, and the thing seemed to be powered by some kind of plasma, a gas made up of ionized atoms. It was moving, he estimated, at 4,500 miles per hour. He quickly lost interest in whatever else was at the target site.

A similar event happened to Ingo Swann once, while he was remote-viewing a Soviet submarine, trying to determine its location. He described the sub, but then remarked that he saw something in the atmosphere above it, something that seemed to be shadowing the sub. What was it? asked Puthoff. Swann shrugged and sketched a flying saucer shape.*

"Accidental" results like these led Puthoff and other officials—even Bob Monroe—to specifically target remote viewers against UFO incidents. McMoneagle, going down to his zone to find what he believed would be some operational target, was often surprised to find himself looking around the cramped, curved interior of an unearthly ship, filled with skinny, large-eyed humanoids—who often stared back at him, wondering what the hell he was doing there. Facing off with aliens was a rough business, it seemed, and on several occasions, McMoneagle returned from the experience drenched in sweat and xenophobic stress.

---

* In *Out There*, a book about UFOs published in 1990, author Howard Blum places this bizarre event (without giving names) at a meeting of SRI and assorted Pentagon and White House officials at the Old Executive Office Building, in 1985. However, according to a former source from the program, that meeting and the surprise description of a UFO by Swann actually happened separately.

Pat Price had also done a great many UFO-related targets, and had even ventured out spontaneously, in his nightly reveries, to spy on flying saucers as they (supposedly) cruised in and out of Alaskan mountains. But Ingo Swann, asked by Puthoff if he would try to confirm some of Price's results, almost always refused. His argument was that UFO occupants—aliens—if they sensed him psychically spying on them, might swoop down to spy on *him,* invading his mind, possessing his soul. Ed Dames might have welcomed such a confrontation, but not Swann.

Still, despite Swann's apparent skittishness about extraterrestrial targets, he had given his favorite student Tom Nance a few during training. These included sites on the dark side of the Moon, and in the Cydonia region of Mars, where there were a number of strange-looking topographic features, including "pyramids" and a mountain that, some said, resembled Senator Ted Kennedy's face. Nance, for whatever prosaic or paranormal reason, had come up with results suggesting that some kind of humanoid civilization had lived at Cydonia, or perhaps even lived there now.

McMoneagle was given the same targets by Bob Monroe, with similar results. He even drew the humanoids in detail, and called them "They." McMoneagle would later tentatively suggest, on the basis of his RV sessions, that a race of humanoids had fought for survival on Mars, had dispatched some kind of space-lifeboat to Earth, and had perhaps built the great pyramids of Egypt. He would also speculate that UFOs in modern skies were actually human-piloted craft from the future.

Some time later, in the early 1990s, Ingo Swann would tell a few close friends and former colleagues about a series of official taskings he said he had been given, taskings which related to the extraterrestrial question.

The story, as Swann told it, began one day in about 1983 while he happened to be home in New York. He received a call from a trusted friend on Capitol Hill—a U.S. congress-man, according to one version of the story—who asked him if he would do a job for some colleagues who needed a skilled remote viewer's assistance. Swann's friend, who had come to him with requests before, didn't specify what the job was about, and may not have even known, but he assured Swann that his colleagues could be trusted and would pay the remote viewer for his time.

Shortly thereafter, following his friend's instructions, Swann stood on a street corner outside a museum in Manhattan. Two men with pseudonyms picked him up in a car, placed a blindfold on him, and drove him for a few hours out of town. When the blindfold was taken off, Swann was in a large underground installation. No one wore a uniform, but from the haircuts and the physiques, and the way people took orders, he decided that at least some were U.S. Marines.

Swann was led into a windowless room, was introduced to some people, and was then allowed to settle himself before starting his remote viewing. The target was described only as a pair of coordinates. They were *lunar* coordinates, for Swann was being asked to remote-view a place on the moon.

He soon did, and more coordinates were given to him. Before the day was out, Swann had described a variety of monumental objects, not human-made but not natural either, scattered across the cold surface of Earth's dusty cousin. Swann, according to the story, was then paid several thousand dollars in cash, and was driven back to his apartment in New York.

It was an outlandish story, but this was just the beginning. Swann would tell of a later mission, in which the same mysterious outfit had flown him to Alaska, then had taken him by helicopter to a remote lake. Something strange happened here at this lake, his pseudonymous companions told him. It happened like clockwork—in fact, it was about to happen now. As Swann stood there, he saw a mist form over the lake, and then an unearthly triangular object rose out of the lake, sucking up water and shooting out bright beams of light, and then zoomed off into the distance. Well, his companions asked Swann, now that he had seen this strange thing, perhaps he could remote-view it and tell them what it was? Swann impatiently explained that that was not how remote viewing worked. He was too front-loaded now with information about the target to be able to remote-view it accurately, and in any case was too frightened by the experience to want to do any further remote viewings of extraterrestrials or their craft.

Swann would later describe these episodes in a few dozen pages of novelistic prose that he circulated among some friends. It sounded absurd, like the plot for some *X-Files* episode—yet it was true that there had been UFO-related targets among the *official* taskings brought to SRI and Fort Meade over the years. The feedback envelope, in these cases, might contain a spy-satellite photograph of some unusual, unidentified object in near-Earth orbit, or even a photo of a strange light in the sky, taken from the ground.

One day near his retirement from the Army, Joe McMoneagle was driven to the Pentagon and escorted to a secure room to do a remote-viewing session against such a target. He was given no advance information. All he knew was that the feedback package was highly classified (thus the need for the secure room). He sat back in a chair, went into a light trance, and dropped down to his zone. He saw a strange, complex high-performance aerial vehicle, apparently not of this earth.

Afterwards, his taskers opened the feedback envelope and showed him the photo inside, which had been taken a few weeks before by one of the latest-model U.S. spy satellites. The photo depicted a strange object that had seemed to zig and zag in front of one of the satellite's wide-angled tracking cameras. Some Pentagon officials had already declared it to be merely a "weather balloon," but McMoneagle considered that explanation laughable.

Around this time, someone brought to the Fort Meade unit a similar, albeit less sensitive photograph from the National Photographic Interpretation Center. Mel Riley, monitored by Ed Dames, worked a CRV session against the target and sketched a disk-shaped craft with a rounded bottom. After finishing the session, for which he had been given only random-number "encrypted coordinates," Riley was shown the feedback photograph. It was an overhead reconnaissance photo, from a plane or satellite, taken at an oblique angle to the ground. It depicted an object flying or hovering at low altitude, not far from a large lake. Dames had been told only that the object was considered an "enigma" by the Pentagon.

In time, Dames would generate many of his own UFO-related targets for the remote viewers, using famous UFO close-encounter and sightings cases as targets. On the basis of these sessions, he would conclude that extraterrestrials had numerous bases around the globe—in mountains, in deserts, under the oceans. He would later say:

If you have no opinion at all on whether a vehicle that is moving in from deep space is a bolide [meteor] or an intelligently-driven machine, and you use remote viewers who, across the board, say this is a hollow vehicle and there are humanoids in it and here's what they look like . . . that is quite a moving experience when you did not believe in the existence of extraterrestrial life to begin with.

But of course, few remote viewers could ever have been described, at any part of their adult lives, as not believing in the existence of extraterrestrial life.

* * *

In his experimentation with remote viewing, Dames developed something he called the "open search." Instead of writing down a specific target description—say, "the Eiffel Tower"—and then assigning it random-number "coordinates" and putting the description with the random numbers in an envelope, Dames simply assigned coordinates to the words "open search," and put that in the target envelope. In Dames's mind, the use of "open search" as a target would free the remote viewer's psi perception to soar up and away, looking for anything that was particularly interesting out there in the Matrix. It could be something that had just happened, or was happening, halfway around the world; or it could be something that was about to happen. In practice, Dames felt that it was the ideal technique for monitoring the alien spaceships that he believed were busy flitting in and out of Earth's atmosphere. It was, in other words, a sort of enigma detector.

One day, Dames had the enigma tables turned on him. He brought Paul Smith into the CRV room, and gave him the coordinates for an "open search." All Smith knew was that he had two random numbers. It seemed like a regular target.

Smith cooled down, playing heavy metal music on his Walkman, and when he was ready, Dames read him the random numbers. Smith did his ideograms, and his Stage Twos, vocalizing basic sensory impressions; then came dimensionals, and Stage Three sketches, and Stage Four tabulations. The session was no more than fifteen minutes old when Dames began to grow disgusted. Smith wasn't describing anything that sounded extraterrestrial. His sketches and descriptions seemed to involve a U.S. naval vessel, a missile, an explosion, a tragic loss of life. At times during the session, though his demeanor suggested nothing more than a man thinking aloud while doing routine desk work, Smith was nearly bilocating. He felt almost as if he were on board this ship, amid the explosion, amid an orange blast of chaos, confusion, dismemberment, death. Dames didn't really take it seriously. He assumed that Smith was in Aol drive.

After the session was finished, Dames took the sketches and descriptions, wrote up a brief cover analysis, and filed them away. He regarded the session as a waste of time.

The date was Friday, May 15, 1987. Forty-eight hours later, in the Persian Gulf, a U.S. Navy guided-missile frigate, the *Stark*, was hit by a French-made Exocet missile fired from an Iraqi warplane. Two dozen of the *Stark*'s crew were killed immediately, and another thirteen died later of their injuries.

Smith's session had been done at a time when there was already significant anxiety, in the military and the general public, over the Iran-Iraq War and its threat to U.S. naval vessels in the Persian Gulf. Although certainly surprising, it wasn't clearly an example of paranormal precognition. Even so, it was touted as a success in various briefings by DIA officials—who were probably unaware of the session's origin as an enigma-hunting exercise.

Ed Dames was, if anything, proud of his status as a troublemaker within the unit, a maverick who dared venture into unknown realms. But he was also developing another kind of reputation—a reputation for becoming too involved in his monitoring of RV sessions, for pushing the viewer, however unconsciously, towards whatever target description he, Ed Dames, happened to favor. Occasionally Dames knew in advance of the session what the target was, but even when he was "blind" at first, he tended to develop strong opinions as the session went on. A few of the viewers began to see him as a significant source of Aol.

There was one episode, in late 1987, which some regarded as a good illustration of this problem. The branch chief at the time was a genial lieutenant colonel named Bill Xenakis, who had taken over after Bill Ray left, earlier in

1987, and would run the unit until Fern Gauvin took over in 1988. Xenakis called in Dames and explained that an ops-type target had just come in. He told Dames only that the target was a possible event.

Dames set up the target in the usual fashion. Xenakis had given him two four-digit random numbers to use as coordinates, and now he wrote them on the outside of an envelope. Then he wrote "possible event" and the coordinates on a slip of paper, sealed it inside the envelope, and went over to the CRV room to start running viewers against the target: Riley, Smith, Buchanan, and Gabrielle Peters.

Dames soon noticed that the viewers' descriptions of the target were remarkably consistent. Their impressions all seemed to involve some kind of unusual aerial vehicle. It had a large payload—box-like objects of various sizes—and the colors red and white featured prominently. The pilot was obese, and the vehicle seemed to be open-topped, with sled-like runners underneath. It was going to come across the northern U.S. border sometime a few weeks in the future. It was going to come down over Canada, down from the Arctic pole.

Some of the data generated by the viewers were very strange, but Dames decided it was probably analytical overlay. For instance, Paul Smith said for some reason that there were livestock associated with the target. Riley drew the vehicle with eight strange objects out in front of it. It didn't matter; it was obvious to Dames what was going on here: Some kind of terrorist attack was being planned. The target was apparently an ultralight plane or a specially modified helicopter, loaded with an atomic bomb—or bombs—and designed to fly under U.S. and Canadian radar surveillance. Stage Four data, designed to pull out intentions and purposes associated with the target, suggested that the device was meant to fly into the United States somehow, surreptitiously, by night. Dames guessed that a

Middle East country was involved, maybe Syria or Iran or Libya.

Dames was in the CRV room with Riley when he decided it was time to act. He told Riley he was going to run over to 4554, the nearest INSCOM building, and get access to a secure phone so he could alert his friends elsewhere in the intelligence community. To Riley, he seemed to be worried that Xenakis and others at DIA would suppress the data as unreliable if he tried to go through their channels. A terrorist nuclear attack on the United States . . . This was big.

Xenakis, meanwhile, was watching the session from the control room, trying not to allow his laughter to be heard across the hall in the CRV room. When Dames came out into the front room of the ops building, on his way to find a secure phone, Xenakis and everyone else were waiting for him, wearing big grins.

It had been Mel Riley's prank, a measure of revenge for all the brain-bending bilocations he'd had to endure on advanced training targets. The prank was that the target's identity had been known to the viewers all along. It was not a terrorist attack; it was Santa Claus and his sleigh. Each viewer had simply gone through the usual structure of a CRV session, describing Santa's raw attributes, and even making rough sketches of the sleigh and reindeer, but never actually naming the target. The idea had been to see what interpretations Dames would make, when presented with such unusual material. Xenakis had agreed to go along, and Dames, it seemed, had fallen right into it.

When he realized that he'd been fooled, Dames good-naturedly laughed it off. But as time wore on, and the unit's problems worsened, Dames seemed to laugh less often. By the middle of 1988, his three-year tour in Sun Streak, which had started in early 1986, was nearing an end. He now realized he didn't intend to stay for a second tour.

* * *

Back in about 1983, as one of the reactions to General Stubblebine's initiatives, the Army Research Institute had asked for a study of all the alternative, New Ageish techniques being promoted at INSCOM, including remote viewing. Jack Vorona, Dale Graff, and Hal Puthoff had hoped to arrange for a relatively receptive, open-minded scientist to head the remote-viewing part of the study. But the Army Research Institute had instead chosen George Lawrence, a Pentagon researcher who was widely considered a skeptic about psi. Lawrence had led the three-man team from the Pentagon that had visited SRI in early 1973, to investigate Uri Geller. After a brief look, Lawrence and fellow team member Ray Hyman, a psychologist at the University of Oregon, had skeptically dismissed the Israeli spoonbender and his feats.

For the Army Research Institute study, Lawrence proposed that Ray Hyman should head the analysis of remote viewing. Hyman was by this time a member of a controversial anti-psi group that called itself the "Committee for the Scientific Investigation of Claims of the Paranormal" (CSICOP).*

Hyman's conclusions therefore seemed easy to precognize, and Vorona and Graff saw to it that he was effectively shut out of the remote-viewing program. He was given no access to classified data, and was referred instead to Colonel John Alexander, who could give him only a few files on secret Soviet psi work.

The result was that Hyman ended up analyzing the sparse data published in the open parapsychology literature, much of which were long out-of-date. Hyman nevertheless drew a strong, angry-sounding conclusion:

---

* CSICOP's members included the showman James Randi, the science writers Leon Jaroff, Martin Gardner, and Philip Klass, and the astronomer Carl Sagan.

By both scientific and parapsychological standards . . . the case for remote viewing is not just very weak, but virtually nonexistent. It seems that the preeminent position that remote viewing occupies in the minds of many proponents results from the highly exaggerated claims made for the early experiments, as well as the subjectively compelling, but illusory correspondences that experimenters and participants find between components of the descriptions and the target sites.

Subjectively compelling, but illusory . . . Those in the program who had witnessed some of the great, eight-martini remote viewing sessions of the past, both classified and unclassified, simply shook their heads when they saw that phrase. In Hyman, they believed, they had an adversary who was utterly, religiously resistant to the concept of psi. He was a true unbeliever.

In any case, Vorona and Graff and other proponents of the program ducked down and weathered the storm. When they needed to convince someone, say, a senator or a White House official, they simply dipped into their treasure trove of classified remote-viewing data, which seemed compelling enough to convince almost anyone.

But further storms were to come, and this time the program's "special access" status* would be no help. Late in 1987, the new secretary of defense, Frank Carlucci, announced that he expected to cut $33 billion from the next Pentagon budget. The last great burst of Cold War defense spending was over, and the search was on for savings. The search was on for potentially embarrassing units and programs, too. Carlucci didn't want anything like the recent

---

* Sun Streak was not actually on the roster of the intelligence community's Special Compartmented Information programs. Vorona, Graff, and others effectively gave the program special-access status by controlling the list of people who knew about it.

Oliver North arms-for-hostages fiasco, or the Army's Yellow Fruit corruption case, happening on his watch. The political situation was therefore ominously similar to that which had caused the CIA, a decade before, to cut off funding for the remote-viewing program.

Sometime in 1988, around the time that a flurry of brief reports of Pentagon dabbling with psi appeared in the media, a Pentagon Inspector General's team arrived at the DT-S offices at Fort Meade, announcing their intention to look into the unit's operations and general practices. Riley and the other remote viewers were ordered by their bosses to make themselves scarce whenever any "IG" people were around. When the IG people weren't around—in fact, months before they arrived, and even after they had left— one of the unit's senior members busied himself at the document shredder.

What was being shredded? Opinions varied. Some said it was some of Angela Dellafiora's flakier channelled data, or Robin Dahlgren's tarot-card data. Others said the shredded data were from practice sessions against targets—Mother Teresa, say, or President Reagan—whom the DIA was not supposed to have "spied" upon. Still others believed that the shredded data were from old operational sessions.

Regardless of what was shredded, the outcome for the remote viewers was negative. The Inspector General's report concluded that DT-S was not ready to become an operational intelligence-gathering unit. The report recommended that the unit be shut down.

Ed Dames left DT-S in the late summer of 1988. Riley and the others threw a party for him, presenting a plaque they had made; it cited his "untiring, selfless, dedication to the study of, and understanding of, alternate universes and parallel dimensions."

Dames also received a Meritorious Service Medal from the DIA, of which he was just as proud. The MSM was mainly a straightforward recognition of ordinary service, and its citations were sometimes written by the recipients' colleagues in the unit. In any case, Dames's citation read like an appropriate epitaph for a program that seemed to have become increasingly separated from military reality.

> His total dedication to the highest ideals of service and his selfless commitment were always evident in his performance of the duties and responsibilities inherent in his position as Project Officer for a special project within the Directorate for Scientific and Technical Intelligence. Captain Dames brought to the Directorate a bank of knowledge and experience in the management and handling of intelligence and security affairs. This ability proved to be absolutely vital to effective integration of this unit into the Defense Intelligence Agency mission. Captain Dames was crucial in his fusion of his unit's unique "cutting edge" technology with the ongoing critical National Intelligence efforts of the Directorate. His efforts resulted in an intelligence product of great value to the National Intelligence Community. Captain Dames's operational and analytical skills were instrumental to the successful execution of 47 major intelligence projects which involved more than 800 individual collection missions. . . . Most significantly, Captain Dames was instrumental in penetrating a key foreign threat decision-making body [presumably the Soviet Defense Council]. The consequences of this singularly profound effort contributed immeasurably to the national security of his country. . . .

Jack Vorona, who had increasingly clashed with Harry Soyster and other top DIA officials over the remote-viewing program, announced his retirement at the end of 1989. For the remote viewers, the announcement was unexpected, and at Vorona's farewell party, there was a certain funereal atmosphere. At about the same time, it became clear that SRI's ten-million-dollar Pentagon contract, which had been running since 1986, was not going to be renewed, despite some favorable reports from the program's oversight committees.

From Capitol Hill, Dick D'Amato would manage to keep the Fort Meade side of the program alive, and it was assigned for a while, "experimentally," to the office of the Army's deputy chief of staff for intelligence.* But the remote viewers could see now that DT-S, far from contributing immeasurably to the security of their country, had faded irretrievably from significance.

Mel Riley, who had been in retirement mode for a while now, decided that he had had enough. His twenty years were up. He put in his retirement papers, and, as it happened, left the Army just before the first rumblings of the Gulf War, in July of 1990. With his wife, Edith, he moved back to Wisconsin, to a small town with a relaxed pace, amid woods and lakes, away from all the stress, all the craziness.

---

* The DCSI was a new, three-star position created in 1985 to replace the old two-star ACSI position. From September 1989 through the mid-1990s, the position was held by Lieutenant General Ira C. Owens.

EPILOGUE

One flew east. One flew west. One flew over the cuckoo's nest.

> —Ed Dames, after learning that
> Dave Morehouse had been
> admitted to a psychiatric ward

ALMOST FOUR YEARS LATER, I SAT IN INGO SWANN'S STUDIO IN lower Manhattan, surrounded by samples of his artistry. In one painting, a bluish gray, classically sculpted bust of a scowling, bearded man—he could have been Jesus, or Socrates, or perhaps Swann himself—hovered above a landscape filled with pyramids. There were halos around his head, buzzing with zodiacal symbols, and yellow beams of energy burst sideways out of his temples and upwards from his forehead; and from beneath him, from the bottom of his little pedestal, prismatic blue and yellow and red beams poured down like the end of a rainbow onto a great . . . brain-like thing . . . that was lying there, soaking up this hallucinatory cascade of colors.

Over at the other end of the studio, by the street, there was another oil painting, a large triptych, all comets and stars and sea, with high and frothy and lacy and soaring waves as if this were a low-gravity planet somewhere. And hanging on another wall, on the Lower East Side side, in fact, was a rendering of a strange three-part entity: the first part a darkly bearded young man, naked and well muscled, his body very pink and barred with mauve stripes; the second part a snake with the leather-capped head of another, more rapacious-looking bearded man atop it; and finally, thirdly, a young woman, nude and tautly perfect, her head thrust backward in an orgiastic pose . . . and the backdrop to the outrageous trinity was a vast sea of water and stars, with cliffs to the right and a gigantic pink tower, spouting a geyser of star-stuff high into the atmosphere of this dusky neverland.

An easel and a blank canvas were set up to one side of the room, and paints were mixed and ready, but the air down here smelled less of paint than of cigar smoke and, faintly, stale champagne. I couldn't tell where the champagne smell was coming from, but there was a layer of the cigar smoke just under the ceiling; and poking up into this mini-stratosphere was a bulging cumulonimbus formation, rising from the long table where a paunchy, bearded man of sixty was sitting, clad in an old T-shirt and sweatpants, clenching in his teeth a Tiparillo cigar.

"Twenty-nine degrees, twenty-five minutes, seven seconds north," said Ingo Swann. "Ninety-eight degrees, twenty-nine minutes west."

Across the table, I wrote the numbers down. After my hand formed the "W" for "west" it moved sideways across the page, making a flat line with three angular, box-like protrusions. "Angles," I said. "Structures."

"That's a correct ideogram," said Swann.

And now I was in Stage Two, waiting for basic sensory perceptions from the target to tickle my synapses. "Wood feel . . . concrete feel . . . dust . . . massive." I realized I was already out of the standard structure—dimensionals like "massive" weren't supposed to surface so soon.

But before I could react I was hit by two images that I treated as Aols: "Aol break, dome . . . Aol break, nuclear cooling tower." There was probably something domelike at the site, but I had to get those Aol images out of my head, or they would start to distort the data.

After a short pause, I found myself doing a Stage Three sketch, letting my hand draw what it wanted: two lines across the page, a line down at a right angle, and a curved shape, like a crescent moon. "Curves," I said, and another image popped in: "Aol break, bunkers." I drew a shape like a Quonset hut. There were too many Aols here. I was going too fast. I needed to take the coordinates again.

Swann read them to me, and this time I skipped the ideogram, moving straight into stage two—"bark . . . browns . . . grays . . . smell of masonry . . . stone . . . bulk . . . steel . . . chrome . . . smells . . . acrid. Aol break, shipyard." I started to sketch some more angles, and curves, but it was still too abstract. I declared a break and, after another pause, took the coordinates again.

This time I sketched a tall column, and then put a top on it. The top grew another leg, and the shape became a table. I sensed that there was water nearby. There was some kind of building—or buildings?—at the target, but I was confused about the precise shape.

On a new page I sketched a large cylindrical object. That felt like one of the buildings. But I sensed something else: "Girders . . . struts . . . something falling . . . sparks . . . metal." I drew a metal tower, as seen from the ground. "Aol break, radio tower."

Now I sketched a road, and what could be a railroad, leading up to a tall, narrow, column-like tower, and next to it a squat, cylindrical building. "Aol break, stadium. Aol break, oil storage [tank] with railroad."

Swann now handed me a knife and some white modelling clay, and invited me to model the target. As I started to shape the clay to form the two buildings, more impressions came in. I sensed that the tower had something on top of it. "Aol break, water tank. Revolving restaurant?"

I ended up modelling the tower with the water-tank/ revolving restaurant on top, and next to it the larger, flattish cylindrical object.

When I was finished, Swann slid the feedback folder across the table. Inside, I found a photo from an old issue of *National Geographic*, of a tower in downtown San Antonio with a revolving restaurant on top, and next to it the large, cylindrical, domed city convention center. Checking a map later, I saw that the narrow San Antonio River— "water nearby"—was two thousand feet away.

Ingo Swann had left SRI in 1988, and was now retired, living quietly down in the Bowery section of Manhattan, writing occasional books and essays, and, from a distance, watching the remote-viewing program sink into oblivion. After a few interviews, he agreed to train me over several weeks in April and May 1994. I wanted to learn about remote viewing from the remote viewer's perspective, and he in turn wanted me to learn from the right teacher.

Remote viewing with someone who already knows the target, and provides occasional feedback during the session, is like riding a bicycle with training wheels on. Even so, I had the impression that my results were not all due to coaching from Swann. In one session, I described a site within twenty seconds—a hot springs in Arkansas, it turned out—based on three impressions, all correct: "terrain . . . white . . . sulfur smell." After the training ended, I had my girlfriend fax me coordinates of sites all over the world, and in solo sessions, without a monitor to give me feedback, I described the targets well enough to overcome even her skepticism. My remote viewings weren't reliable or detailed enough to justify my employment as a full-time psychic spy, but I was reasonably convinced that, as General Thompson would put it, "there's something there."

I knew I couldn't perform the in-depth, long-term research that that "something" deserved, but as someone writing about remote viewing and remote viewers, I wanted to get a feel for all the variety and the strangeness of their experiences. Which brought me, inevitably, to Ed Dames.

Dames was now living in Albuquerque, New Mexico, and had led an interesting life since leaving DT-S in 1988. First he had worked at another secret unit, this one an INSCOM "strategic deception" and counter-narcotics unit known as Team Six. Dave Morehouse had joined him there, briefly, in 1990. On the side, the two officers had also formed a company, Psi-Tech, with the idea of using moonlighting remote viewers as a kind of psychic investigation team for private clients. Morehouse, Paul Smith, Mel Riley, Lyn Buchanan, and others would provide the raw data, and Dames would analyze it all. Dames convinced the retired General Stubblebine to serve, for a time, as chairman of the board.

Unfortunately, Psi-Tech's clients were relatively scarce, and were usually out on the New Age fringe of things. A wealthy man in Baltimore asked Dames to remote-view the mysterious "crop circles" appearing in wheat fields in Southern England; Dames provided the man with data suggesting that the circles were caused by flying-saucer-like devices skimming aerobatically over the wheat fields. Later, a group from the former Soviet Union asked Psi-Tech to remote-view the disappearance of a Russian space probe near Mars. Dames again implicated aliens.

Dames, along with Morehouse, seemed increasingly preoccupied with extraterrestrial matters, and tried to use remote viewing to locate "alien bases" on Earth. There was one base in Alaska, the remote viewing suggested, and one off the coast of South America, and at least two in northern and western New Mexico—where Dames and Morehouse went out into the desert, in search of evidence. In late 1991, Dames retired from the Army, separated from his wife Christine, and moved to Albuquerque. A year and a half later, in March 1993, he appeared at a local UFO conference and announced that a colony of pregnant Martian females lay beneath the New Mexico desert. Sometime between April and August, he predicted, these Martians would give birth and emerge aboveground. "We're sure it's going to happen," he told his audience. "We've alerted the media, and teams of doctors, technicians, and documentary filmmakers are on call and in place to respond at a moment's notice. . . . President Clinton will announce it and everyone in the world will know!"

But August 1993 came, and went, and no aliens appeared. Dames, apparently running out of money, began to turn Psi-Tech into a remote-viewing training company, and offered a week-long course for about $3,000. His students included a UCLA English literature professor; an executive at an Albuquerque-based mining company; and Courtney Brown, a political science professor at Emory University in Atlanta. Brown became so enamored of remote viewing, and of what he thought it could do, that he decided to use it to explore the history of interactions between the aliens and planet Earth—among other things detailing the various races of aliens, such as the big-headed "Grays," and the blond and blue-eyed "Nordics." Brown would later publish a book about it all, titled *Cosmic Voyage*.

I arrived in Albuquerque in July 1994, and spent a few days with Dames, practicing remote-viewing the Psi-Tech way. The advantage of practicing with Dames was that he used random-number "encrypted coordinates" instead of actual geographical coordinates, thus making the technique a bit more rigorous. But as expected, I was mostly given unusual, often extraterrestrial targets. In some cases, I was surprised to learn that I had described precisely what

Dames had expected me to describe, and what other students before me had described—for example, a high-speed vehicle under the surface of Mars. I assumed that this had come from inadvertent cues from Dames during the session, but there were times when the information seemed to pop into my consciousness so unexpectedly and spontaneously that I couldn't help wondering whether "telepathic overlay" was also a factor.

The only really satisfying session, down in Albuquerque, came when I took out a pair of random numbers that had been faxed to me by my girlfriend; they represented a site she had chosen, somewhere in the world. Neither Dames nor I knew what it was. With Dames as monitor, I targeted the site, and described a place on an island, near a cliff that ran down to the sea. There seemed to be some kind of construction going on at the site; the buildings were unfinished.

The site, I learned later, was a ruined temple to Athena, on a hill overlooking the Mediterranean, on the island of Rhodes. The "construction" I had sensed was possibly an AoL; the buildings at the site were actually undergoing *de*construction by the elements.

My days in Albuquerque were busy, intense with remote viewing, and I was insomniac most nights. After half a week I was "bouncing off the walls." Between sessions, I would go outside the little office suite center where Psi-Tech had its one-room office. I would walk over to a large granite boulder on the edge of the parking lot, sit on it, and stare at a tree a few hundred yards away, and the Sandia Mountains behind it. The tree seemed extraordinarily green. The mountains seemed immensely stark. The sky seemed incredibly blue. While I quietly semi-hallucinated, Ed Dames would talk, a hundred yards away through the heat, on his cellular phone, checking his messages, chatting with his new girlfriend, a former Psi-Tech student who lived in Beverly Hills. One afternoon, Dames came over after a chat on the phone, and informed me quietly: "I have a meeting with the Gray leadership next month. The ones in uniforms."

"Uh-huh," I said, giving him the same blank stare I had been applying to the mountains.

He looked up at the mountains, then chuckled softly, shaking his head. "You can't tell anybody about this. They'll put you in a straitjacket."

"Yes." I laughed. "Yes."

Ed Dames wasn't always off communing with aliens in the desert, and on the whole he was intelligent and friendly, and interesting. There are a lot worse people to shoot the breeze with, over a few beers. But I couldn't help thinking that if I continued to remote-view at the pace he set, day after day, year after year, my mind would eventually become clouded by ETs and spirits, pregnant Martians, the certainty that I was Chosen and could do no wrong. I would wrestle, down in that ancient, Boschean abyss, with the sprites and demons that always seem to linger around psi.

I'd like to think I sensed them once. It was on my last day in Albuquerque. Unknown to me, Dames had chosen his own psyche as the target—"Ed Dames/Deep-Mind"—and I was perceiving grayness, whiteness, wetness, even "madness," and things seemed to rush past me constantly, always beyond my reach. Somewhere along in the session I detected laughter.

Afterwards, Dames remarked with a smile that other remote viewers had also heard laughter down in Ed Dames/Deep-Mind. "It reminded me of a bunch of little gremlins in the background," Mel Riley later told me.

And what did you think of that, Mel?

"Nothing. It's all part of remote viewing. You've got to maintain a sense of humor. If you don't, you go crazy."

* * *

By the time the Gulf War began in early 1991, only four remote viewers were left at Fort Meade: Lyn Buchanan and a DIA civilian named Greg Sloan, plus Angela Dellafiora and Robin Dahlgren. They received occasional taskings during the war, especially when the Pentagon decided it needed to hunt down Saddam Hussein's mobile SCUD launchers in western Iraq. The research side of the program had now been revived by Ed May, under the auspices of another think tank, Science Applications International Corporation (SAIC). Ken Bell and Joe McMoneagle, under contract to SAIC, were also asked to help find Iraqi SCUDs.

The SCUD search was a classic example of how remote viewers could, in principle, be useful militarily. If remote viewers' data could narrow the "search window" even slightly, they would save the Pentagon millions of dollars in costs for the massive SCUD-hunt—which involved hundreds of aircraft sorties per day, plus roving units of British and American commandos on the ground. Such a payoff would make the RV program's own budget, now about a million dollars per year, seem well worth it. But as was now almost always the case, remote viewers' results probably never made it to battlefield commanders based in Saudi Arabia.

Ironically, around this time the program switched to a new and grander-sounding code name. "Sun Streak" came off the rubber stamps, and was replaced by "Star Gate." It was a name the program would never live up to.

Paul Smith spent the Gulf War in the thick of things, with a helicopter assault unit attached to the 101st Airborne Division. When the ground campaign began, Smith and his unit were among the first into Iraq, and quickly captured an Iraqi battalion—one of the many that collectively threw down their arms in surrender that day. Smith stayed in Iraq for a month after the cease-fire, camped south of Basra. Then he came home, and found another job at the DIA, a job that had nothing to do with remote viewing.

The following year, 1992, Lyn Buchanan reached his twenty-year service mark and retired from the Army. He joined up with General Stubblebine, who had divorced his first wife and moved in with a psychiatrist in New York who specialized in "UFO abductions." Buchanan went to work for Stubblebine, among other things holding remote viewing workshops at various UFO enthusiast and New Age conferences. Eventually, there was a falling-out, and Buchanan and his wife moved back to Maryland. He did computer work for the government, and set up his own remote-viewing training company, Problems Solutions Innovations (PSI).

After Buchanan had departed DT-S, only Greg Sloan, Angela Dellafiora, and Robin Dahlgren were left. There were no efforts to recruit additional remote viewers. Dale Graff was officially the branch chief. In the summer of 1993, Graff resigned; he was replaced by a DIA HUMINT specialist named Al Garfield, and funding continued, but the end seemed near.

Mel Riley kept in touch with these developments, from up in Wisconsin, but wasn't much disturbed by them. It had long been clear what was going to happen. The remote-viewing program was now receding into the past, as far as he was concerned. Perhaps it would be revived someday; perhaps not. Whatever happened, he had played his part, and it had been interesting while it lasted.

Riley now worked at a museum in a town near his home, serving as assistant curator. He helped maintain the exhibits of Native American and pioneer life, and organized new exhibits, and guided tourists and schoolchildren around the place. His wife, Edith, worked as a nurse in a nearby hospital. The two of them, hosting relatives now and then, lived in a cozy house whose backyard was lapped by a branch of central Wisconsin's Wolf River. Riley could

take his canoe, on a summer afternoon, and paddle up-
stream until the river narrowed and became a shallow wilderness rapid, and then when he could go no farther he
would relax and drift back home again. There were rivers
and lakes everywhere around there, swimming with trout
and northern pike, and crawling with crawfish. There were
deep woods, and quiet pine glades where he hunted in the
fall. There was always venison, and perhaps a rabbit or two,
in the Riley freezer.

Riley had always been fascinated by Indian lore, and
now as he mellowed into middle age he read even more
deeply on the subject, and practiced Native American
dances and handicrafts. Some of the local tribes, surprised
by his seriousness about their culture—he was now more
knowledgeable than many of them—began to treat him
almost as one of their own. He made or was given ornate
costumes and headdresses, and constructed a large and
very authentic-looking tepee in his backyard. He was invited to festivals and ritual dances from which white men
were normally excluded. A local medicine society, a society
of Indian healers and magicians, even gave him an otter-
skin "medicine bag." If something difficult needed doing—
a change in the weather, the healing of a sick relative—
Riley would sequester himself, calmly focussing his Indian
medicine on the situation.

Greg Sloan, whom Riley stayed in touch with over these
years, also developed an interest in Native Americana, and
by 1994, in the throes of a divorce and the breakdown of
DT-S, asked to take part in a Sun Dance. A Sun Dance is a
crucifixion-like ritual, in which a man, via small metal
hooks in his skin, is tethered to a post for several days and
must dance, bleeding and hungry, having visions, until the
hooks work their way out of him. The Sun Dancer symbol-
ically takes upon himself, wrestles with, and somehow re-
solves by his suffering, the sins and misfortunes of the
people around him. Sloan, a tall, dour man in his mid-

thirties, with dark hair and a thick mustache, would dance the Sun Dance under blazing heat three years in a row. Riley just watched, not really approving, not really disapproving . . . just watching life, in all its strangeness, as it unfolded before him.

Former Stubblebine aide John Alexander, now retired from the Army and working on "non-lethal weapons" programs at Los Alamos, co-wrote a successful book in 1992, *The Warrior's Edge*, about the alternative world and soldiering. Ed Dames eventually decided he could do at least as well with a book on remote viewing. Ingo Swann hooked him up with a literary agent he knew, Sandra Martin. Dave Morehouse, who had been discussing the remote-viewing program with investigative journalist Dale Van Atta since 1989, was also invited to join the project.

Dames and Morehouse worked on the book for a while, but they didn't get far, and eventually agreed to turn over the writing to Jim Marrs, a former Texas newspaper reporter who had written *Crossfire*—a Kennedy assassination-conspiracy book that had been one of the inspirations for Oliver Stone's film *JFK*. Marrs wrote a proposal for an exposé of the remote-viewing program, and sold it to Harmony Books (an imprint of Crown Publishing) for a $100,000 advance, which he split with Dames and Morehouse.

Remarkably, Morehouse was still in uniform at this point, as a training officer with the 82d Airborne Division at Fort Bragg, North Carolina. He seemed to believe that he could continue his military career even as he benefitted financially from exposing a classified program. When the deal with Harmony came through (Morehouse heard about it over his field phone, while on exercises in North Carolina) he used his share of the advance to lease a Mercedes. Through Sandra Martin, he began negotiating with NBC for a movie-of-the-week deal based on his experiences as a military psychic.

Eventually, Morehouse's apparent love of dangerous situations caught up with him. In early 1994, an irate girlfriend filed a complaint with Fort Bragg authorities,* and Morehouse was charged with a number of offenses against the military code, including adultery, sodomy, the theft of an Army computer, and above all, conduct unbecoming an officer. In initial statements to Fort Bragg authorities, the woman mentioned that Morehouse had bragged about his highly classified work at DT-S and other units, had claimed that he could psychically spy on her at will, and had told her about the book he was writing with his friend Ed Dames. Mention of the book deal—which appeared to involve a deliberate disclosure of classified information—set off further investigations of Morehouse by INSCOM, the Army Criminal Investigation Division, and the Defense Investigative Service. Morehouse now faced a likely expulsion from the Army, and a possible jail sentence.

A few days after Fort Bragg authorities had decided to send Morehouse to a full court-martial, Morehouse checked into Walter Reed Army Medical Center in Washington, D.C. He gave the impression that he was having visions of angels, and was depressed and suicidal. He was no longer competent to stand trial, his lawyers now contended. Remote viewing had destabilized him, and now he had gone over the edge. Morehouse and Sandra Martin now also began to claim to friends that shadowy government operatives were harassing them, trying to shut them up. In one case, Martin told me, some Pentagon operative

---

* The woman was the wife of an enlisted man who had been Morehouse's driver, and who, ironically, had sought counselling from Morehouse for his marital problems. In testimony for the court-martial, the woman quoted Morehouse as having urged her to "live close to the flame" as he did.

had tried to intimidate her on the New York subway, standing over her and warning her "to stop representing Dave."

The remote-viewing community was generally skeptical about all these stories, but by the time Morehouse came out of the hospital, months later, he had what appeared to be a powerful defense strategy in place: The court-martial would become an investigation and exposure not of his wrongdoings at Fort Bragg, but of the classified, politically embarrassing remote-viewing program. A lot of dirty government laundry was going to be aired.

As Morehouse's lawyers began to request special clearances to look into the remote-viewing program, and to interview former participants, the Army classified the proceedings, and attempted to keep them from reaching a trial. Within a few months, Fort Bragg authorities had struck a deal with Morehouse. In lieu of a trial on the Fort Bragg misconduct charges, he resigned from the Army with an "other than honorable" discharge that left him neither pension nor benefits. He officially separated from the Army in January 1995, and went to work for Sandra Martin in New York.

Ed Dames was now living in Beverly Hills with his girlfriend, the estranged wife of the actor Brad Dourif.* After seeing a draft of the Jim Marrs book in the spring of 1995, Dames complained that it was heavily fictionalized, and focussed too much on Morehouse. Harmony eventually cancelled the book.

Morehouse, undaunted, started to write his own book, *Psychic Warrior,* and by the fall of 1995 he had sold it to St. Martin's Press. Morehouse now alleged that he had developed psychic powers after being hit on his helmet by a bullet while on a training exercise in Jordan in 1987. He had then been asked to join DT-S, where he had performed

---

* Dourif played Billy in the film *One Flew over the Cuckoo's Nest.*

various impressive paranormal feats.* In early November 1995, Morehouse and a new agent pitched this tale to Hollywood film studios. Several made bids, including Oliver Stone, who narrowly lost out to Interscope Communications. According to *Variety*, Interscope agreed to pay Morehouse $300,000, plus another half million or so when the film was made. Morehouse began working on the book, the screenplay, and a Saturday morning children's cartoon show for Hanna-Barbera—involving a team of superheroes who use psi and other non-lethal powers to combat their foes.

In 1994 Dick D'Amato tried to move the remote-viewing program into the CIA's budget, under the Agency's Office of Research and Development—where Ken Kress, the engineer who had originated the remote-viewing program twenty-two years before, now worked.

But Kress couldn't save the program, even if he had hoped to. The Office of Research and Development—and the CIA as a whole—didn't want it. Dick D'Amato was not someone who could be easily defied, but the Agency agreed to accept the remote viewers on the condition that an outside review would first take place. The review was conducted by a small consulting group, the American Institutes for Research (AIR), which often did work for the Agency.

AIR President David Goslin, who coordinated the review, had overseen the controversial Ray Hyman study of remote viewing in the late 1980s, and was known by some as another skeptic about psi. In any case, by the time the study began, the Democrats—led by D'Amato's boss, Sena-

---

* Morehouse's former colleagues remember his story about the Jordan incident; but they say that Morehouse told them the bullet impact only gave him a headache afterwards. Morehouse apparently never mentioned to his colleagues at DT-S any prior paranormal experiences.

tor Robert Byrd—had lost the Senate to the Republicans. The CIA could now do what it liked with the program.

In analyzing the program for the AIR study, Goslin interviewed the three remaining remote viewers, and several anonymous intelligence officials who had tasked them during the period 1993–94. Goslin also commissioned an outside appraisal of the recent remote-viewing research by two academics—pro-psi statistician Jessica Utts from the University of California at Davis, and anti-psi psychologist Ray Hyman.

Predictably, Hyman and Utts disagreed on whether there was sufficient scientific evidence for the validity of remote viewing. Hyman said there wasn't; Utts said there was. On the separate question of remote viewing's utility in intelligence work, David Goslin concluded from his analysis of the 1993–94 operations that it had not been useful.

The AIR study eventually made the news in late November 1995, and prompted ABC's *Nightline* and *The Washington Post* to run stories on the psychic-spying program. A bubble of media interest followed, lasting several days. Joe McMoneagle, Keith Harary, Ed May, Dale Graff, and others suddenly emerged to give their sides of the story. Why did the AIR report focus only on the last, worst years of the program? they wondered. Why wasn't the CIA willing to admit all the successes the program had produced in previous years? Why didn't they just kill the Fort Meade unit and rely on the better, freelance remote viewers?

But the mainstream media in America didn't seem interested in disputing the CIA's negative conclusions, and the bubble of interest quickly subsided. The *Post* ended its coverage with a story by its science staff, suggesting that remote viewing was bogus, a mixture of fraud and delusion.

Those on Capitol Hill who had supported the program meanwhile ran for cover. Some refused to return reporters' phone calls. Others, like Dick D'Amato and Senator Byrd, offered only a weak defense of the program: It had involved very little taxpayer money, they said. It had never really been used operationally. It had never been taken too seriously. And anyway, it was all over now.

A year or so after they were vacated, I drove over to the remote-viewing unit's old buildings at Fort Meade. There was snow on the ground, and it was clear that no one had been up the driveway in weeks, if not months. Paint flaked off the sides of the buildings, and the aluminum chimneys atop 2561 were now stooped by wind and time.

I parked in front, and walked around the two buildings. Along 2560, the ops building, there were windows outside each of the RV rooms, but through the security bars and window glass only bricks were visible. Finally I was able to get a glimpse inside, through a window that looked into the building's entrance room, where Mel Riley's desk had once stood. I saw a beige carpet, a dusty chair, and an open door inviting me into the corridor with the RV rooms. Had the building's door not been locked, I would gladly have gone in. I wanted to linger in those rooms, meeting the ghosts conjured up in all those years of remote viewers' reveries. What outrageous stories *they* could tell!

ACKNOWLEDGMENTS

In years to come I shall wince at the remembrance of how much time, assistance, and recollective effort I demanded from my sources for this book, and how little—this little book, in fact—I have been able to give them in return. I am grateful to all of them (those I'm permitted to mention are listed on the next three pages), but I want to acknowledge a special debt to Skip Atwater, Hal Puthoff, Mel and Edith Riley, and General Ed Thompson, who were heroically co-operative.

I also want to thank my editors, Stephanie Gunning and Mike Shohl at Dell; fellow researchers Bill LaParl and Marcello Truzzi; Gerri Harcarik at the U.S. Army's Center for Military History; Wendy Sparks at the Ronald Reagan Library; the staff of the cartographic branch and the still photo branch of the National Archives; Joe Haytas at the Defense Visual Information Center; William Pearce at the INSCOM Freedom of Information Act Office; and Virginia Grenier of the Fort Bragg FOIA office.

INTERVIEW SOURCES

A number of sources who spoke on background are not included in the list below. Also, not all those listed below spoke on the record all the time.

Colonel John Alexander, USA (Ret.). A senior aide to Major General Albert Stubblebine, chief of the Army's Intelligence and Security Command (INSCOM), 1982–84.

Captain Fred H. "Skip" Atwater, USA (Ret.). Operations and training officer at Fort Meade unit, 1978–87. Atwater was also instrumental in founding the unit.

First Sergeant Leonard "Lyn" Buchanan, USA (Ret.). Remote viewer, Fort Meade unit, 1984–92.

Bonnar "Bart" Cox. Director of Information and Engineering Science Division at Stanford Research Institute (SRI), 1973–76. Participated as experimenter in early remote-viewing research.

Major Edward Dames, USA (Ret.). Remote-viewing

trainee at SRI, 1983–84. Assistant operations officer at Fort Meade unit, 1985–88. Founded Psi-Tech, a commercial remote-viewing venture, 1989.

Christine Dames. Ed Dames's ex-wife.

Fernand Gauvin. Remote viewer, Fort Meade unit, 1978–81. Assistant operations officer, 1986–88; branch chief, 1988–89.

Uri Geller. Psychic investigated at SRI, 1972–74.

Dale Graff. Air Force civilian analyst, later a senior DIA official who supported remote-viewing program, 1977–89. Branch chief of Fort Meade unit, 1989–93.

Lieutenant General Daniel O. Graham, USAF (Ret.). Director of the Defense Intelligence Agency, 1974–76. (Deceased.)

Keith Harary. Psychic, now a psychologist, who took part in remote-viewing development and operational work at SRI, 1980–82 and in late 1980s.

Ron Hawke. A physicist at Lawrence Livermore Laboratory. Part of a group that conducted psi experiments with Uri Geller, 1974–75.

Louis Jolyon-West, M.D. Professor of psychiatry at UCLA and an expert on dissociative phenomena. Member of medical oversight board for Science Applications International Corp. remote-viewing research in early 1990s.

Commander C. B. "Scott" Jones, USN (Ret.). Former senior aide to Senator Claiborne Pell (D-RI), adviser on psi-related matters. Ran a group of psychics that performed contract work for several federal agencies in early 1980s.

Sam Koslov. Science adviser to the secretary of the navy, 1976–77.

Chief Warrant Officer Joseph McMoneagle, USA (Ret.). Remote viewer with Fort Meade unit, 1978–84; SRI unit, 1985–89; SAIC unit, 1990–95.

Professor Michael Persinger. Psychologist at Laurentian University, Ontario, and informal consultant to SRI, early

1980s. Persinger has studied the link between neurophysiological processes and mystical or paranormal experiences.

Hal Puthoff. Laser physicist and former NSA employee who started psi research program at SRI in 1972 and headed it until 1985.

First Sergeant Mel Riley, USA (Ret.). Remote viewer, Fort Meade unit, 1978–81, 1986–90.

Ron Robertson. A security officer at Livermore Lab during 1970s. Part of a group that conducted psi experiments with Uri Geller.

Geraldine Stubblebine. Ex-wife of Major General Albert Stubblebine, USA (Ret.), head of INSCOM, 1981–84.

Ingo Swann. Remote viewer, SRI, 1972–88.

Russell Targ. A laser physicist who was Hal Puthoff's assistant at SRI, 1972–82.

Major General Edmund Thompson, USA (Ret.). Head of the U.S. Army Intelligence Agency, 1975–77; assistant chief of staff for intelligence, 1977–81; DIA deputy director for management and operations 1982–84. A key supporter of the remote-viewing program.

Robert Van de Castle. Retired professor of psychology at University of Virginia. Evaluated Uri Geller at SRI for Pentagon's Advanced Research Projects Agency.

John Wilhelm. Former *Time* science correspondent, author of 1976 book *The Search for Superman,* about early (unclassified) psi research at SRI.

PSEUDONYMS

The following names mentioned in the text are pseudonyms:

Bill and Judy Alvarez
Frances Bryan
Nick Clancy
Peter Crane
Don Curtis
Laura Dickens
Bud Duncan
Donald Ebsen
Norm Everheart
John Fairchild
Frank Gaines
Al Garfield
Bob Grant
Steve Hanson

Richard Henderson
Steve Holloway
Walt Jerome
Richard Kennett
Colonel Kowalski
Mary Long
Dawn Lutz
Peter Maris
Jim Morris
Tom Nance
Debbie Norfeld
Bill O'Donnell
Doug Pemberton
Gabrielle Peters
Don Porter
Janice Rand
Ed Rogers
Mike Russo
Greg Sloan
Stan Snyder
Nancy Stern
Ted Wheatley

NOTES

All quotes in the text are from personal interviews unless otherwise noted.

Epigraph, Book One

xiii Charlie Rose, in Stuckey 1979.

Chapter 1 The Zone

1 Riley's morning: Reconstructed from Riley's recollection of what that morning had probably been like for him. He did not always use the suitcase ritual and the diving ritual.

3 Special Actions Branch: INSCOM 1981b.

3 an Army memorandum: ibid.

5 Chinese nuclear weapon: Riley; Atwater; McMoneagle; Graff 1995; and two researchers formerly associated with the program.

Chapter 2 The Dream Team

7 Young Riley: Riley.

9 Riley did well: Riley; Burroughs 1974.

10 Systems Exploitation Team: Riley; Atwater; Thompson.

11 Atwater: Atwater.

11 ASA and NSA: A former senior Pentagon official.

13 Atwater's proposal: Atwater. Thompson remembers that the psychic spying unit was actually his idea.

14 Thompson's enthusiasm: Thompson.

14 Gondola Wish: Riley. Atwater vaguely remembers it.

14 Atwater was given: Atwater.

14 first task: Atwater; Riley; Thompson; a former SRI source.

15 SRI researchers had already: Puthoff; Atwater; Thompson.

15 Back in Washington: The account of the screening and selection process comes from the recollections of Atwater, Riley, and McMoneagle.

17 The group: Atwater; Riley; McMoneagle.

17 Gauvin: Gauvin.

18 frustrating slowness: Riley.

19 word came down: Riley. Atwater remembers a lag while the human use issues were sorted out.

19 mind control: Ranelagh 1986.

20 six to SRI: Atwater; Riley.

20 Hanson: Atwater.

21 chocolate RV: Riley; Atwater.

21 more interesting targets: Riley.

22 Thompson's RV session: Riley; Thompson.

23 Gondola Wish support: A former senior Army official.

23 practical annoyances: Riley; Atwater.

25 Army memo: INSCOM 1981b.

25 high-level interest: Thompson, Atwater, and McMoneagle all remarked that the interest came in part from

other areas of the intelligence community. Riley told me he suspected that the CIA had much to do with it and wanted to use the Army to hide its own potentially controversial interest in psi. Two other former participants in the program also provided information on Pentagon/CIA plans in this area.

25 originally envisioned function: Oddly Thompson recalls that the unit was originally meant for offensive spying, not opsec. It may have been that Thompson simply didn't know much about the unit until late 1978.

25 budget, manpower slots: Atwater; Riley; McMoneagle; INSCOM 1981b. These were drawn ad hoc from the budget for General Thompson's office. No official manpower authorization for the unit existed until 1981 (INSCOM 1981b).

25 Special Actions Branch: This name is mentioned in INSCOM 1981b as INSCOM's temporary "vehicle" for the unit 1979–81.

25 Grill Flame: Atwater; Riley; INSCOM 1981a,b. There is some confusion over the origin of the code name Grill Flame. Atwater thinks it was from an Army code name list (because he knew of a separate Army project code-named Grill Frame), while another former participant remembers it as a code name taken from a DIA list. Graff told me he wasn't sure. INSCOM 1981b refers to "DOD project Grill Flame."

25 secrecy was designed: This was the view expressed to me by every source who participated in the program, from remote viewers to program managers.

26 Chinese nuke: Details of this operation come from Riley, Atwater, Graff 1995, and two researchers formerly affiliated with the program.

26 McMoneagle's zone: Atwater. I also have heard an audio recording of one of McMoneagle's sessions.

Chapter 3 PSI-INT

30 HUMINT on the wane: See Emerson 1988, Woodward 1987.

31 broach these matters: Riley; Atwater.

32 Trent: Riley, Atwater; McMoneagle.

33 Protocols for remote viewing: Atwater; Riley.

35 unique talents: Atwater; Riley; McMoneagle.

35 Trent under truck: Atwater.

36 limitations on RV: Atwater; Riley; McMoneagle.

37 kept busy: Atwater, Riley.

37 mapping foreign sites: Atwater; Riley; McMoneagle.

37 search problems: Atwater; McMoneagle; Riley.

37 U.S. consulate: Atwater. Graff 1995 refers to this as a CIA operation, but Atwater remembers its being an NSA job, and a CIA source in a position to know doesn't remember it as an agency tasking.

38 difficulty of search problems: McMoneagle; Atwater; Riley; Puthoff.

39 a nuclear weapon: Riley remembered the bomb dropping into the Mediterranean. A researcher associated with the program vaguely remembered the incident and recalled that the bomb had dropped into the Atlantic off Spain.

39 Skylab: McMoneagle; Atwater.

40 Navy A-6: Atwater; Riley.

40 U.S. helicopter down in Peru: Riley.

41 agent in Eastern Europe: Atwater.

42 KGB illegal: A former CIA official; Riley; Atwater; Graff 1995.

46 "interesting civilization": Atwater.

47 Korean talks: Atwater.

48 Moscow embassy building: Atwater; Riley.

49 walking off the job: Doder 1983.

50 Top Hat reconstruction: Hockstader 1996.

50 XM-1 tank: McMoneagle.

51 Air Force approached Atwater: Atwater. Riley remembers also drawing an angular, sparrowlike plane, which he later recognized as the F-117 Stealth light bomber.

52 psi countermeasures: Atwater. Riley says he later suggested facetiously that the unit should wear Mickey Mouse masks to disguise its own work from Soviet remote viewers.

54 briefing for Odom: Atwater.

54 Perry: Two sources formerly associated with the program.

54 officials at the DIA and CIA: For CIA, see the discussion in Chapter 14. For DIA, I am referring to Dale Graff, whose early psi experiments I discuss briefly in Chapter 15.

55 Charlie Rose: Stuckey 1979, a former senior Pentagon source, Targ, and another management-level source from the program.

55 *Omni* interview: Stuckey 1979.

Chapter 4 Joe of Arc

56 T-72 operation: Atwater; Riley. Weiser 1994 quotes sources who suggested that the first T-72s were acquired (through Poland) only in 1987, by the CIA. But when I asked a knowledgeable former senior Pentagon official to confirm or deny that the first T-72 had been acquired sooner, perhaps around 1980, he simply declined to comment.

57 Weiser article: Weiser 1994.

59 Young McMoneagle: Unless otherwise noted, the source is McMoneagle, in interviews. Atwater and Riley provided some details of his RDF work, which McMoneagle himself was unwilling to discuss. Atwater also mentioned McMoneagle's apparent lapses of memory regarding Vietnam.

61 white light: McMoneagle 1993, p. 108.

63 Near-death experience: McMoneagle, p. 28ff.

64 new person: McMoneagle 1993. The temple in Japan story comes from an interview.

65 remarkable realism: Atwater; McMoneagle. I also have seen and heard some of the raw results of McMoneagle's sessions.

65 agent based in Europe: Atwater. McMoneagle gives an altered, degovernmentalized version of this event (the target is supposedly in California, on Highway 1) in McMoneagle 1993, pp. 209–10.

66 FBI job: A former CIA official. The official mentioned that the case was brought to him by someone in "law enforcement." Given this and the other details of the case, it seems safe to infer that the tasking officer was from the FBI, which has the primary responsibility for the domestic tracking of Soviet spies. McMoneagle also remembered the case but didn't provide details.

69 three-digit code numbers: Atwater; McMoneagle.

70 Severodvinsk shipyard: Atwater; Graff 1995. McMoneagle confirmed some details.

Chapter 5 Bouncing off the Walls

73 spaced out: This anecdote comes from Riley.

74 RV aftereffects: Riley. I also had my own experience with intensive remote viewing during April and July 1994 (see Epilogue).

75 more liable to slip: West; Riley; Dames.

75 human use rules, Hartsell: Riley.

76 CIA's Iranian agent: Emerson 1988, pp. 20–21.

76 RV and Iran crisis: Riley; Atwater.

80 Jackie Keith: Riley; Atwater.

81 Air Force colonel: Riley; Atwater.

81 sea change: Atwater; Riley.

Epigraph, Book Two

83 Hal Puthoff.

Chapter 6 Puthoff

85 Puthoff's life: Puthoff.

87 $70 million in government contracts: Wilhelm 1976; Jaroff 1973a.

88 magnetometer incident: Puthoff; Puthoff and Targ 1977. Swann provided a more dramatic account, which involved graduate students fleeing the lab in distress. In an interview in 1994 Arthur Hebard, builder of the magnetometer, disputed that Swann had done anything paranormal in his laboratory and blamed the disturbance in the output (which he says he later reproduced) on a glitch in a helium coolant line. Hebard's account is contained in Randi 1982.

90 Elisha: 2 Kings 6:8–12.

90 oracles: Targ and Harary 1984.

90 John Dee: Deacon 1968; McRae 1984.

90 Czechs, Russians, Germans: Ebon 1983; Lyons and Truzzi 1991.

90 Nautilus story: A lengthy account of the Science et Vie affair is given in Chapter 3 of Ebon 1983. It is also referred to by Ostrander and Schroeder 1970.

92 Khrushchev: Soviet émigré Nikolai Kokhlov, allegedly a former KGB officer, in Starr and McQuaid 1985.

92 effect of Nautilus story: The sudden growth of Soviet parapsychology in the 1960s is discussed in Ostrander and Schroeder 1970, Lamothe 1972, and Ebon 1983.

92 Vasiliev quote: Groller 1986.

92 Kogan: Puthoff, Puthoff and Targ 1976.

93 Milan Ryzl: Puthoff; Puthoff 1984a, p. 92.

93 Naumov claims: Ostrander and Schroeder 1970.

94 DIA report: Lamothe 1972.

95 CIA skepticism: A former senior CIA official.

95 Kirlian photography: Ostrander and Schroeder 1970; Ebon 1973.

95 Kogan seemed more serious: Puthoff. Thompson also referred in interviews to the fact that much of Soviet psi research suddenly "went classified" in the late 1960s.

95 Nixon tale: Gottlieb's testimony was on September 21, 1977, before Senator Edward Kennedy's Subcommittee on Health, reported in Ebon 1983, pp. 116–17. Gottlieb denied Nixon's involvement when asked directly by Kennedy but elsewhere said, "[T]he president when he came back described some unusual feelings he and others had and asked if I would be able to give counsel." A former senior CIA official told me that he rejected the White House's request to look into the matter, arguing that it was inappropriate for the CIA to be involved in White House medical issues. According to the official, he suggested that the White House contact a domestically oriented medical authority such as the U.S. surgeon general.

96 more monitoring of psi: A former senior CIA official; Puthoff.

96 Puthoff approached: Puthoff, a former senior CIA official.

97 October '72: Puthoff; Swann; Puthoff and Targ 1977. I first confirmed the CIA connection from former senior CIA and Pentagon officials. Following the broadcast of Schnabel and Eagles 1995, the CIA officially admitted its involvement in a press release (September 6, 1995).

Chapter 7 The Coordinates

98 Young Swann: Swann.

99 early SRI failures: Swann; Puthoff.

99 ESP teaching machine: Swann. A description of the teaching machine is given in Puthoff and Targ 1977 and Gardner 1981, p. 75.

100 Targ: Targ; Puthoff; personal observation.

100 other experiments: Swann; Puthoff.

101 coordinate idea: Swann; Puthoff.

102 Puthoff and Targ relented: Puthoff; Swann; Puthoff and Targ 1977.

102 first experiments: These data, some of which are referred to in Puthoff and Targ 1977, come from documents I was shown by Swann. The results of the final run of ten targets was published in Puthoff and Targ 1973.

103 Targ and phone: Swann. Possibly this is only a retrospective revenge fantasy.

104 tightened protocol: Puthoff; Swann.

104 May 29: The account of the SRI side of this event comes from Puthoff and Puthoff and Targ (1973, 1975, 1977), who omit mention of the actual target. The anecdote about Price and the police dispatcher comes from Targ 1996. The account of the CIA side comes from a former senior CIA official. (The official told me that "Bill O'Donnell" was not involved in evaluating psi research, and initially didn't know why "Kennett" had asked him for coordinates. Puthoff, however, remembered that O'Donnell later visited SRI with Kennett, and he understood that O'Donnell also was involved in the psi research evaluation.)

The results of the remote-viewing sessions were published in SRI's reports to the CIA (Puthoff and Targ 1973, 1975), which were only recently declassified. The target site, the Naval Security Group Activity base at Sugar Grove, West Virginia, has never been officially confirmed, though I was able to match it to the RV descriptions. After identifying Sugar Grove as the target site in Schnabel and Eagles 1995, I then obtained confirmation from several sources formerly associated with the remote-viewing program.

There are some oddities about this case. For one, I was unable to find any record of the personnel named by Price—Hamilton, Nash, and Calhoun—in the Army, Air Force, or Marines (the ranks imply that they were not Navy). Moreover, the actual coordinates given to Swann and Price described a place about ten miles to the southwest of Sugar Grove, on Bullpasture Mountain, in Virginia. Swann claimed to me that the names, the project code words, and the coordinates indicated by Price were later *changed* in SRI's reports of the incident, to protect the security of the target. But Puthoff denies this and says he doesn't even remember checking the accuracy of the coordinates.

105 TSD/OTS, ORD: Two sources formerly associated with the RV program.
108 Pat Price: Puthoff; Swann. The dispatcher story comes from Targ 1996.

Chapter 8 The Shamans

114 Washington visitors: Puthoff; Swann. This occurred over the next few years.
116 dissociative disorders: West 1967; American Psychiatric Association 1987.
116 shaman and ball of fire: Eliade 1964, p. 100.
116 modern UFO shamans: Schnabel 1994; Persinger 1989.
117 Swann shamanic: The details of his life and beliefs come from Swann.
117 Swann's past life: Swann 1973, p. 8.
117 ordinary joe: Puthoff and Targ 1977 and Puthoff in initial interviews.
117 Price shamanic: Swann; Wilhelm 1976; a former CIA official; Puthoff.
118 Kalweit quote: Kalweit 1987, pp. 203–04.

118 Eliade quote: Eliade 1964, p. 257.

118 three-digit code number: Puthoff.

119 Kerguelen story: Swann; Puthoff; Puthoff and Targ 1973, 1975. Swann claimed that his data drew a diplomatic protest from the French and the Soviets, but Puthoff and Targ and a former CIA official denied this.

120 CIA officials briefed: Targ 1996; another former member of the program.

121 Semipalatinsk story: Puthoff and Targ 1975; a former senior CIA official; a former DIA official; Puthoff. The quotes from Price and the description of him in the remote-viewing room come from Targ 1996. Robinson 1977 was the source for much of the description of the Semipalatinsk site. A former DIA official vouched for Puthoff's claim that the gores/spheres were not known to U.S. intelligence before Price's description of them in the summer of 1974.

125 Price RVing in bed: Puthoff.

125 Swann and workings of psi: Puthoff; Swann. The comparison of Price and Swann comes from Puthoff, a former senior CIA official, Puthoff and Targ 1977, and Targ 1996, as well as my own observations of Swann.

126 Swann and alphanumerics: Swann; Puthoff.

127 "manipulator": Swann.

127 Swann usually absent: Swann; Puthoff.

128 Swann won't return: Swann. Puthoff remembers the drive to the airport.

Chapter 9 The Trickster

129 Geller at SRI: The account of Geller's first visit to SRI comes mainly from interviews with Puthoff, supplemented by Puthoff and Targ 1977, Wilhelm 1976, and interviews with Geller.

131 Geller's life: Geller; Geller and Playfair 1986; Gardner 1981; Randi 1982.

132 Dayan: Geller and Playfair 1986, pp. 194–95.

133 Yariv denial: Wilhelm 1976, p. 177.

133 Elisha: 2 Kings 6:8–12.

134 CIA interested: Puthoff admitted that his contract "sponsor" was interested in Geller. A former senior CIA official also noted the agency's interest in Geller.

134 wild surmises: Puthoff.

134 Geller's secret meetings: Geller.

134 Israelis visit: Puthoff.

135 Puthoff paranoid: Puthoff ("more paranoid" is a direct quote). Geller says that the Israeli intelligence men were genuinely interested in hearing SRI's opinions since they hadn't been able to keep him in Israel to perform their own experiments.

135 some visits not reported: Geller recalls being asked by Puthoff and Targ, on several occasions, not to sign in as an official visitor at SRI. (A similar policy was used for the Fort Meade remote viewers, who were asked to sign in under the name Scotty Watt.)

135 Geller's feats at SRI: Puthoff, Wilhelm 1976, and Puthoff and Targ 1977.

136 "Geller caught" rumor: Swann; Puthoff.

137 SRI suspected fraud: Puthoff.

137 mythology of shamanism: Campbell 1984, p. 168.

138 Najagneq, for example: Ibid., p. 169.

138 mystifications, theatrical scenes: Ibid., p. 171.

138 trickster themes: For example, Ellenberger 1970, Ross 1989, Schnabel 1994.

138 Jung's trickster: Jung 1959.

138 heat from skeptics: Puthoff.

138 Advanced Research Projects: Puthoff; Wilhelm 1976; Van de Castle.

139 no CIA money for Geller: Puthoff.

139 Kennett: A former researcher associated with the program and a former senior CIA official.

140 Mexico, New York, etc.: Geller and Playfair 1986; Geller. I saw Geller's house during a visit in December 1994.

Chapter 10 Remote Viewing

141 Precognitive remote-viewing protocol: Puthoff and Targ 1976, p. 347.

142 glider: A former senior CIA official. Puthoff and Targ (1977, p. 57) write that the target was a moon and stars symbol, scavenged from a piece of material in a garbage dump.

142 SRI contracts: Puthoff.

143 need to publish: Puthoff; Swann.

143 "many consider the study": Puthoff and Targ 1976.

143 Early psi research: Ellenberger 1970 contains a good account.

145 psi shut out at turn of century: This is my opinion.

145 Rhine: See Broughton 1991.

146 paradigm failed to shift: This is my opinion.

147 coordinates dubious: Puthoff.

148 October 4: Puthoff and Targ 1975, 1976, 1977; Wilhelm 1976.

148 Puthoff comments: Puthoff 1996. Oddly, in my discussions with Puthoff on this issue in 1994, he admitted that the coordinate experiments came first. One source of confusion may be a sketch (Puthoff and Targ 1977, p. 12) from an early outbound type of experiment (the remote viewer was Russell Targ, of all people) that was misdated "Friday 4/12/73" when the year was actually 1974.

149 Puthoff wanted new term: Puthoff.

149 variety of expressions: These terms come from Puthoff and Targ 1974, 1975, 1976.

149 Puthoff came up with RV term: Puthoff. Swann also claims to have invented the term *remote viewing*, but Puthoff insists to the contrary.

149 nine outbound sites: These experiments are recounted in Puthoff and Targ 1975, 1976, 1977; Wilhelm 1976.

150 variables didn't matter: Puthoff. Incidentally, in Puthoff, Targ, and May 1979, the SRI researchers acknowledge that they still haven't tested RV in cases where the viewer is *magnetically* shielded.

150 Osis experiment: Puthoff.

150 session four: Cox; Puthoff; Puthoff and Targ 1975, 1976, 1977; Targ and Harary 1984; Wilhelm 1976.

152 Rinconada time warp: Targ 1996; Puthoff and Targ 1975, 1977.

152 everyone could do RV: Puthoff; Puthoff and Targ 1977.

152 four ordinary people: Puthoff; Puthoff and Targ 1974, 1975, 1976, 1977; Swann.

153 sexual unorthodoxy: See Campbell 1984.

153 odds too high: For example, Marks and Kammann 1980; Hyman 1989; Puthoff, Targ, and May 1979.

153 Hammid wasn't as good: Puthoff.

154 Hammid precognition: Puthoff and Targ 1974, 1975, 1976, 1977.

154 a similar experiment: Duane and Behrendt 1965.

154 Her brain waves: Puthoff; Puthoff and Targ 1974, 1975, 1976.

155 invisible inks: Puthoff and Targ 1975.

155 Hammid queen of RV: Puthoff.

155 submersible: Puthoff; Swann; Schwartz 1979.

155 Targ stood in: Puthoff; Puthoff and Targ 1975, 1976, 1977 (p. 12). Targ's sketch was the one misdated "Friday 4/12/73" when it was actually 1974.

156 *Nature* paper: Puthoff and Targ 1974.

156 IEEE paper: Puthoff and Targ 1976.

156 Robert Lucky: Puthoff.
156 Psychic stuff is really: Stuckey 1975.

Chapter 11 You Can't Go Home Again

157 clinical evaluations: Puthoff; a former senior CIA official; Puthoff and Targ 1975.
158 Swann and Price resisted: Puthoff and Targ 1975. Skepticism about modern psychological and psychiatric methods is part of the belief system taught by the Church of Scientology, to which both Swann and Price then belonged.
158 EEG asynchronicities: A former CIA official.
159 both bounced around: A scientist formerly associated with the program remarked on this aspect of the SRI psychics in general. Data on Swann's and Price's movements comes from Puthoff; Swann; Wilhelm 1976; and Puthoff and Targ 1977.
159 the shamanistic crisis: Campbell 1984, p. 253.
159 schizophrenia patient: Puthoff.
161 Psychotronic conference: Puthoff; Swann.
161 Duane Elgin: Puthoff; Stuckey 1975. Some reference is made to Elgin in Puthoff and Targ 1977.
162 Elgin quote: Stuckey 1975.
162 Lawrence Livermore affair: This account comes primarily from a high-level source formerly associated with the remote-viewing program. Two other sources, plus Robertson and Hawke, provided some corroboration, especially of the technical details of the experiments with Geller. Robertson claimed not to know about some of the stranger paranormal events (the voice on the tape, the apparitions), while Hawke refused comment on all of these strange events, citing a desire to write about his experiences with Geller in detail after he retires from Livermore Laboratory. The episode is also referred to, very briefly and with a less

dramatic conclusion, in Puthoff and Targ 1977, pp. 164–65. My primary source suggested that the Puthoff and Targ 1977 conclusion was fictionalized, perhaps to protect those involved. That doesn't mean that it was.

Chapter 12 An Eight-Martini Evening

170 Hearst case: The account of this episode comes from Puthoff. My sources for the details of the kidnapping itself and the SLA characters like William Wolfe were the many news reports of the case, 1974–75.

173 Swann in New York: Swann, Wilhelm 1976, p. 202.

173 Swann's missing person cases, etc.: Swann.

173 Swann's predictions: Puthoff and Targ 1977; Swann.

174 Swann's return to SRI: Swann; Puthoff.

175 Price goes east: Puthoff.

175 Price and CIA: A former CIA official. Another source confirmed generally that Price worked for Everheart and OTS, and Director of Central Intelligence Stansfield Turner referred to Price, without naming him, in Coates 1977 and in a brief 1995 discussion with me during the filming of Schnabel and Eagles 1995.

Chapter 13 Evil Rays

181 epigraph: Bridges 1949, p. 264.

181 Price's corporate plane: A former CIA official.

181 Price's land buy: Ibid.

182 Price heads west: Puthoff.

182 Price warned about heart: Puthoff; Puthoff and Targ 1975; a former CIA official.

182 Price looked old: See the photo of Price in the photo section or the one in Puthoff and Targ 1977, p. 47.

182 Las Vegas: Puthoff.

183 mystery man: Two sources formerly associated with the RV program. An extremely dramatic account

(which these sources say is false) appeared on the Internet in late 1994 under the name Terry Milner. Milner, who said he was writing a book and had a source who had been close to Price, implied that Price had been assassinated by the KGB. Milner refused my request for an interview.

184 Larry Collins: Collins 1988.
184 Soviet research: Ebon 1983; Starr and McQuaid 1985; Lyons and Truzzi 1991.
185 Naumov jailed: Ebon 1983, p. 122.
185 Soviet screening program: Charlie Rose, in Stuckey 1979, plus Alexander, Swann.
185 Central Asian woman: Ebon 1983.
186 Bulgarian seeress: Lyons and Truzzi 1991, p. 201.
186 Communist psi theories: Ebon 1983.
186 Kogan and ELF: Puthoff; Puthoff and Targ 1975, 1976.
187 brutal and sinister: These anecdotes come from Ebon 1983; Starr and McQuaid 1985.
187 human subjects: Two sources associated with the RV program.
188 remote influencing: Ebon 1983; Starr and McQuaid 1985; Ostrander and Schroeder 1970.
189 wilder stories: Swann.
189 psi machines: Ebon 1983; Groller 1986; Alexander 1980; Puthoff.
190 U.S. skepticism: A former senior CIA official.
190 *New York Times:* Lewis 1977. Puthoff told me that he suspected Brezhnev was referring either to psi or to electromagnetic mind-altering devices.
191 Soviet *IEEE* wrangle: Puthoff; Targ and Harary 1984.
192 Prague conference: Puthoff; Swann.

Chapter 14 The Unbelievers

193 questioned privately: Jaroff 1974.
194 Laura Dickens: Puthoff. Puthoff and Targ 1976 refer to

this person as V1, a woman, while Puthoff and Targ 1977 refer to V1 as a man. Both now indicate that V1 was a woman. Puthoff says they referred to her as a man in their book *Mind Reach,* where a more extensive and potentially embarrassing account of her experiences was given, in order to protect her identity further.

197 SRI skeptics: Puthoff. See also Randi 1982.

197 Jaroff: Jaroff 1973a.

197 fascism worries: Wilhelm 1976, p. 159; Wilhelm.

197 editors of *Nature: Nature* 1974.

198 valid criticisms: See Marks and Kamman 1980; Hyman 1989; Randi 1982; Puthoff, Targ, and May 1979.

198 religious conspiracy theory: See Collins and Pinch 1982, pp. 43–44, for an interesting sociological discussion of the debate.

198 *Time* cover story: Jaroff 1974.

198 both had joined: Puthoff; Swann.

199 Hubbard and Dianetics: See Corydon and Hubbard 1987 and Wallis 1977, for example.

199 Puthoff and Swann resign: Puthoff; Swann.

200 Scientologists everywhere: Swann; Wilhelm 1976.

200 coal company deal: A former CIA official.

200 Kennett and remote viewing: A former CIA official.

201 skeletons, MKULTRA: On Gottlieb and MKULTRA, the source is Ranelagh 1986. On the relevance of this to remote viewing, the sources are two former CIA officials and Puthoff.

203 Gottlieb, Colby, McMahon: A former CIA official; Puthoff.

203 OTS still involved: A source formerly associated with the program.

203 Dave Brandwyne: A former CIA official and another source formerly associated with the program.

204 funding drought, long hours: Puthoff.

204 Richard Bach: Puthoff. Bach also comments on his re-

mote-viewing experiences at SRI in a foreword to Puthoff and Targ 1977.

205 "the logo of the company": Puthoff and Targ 1977, pp. 91–93.

205 Office of Naval Research: Koslov; Puthoff; Wilhelm 1977.

206 Dale Graff and submersible: A former DIA official; Puthoff, Targ, and May 1979, Schwartz 1979; Swann.

210 John Wilhelm article: Wilhelm 1977.

210 Stansfield Turner: Coates 1977.

Epigraph, Book Three

213 Stubblebine 1992.

Chapter 15 The Super God in the Sky

215 Epigraph: From Reuters North American Wire, September 20, 1995. (Carter, whose account is erroneous in several respects, was speaking to a group of college students.)

215 metal-shielded room: Puthoff.

215 tasking from Thompson: This account comes from two sources formerly associated with the RV program and from Graff 1995.

219 Carter's reminiscence: Reuters North American Wire, September 20, 1995.

219 half a dozen sources: A source formerly associated with the RV program.

219 lines tangled: Puthoff.

220 Atwater and Watt: Atwater.

220 Sleeping Beauty: Collins 1990.

220 Atwater targeted McMoneagle: A source formerly associated with the RV program.

221 Price sighting rumor: A source formerly associated with the RV program.

221 Swann's SRI territory: Swann; Puthoff.

221 budget: Two sources formerly associated with the program.

221 Puthoff only one briefed: Puthoff.

221 operational taskings: A source formerly associated with the RV program.

222 Class A, B, C targets: Swann; Puthoff.

222 Swann biowar sites: Swann; a source formerly associated with the RV program.

222 human subjects: A source formerly associated with the RV program remembered the site in forest session but specifically did not recall any confirmation from the tasking agency. A former CIA source did not recognize the description of the site given by Swann, and vehemently denied that remote viewers had had anything to do with U.S. revelations of the Soviet biological weapons program.

222 Obolensk: Barry 1993.

223 biowar targets: A source formerly associated with the RV program.

223 lengthy list of such sites: Barry 1993.

223 *Typhoon* submarine: A source formerly associated with the RV program.

223 Swann erroneous: One source from the program told me that Swann had participated in this operation. Swann himself told me and several others the story about the deadly premature blast. The connection between the two accounts is my inference.

223 Langford, Swann targeted subs: A source formerly associated with the RV program.

223 the lost nuke: Another source formerly associated with the program.

224 MX episode: Two sources formerly associated with the RV program, plus Graff 1995. The material on the history of the MX program itself comes from various news reports of the time, plus the Warren AFB public

relations office. The assertion regarding the likely factors in Reagan's decision is my opinion, based on news reports from 1983 that make it plain that the shell-game scheme faced strong opposition in Congress and among landowners in Utah and Nevada.

Chapter 16 Aol

229 epigraph: Boyd 1990, p. 71.

229 rocket motor: Puthoff; Swann.

230 nuclear test: Puthoff.

230 other experiments: Puthoff; Puthoff, Targ, and May 1979.

231 AAAS paper: Puthoff, Targ, and May 1979.

231 magnetic field: Puthoff; Persinger; Swann. See also Schaut and Persinger 1985 for a review of Persinger's work on this subject.

232 geomagnetic field meter: Puthoff.

232 correlation too small: Puthoff.

233 Chinese experiment: Puthoff. Oddly Puthoff and colleagues were less skeptical in discussing this experiment in Hubbard, May, and Puthoff 1986.

234 Swann's work: Puthoff; Swann. Certain aspects of Swann's work are discussed by Puthoff and Targ 1975, 1976, 1977 and Puthoff, Targ, and May 1979.

234 two-thirds accurate: Puthoff, Targ, and May 1979.

234 two-thirds optimistic: Mumford, Rose, and Goslin 1995. Even McMoneagle 1996, while generally agreeing with Puthoff's accuracy figures, has noted that "the very best world class remote viewers under laboratory conditions tend to run 50/50 as to whether they are on or off target."

235 calibration worthless: Atwater; Riley.

236 Adrienne: Puthoff; Puthoff and Targ 1977.

236 Everheart: A former senior CIA official.

237 "Frequently she will make": Sinclair 1930, p. 125.

237 left-hemispheric damage: Puthoff and Targ 1977, pp. 122–23. Their emphasis then on "hemispheres," as opposed to more precise functional demarcations of the brain, is something they would now revise, according to Puthoff.

238 "It seems reasonable to assume": Puthoff and Targ 1977, p. 41.

238 "Enough data . . . has [sic] been gathered": Puthoff and Targ 1975.

239 Roney-Dougal: Puthoff.

239 Dixon: Dixon 1971.

242 Arnheim, Stage One: Swann and Puthoff were the main sources, but a simple comparison of Swann's staged method with the discussions in Arnheim 1974, especially the passages around pp. 43, 63, and 171, was also very helpful.

243 Arnheim quote: Arnheim 1974, p. 43.

245 Stage Two, etc.: Swann; Puthoff.

248 RV session: This is just for illustration purposes; it is
–51 not a real session. Against this type of target a CRV session would almost always be longer and "noisier."

252 McMoneagle best at names: Personal observation; McMoneagle 1996.

253 Sinclair quote: Sinclair 1930, p. 134.

253 Warcollier: Warcollier 1948.

255 Swann training: Swann; Puthoff.

256 Mount St. Helens: Swann.

256 moon shot: Harary.

Chapter 17 Blue

257 high-priority target: Two sources formerly associated with the RV program, plus Graff 1995. Harary, citing security obligations, refused to discuss this with me when I first interviewed him in July 1994, but he later commented on it publicly during an appearance on

Larry King Live on November 29, 1995. Lyons and Truzzi 1991, who briefly refer to the episode, report that there was some skepticism at the NSC over the usefulness of Harary's data.

258 Harary's background: Harary; Puthoff.

260 Harary versus Swann: Harary; Puthoff. Swann made it clear in interviews that he disliked Harary and often claimed that he had "had Keith fired from the program."

260 wanted controlled studies: A not very well-controlled study in this area was reported in Puthoff 1984a, pp. 89–90.

261 experiments without coordinates: Puthoff; Harary; Puthoff and Targ 1975, 1977, 1979.

261 "Why don't you just say 'target'?": Puthoff; Harary.

262 infighting at SRI: Harary; Swann.

263 wanted their own project: Harary; Swann; Puthoff.

263 Langford still RVed: A source formerly associated with the RV program.

263 Targ's demise: Harary, Swann, and another source formerly associated with the RV program. A copy of the memo was provided to me (but not by Puthoff).

264 Targ's high moral reasons: See, for example, Targ's remarks in Anderson 1984.

264 Soviet tour: Harary; Targ and Harary 1984; Anderson 1984.

265 concerns at SRI and DIA: Two sources formerly associated with the RV program.

265 Targ's work in Moscow: Anderson 1984. Although Targ's work may have been innocuous, Colonel John Alexander later told me that the Institute of Theoretical Problems was deeply involved in military-oriented research.

265 Delphi Associates: Harary; Harary 1992.

266 lawsuit, angry correspondence: Harary 1992; Targ 1992.

Chapter 18 Spoonbender

267 Buchanan story: Buchanan. Stubblebine referred to it at a New Age conference ("TREAT IV") in March 1992. McMoneagle also remembered parts of the story.

268 Lee Marvin's brother: Emerson 1988, p. 103.

271 Jim Wright: Levine, Fenveyesi, and Emerson 1988.

271 Charlie Rose: McRae 1984, pp. 47–49.

271 John Tower: a source formerly associated with the RV program.

271 Claiborne Pell: numerous sources, including Jones; McRae 1984; Levine; Fenveyesi; Emerson 1988.

272 Science and Technology Committee: Targ and Harary 1984, p. 4.

272 Noreen Renier: Levine; Fenveyesi; Emerson 1988; McRae 1984.

273 Reagan and astrologers: Truzzi.

273 "This is a very psychic White House": Jones.

273 Scott Jones's psychics, "Cat" story: Jones.

273 Tannous: A former senior CIA official.

273 Mrs. MacArthur: A former senior CIA official.

275 West Point man: This is from a background sheet on the general provided by the U.S. Army's Center for Military History.

276 beyond lateral thinking: Geraldine Stubblebine.

276 New Age thinking: Alexander; INSCOM 1983; Druckman and Swets 1988; Squires 1988.

277 The New Mental Battlefield: Alexander 1980.

277 Richard Groller: Groller 1986.

277 Tom Bearden: McRae 1984, chap. 6.

277 Fire Support Mission . . . : Ibid., p. 129.

277 Task Force Delta: Ibid., chap. 6; Squires 1988.

278 "I am one of the tribal elders": McRae 1984, p. 125.

278 get them thinking laterally: Alexander.

279 spoon-bending party: A former senior Pentagon official.

279 retreat for officers: Alexander.

280 Det-G, etc.: These bureaucratic shifts are noted in IN-SCOM 1981a, b.

280 Center Lane: Dames; Atwater; Puthoff 1996; other sources formerly associated with the program.

280 Watt, Jachim, Busby: Atwater; McMoneagle; Dames.

281 searched talent pool: Atwater.

281 Nance, Cowart: Swann; Atwater; McMoneagle; three other sources.

281 old-timers: McMoneagle; Atwater.

281 doubts about Swann's technique: McMoneagle and another source.

281 Bell leaves: Ibid.

282 McMoneagle still argued: McMoneagle.

282 McMoneagle sole viewer: McMoneagle. Atwater agrees that this is plausible. McMoneagle and another source (who may simply be parroting McMoneagle) charge that the three-digit identity codes were used in this period in a way that misled clients into thinking that there was more than one viewer providing similar information.

282 Carlos: Three people (DIA, CIA, and another office) formerly associated with the RV program.

282 bloody clothes: Alexander; Dames.

282 hysteria over terrorism: Woodward 1987, pp. 182–83; also Emerson 1988.

283 RVers caught up in worries: Three people (DIA, CIA, and another office) formerly associated with the RV program.

284 Dozier case: Emerson 1988, pp. 63–70, briefly mentions the use of psychics in this episode, without giving names. He is the main source for the raided family story and the account of the SIGINT operation. I also had five sources from within the program: Atwater,

McMoneagle, and sources from the DIA, CIA, and another part of the program. Atwater is the source for the Ted Wheatley story. McMoneagle is the source for the claim that McMoneagle's data were ultimately accurate.

286 Fadlallah: Emerson 1988, pp. 195–99. The CIA denied involvement in the eventual bombing of Fadlallah's house.

286 Landbroker: INSCOM 1984c; Emerson 1988, pp. 111–12. Emerson refers in passing to the use of psychics. McMoneagle, Atwater, and another source confirmed that McMoneagle was the viewer. Some of the unit's RVers in training listened in from the control room during the session. McMoneagle claimed to me that some of his data on the Noriega villa "will never be declassified."

288 Thousandth RV session: Atwater.

288 lonely business: McMoneagle; Atwater.

288 Cowart, Trent: Atwater; McMoneagle; Riley; Swann.

288 new recruits: Atwater; McMoneagle; Dames; Swann; Buchanan; another source.

Chapter 19 Obi Swann

291 Ed Dames: Dames; personal observation.

291 out-of-body experience: Christine Dames.

292 Dames interested in RV training: Dames; Swann; another source.

293 Dames's initiation and training: Dames. Other trainees who went through the same experience, plus Swann and Atwater and another source connected to the program, provided additional information and insights.

294 Atwater's mother: Atwater.

295 Bob Monroe story: Monroe 1971; Atwater; official

Monroe Institute literature; Druckman and Swets 1988.

296 Atwater's first visit: Atwater.

296 sharing Hemi-Sync tapes: A former senior Army official; INSCOM 1984a, b.

297 Buchanan's OBE: Buchanan. Dames and others remember him talking about it.

297 outrage, brainwashing, hysteria: Dames; Atwater; Buchanan; another source who took the course.

298 life would never be the same: Dames.

298 Hemi-Sync experience: The descriptions of the tone states comes partly from the Monroe literature but mainly from my own impressions. I took the course in 1995, listening to the same tapes that Dames, Smith, and the others listened to.

299 dark circles: These are evident on a 1984 lecture Monroe videotaped, which I saw in 1995. One of Monroe's daughters-in-law, who was a trainer at the course, described his sleep patterns for me.

299 McMoneagle research: McMoneagle 1993; Dames; and two other sources from the program.

300 Jesus, Miranon: I read the transcript of the Jesus session and heard the Miranon story when I was at Monroe in 1995.

301 Inga Arnyet: Atwater. Dames tells a dramatized version of this story in which there were several "KGB extrasensors."

301 Swann not ready: The sources on Swann's initial trainees are Swann, Dames, and two others from the program.

302 NSA backed out: Swann suggested to me that this was because Norfeld had done poorly in training. Others (one source from the research side, and two from the operations side) said that NSA had backed out for internal political reasons. McMoneagle specified that it

was because the Norfeld–Henderson venture hadn't received proper authorization.

302 secretive agency: Dames and Swann later implied that these trainees were from the special operations Delta Force, but a source in a better position to know denied this. McMoneagle said the Delta Force story was "a figment of somebody's imagination."

302 last four trainees: Swann, Dames, and another source familiar with the training program.

305 Kwajalein bilocation: A former member of the RV program.

306 Dames as "protégé": Dames, in ordinary interviews and in Schnabel and Eagles 1995.

306 Swann's true protégé; Swann, two other sources from the program.

306 Nance: Dames; Riley; Atwater; another source.

306 Nance's sessions: When I first interviewed Swann at his home in late 1993, I was able to see and take notes on many sessions Nance had done while in his advanced stages of training, including the May 1984 series.

308 Nance at Tulum: Swann.

Chapter 20 Flameout

309 Mel Riley in Germany: Riley; Atwater.

310 Rolya and Thompson on good terms: Thompson.

310 Odom: Alexander, Atwater; Dames.

310 Odom in control: Alexander.

310 RVers unhappy with Stubblebine: Atwater; McMoneagle; Dames.

311 Alex Tannous: Atwater; another source from the program.

311 Stubblebine's recruits: Atwater; McMoneagle; Buchanan; Dames; another source from the program.

312 Stubblebine rescinds orders: Buchanan.

313 Stubblebine at Monroe: Dames, Buchanan, and another former member of the program.

314 senior officials worried: Geraldine Stubblebine and a former senior Pentagon official.

314 Yellow Fruit scandal: Atwater; another former member of the program. Some cite this as the primary reason for Stubblebine's ouster, although Alexander, who was closest to Stubblebine, cites the Monroe incident.

314 Richard Kennett: A former CIA official.

315 Pemberton case: Atwater; Dames; another former member of the program.

316 Olson: Ranelagh 1986, p. 209.

316 Odom used Pemberton incident: Alexander.

316 unit doomed: Atwater; Dames; another former member of the program. Soyster later made his views clear in Smith 1995.

316 CIA briefing, 1984: Three officials formerly associated with the program.

318 McMahon distancing: A former senior CIA official.

318 van with nuke: A source formerly associated with the program.

319 program survived: Dames, Riley, Atwater, and two other sources from the program.

320 SRI fared better: A source formerly associated with the program. Ed May 1996 refers to the five-year contract.

321 Puthoff guarded: Puthoff.

322 RV fund-raiser: Ibid., Puthoff 1984b.

322 Puthoff's career change: Puthoff.

323 McMoneagle retired: McMoneagle; McMoneagle 1993.

325 heart attack: McMoneagle 1993, pp. 143–44.

Chapter 21 The Witches

327 bilocation: Riley.

328 RDF: Riley.

328 Atwater arranged transfer: Atwater; Riley.

329 new faces at unit: Dames, Atwater, Riley, and another source from the program.

330 Kincaid story: Atwater and another source. Dames tells a different, more dramatic version of the helicopter story.

331 ERV, CRV, and random numbers: Atwater, Dames, Riley, and another source from the program.

332 Qaddafi and Noriega searches: Dames; Buchanan; Riley; another source from the program.

333 "Ask Kristy McNichol": Buchanan.

334 high-tech weapons sites: Graff 1995; Dames; two other sources from the program.

334 Lebanon hostage crisis: Dames; Riley; another source from the program.

334 Silkworm missiles: Dames; Riley.

334 counternarcotics: Three former members of the program; Graff 1995; Dames; Atwater; Riley.

335 POW search: Atwater. Dames, oddly, later claimed to believe that there were POWs still in Vietnam.

336 Atwater's retirement: Atwater.

337 RV too flaky: Soyster, in Smith 1995. Soyster's opposition to the program was remarked upon by virtually every source I had from DIA, SRI, and Fort Meade.

337 traveled around country: Riley; three other former members of the program.

338 supportive senators: These were identified by several sources from the program, including McMoneagle.

338 no one sanctioning: Riley; Dames; Buchanan; another source from the program.

339 search problems: McMoneagle. This is evident from Graff 1995 and from other former remote viewers' descriptions of the targets they were given.

339 unit past its prime: McMoneagle and another source. Graff, May, and the CRVers blamed the decline largely on management and morale problems.

339 Severodvinsk redux: McMoneagle. Graff thinks this is

unlikely, among other reasons because it would have been easier for someone simply to invent new data.

340 Gauvin and decline: Riley, Atwater, Dames, and two other sources from the program.

341 Gauvin's pluralism: Gauvin. A former member of the unit noted that Atwater and Ray were less tolerant of the exotic methods, at least within DT-S.

341 Angela Dellafiora: Dames; Riley; Buchanan; Atwater; McMoneagle; another source.

342 U.S. Customs Service: Atwater; three other sources from the program; Graff 1995.

343 Libyan ship: Two sources from the program; Graff 1995.

343 hijacked from Rome: Graff 1995; another source.

343 Angela's data preferred: A former DIA official.

343 reaction by male CRVers: Dames; Riley; Buchanan; another source from within the program. Graff claimed that the reaction was pure jealousy: "They were babies."

344 Higgins case: Graff 1995; Buchanan; Riley; another source.

344 Angela coached: Buchanan; Dames; Riley; another source.

345 mesmerizing influence: Ibid.

345 Gauvin's private sessions: Riley.

345 Vorona's visits: Dames; Riley; Buchanan; another source. Graff confirmed that on certain (operational) matters Dellafiora alone was consulted, sometimes directly by senior officials.

345 Vorona's defense: Vorona 1995; Graff; another source from the program who apparently had been speaking to Vorona.

345 CRVers thought it odd: Riley; Buchanan; Dames, two other sources.

346 Dahlgren: Riley; Dames; Buchanan; two other sources.

347 Dahlgren and D'Amato: Buchanan; Riley; two former

DIA officials; McMoneagle; May 1996; a former member of the SRI program.

347 Pandolfi's skepticism: Pandolfi.

347 Pandolfi shut out: Graff.

347 Pandolfi on Capitol Hill: Pandolfi.

348 D'Amato and senators: Smith 1995.

Chapter 22 A Haunted House

350 RVers bored: Buchanan; Riley; another source.

350 Morehouse: Buchanan, another remote viewer.

351 Dames's targets: Dames; Riley; Buchanan; another source; Christine Dames.

354 Kincaid story: Riley; Dames. Atwater remembers it was a different relative.

354 Ray: Riley; Dames; Buchanan; Atwater.

355 Dellafiora on Mars: Dames.

355 Dames's long interest: Dames.

356 senior management levels: This is common knowledge in the UFO research community, and people like Puthoff and Graff are often accused of having "inside knowledge" about UFOs. Stubblebine's interest is evident from Stubblebine 1992, among other things. The sources for D'Amato include a former senior intelligence official and two congressional staffers.

356 Paul Tyler: Tyler served as master of ceremonies for the 1992 annual Mutual UFO Network symposium in Albuquerque, New Mexico. The quote is from Tyler 1993.

357 Superdome: Puthoff; Targ and Harary 1984, p. 41.

358 McMoneagle's metallic craft: McMoneagle 1993, p. 211.

358 UFO and submarine: A source formerly in the program; Swann.

358 targeting RVers against UFOs: Puthoff; McMoneagle 1993; Swann; Dames.

359 Swann's fears: Puthoff; Swann.

359 Nance: Dames; Swann; another source.

359 Bob Monroe: McMoneagle 1993, p. 174.

359 craft from the future: McMoneagle.

359 Swann's X-Files story: Two sources familiar with the story, including one who has read Swann's written account.

361 McMoneagle at Pentagon: Dames; Atwater. McMoneagle discussed the incident in very general terms.

362 Riley RVs UFO: Riley; Dames; another source from the program.

362 Dames's own UFO targets: Dames; Riley; Buchanan; Graff; another source.

363 open search: Dames; Riley; another source; Graff 1995.

364 Dames a source of AoI: Buchanan; Riley; two other sources.

365 Santa Claus prank: Riley; Buchanan; another source.

367 Vorona, Graff, Puthoff hoped to arrange: A source formerly in the program.

367 instead George Lawrence: May 1996.

367 Hyman shut out: Two sources formerly in the program.

367 Hyman's report: Druckman and Swets 1988. See also Hyman 1989.

368 treasure trove: A source formerly in the program.

368 special-access status: A CIA source.

368 Carlucci, IG team: Dames; Riley; Smith 1995. Carlucci's budget cut announcement was reported in *The Washington Post* on December 5, 1987.

369 shredding: Dames; Riley; Buchanan; another source.

369 Dames's plaque: Riley; Dames. I've seen the plaque.

370 Vorona's retirement: Riley; Buchanan; another source.

371 SRI's Pentagon contract: The contract is referred to in May 1996.

371 DCSI's office and RV: A source formerly in the program.

371 Riley leaves: Riley.

Epilogue

372 "One flew east": Riley.

376 Dames's interesting life: Dames; Riley.

376 UFO bases: A former remote viewer. Dames also told me about the New Mexico bases.

377 Dames at UFO conference: Duce-Ashe 1993.

377 Dames's clients: I spoke to all three.

380 SCUD hunt: McMoneagle, a DIA source.

381 Al Garfield: Two sources from the program.

381 Mel Riley: Riley.

383 Dames's book project: Dames; Swann, Sandra Martin.

383 Morehouse and Dale Van Atta: A former remote viewer.

383 Morehouse story: The NBC deal—Sandra Martin. Morehouse's stay at Walter Reed—Martin, Dames, and another source (and I visited Morehouse there briefly in May 1994). Claims of a Pentagon harassment campaign—Martin, and Dames repeated to me the allegations he had heard from Morehouse. Morehouse's legal problems and maneuvers—(a) Martin, (b) Dames, (c) Morehouse's lawyer Barry Steinberg, (d) the seven-hundred-page case file from the Morehouse investigation and court-martial at Fort Bragg, and (e) a heavily redacted set of documents from INSCOM's investigation. (These two sets of documents are available by requests under the Freedom of Information Act.)

383 Morehouse on field phone: Morehouse, in comments on the Internet, December 1995.

385 Dames helps kill Marrs book: Dames, Riley, and two sources in New York publishing circles.

385 Morehouse's book: Morehouse; publishing sources; Fleming 1995.

385 Morehouse now claimed: Fleming 1995.

386 Oliver Stone: A source in publishing circles.

386 children's cartoon show: Buchanan, who was told this by Morehouse.

386 end of program: Graff; Puthoff; Pandolfi; McMoneagle; Mumford, Rose, Goslin 1995; May 1996.

387 supporters ran for cover: Smith 1995; Graff.

BIBLIOGRAPHY

Alexander, John
1980. The new mental battlefield. *Military Review* (December).

American Psychiatric Association
1987. *Diagnostic and Statistical Manual of Mental Disorders* (3d ed., rev.).

Anderson, Ian
1984. Strange case of the psychic "spy." *New Scientist* (November 22).

Anderson, Jack
1981a. Pentagon invades Buck Rogers' turf. *Washington Post* (January 9).

1981b. Yes, psychic warfare is part of the game. *Washington Post* (February 5).

1984a. Psychic studies might help U.S. explore Soviets. *Washington Post* (April 23).

1984b. "Voodoo gap" looms as latest weapons crisis. *Washington Post* (April 24).

1984c. Pentagon, CIA cooperating on psychic spying. *Washington Post* (May 3).

1985. U.S. still in psychic research. *Washington Post* (October 24).

1989. CIA secrets and Customs agent's firing. *Washington Post* (February 15).

1995. Psyched up for spies' crystal ball. *Washington Post* (November 2).

Arnheim, Rudolf

1974. *Art and visual perception.* Berkeley: University of California Press. (First published 1954.)

Barry, John

1993. Planning a plague? A secret Soviet network spent decades trying to develop biological weapons. *Newsweek* (February 1).

Blum, Howard

1990. *Out there: the government's secret search for extraterrestrials.* New York: Simon and Schuster.

Boyd, Brian

1990. *Vladimir Nabokov: the Russian years.* London: Vintage.

Bridges, E. Lucas

1949. *Uttermost part of the earth: Indians of Tierra del Fuego.* New York: Dutton. (Pagination in notes from 1988 edition, published by Dover Books in New York.)

Broad, William

1984. Pentagon is said to focus on ESP for wartime use. *New York Times* (January 10).

Broughton, Richard

1991. Parapsychology: the controversial science. London: Rider.

Burroughs, Colonel Lorenzo, USAF

1974. Letter of commendation to SPC-5 Melvin C. Riley. (The letter merely refers to Riley's "outstanding accomplishment," which was classified.)

Campbell, Joseph
1984. *The historical atlas of world mythology*, vol 1, *The way of the animal powers*. New York: Times Books.

Coates, James
1977. Psychic spy died: no word since. *Chicago Tribune* (August 10).

Collins, Harry, and Trevor Pinch
1982. *Frames of meaning: the social construction of extraordinary science*. London: Routledge.

Collins, Larry
1988. *Maze*.
1990. Mind control. *Playboy* (January).

Corydon, Bent, and L. Ron Hubbard, Jr.
1987. *L. Ron Hubbard: messiah or madman?* Secaucus: Lyle Stuart.

Dames, Ed
1992. Lecture on remote viewing, TREAT-IV Workshop, Atlanta, Georgia (March 9).

Deacon, Richard
1968. *John Dee: scientist, geographer, astrologer, and secret agent to Elizabeth I*. London: Muller.

Dixon, Norman
1971. *Subliminal perception*. New York: McGraw-Hill.
1979. Subliminal perception and parapsychology: points of contact. *Proceedings of the XXVII Annual International Conference of the Parapsychology Foundation, Inc.* New York, N.Y.

Doder, Dusko
1983. Soviets stop building U.S. embassy over use of bugging detector. *Washington Post* (May 27).

Druckman, Daniel, and John A. Swets
1988. *Enhancing human performance: issues, theories, and techniques*. Washington: National Academy Press.

Duane, T. D., and T. Behrendt
1965. Extrasensory electroencephalographic induction in identical twins. *Science* vol. 150, p. 367.

Duce-Ashe, Carolyn
1993. TREAT speaker turns heads. *UFO*, vol. 8, no. 3. (Duce-Ashe reported remarks by Ed Dames at the fifth Treatment and Research of Anomalous Trauma conference, Santa Fe, New Mexico, March 21.)

Ebon, Martin
1975. Ingo Swann, parapsychology's most popular "guinea pig." *Probe* (November).
1983. *Psychic warfare: threat or illusion?* New York: McGraw-Hill.

Eliade, Mircea
1989. *Shamanism: archaic techniques of ecstasy.* London: Arkana. (First edition 1964.)

Ellenberger, Henri
1970. *The discovery of the unconscious: the history and evolution of dynamic psychiatry.* New York: Basic Books.

Emerson, Steven
1988. *Secret warriors: inside the covert military operations of the Reagan era.* New York: Putnam.

Fleming, Michael
1995. G.I. psychic sells tale. *Daily Variety* (November 16).

Gardner, Martin
1981. *Science: good, bad, and bogus.* Buffalo: Prometheus Books.

Geller, Uri, and Guy Lyon Playfair
1986. *The Geller effect.* New York: Henry Holt.

Graff, Dale
1977. A journal of psychic experiments. Unpublished typescript.
1995. "Operational project summary." An unofficial list of nineteen apparent RV successes, 1974–93, provided to CIA-sponsored investigators in the summer of 1995 and later obtained by a few members of the media. (I did not obtain this document from Graff.)

Groller, Richard
1986. Soviet psychotronics: a state of mind. *Military Intelligence* (October–December).

Harary, Keith

1992. The goose that laid the silver eggs: a criticism of psi and silver futures forecasting. *Journal of the American Society for Psychical Research*, vol. 86 (October). Response to Targ's response follows.

Hockstader, Lee

1996. "Top Hat" to cap off Moscow embassy saga. *Washington Post* (February 22).

Hubbard, G. Scott, Edwin C. May, and Harold E. Puthoff

1986. Possible production of photons during a remote-viewing experiment. In *Research in Parapsychology 1985*, ed. Debra H. Weiner and Dean I. Radin. Metuchen, N.J.: Scarecrow Press.

Hyman, Ray

1989. *The elusive quarry: a scientific appraisal of psychical research.* Buffalo: Prometheus Books.

Jung, Carl

1959. *Four archetypes.* London: Ark. (published 1986), vol. 9, *The collected works of C. G. Jung,* ed. Herbert Read, Michael Fordham, and Gerard Adler.

Kalweit, Holger

1992. *Shamans, healers, and medicine men.* Boston: Shambhala. (First edition 1987, trans. Michael Kohn.)

INSCOM

1981a. Cable from the Army's ACSI, Major General Ed Thompson, to the commander of INSCOM, Major General William Rolya. The cable notes that an (unnamed) undersecretary of the army has approved the transfer of control of the Fort Meade Grill Flame unit from the office of the ACSI to the commander of INSCOM (February 11).

1981b. "Formalization of project GRILL FLAME." Cover memorandum and letter of instructions regarding Fort Meade unit. Unit transferred to control of INSCOM Operations Group, formalized as "Detachment G" (September 10).

1983. "High Performance Task Force Report." (March)

1984a. "Guidance regarding use of Hemi-Sync tapes" (June 29). Response to letter from INSCOM Chief of Staff requesting information on use of Hemi-Sync tapes by INSCOM personnel.

1984b. "Guidance regarding use of Hemi-Sync tapes." New guidelines limiting Hemi-Sync use (July 6).

1984c. Memoranda summarizing Project Landbroker. (Some documents, from 1988, were generated during Army dispute with former Landbroker participant Edward Malpass.) Released to the author after a FOIA request, 1995. Pages heavily redacted.

Jaroff, Leon

1973a. The magician and the think-tank. *Time* (March 12).

1973b. Reaching beyond the rational. *Time* (April 23).

1974. Boom times on the psychic frontier. *Time* (March 4).

Lamothe, John D.

1972. Controlled offensive behavior—USSR. (DIA report on Soviet psi research and development.)

Levine, Art, Charles Fenyvesi, and Steven Emerson

1988. The twilight zone in Washington. *U.S. News & World Report* (December 5).

Lewis, Flora

1977. Émigré tells of research in Soviet in parapsychology for military use. *New York Times* (June 19).

Lyons, Arthur, and Marcello Truzzi

1991. *The blue sense: psychic detectives and crime.* New York: Mysterious Press.

Marks, David, and Richard Kammann

1980. The psychology of the psychic. Buffalo: Prometheus Books.

May, Edwin

1996. The AIR review of the Department of Defense's

Star Gate program: a commentary. *Journal of Scientific Exploration*, vol. 10 (Spring).

McMoneagle, Joe

1993. *Mind trek*. Norfolk: Hampton Roads Press.

1996. Hemi-Sync's impact on remote-viewing. *TMI Focus* (Monroe Institute newsletter), Spring issue.

McRae, Ronald

1984. *Mind wars: the true story of government research into the military potential of psychic weapons*. New York: St. Martin's.

Monroe, Robert

1971. *Journeys out of the body*. New York: Doubleday.

Mumford, Michael, Andrew Rose, and David Goslin

1995. An evaluation of remote-viewing: research and applications. American Institutes for Research (September 29).

Nature

1974. Investigating the paranormal. *Nature* vol. 251, no. 18 (October), pp. 559–60.

Newsweek

1974. Parapsychology: the science of the uncanny. *Newsweek* (March 4).

Osis, Karlis

1972. New ASPR research on out-of-body experiences. *ASPR Newsletter*, no. 14 (Summer).

Ostrander, Sheila, and Lynn Schroeder

1970. *Psychic discoveries behind the Iron Curtain*. Englewood Cliffs, N.J.: Prentice Hall.

Persinger, Michael

1989. Predicting the details of visitor experiences and the personality of experiences: the temporal lobe factor. *Perceptual and Motor Skills*, vol. 68, pp. 55–65.

Puthoff, Hal

1982. SRI internal memorandum April 19. (This was not provided to me by Puthoff.)

1984a. Remote viewing studies at SRI International. From

Proceedings: Symposium on Applications of Anomalous Phenomena, ed. C. B. Scott Jones (Leesburg, Va., November 30–December 1, 1983), published by Kaman Tempo, a division of Kaman Sciences Corp., Alexandria, Va.

1984b. ARV applications. *Research in parapsychology 1984*, ed. Rhea White and Jerry Solfvin. Metuchen, N.J.: The Scarecrow Press.

1996. CIA-initiated remote-viewing program at Stanford Research Institute. *Journal of Scientific Exploration*, vol. 10 (Spring).

Puthoff, Hal, and Russell Targ

1973. Project Scanate: exploratory research in remote viewing. SRI report sent to CIA (c. August).

1974. Information transmission under conditions of sensory shielding. *Nature*, vol. 251, no. 18 (October), pp. 602–07.

1975. Perceptual augmentation techniques. (A series of reports for the CIA's Office of Research and Development, under a contract that ran 1974–75.) Final report, December. Declassified by the CIA, July 1995.

1976. A perceptual channel for information transfer over kilometer distances: historical perspective and recent research. *Proceedings of the IEEE*, vol. 64 (March).

1977. *Mind reach*. New York: Delacorte.

Puthoff, Hal, Russell Targ, and Edwin May

1979. Experimental psi research: implications for physics. Paper presented at meeting of AAAS, Houston, Texas (January 3–8).

Randi, James

1982. *Flim Flam!* Buffalo: Prometheus Books.

Ranelagh, John

1986. *The agency: the rise and decline of the CIA*. New York: Simon and Schuster.

Reuters

1995. Carter says psychic found lost plane for CIA (September 20).

Robinson, Clarence
1977. Soviets push for beam weapon. *Aviation Week and Space Technology* (May 2), pp. 16–23.

Ross, Colin
1989. Multiple personality disorder. New York: Wiley.

Schaut, G. B., and M. Persinger
1985. Subjective telepathic experiences, geomagnetic experiences, and the ELF hypothesis: part I, data analysis. *Psi Research* vol. 4, pp. 4–20.

Schnabel, Jim
1994. *Dark white: aliens, abductions, and the UFO obsession.* London: Hamish Hamilton.
1995. Tinker, tailor, soldier, psi. *The Independent on Sunday Review* (August 27).

Schnabel, Jim, and Bill Eagles
1995. *The Real X-Files.* A one-hour documentary for Channel Four TV (U.K.). Schnabel was the writer and narrator, and Eagles the director. The executive producer was Alex Graham of Wall to Wall TV, London. First broadcast August 27. An edited version was first broadcast in the United States on Discovery Channel, March 12, 1996.

Schwartz, Stephan
1979. Deep quest. *Omni* (March).

Sinclair, Upton
1930. *Mental radio.* London: Werner Laurie.

Smith, R. Jeffrey
1995. A handful of senators kept DIA's psychics at work. *Washington Post* (December 1).

Squires, Sally
1988. The Pentagon's twilight zone. *Washington Post* (April 17).

Starr, Douglas, and E. Patrick McQuaid
1985. Psi soldiers in the Kremlin. *Omni* (August).

Stubblebine, Albert
1992. Lecture on remote-viewing. *International Symposium on UFO Research* (May).

Stuckey, William

1975. Psychic power: the next super-weapon? *New York* ("year-end issue").

1979. Psi on Capitol Hill. *Omni* (July).

Sullivan, Gail Bernice

1976. Remote viewing: on a clear day, they can see 2,480 miles. *San Francisco Examiner* (December 28).

Swann, Ingo

1973. Interview. *Psychic* (March–April).

1975. *To kiss earth goodbye.* New York: Hawthorn.

1978. *Star fire.* New York: Dell.

1981. Are Russians winning the psychic war? *Fate* (December).

Targ, Russell

1992. Targ's response to Harary's article. *Journal of the American Society for Psychical Research,* vol. 86 (October).

1996. Remote viewing at SRI in the 1970s: a memoir. *Journal of Scientific Exploration,* vol. 10 (Spring).

Targ, Russell, and Keith Harary

1984. *Mind race: understanding and using psychic abilities.* New York: Villard.

Time

1984. An E.S.P. gap. *Time* (January 23).

Tyler, Captain Paul (USN, Ret.)

1993. Remarks at October meeting of New Mexico MUFON chapter. Reported in *NM MUFON News,* no. 12 (January 17, 1994).

Vorona, Jack

1995. Spy stories. Letter to *The Independent on Sunday* (October 1).

Warcollier, René

1948. *Mind to mind.* New York: Creative Age Press.

Wallis, Roy

1977. *The road to perfect freedom.* Colorado Springs: Colorado University Press.

Weiser, Benjamin
1994. Poland helped U.S. buy Soviet weapons. *Washington Post* (February 14).
West, Louis Jolyon
1967. Dissociative reaction. In *Comprehensive Textbook of Psychiatry*. Baltimore: Williams and Wilkins Company, pp. 885–99.
Wilhelm, John
1976. *The search for superman.* New York: Pocket Books.
1977. Psychic spying? *The Washington Post* (August 7), Outlook section.
Woodward, Bob
1987. *Veil: the secret wars of the CIA.* New York: Simon and Schuster.

INDEX

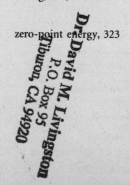